Standing on an Isthmus

Standing on an Isthmus

Islamic Narratives on War and Peace in Palestinian Territories

S. Ayse Kadayifci-Orellana

LEXINGTON BOOKS

A division of
ROWMAN & LITTLEFIELD PUBLISHERS, INC.
Lanham • Boulder • New York • Toronto • Plymouth, UK

LEXINGTON BOOKS

A division of Rowman & Littlefield Publishers, Inc.
A wholly owned subsidiary of The Rowman & Littlefield Publishing Group, Inc.
4501 Forbes Boulevard, Suite 200
Lanham, MD 20706

Estover Road
Plymouth PL6 7PY
United Kingdom

British Library Cataloguing in Publication Information Available

Library of Congress Cataloging-in-Publication Data

Kadayifci, Ayse S.
Standing on an isthmus : Islamic narratives on war and peace in Palestinian territories / S. Ayse Kadayifci-Orellana.
p. cm.
Includes bibliographical references.
ISBN-13: 978-0-7391-1111-6 (cloth : alk. paper)
ISBN-10: 0-7391-1111-6 (cloth : alk. paper)
1. Arab-Israeli conflict 2. West Bank–Politics and government. 3. Gaza Strip–Politics and government. 4. Self determination, National–West Bank. 5. Self determination, National–Gaza Strip. I. Title. II. Title: Islamic narratives on war and peace in Palestinian territories.
DS119.76.K253 2007
956.9405'4--dc22 2007023941

Printed in the United States of America

The paper used in this publication meets the minimum requirements of American National Standard for Information Sciences—Permanence of Paper for Printed Library Materials, ANSI/NISO Z39.48–1992.

Dedicated to my beloved daughter Sofia Leyla Orellana

Contents

Chapter 1

Introduction

When I first started studying and researching the Israeli-Palestinian conflict for my dissertation, the peace process was barely limping forward under the policies of Netanyahu, but there was still some hope that peace would prevail. Hopes that Palestinians and Israelis would resume the peace process were fortified when Ehud Barak became the Israeli Prime Minister in July 1999. With renewed vigor, both sides signed the Sharm al Sheikh Memorandum, which envisioned them reaching a framework for agreement on the permanent status of difficult issues such as Jerusalem, refugees, settlements, borders, and water- by February 2000. At the end of this round, it was anticipated that a full-fledged agreement would be signed.

Similar to the previous stages of the peace process, implementation of the agreement proved to be very difficult. By early 2000, only some of the deadlines were met, while others seemed progressively more impracticable. Increasing Palestinian disenchantment with the peace process (due to a decrease in living standards, increasing unemployment and restriction of movement, accompanied by a rising numbers of settlers, among others) undermined their anticipation for a just peace. Added to this was the rumor that Palestinian leadership had already compromised on territory.

The Camp David Summit meeting took off amidst this social *angst*. After 15 days of exhaustive negotiations the meeting failed to produce the hoped-for agreement. The declaration of a Palestinian state, envisaged to take place in September 2000, was postponed indefinitely under international and regional pressure, and the West Bank and Gaza exploded into violence by October. Ehud Barak resigned in December and Ariel Sharon, a right-winger, was elected as the Prime Minister of Israel on February 6, 2001, signaling that overwhelming majority of the Israeli population now favored a tougher approach to the conflict.

jority of the Israeli population now favored a tougher approach to the conflict. The continued escalation of conflict between Israelis and Palestinians since then has dissolved all hopes for a peaceful future. Israel re-occupied almost all of the West Bank in March and June 2001, raided Palestinian cities indiscriminately killing many civilians as well as militants, including notorious Hamas leaders such as Sheikh Ahmed Yassin and Abd al-Aziz al Rantisi. Moreover, Israel initiated the construction of the internationally contested wall between Israel and the Palestinian Territories. In response, militant groups such as Hamas, Islamic Jihad, and al Aqsa Brigades stepped up suicide attacks in Israeli cities and settlements, killing many civilians as well. In order to stop the violence the Quartet (United States, Russia, the United Nations and the European Union) drafted a "roadmap" for the Middle East settlement. However diplomatic initiatives were put on hold as a result of the complications related to the US-led war in Iraq in April 2003.

Death of Yasser Arafat in November 2004 initiated a new current in the region. On January 9, 2005 Palestinians had their first presidential elections in nine years to replace Arafat. Mahmoud Abbas, (also called Abu Mazen), a long-time aid of Arafat was elected as the new head of the Palestinian Authority, revitalizing hopes for resuming the peace process in the region. Following his election, he was able to negotiate a truce with the militant groups and to convince them to halt military operations against Israelis, provided that it is mutual. However, this truce did not last long either, as Abbas needed to get something substantial from the Israel in return to convince the Palestinian population and to secure his credibility. Attempts of the Quartet, consisting of US, Russia, United Nations and the European Union to revive the Peace Process have been fruitless also.

The most dramatic development in the region, however, was the results of the Palestinian Legislative Council elections of January 25, 2006, where Hamas was the winner. Winning 74 seats provided Hamas with the majority of the seats and the ability to form a majority government. Although this development was heralded by the municipality elections of 2004 and 2005, international community was greatly disappointed with these results and expressed its disappointment by stopping international aid, so crucial for providing basic services and paying the wages, among other things. Cutting off its financial resources left the new government in dire straits and have worsened the living conditions of already extremely poor Palestinian society.[1] In addition, violent clashes between Hamas and Fatah fractions have cost the lives of many Palestinians. Although an agreement was reached between Hamas and Fatah in Mecca in February 2007 and the formation of a new government is underway, it is not clear how long this agreement will last and how it will impact the Peace Process in the Middle East. Still, peace in the Middle East will be a distant hope and as long as the main issues of the conflict remain unchanged, and both Palestinian and Israeli leaders do not take some concrete steps towards reconciliation, violence will erupt once again.

Moreover, in order to revive optimism and hope in peace, it is necessary to recognize and address the limitations of the previous peace process. One of the major shortcomings of the Oslo peace process was that it took place merely between Israeli officials and the PLO, not between Israeli and Palestinian communities. Thus it could only reach a settlement, and not reconciliation at the societal level.[2] Implementation of the agreements proved to be much harder then signing of agreements. Mediators had pulled out once a settlement was reached and an agreement was signed. No mechanism was set up to monitor or enforce the implementation of the agreements and no services were offered to assist reconciliation between the communities. These were left in the hands of the parties alone and the parties neither had the time nor the programs to bring the "Spirit of Oslo" back to Israel and Palestine.[3] The negotiators also faced serious "reentry" problems in convincing their constituencies of the benefits of the agreements and that it was possible to reach a mutually acceptable solution to the conflict.

There has not been a systematic and coordinated reconciliation between both the Israeli and Palestinian people even though there have been an increasing number of dialogue groups involving Arabs and Jews, especially in the USA. The peace process excluded peace activists, grass-roots leaders (including religious leaders), and hard-liners on both sides. The negotiators failed to account for the civil society and alternative leaderships that have been gaining support among the populations. The rise of Islamic movements in the Occupied Territories and the right-wing movement within Israel were especially underestimated. Critical developments, such as signing of the First Alexandria Declaration of the Religious Leaders of the Holy Land on January 21, 2002, went unnoticed and cultural and religious sources that could provide a basis for reconciliation were ignored. Failure to recognize the need for communal reconciliation, accompanied by a failure to address the deepening feeling of desperation and frustration of the Palestinian people, proved to be very costly.

Extremist Islamic groups, particularly Hamas, were quick to exploit the disappointment with the peace process. These groups instigated a relentless series of suicide attacks, and the Israeli government, then led by Sharon has responded with equally ruthless measures that devastated Palestinian society mentally and physically. Since both Islamic and Jewish groups pushing for radical measures are moved by their faiths, religion in this conflict is viewed as a propellant, or the underlying problem. Consequently, in their analysis, conflict resolution pundits assumed religion was a detrimental factor, and practitioners relied on secular approaches that rested on problem-solving methods and reason.

Regrettably, human behavior in conflict situations can hardly be described as rational or reasonable. Galvanized by hatred, anger and fury, conflict-ridden individuals commit horrific acts of violence and revenge, such as suicide attacks, mutilation of the enemy, torture, targeting civilians without discriminating age or gender, and so on. Often, religion is abused to construct negative enemy images and justify such acts of extreme cruelty. For instance, religion has been used to justify violence and oppression of other groups during the conflicts of Sri Lanka, Ex-Yugoslavia, Rwanda, South Africa, among many others.[4] However, this source of violence and conflict can also be a resource for stopping violence, resolving the conflict, facilitating reconciliation, and establishing peace.

This work contributes to conflict resolution theory by problematizing the relatively untouched concept of "legitimacy", and by introducing hermeneutics as an analytical tool to the field. To that end, here I explore the process of the legitimation of narratives of peace and war during conflict, looking at Islamic narratives in Palestine as a case study. I argue that the question of "legitimacy" is key to understanding when war or peace is justified within a society and those leaders who attempt to engage in war or maintain conflict need to justify their decisions by establishing regimes of truth to mobilize the population towards their objectives. The underlying assumption is that culture and religion *do* matter in conflict and conflict resolution. Cultural and religious constructs can either promote "cultural violence" by encouraging, provoking, or justifying violence, or they can be resources for "cultural peace" by promoting and encouraging coexistence and peace, or by delegitimizing and undermining oppression and violence.

Religion plays a significant role in Middle Eastern traditional approaches to peace and conflict resolution, since religious affiliation of the peacemaker affects his/her status, and traditional and religious belief systems are considered more credible sources. Analyzing this process of legitimation also provides insights regarding the legitimate conflict resolution mechanism that is acceptable to the parties to the conflict. For this purpose, this work examines the potential role of the traditional ways of dealing with conflict such as *musalaha* (reconciliation), *tahkim* (arbitration), and *hudna* (truce). Answering these questions also serves to uncover the uncanny relationship between conflict and religion, and contributes to the understanding of how religious (in this particular case, Islamic) beliefs, commitments, or traditions shape or influence concrete social actions—such as motivating conflictual or peaceful behavior—and to what extent. Moreover, it helps us to understand what human needs religious texts and images fulfill.

In conflict situations—especially in intractable conflicts—transition from war-like behavior to peace behavior is very hard, since the parties have invested significant resources to continue the conflict. Additionally, signing an agreement between political leaders is hardly enough for a sustainable peace. Since the communities of the rival parties are under the influence of a history filled with resentment, dehumanization, anger and rage, it is very difficult to change the conflictual psychology of the communities. Changing negative images into a positive one is usually very hard, as the individuals have deep injuries and traumas as a result of the long-standing violence. Hence, for peace to be sustainable and lasting there is need to change the negative perceptions of the "other," and to establish constructive relations between the communities. This requires justification for altering the negative mind frames concerning the "other," in addition to addressing the needs and interests of the parties. As remarked by Lederach, "[n]egotiation becomes possible when the needs and interest of all those involved and affected by the conflict are legitimated and articulated," and "mediation can and should facilitate the articulation of legitimate needs and interests of all concerned into fair, practical, and mutually acceptable solutions."[5]

Thus, for peace to be sustainable it must be seen as legitimate by the communities involved, and the leadership that sign the agreement must also be considered legitimate by the majority of the community. In addition, intervenors in the conflict and the process of third party assistance must be viewed as legitimate and be accepted by the communities involved. This view was supported by my research and perhaps best articulated by Dr. Azzam who stated that "people must agree with the negotiators and the negotiations; when no one supports the leaders, it is no use to have such negotiation."[6] Therefore, I suggest that conflict resolution theory should include an analysis of the nature of leadership, sources of legitimacy and authority, and identify those leaders who have the courage to advocate peace with the "enemy."

To that end, I explore the sources of legitimacy and authority within the context of Palestinian society. For my exploration, I utilize Max Weber's analysis regarding the sources of legitimacy, and legitimate authority. I argue that different communities derive legitimacy from different sources; religion, culture and the evolution of the society impact the community's sources of legitimacy. The sources of legitimacy in the Palestinian society are based on subjective sources, particularly a mixture of religion and custom. Islamic sources (e.g. the Quran, the *Hadith*, and the *Sunna*) play a crucial role in the process of legitimization. Until recent years Western conflict resolution theory and practice have been dominated by a secular, rational, and problem-solving approach, and scholars viewed religion and culture as problematic, or ignored them altogether. Yet, ignoring religion and culture also means ignoring vast sources of values, traditions and institutions that can form the basis for reconciliation between enemies. As the Mufti of Jerusalem pointed out, "to resolve conflicts it is necessary to pay attention to the customs. Every society has its own customs, and these customs must be taken into account..."[7] Moreover religio/cultural values, traditions and institutions can assist healing deep social and personal injuries and traumas. However, this does not mean that contributions of conflict resolution theory should be ignored either. As Marc Gopin aptly states "it is self evident that official processes of diplomacy and rational methods of negotiation are indispensable to the solution of any conflict involving states and/ or large number of people who live within particular geographic boundaries."[8] But he correctly adds: "it is equally true that right beneath the surface of most human exchanges is a myriad of constructs of reality, of the collective self and of the "other" by each and every party to a conflict, including intervenors."[9] These constructs, whether cultural or religious, may perpetuate conflict by dehumanizing the other and justifying violence, or may promote peace and nonviolence by emphasizing common humanity and encouraging co-existence.

In many of the post-Cold War conflicts, religion is one of the central identifying characteristics of communities in conflict. This is especially true for the Israeli-Palestinian conflict, which has enormous religious tension. The politization of religion in Israeli-Palestinian conflict—as it is the case with many other conflicts—is facilitated by ambiguities in religious texts and doctrinal sources on war and peace. Religion is one of the main determinants of identity for both Israelis and Palestinians and the majority of both communities view religion as an integral aspect of their culture. Thus religion seems to be one of the major problems in this particular conflict. However, the aim of understanding the role of religio-cultural texts and institutions is not to depict a pessimistic picture of the Israeli-Palestinian conflict, but rather to highlight the much greater potential available for a more systematic and coordinated mobilization of religio-cultural resources and capacities for conflict resolution and peace-building.

Religion touches upon deep levels of identity. Religious feelings can mobilize people faster then any other element of their identity. The moral and spiritual forces of religion encourage people to act and change.[10] Rituals are powerful means of communication, in which followers of a religion connect to their spiritual sources and observe their values and beliefs.[11] "When a moral message serves to mobilize mass action, or when the moral messenger backs its words with effective leadership of its own, the religious actor can become a significant catalyst for change."[12] In societies like the Palestinian society, religious institutions represent a significant portion of the population and possess moral legitimacy as well as the capacity to reach and mobilize adherents throughout the community. For these reasons religion needs to be a domain of inquiry in conflict resolution theory and conflict resolution scholars must develop methodologies to constructively interact with the religious leaders, scholars, and even fundamentalists. This means hermeneutically engaging with these groups within a conflict resolution framework, and including an analysis of religious texts, myths, symbols and traditions, together with various institutions that legitimize or delegitimize violence.

Every religious discourse contains a variety of narratives. The constellation of power relations and leaders enables a certain narrative to emerge as the dominant one at a particular period. Since these different narratives, based on various interpretations of religious texts, compete with each other for hegemony in the political and social arena there is a need to understand the process of how one narrative becomes hegemonic. Thus explaining the role of effective history for the Palestinian community, their religious and cultural meaning-making processes, together with the role of formal and informal institutions and the financial support these institutions receive becomes important for understanding potential resources for peace-building. This analysis also shows that the process is not predetermined and static but can change as a result of careful and coordinated peace making and reconciliation efforts.

In that line, I examine competing readings of Islamic texts on peace and conflict resolution to understand which elements contribute to social acceptance and dominance of one particular narrative over others. I investigate the relationship of effective history, power and institutional practices in this process. In particular, I analyze how different groups in the Palestinian Territories justify their perspectives of the conflict and its resolution, utilizing cultural and religious texts, vocabulary, symbols, and institutional sites.

Conflicts are real. They affect real people. Real people die, real people decide to take up arms and kill, real people become refugees, and it is real people that suffer. What is interesting though is: "how do people make sense of events, what makes them decide how to act, to kill or to die for, and how do they interpret and give meaning to wars?" This study rests on the belief that, understanding the process of interpretation, especially at critical times, such as conflicts, is crucial for conflict resolution studies. This book offers a framework for understanding the dynamics of mass mobilization towards peace and war, and uncovers the process of how individuals interpret their realities and act upon their interpretations, through a Gadamer-based hermeneutical approach that includes a Foucauldian understanding of power.

Hermeneutics as the theory of the operations of understanding in their relation to the interpretation of texts[13] aims at understanding the meaning making processes and actors' definitions of a situation. The Gadamerian hermeneutical approach captures the inter-subjective and continual process of interpretation, which is conditioned by religious and cultural traditions, myths, texts and also historical experiences of the community. In the process of the legitimization of narratives, different interpretations compete with each other for discursive dominance.

This competition takes place at institutional sites, whereby truth, knowledge, and beliefs are produced and legitimated. Power relations and technologies of power play a key role in elevating one truth over another, and render one narrative more important then others. Textual (religious and cultural texts), contextual (religious, cultural constructs, and effective history) and power relations embedded within the society delimit what can be said and not said. In other words, they form the possibilities and constraints for emerging narratives. Various institutional sites become important locales for reaching out to the population, and for the production, reproduction, and legitimization of narratives. At these institutional sites, various technologies of power or tactics are employed to establish regimes of truth. In this process, different groups utilize cultural and religious vocabulary and symbols that the population is familiar with and considers legitimate. Additionally, these groups utilize pre-existing social structures as resources to mobilize the society. The effectiveness and popularity of the institutions these groups are affiliated with assist them in reaching out to the community as well as giving them credibility and legitimacy.

There are a variety of possible explanations as to why people choose one religious response to a conflict over another. Some of these explanations are related to cognitive and emotional needs that may be met by particular religious imagery, symbolism, or text. Social motivations and personal experiences also play crucial roles in determining affiliations with a group that espouses a certain approach to religious texts. Violent or politically coercive aspects of a particular religious response may be not as important as other benefits received from a particular group. For example, most Hamas supporters, including Christian Palestinians, emphasized the effectiveness and quality of the services provided by institutions that were affiliated by Hamas rather then the violent and coercive aspects of the organization. They argued that Hamas was the only group that was doing work to relieve the suffering of the Palestinian people. Therefore, I argue that institutions play an important role in the legitimation of narratives and in controlling the discursive space, and thus, conflict resolution theory should also include an analysis of the role of institutions in the legitimation of narratives and peace-building.

Finally, based on the findings of my work, I argue that religion can play a constructive role in reconciliation and peace-building in the region. Religious involvement in peacemaking initiatives can prepare and equip conflict resolution practitioners and diplomats for much more proactive roles in transforming the conflict. Gopin supports this argument by stating that "a close study of the sacred texts, traditions, symbols and myths that emerge in conflict situations may contribute to theoretical approaches to conflict analysis by providing a useful frame of reference for conflict resolution workshops, and interfaith dialogue groups, and by creating a bridge to the unique cultural expression of a particular conflict."[14]

The questions, then, become: how can we utilize religion as a resource for peacemaking? Is there a way to empower those groups and individuals that support a nonviolent Islamic approach to actively pursue a just peace for all parties involved? This book concludes by offering a framework of conflict resolution that is derived from hermeneutically engaging in religio-cultural texts and traditions concerning conflict resolution in the Palestinian Territories.

Method and Conclusion

The discussion of hermeneutics has three major conclusions for this work. The first conclusion relates to its epistemology and methodology. Epistemologically this project situates itself within the tradition of "perspectivism." Perspectivism, derived from Friedrich Nietzsche's works in general, here refers to the view of the object of study from where the subject or the observer stands in relation to it. It does not argue whether 'truth' exists or not, but it is based on the contention that the embeddedness of the observer within a particular historical, religious/cultural context and his/her experience in the world influences the ways s/he makes sense of it.

For Nietzsche, knowing the world is always being in the world: there is only a perspective of seeing, only a perspective of "knowing"; and the more effects we allow to speak about one thing and the more eyes we can use to observe one thing, the more complete will our "concept" of this thing and our "objectivity" be.[15] These perspectives are formed as a result of our positioning in relation to our horizons, and are therefore affected by our cultural/religious, sociological, and historical context as well as personal experiences. It is thus important to employ a variety of perspectives and effective interpretation in the service of knowledge. Therefore, for Nietzsche it is nonsensical to talk about a subject that is timeless, will-less, and disinterested.

Perspectivism in that sense refers to an "activity of knowing" which unites the knower (the subject) and the known (object), and it is sensitive to the cultural embeddedness and physical embodiedness. This epistemological standpoint rejects the idea that there is a separation between cognitive and affective constitution and supports the argument that different forms of knowing involve different forms of effects. It also rejects the Cartesian distinction between object and subject. Perspectivism is an approach that is self-reflexive: conscious of where one stands in relation to the matter that it deals with, his/her relationship with it or his/her cultural/ historical situatedness. This view allows for multiplicity of meaning and possibilities. It also allows re-engagement with the subject matter from different angles in order to understand and make sense of it. It does not deny or affirm the existence of a "truth" out there, but argues for the possibility of multiple interpretations of truth.

Perspectives, as understood in this context, refer to complexes of judgments about the world and different judgments involve different styles of reasoning. Perspectives are rooted in the ways of acting in the world and they also articulate the acting subject (the agency). Therefore, perspectives are constitutive of the form of agency and the form of agency is constitutive of the perspectives. Such an approach is sensitive to the historical and cultural situatedness of the subject.

Epistemology of perspectivism is in line with the hermeneutical approach of Gadamer, who sees hermeneutics as a universally ontological condition.[16] In this ontological condition, individuals interpret the world out there based on their horizons and from the particular vantage point the observer stands on. This horizon constitutes the perspective of the observer and is comprised of the historical, cultural, religious, linguistic, and social background of the observer, while also including his/her prejudices.

Recognizing this leads to the conclusion that this study represents one of many possible perspectives regarding the study at hand and does not claim to be the only 'truth' out there. Besides, it also leads to the acknowledgment that this work is a product of the historical situatedness of its author. As a Turkish woman, who studied in United States of America and considers herself to be a Muslim, the author recognizes that this work is not free of prejudice. Yet, I use the term prejudice here in a positive sense, as "biases of our openness to the world."[17] Prejudices are taken here, as "conditions whereby we experience something— whereby what we encounter says something to us."[18] It is about how our experience in this world and our perspectives comes into life. Therefore, I attempt to adopt a self-reflexive approach and be aware of the way I am influencing the study and the way I am influenced by it.

The methods that were employed for this study are manifold. This work adopts a "qualitative case study" as a research design. Here "qualitative" refers to a multi-method focus that involves an interpretive and naturalistic approach.[19] Naturalistic approach means that the subject matter is studied in its natural setting. Although perspectivism as an epistemological standpoint does not claim to hold the absolute truth, it is not based on an imagination without any concrete base. Thus, the study here is based on an empirical fieldwork conducted in Israel and Palestinian Territories during the summer of 2000. The locale of this study has been mainly East Jerusalem, the West Bank cities of Bethlehem, Hebron, and Beit Jala. During this process, I have attempted to make sense of the phenomena that I studied in terms of the *meanings* employed by the people I have interviewed and observed.

I have employed a variety of methods, empirical materials and observations in a single case study to gain an in-depth perspective of my initial research question: when does one particular narrative become legitimated and why? Within this research design, an in-depth case study approach enabled me to find out what is common and what is particular about legitimation of narratives of war and peace based on the Islamic tradition among the Palestinians. In my analysis, I included the nature of my case, its historical background, the physical setting, as well as its economic, political, religious and cultural contexts.

The basic method of data collection rested on semi-structured interviews with the persons that are directly involved in local organizations and are engaged in social movements, as well as local people who are not directly involved in these organizations. Two sets of questions were prepared for two different groups. The first group consisted of "middle range leaders," which includes local religious leaders such as imams, muftis and religious scholars, directors of organizations for conflict resolution and peace, and community leaders from the refugee camps. This group is particularly important because they are involved in organizing, coordinating the public, influencing them through meetings, sermons, social services, and lectures.

The second group involved members of the community who are targeted by the local leaders, such as students, merchants, and women. The second set of questions was designed to understand how these people are influenced and attracted by the messages of the local leaders. Both groups have shown willingness to share their perspective of the conflict and its resolution, their frustration and how they interpret the religious texts and the current situation.

The questions asked were semi-structured, which enabled the persons to be creative and gave them the flexibility to add what they consider to be necessary. It is my belief that semi-structured interviews were best suited to my data collection because a structured interview would have been limiting and constraining the dialog that I hoped to generate. The semi-structured interview approach led to in-depth conversations and helped me to *understand* their complex behavior without imposing any a priori categorizations that might have limited my inquiry. Furthermore, this approach allowed me to see the dilemmas and interaction of complex situations that the Palestinian population encounters.

The interviews were conducted in a comfortable and informal environment, where the author was able to learn how the interviewees feel and think about the conflict, Islam, and Israelis. During my stay in the West Bank, I stayed at a Bible College, which gave me access to the Christian Palestinian community as well as an opportunity to observe the interaction between Muslim and Christian Palestinians. At different occasions, my background as a Muslim women and my knowledge of the Quran and *Hadith* literature gave me access to various Muslim community leaders at Mosques and other settings. At times I was asked to recite from the Quran to "prove" that I was a Muslim and "know" what I was talking about. Passing these initial tests enabled me to gain credibility among the members of the society and gave me the chance to have in-depth conversations about issues presented in this thesis.

Being a women researcher also assisted me in many ways. It gave me an easy access to female Palestinians whom I interviewed. At various occasions I was invited to the homes of the Palestinians where I interviewed and met with their families. This helped me to observe the Palestinian life in-depth from a different angle and resulted in stimulating conversations regarding the daily life of Palestinians, their relationship to Islam and the "other," as well as conflicting views within the Palestinian society. Unfortunately, it was not possible to tape-record the interviews due to the sensitive nature of the topics and the risk it held for those who were interviewed. Yet, these conversations were supported with a journal, recordings of the observations and events that took place during my stay in the region.

The period of these interviews coincided with the Camp David meetings between July 11 and 24, which enabled me to follow the Palestinian news and people's reactions to and expectations from it in person. The Camp David Summit that took place in United States, where Israeli Prime Minister Barak and the Palestinian Leader Arafat came together to discuss the final status issues were of critical importance, and its failure was one of the reasons for the Peace Process to collapse. Being in the West Bank gave me the opportunity to talk to Palestinians about their views of and expectations from this meeting, together with their ideas about the future of relations between Palestinians and Israelis.

Most of my interviews were conducted in English, since most of the Palestinians I interviewed (including the Imams) were proficient in this language. However, my interviews relied heavily on Arabic terms regarding religious concepts. I am particularly indebted to Nidal and Nayef, who offered their help as my guides and at times as my translators of cultural mores, jargon, and language, and also connected me to various individuals, including students and imams, whom, without their help, I would not have access to. Nidal, who was a graduate of sociology, also assisted me in designing the right questions and approaches in a complex setting such as the West Bank and East Jerusalem. All my informants and interviewees were informed about the nature and the goals of my research. Due to the sensitive nature of this research, they will remain anonymous (their real names will not be used, or only their first names will be used), to protect their identities, unless they agreed otherwise.

A second trip to the region, this time including a trip to Gaza, was planned to further deepen my research and conduct interviews with other Islamic leaders. However, the breakout of Al-Aqsa *Intifada* made it impossible to conduct any research in the region. The situation has not changed since then. Therefore one of the major shortcomings of this work is that the number of interviews conducted and the period spent in the region is limited. In order to compensate this shortcoming, I have interviewed various Palestinians individuals and met with officials who took part in the Palestinian negotiation team in Washington DC.

Newsletters and brochures that local organizations produce and distribute also support this research. Observing the activities and strategies of these organizations to mobilize people towards their constructed ends, the speeches delivered by the local leaders, as well as educational tools (for example, history books) are also part of the data utilized here. The data also focuses on how the population receives these strategies and activities, and how they affect the way people think about events and the conflict in particular. Listening and collecting tapes of sermons, which is a very popular way of communicating religious ideas and thoughts not only within Palestinian Territories but also outside of Palestine, is another source that is used in this project. Many sermons can also be found at various Internet sites, together with the speeches and essays of some important religious leaders. Looking at popular literature, arts, and music, and observing sermons, radio and TV programs are also important tools to understand how the process of legitimation of various narratives takes place. The collective conscience and consciousness are developed, reproduced, and perpetuated through popular culture and they serve to represent and create the collective mood.

A deep reading of the sacred texts such as the Quran, the Sunna and the Hadith also supports this research. This is important for understanding the nuances between various interpretations of the texts and how they are utilized under different conditions and in different eras for different purposes. Various historical documents, and history textbooks that are used in the schools of the region are also utilized during the research in order to develop an understanding of how history was constructed from the perspective of the Palestinians and how it serves to understand their current perspective. The way that history is constructed is very important to understand the perspective of a group, and a deconstruction of this history will serve to unveil various issues that are latent.

International and local newspapers have also been incorporated to the research in order to follow the developments and how they are represented in different sources. A thorough exploration of the literature on the history of the region, history of the conflict, hermeneutics, sociology, conflict resolution, Islam, religion in general, and conflict resolution practices in the region supplements the previously mentioned methods. This way, the author utilizes the knowledge that was produced previously and detects those areas where there needs a contribution and what is missing.

The data gathered from the fieldwork and the interviews are subject to the critical interpretation of the author, together with the documents and secondary sources used in the research. How the perspective of the author influences the interpretation of this data will be made clear throughout the text. This self-reflexive consciousness of interpreting the data related to the study constitutes the first-level application of hermeneutics.

There is another important conclusion in the discussion of hermeneutics that relates to the content of the work. Observing the Islamic social movements in the Palestinian Territories, we see competing groups with their own interpretation of what peace/war means and how peace should be attained. In their competition for legitimization, it becomes important to understand what this particular conflict means for the population involved and how they define peace. In this sense, the conflict itself becomes a text for interpretation, and developing an understanding of how the Palestinians interpret this conflict requires a critical hermeneutic approach, where culture, religion and historical situatedness are incorporated.

We have seen the waves of Pan-Arabism, Palestinian nationalism, and Pan-Islamism in the region. The current situation suggests that the needle of the compass has turned toward Islamic social movements. This means that Islamic social movements are gaining velocity and becoming a major discourse. The rise of suicide attacks targeting Israeli civilians under the banner of Islam, especially since the Al-Aqsa *Intifada*, and the rise of support for such actions back this observation.[20] As a result, it becomes important to understand what this conflict means to the population involved and how they define peace. However, the Islamic social movements are not a unified whole. There exist various different interpretations of peace and proposals for action. For that reason, it becomes crucial to understand the dynamics behind the process, as well as when and why one narrative becomes legitimized rather then others. This requires a careful examination of the meaning-construction process, which is situated in the unique historical and cultural/religious context of the Palestinian Society. Examining this process of legitimization and how Palestinians makes sense of the conflict constitutes the second level application of the hermeneutical approach.

The development of Islamic narratives entails also a study of Islamic scholarship concerning interpretation of the Scripture. Interpretation (*ijtihad* and *tafsir*) has played a significant role in the development of Islamic Law (*Shariah*) as well as Islamic philosophical tradition and mysticism (sufism), and has been an integral part of Islamic sciences in general throughout its history. The most influential scholars include, but are not confined to, Al-Farabi, Al-Ghazzali, Ibn Arabi, Al-Mawardi, and Ibn Rushd. Currently a new group of scholars have been working on interpretation of the texts within the Islamic tradition to develop new approaches that deal with contemporary developments of the modern world. Some of the critical scholars include Fazlur Rahman, Amina Wadud, Farid Essack, Mohammed Arkoun, and al-Ghannouchi. The history and the current development of the Islamic interpretation display various similarities and also differences from its Western counterparts. A dialogue between these two traditions will contribute to our understanding of the hermeneutical tradition in general, and various developments within Islam in particular. Therefore, focusing on a critical dialogue with the interpretive tradition as developed from within the Islamic tradition to evaluate the legitimacy of Islamic narratives concerning war and peace will constitute the third and final-level application of hermeneutics in this study.

Nevertheless, another limitation of this work is that it only focuses on the Islamic narratives of peace and conflict resolution and it leaves out Christian, Druze and Jewish perspectives. Developing a conflict resolution strategy in the region requires similar works to be done among the Christian, Druze and Jewish communities that interact in the region. All of these traditions incorporate visions of peace as well as narratives that justify war and violence under certain circumstances. A research that extends to cover all these traditions would have enlarged this project to an unfeasible extend both in terms of time and finances as well as volumes. Therefore, this research is limited to focusing on the Muslim-Palestinian community that lives in West Bank, Gaza, and East Jerusalem. However, it is important to initiate an internal dialogue within these religious traditions as well as initiating a dialogue between them to promote peace in the region.

Finally, the author of this study sees the field of conflict resolution and peace studies as a normative project that aims to develop strategies to resolve conflicts nonviolently. Furthermore, she also contends that it is the responsibility of the activists and scholars to understand how violence is justified in different communities, develop strategies to resolve conflicts and to empower those groups and leaders who are working to establish peace through nonviolent means. Therefore, after the analysis of when and why one particular Islamic narrative of peace or war becomes legitimated within the Palestinian Territories, this study concludes by introducing a framework for conflict resolution model that emerges from within the work and the conflict itself. This framework is based on the findings of this research in terms of the relationship between narratives, legitimacy and power within the context of Palestinian society. It is also built upon the religious/cultural traditions that influence the process of legitimation, power relations, and authentic conflict resolution mechanisms that are embedded within the long history of the region. Yet, this conflict resolution framework, which will be presented in the conclusion briefly, is not developed exhaustively, since this would have expanded this book another volume. A more detailed analysis on combining conflict resolution models developed in the West and indigenous conflict resolution mechanisms of the Middle East deserves to be the topic of another extensive work.

Endnotes

1. See Allan Johnson "UN Alarm at Palestinian Poverty" in *BBC* Ferbruary 22, 2007

2. W. Zartman. "Explaining Oslo" *International Negotiation* vol. 2 (1997), 195-215, 208.

3. Zartman 1997. 209.

4. For more information see Kadayifci-Orellana "Religion, Violence and the Islamic Tradition of Nonviolence" in *The Turkish Yearbook of International Relations.* No. 34. 2004; 23-62

5. J. P. Lederach, *Preparing for Peace: Conflict Transformation Across Cultures.* (Syracuse: Syracuse University Press, 1995). 14.

6. Interview with Dr. Sheikh Azzam Hebron July 20, 2000.

7. Interview with the Mufti of Jerusalem. Jerusalem. July 5, 2000.

8. Marc Gopin, *Holy War Holy Peace* Oxford University Press, 2002, 37.

9. Gopin 2002.

10. Abu-Nimer, Mohammed. *Nonviolence and Peacebuilding in Islam* (Florida: University Press of Florida, 2003), 17.

11. Abu-Nimer 2003., 18.

12. Cynthia Sampson, "Religion and Peace Building" in *Peacemaking in International Conflict: Methods and Techniques.*_W. Zartman and L. Rasmussen eds. (Washington DC:United States Institute of Peace Press, 1997), 281.

13. Paul Ricoeur, *Hermeneutics and the Human Sciences*: Edited and Translated by John (London and New York: Cambridge University Press, 1982), 43.

14. Marc Gopin,. Between Eden and Armageddon: The Future of World Religions, Violence, and Peacemaking. (Oxford University Press, 2000), 15.

15. Friedrich Nietzsche *Genealogy of Morals* Walter Kaufmann trans. (New York: Vintage Books, 1989), 110.

16. For a detailed discussion on Gadamer's hermeneutical approach see Chapter 2.

17. Gadamer, Hans-Georg "Universality of the Hermeneutical Problem" in *Philosophical Hermeneutics: Hans Georg Gadamer* translated and ed. By David E. Linge. (Los Angeles: University of California Press, 1997), 9

18. Gadamer 1997.

19. Norman K Denzin and Yvonna S. Lincoln "Introduction: Entering the Field of Qualitative Research" in *Handbook of Qualitative Research* (London: Sage Publications, 1994), 2.

20. According to Christopher Dickey, the polls in 2002 show that the support for suicide attacks has risen to 80 percent. See Christopher Dickey "Inside Suicide Inc." *Newsweek* at http://www.msnbc.com/news/735266.asp, 2002, 2.

Chapter 2

Theoretical Reflections: Legitimacy, Conflict Resolution and Hermeneutics

War and conflict as social phenomena, lurking in all aspects of social life have been studied from various perspectives thereby giving rise to competing paradigms among scholars. Among these perspectives, conflict resolution field attempts to understand the sources of human conflicts and to transform their destructive aspects into constructive relations between states or communities. Conflict resolution, originally developed by the Western middle class to resolve conflicts in industrial relations, was applied to international conflicts in late 1960s and early 1970s.The traditional conflict resolution approaches to conflict and war are derived from the "realist" international relations tradition, which sees war as "nothing but a duel on a larger scale, an act of force to compel the enemy to do the will, a true political instrument" in Clausewitzian terms.[1]

Realists, believing in that there is an objective truth or a reality, have been aspiring to discover the right scientific method for explaining the world. Positivism has been the dominating epistemology of conflict resolution since its emergence. Positivist epistemology in international relations field uses a deductive reasoning that entail propositions linking sets of variables, which are tested against empirical observations. Those interrelated hypotheses that pass the empirical test are formulated into an empirical theory. Based on the Cartesian fact-value distinction, the methodology that comes with this epistemology is characterized by the search for explanation based on cause and effect analyses. In order value distinction, the methodology that comes with this epistemology is characterized by the search for explanation based on cause and effect analyses. In order to discover objective laws, "[t]he object for an explanation or the dependent variable requires the identification of independent variables which 'explain' the phenomenon under observation."[2] Theories are modified or rejected if anomalies occur. This epistemological and methodological grounding does not allow space for phenomena such as culture or religion, since they seem to be too subjective and cannot be operationalized from a positivist perspective.

The traditional toolbox[3] and the practice of conflict resolution are informed by various assumptions, although the traditional Western[4] approach has been undergoing a major transition,[5] and its central assumptions are being called into question. These assumptions include: conflict is a normal, endemic feature of social interaction; it is not inherently good or bad, but can be constructive or destructive; facing conflict is necessary and is recommended; humans are rational beings that tend to maximize self interests; individual interests, positions, needs and desires are important; rationality and rational choice is crucial and settling of conflicts based on rational planning is preferred; written agreements are central; legal formality and procedures are essential; parties are task oriented and should focus on negotiable issues; and material resources are important.[6]

Conflict resolution starts with the attempt to explain the causes of conflict in social life, and then moves into analyzing conflict dynamics, namely its escalation and de-escalation. Since conflict is seen as a generic phenomenon that takes place at various different levels of society, isolating the conflict system has been the major mode of inquiry. Based on the assumption that humans are able to change their behaviors and attitudes, the traditional conflict resolution approach carries the belief that the settlement of differences and the making of peace is something that can be learned and improved. Consequently, the field focuses on the 'resolution' of the conflict by changing the attitudes of the policy makers, the main idea being to uncover the causes of the conflict, factors that escalate it, and to transform the conflictual relation into a cooperative one. To this end, finding a ground for dialogue and communication between the parties is a critical factor in conflict resolution process.

The traditional tools of conflict resolution vary from procedures of international law, arbitration, negotiation, mediation, and problem solving to facilitation. Implicit in the study of traditional Western conflict resolution and development of this toolbox, is the idea that the procedures of social science make it possible to achieve a general, analytic description and understanding of the properties and processes of conflict. These approaches see conflict as inevitable in all societies, but make a distinction between destructive and constructive conflicts, arguing that conflict resolution should embrace creative and nonviolent consequences of conflict and minimize its destructive consequences. The development and testing of empirical theory about the conditions of conflict and peace become the ultimate intellectual task of conflict analysis, since the ultimate objective of conflict resolution is to reduce human misery.

In this framework, conflict resolution scholars give priority to "reason" and hold the belief that since humans are beings endowed with reason it is possible for them to come to an agreement after a process of rational argumentation. Rational argumentation comes with "giving good reasons" that can be rationally debatable. This view assumes that the parties are able to meaningfully communicate the reasons, reason being the "universal" capacity of every individual.[7] This approach is based on the belief that the reasons given for justification of any argument must be open to confirmation or disconfirmation. In this process, parties are considered to be able to leave aside their cultural/religious baggage and to focus on their interests. This framework is challenged as new types of conflicts emerged following the end of the Cold War

The collapse of the Cold War system brought major changes to the arena of international relations. With the end of the Cold War, the bipolar conceptualization of the world ended, and the globalization of information and economic power initiated a new trend of democratization in different parts of the world. The number of interstate wars decreased. However, the number of intrastate conflicts increased considerably. As Lederach points out, today "most current wars are intrastate affairs,"[8] and they are deep-rooted. Indeed, Wallensteen and Sollenberg notes that the intensity of these intrastate conflicts and casualties caused by them have been so high that the first post-Cold War decade has been the bloodiest since the advent of nuclear weapons.[9] Since some of these intrastate wars are viewed as threats to international peace and security in general, resolving them becomes utmost important for the world community. Today, the way we understand conflicts and war has changed dramatically. Recent violence in places like Rwanda, Bosnia, and East Timor, among others, and atrocities committed during these conflicts have led to the redefinition of international conflict and has instigated new approaches in the field of peace and conflict resolution.

The major shift in the nature of conflicts has been the proliferation of ethnic, religious, cultural, and environmental conflicts in recent decades. These conflicts involve people from different cultures and traditions, where the Western way of thinking does not dominate the way these people see the world and make sense of it. These communities live close to each other, or have been put together within the artificial state boundaries. They are traumatized with the impact of colonization and imperialism, and are lagging behind the West in material, technical and scientific terms. They suffer from extreme poverty and economic deprivation and the pressure of the globalizing economy.

Ethnic and religious conflicts are generally defined as identity conflicts. One crucial aspect of identity conflict is that it incorporates psychological, physical, social dimensions, since identity is an intrinsic element of the "self." A perceived threat to "self", or to a sense of security based on a distinctive identity usually overrides rational thought and reason. A wider social recognition of identity and effective participation in social, economic and political processes are recognized today as basic needs of all humanity.[10] Denial of that identity may lead to a sense of victimization and also to conflict.[11] Conflicts that are based on identity are usually much more complicated and harder to resolve than those conflicts over resources. Moreover, since ethnic conflicts take place between communities that live very close to each other, and usually have a history of hostility, it becomes harder to overcome grievances that have been accumulated over the course of history. Therefore these conflicts are long-standing. In order to capture the unique features of these conflicts new concepts such as "intractable" and "protracted" conflicts have been introduced.[12]

Another major shift concerning war has been the emergence of terrorism as a new means of war. Terrorism as a strategy does not allow an overt war with conventional weapons. Although terrorism has been around for a long time now, the way it is viewed especially after the September 11, 2001 attack in the United States have changed significantly. Terrorism as strategy of war has been an integral part of the Israeli- Palestinian conflict for many decades now. Yet, a terrorist for one party may be viewed as a freedom fighter by the other therefore it is a hard task to define what terrorism means to different groups. It is not unusual for a party to attempt to legitimize and justify these acts that might be called terrorism, under the rubric of "self-defense," basing it on various religious and cultural narratives, as is the case with groups such as Hamas and Islamic Jihad, among others.[13]

Finally, the technological developments increased speed and visualization, changed modes of representation of war and conflict. On the one hand, live media coverage of wars blurred the distinction between fact and fiction. On the other hand, it brought the devastation and destruction caused by these wars into the living rooms of many. By control of information, and choosing what to be covered what not to be covered, via embedded journalism for example, media began to take more active part in construction of reality. Means of reproduction have come to be used to generate, mediate and simulate all realities. Particular discursive constructions of "regimes of truth", related to just war and responsibility are represented in every realm of social life. Truth as an instrument and a product of perception is used to define the enemy, security, just war and the good life in a novel way. This mode of understanding turned war into a performance, "a game", as Der Derian puts it[14]. In this novel system of representation of war the individual is situated in a network of power relations through "mise en discourse" with those who claim to have a right to extract and interpret the truth. Consequently, novel approaches in international relations are not after mirroring reality, but recognizing and investigating "the interrelationship of power and representational practices that elevate one truth over another, that subject one identity to another, that make one discourse matter more than the next."[15]

In that line traditional approaches to conflict resolution are also now being reappraised and, in order to deal with the problems of contemporary conflicts, scholars[16] have started to question the basic assumptions of the field and to develop new approaches. Today, scholars in the field of Peace and Conflict Resolution are increasingly talking about the importance of combining peace at the level of official diplomacy with peace at the level of "civil society" and grassroots. We are witnessing a proliferation of the literature of "track-two diplomacy", "transformation", and "citizen diplomacy", among others. The common theme of these approaches is that they all recognize the importance of unofficial diplomacy that includes citizens, and they call for a multidimensional approach that integrates UN peace operations, intergovernmental organizations, regional organizations, NGOs, and grass-root groups in the process of establishing sustainable peace.

These approaches implicitly or explicitly argue that, for peace to be sustainable, it must be supported by the society in general and that both conflict resolution theory and practice should be sensitive to understanding the particular needs, historical, cultural and religious backgrounds of these societies. Not all societies share the same assumptions about conflicts. Many non-Western communities view Western attempts to resolve these conflicts with suspicion, and as the new form of intervention or imperialism. Moreover, trying to apply an approach that is alien and non-understood or not internalized by the communities cannot go further than unsuccessful impositions and will not be sustainable. They might result in settlements as a result of the distribution of power in the world, and coercive measures that have been applied for example in Serbia and Iraq, but they will not be long lasting.

Sustainability of peace means not only "a movement from confrontation to negotiation to dynamic, peaceful relationships", but "also to create a proactive process that is capable of regenerating itself over time—a spiral of peace and development instead of a spiral of violence and destruction."[17] Increasingly, it is recognized that the solution to the conflict must come from the parties themselves, rather then being imposed upon them. Therefore proponents of these approaches call for conflict resolution mechanisms from top-down-high level and bottom up grass-roots methods. This is based on the recognition that although a peace treaty may be signed, unless the individuals of the conflicting parties change their relationships, the peace will be incomplete. This is particularly true for those conflicting communities that live in close proximity, and where the experience of the conflict is immediate in their daily lives, such as Israelis and Palestinians. Therefore, it becomes crucial to combine different levels of the society during the peacemaking processes.

In this respect, Lederach argues that a successful peace process requires integrative initiatives at different levels of society. He distinguishes three levels where building peace can take place: top leadership, middle range leadership, and grassroots leadership. Lederach also states that since the middle range has better access to both top and grassroots leaderships, it is more likely to be successful at integrating these different processes, and thus, bringing about a sustainable peace. A comprehensive approach that connects activities at different levels, such as focusing on high level negotiations led by a highly visible single mediator at the top leadership level, problem solving workshops, peace commissions, insider-partial teams and training in conflict resolution at middle range leadership, as well as local peace commissions, grass-root training, prejudice reduction, psychological work in postwar trauma at grass-root level leadership, is more likely to result in a sustainable peace. The key to the success of this process, according to Lederach, "lies in the *relationship* of the involved parties with all that term encompasses at the psychological, spiritual, social, economic, political and military needs." [18]

Nevertheless, neither of these levels presents a unified idea of peace. These levels of action include groups with very different ideas of peace and resolution of the conflict, which compete to become dominant. Lederach states that "leaders within each level have connections to their "own people" up and down the pyramid, at the same time, have counterparts within their own level who are perceived as enemies."[19] Within each society that experiences a deep-rooted conflict, peace means different things to different people. Different groups come with their own narratives of their conflicts and ways to deal with them. Lederach does not develop how these narratives emerge and gain the support of the population, which is a crucial question that conflict resolution scholars should deal with in order to understand the dynamics of the process and to link different levels of society together to work together towards peace.

At the heart of these issues are the question of "legitimacy" and the acceptability of the peace narrative. Scholars who argue that peace cannot be imposed but must be brought about from within the context of the conflict have recognized this crucial question of 'legitimacy'. Yet, neither Lederach, nor other scholars in the field who focus on these issues deal with the question of how does one particular idea of peace or resolution of conflict becomes more acceptable to the society, or why does one particular idea of peace become the dominant idea within a society.

This question is also closely related to the idea of 'cultural violence' developed by J. Galtung. Galtung identifies cultural violence as those religious, cultural, ideological, or linguistic symbols that legitimize direct or structural violence.[20] Galtung states:

> Much direct violence can be traced back to vertical structural violence, such as exploitation and repression, for liberation, or to prevent liberation. In the background is cultural violence legitimizing both the structural violence and direct violence to undo it and to maintain it[...][21]

In that sense, myths and legends of one cultural group can be manipulated to dehumanize the opponent and justify the oppression and destruction of the other. Kumar Rupesinghe states that "[f]rom flags and anthems to inflammatory speeches and mythical stories, any aspect or particular elements of a culture, which encourage, provoke, or justify violence can be defined in terms of cultural violence."[22] Elements of cultural violence distances the "other" by using cultural myths and symbols to prove superiority of one group against another, to dehumanize the "enemy," and to justify violence. This concept suggests that both structural and direct violence is made possible and reinforced through various mechanisms that are embedded within a society.

Although this concept is crucial to understand how and why violence is legitimated, Galtung has not expanded on how cultural violence operates within the society. As Jacobsen states, Galtung insists "the focus of conflict resolution should be on understanding structural and cultural causes of violence and on understanding the problems of moving from conflict modes (attitudes- behaviors- contradictions) through outcome alternative (withdrawal-compromise-transcendence) to future prevention (empathy-nonviolence-creativity)."[23] Furthermore, he fails to explain how "cultural violence" is produced and reproduced within the society, and how "we" can create the conditions for the emergence of "cultural peace." He categorizes culture simply as "collective subconscious"[24] thus reduces it to a psychological phenomenon, and negates the dynamic, enabling and constraining role that culture plays. His approach takes the structure as the determining force and fails to acknowledge the dialectical relationship between the individual and his/her social institutional, cultural, and socio-political context. He does not explore how culture of violence becomes dominant, or what is its relationship with other narratives in a particular society. The same symbolic constructions that legitimize a culture of violence may also promote mechanisms to resolve conflicts peacefully and may serve to establish constructive relations with the "other". Therefore it becomes imperative to look at these constructions and to understand the how they legitimize conflictual or peaceful relations.

Violent conflict is co-constructed through the actions of the individuals situated in relation to the discursive and institutional continuities that enable the occurrence of war and render it a legitimate human behavior.[25] As Vivienne Jabri states:

> The starting assumption is that violent conflict is not a product of characteristics innate within the "make-up" of human beings or of instrumental reason, nor is it a product of the international system, but derives from the ontological relationship between agency and structure, where war as human action is a product of human decisions made within the context of structured social relations.[26]

War normalizes the abnormalities of peace and involves every individual in the society. As violent conflicts are results of human decisions and actions, any study of conflict must take into account the role of the individual or the acting subject within the structures that allow such violence as continuity in our social life. Ignoring the "institutional and discursive pillars of the society where war emerges and recursively feeds back to reconstitute and reproduce its constitutive elements,"[27] as from a realist perspective, reduces war to a calculated instrumentalist act. For that reason, conflict resolution scholars should seek to divulge the ideological basis of narratives of violent conflict and its relation to practice. They should also incorporate how war is reproduced or reinforced through shared inter-subjective meanings and images together with social institutions that serve to legitimate war and conflict. For that reason, they must study the sources of legitimacy in these communities to understand how religious and cultural symbols are used to justify violence.

Legitimacy and Conflict Resolution

Legitimacy is the phenomenon that people are willing to accept domination on normative grounds on which specific beliefs this acceptance is grounded.[28] Max Weber refers to legitimacy as the "prestige of being considered binding" that a social order enjoys.[29] Legitimacy becomes an important domain of inquiry in many ways for scholars of international relations and peace and conflict resolution. First of all, legitimacy forms the basis of when war becomes justified. Any leadership that attempts to wage war or continue an ongoing conflict needs to justify its discourses of war and its actions to mobilize the population towards that end. Indeed, at times of conflict political and military leaders do not hesitate to draw justification for their actions from their cultural, religious, and historical traditions. Second, legitimacy becomes important for the rightful conduct of war, as it informs the acceptable warfare strategies such as guerilla warfare or terrorizing attacks; choice of weapons such as nuclear weapons or conventional weapons; as well as treatment of prisoners based on the definition of the captured enemies, such as enemy combatant or prisoner of war.

Legitimacy is also important to define the right method of conflict resolution as it informs which mechanisms are considered legitimate, and whose mediation or facilitation is being accepted. How mediators are perceived is crucial for the success of that attempt. Since most of the time mediators come into the mediation process with their won interest and agenda, and at times with power, the third party may become directly involved in the bargaining process, such is the case with the United States in the Israeli-Palestinian conflict. Therefore, parties might have differing opinions of the acceptable intervention process and identity of the interveners. Some societies may view formal mediation attempts by neutral third parties and adjudication mechanism as a legitimate mechanism.

Whereas others may view informal mediation—led by a third party that knows the disputants, their history, and is recognized as having necessary religious, political, or social legitimacy—, reconciliation and healing as more legitimate ways to resolve conflicts.[30]

The concept of legitimacy is not only important for the emergence of narratives of peace and war and their acceptance by the population, but also for determining who is authorized to narrate. Not everybody's narratives are considered legitimate and not everybody has the authority to represent a community; furthermore, not every intervention to resolve the conflict is considered legitimate. Thus, legitimacy is also important to determine who are considered as the legitimate representatives of a party to the conflict and who has the right to intervene and mediate. Or, to put it in other terms, who has the right to represent the parties in the conflict. Leadership identification is always too problematic. This question becomes important in times of conflicts especially when there are various competing leaderships. For example who represents the Palestinian people, Arafat or Hamas? Who is going to be invited to the peace process?

Finally, legitimacy is also important to define the acceptable outcome of a peace process. For the outcome of any peace-building effort, may it be negotiations, mediations, or arbitration, to last and be successfully implemented among the populations involved, it must be considered legitimate and acceptable. Although it is not possible for every member of the community to agree on all issues or all the conditions of peace agreements, a critical majority of the population must consider the outcomes of the conflict termination effort and the conditions of peace as just and acceptable. Therefore, a peace treaty between the representatives of parties is necessary but not sufficient to sustain the peace between communities that have been involved in a conflict. Peace must be acceptable and perceived just by the population in general. This requires the inclusion of those groups that can damage the outcomes (through guerrilla warfare, or terrorism for example) of the peace process.

The "traditional"[31] conflict resolution theories do not question the concept of legitimacy but take it as a given. [32] This work problematizes the concept of legitimacy and argues that the implicated understanding of legitimacy in international relations and peace and conflict resolution is a particular one, developed as a result of specific religious, political, sociological and economic history of the Western societies. In that line, it also argues that different societies have different sources of legitimacy. This affects how different societies perceive what is legitimate and whose authority is legitimated. This, in turn, both constrains and enables various narratives to emerge as legitimate. For that reason, any international relations and conflict resolution scholar who attempts to resolve conflicts in different cultural contexts must take into account what legitimacy means for that particular society.

The concept of "legitimacy" is closely tied with the concepts of authority and power. Traditionally authority is defined as "legitimate power", "as power which is seen as fairly exercised or justly wielded."[33] The most important theorist of the modern idea of legitimacy is Max Weber, who formulated two possible foundations of legitimacy, namely subjective and external.[34] According to Weber, there are three possible bases of subjective legitimacy. These are:

> *i)* affective, which results from emotional surrender;
> *ii)* value-rational, which is determined by the belief in the absolute validity of the order as the expression of ultimate values of an ethical or esthetic or of any other type; and
> *iii)* religious, which is determined by the belief that salvation depends upon obedience to the order.[35]

On the other hand, he defines external bases of legitimacy as guaranteed by the expectation of specific external effects, which are interest situations.[36] He also distinguishes this group into twc categories. If the "validity is guaranteed by the probability that deviation frcm it within a given social group will result in a relatively general and practically significant reaction of disapproval,"[37] he calls it *convention.* "If it is externally guaranteed by the probability that physical or psychological coercion applied by a *staff* of people in order to bring about compliance or avenge violation," he calls it *law.*[38]

Weber also adds that the actors may ascribe legitimacy based on either "*tradition*: valid is that which has always been, or *effectual,* especially emotional, *faith*: valid is that which is newly revealed or exemplary, or *value-rational* faith: valid is that which has been deduced as an absolute, or positive enactment which is believed to be *legal.*[39] And, Weber also states that the legitimacy based on the sacredness of tradition is the oldest and most universal type of legitimacy.[40]

Weber, furthermore, states that different sources of legitimacy lead to different kinds of authority. If the sources of legitimacy are based on rational grounds, that is, "resting on a belief in the legality of enacted rules and the right of those elevated to authority under such rules to issue commands,"[41] the type of authority is called '*legal authority.*'[42] If legitimacy is based on tradition "resting on an established belief in the sanctity of immemorial traditions and the legitimacy of those exercising authority under them," he calls this type of authority '*traditional authority.*'[43] Finally he introduces the term '*charismatic authority*' to describe the types of authority "resting on devotion to the exceptional sanctity, heroism, or exemplary character of an individual person, and of the normative patterns or order revealed or ordained by him."[44] Legal order calls for obedience to the legally established impersonal order. The traditional order calls for obedience to the persons who hold the traditionally sanctioned position of authority, who is bound by the tradition. Whereas in the charismatic order, charismatic leader is the one who is obeyed by the virtue of personal trust within him.[45]

Adam Seligman argues that legitimacy in modern, Western liberal societies is based on *external* sources of legitimacy, "upon a politics of interest as delineated in the writings of Hobbes and Hume."[46] The Western idea of legitimacy is a product of Enlightenment and is constructed by the relationship between authority and the self. The self is construed as a self-regulating moral agent that has rights and is autonomous. This agency is rational and calculative and seeks the maximization of his/her interests. The authority is obeyed and legitimated because it is in the interest of the autonomous individual. In this economic reading of society, there is a contractual relationship based on mutual interests. The legitimacy is thus based on "rational grounds, resting on a belief in the legality of enacted rules and the right of those elevated to authority under such rules to issue commands (legal authority)," to quote Weber.[47] In this secularized view of society, God is invisible in the public sphere, if not dead. Religion becomes a matter of personal conscience and thus privatized.

The idea of legitimation is closely tied to the idea of justice. The way justice is defined distinguishes what is considered legitimate from what is illegitimate. Yet justice is not an absolute. What is considered "just" differs from society to society and from one time period to another. The Western notion of legitimacy led to the development of modern Just War theory to justify war in international relations. Although Just War theory has theological roots in the work of St. Augustine entitled *The City of God*, where he attempted to legitimize war as opposed to the pacific reading of Christianity, the theory was soon adopted by international lawyers, military, policy-makers, moral philosophers, as well as international relations theorists. This theory attempts to legitimate war based on a just cause, *jus ad bellum*, and the permitted conduct of war, *jus in bello*. Thus, justice overrides peace, and peace is defined as the absence of war. Decision to use war as a means 'to correct a wrong' belongs to the 'legitimate authority' which is the state.

It is possible to draw parallels between the idea of modern individual and the conceptualization of the state in international relations. In this parallel, the idea of an autonomous, calculative individual (or the actor) of international arena is the "state." The state is considered a unitary actor that tries to pursue its interests, and these called the "national interests." The autonomy of the individual is projected as "state sovereignty." The state is taken as a given, and it is considered a-historical. In turn, the policy makers, who are purposive actors that seek their goals via calculative reason, lead the decision-making process. The international system is considered to be in a state of chaos, where a contractual order is necessary to contain the violent capacity of man. Therefore a regulatory system is required to administer conflict and war.

The regulative aspects of rules of war, the legality of system defines when war is legitimized and how the civilians and war prisoners should be treated during war. These rules, as codified in the Hague and Geneva conventions, constitute the normative basis of war according to the traditional Western concept of international relations. Thus, the rules of Just War "do not merely render war tolerable, they enable war to take place where the constitutive element is justification."[48] As Jabri states, "the Just War discourse constitutes a set of interpretive schemes and structuring categories which are drawn upon by policy-makers, constituents, military personnel, and social theorists, in the production and reproduction of structures of signification and legitimation which constitute war as an aspect of social system."[49] In the formulation of "just war," the parallel between the authority of the state and the autonomy of the individual provides evidence on the multifaceted features of the conceptualizations of the individual, the state, and the justification of conflicts.

As the analysis above shows, traditional understanding of legitimate discourse of war, which has dominated the field and practice of international relations to this day, is a secular one based on the premises of state sovereignty, legality, and reason. This idea of legitimacy was taken for granted by many of the traditional conflict resolution and peace studies scholars. The repercussions of this approach are evident in the assumptions of conflict resolution theories.[50] The origins and development of this was not considered historical, nor was it ever problematized. Yet legitimacy and justification are culturally contingent and informed by the religious, historical, social, and economic experiences of a particular community. Therefore, in order to understand why one particular narrative of peace or war becomes legitimate it is necessary to look what legitimacy means for that population.

To mobilize support for their acts and policies at times of conflicts the leaders justify their narratives of the conflict through the symbolic orders embedded in their cultural traditions. These symbolic orders and meaning structures, which are inter-linked with structures of domination and legitimation, are mobilized to legitimate the interests of certain groups. In such an environment, narratives of peace and nonviolent conflict resolution compete with the narratives of violence and war. In this process of mobilizing support, shared norms, such as religious norms, are used as the basis for justifying particular narratives.

The individual gives meaning to the world surrounding him/her and social structures enable and/or draw the boundaries of these meanings. The link between the individual and social structure is found in the processes of generating meaning and in the interpretation of the life-world through cultural schemes and symbols. Thus, hermeneutics as the art/science of interpretation and understanding contributes to conflict resolution field because it gives us the tools for uncovering the procedures through which humans interpret the world around them and act upon their interpretations. Uncovering the link between interpretation and action is especially important to comprehend the dynamics of mass mobilization towards war or peace, since the high risks involved require the conviction of the individuals in the legitimacy of the narrative that justifies the conflict. In order to understand the ability of a leadership to mobilize populations, the legitimization process of discourses must be appraised.

Defining Narrative and Discourse

At this point, it is important to insert what it is meant with the notions of "discourse" and "narrative". Although at times "narrative" and "discourse" are used interchangeably, this project prefers the term Islamic "narratives" to distinguish different interpretations of Islamic texts related to peace and war. According to Oxford Dictionary of Philosophy discourse is "a continuous stretch of language containing more than one sentence: conversations, narratives, arguments, speeches."[51] Foucault sees discourse as a body of thought and writing that is united by having a common object of study, a common methodology, and/or a set of common terms and ideas.[52] Discourse as a symbolic order is linguistically and culturally specific and makes it possible for all subjects who have been socialized under its authority to speak and act together. Discourse always has an order but there is not necessarily a single order for all discourses.[53]

"Narrative" constitutes a part of discourse. A discourse can contain more than one narrative within its body. For instance, Islamic discourse of war and peace contains different approaches and different interpretations. From a Foucauldian perspective, Islam as a discourse refers to the body of thought and writing that is united by having a common object of study, a common methodology used by Islamic scholars and a set of common terms and ideas it incorporates which is linguistically and culturally specific. Islam as a discourse makes it possible for all Muslims who have been socialized under its authority to speak and act together. However, there are different interpretations and approaches within this body. Therefore, another terminology that can differentiate between these strands of interpretation is considered necessary for the purpose of this study. Moreover, the excessive use of the term "discourse" in the social sciences conflates the meaning of the term and creates confusion.

In order to clarify the subject matter further, thus, this project prefers the term "narrative." A "narrative" according to Richard K. Ashley "is a representation that arrests ambiguity and controls the proliferation of meaning by imposing a standard and standpoint of interpretation that is taken to be fixed and independent of the time it represents."[54] This definition captures the attempts of different Islamic groups' to represent the "Islamic truth" concerning war and peace. Ashley also adds that, "[a] narrative typically accomplishes this structuring by adopting a perspective from which it privileges the least complex, least ambiguous elements of the text it represents."[55] By the least complex and least ambiguous elements he means "the least-questioned constructs, the dominant tropes, the recurringly heroic figures, the modal forms of subjectivity, the conditions that are then and there objectified as the necessary and fundamental structures of life."[56]

When observing Islamic narratives, one can see what exactly it is that these groups are doing to prove their correctness. Their narratives de-historicize these textual elements and take them as the fixed, identical, and self-sufficient origins of meaning. They become the basic truths, whereas other elements of a text are, to paraphrase Ashley, seen as secondary, contingent, derivative, "superstuctural," or marginal.[57] Ashley also adds "a narrative reasserts closure by imposing a central ordering principle whose categories and standards of interpretation are taken to express the essential and timeless truth integrating all of the historical times and places among which it discriminates."[58]

Ashley's definition of narrative aptly captures the treatment of Islamic texts by different Islamic groups. These Islamic groups present their interpretation of Quran, *Hadith* and *Sunnah* concerning war and peace as the ultimate truth applicable regardless of time and place. To paraphrase Ashley again, they construct a story in which all time, all space, all difference, and all discontinuity are cast as part of a universal project in which the ordering principle is itself redeemed as necessary, timelessly, and universally true.[59]

When there is no official army, as it is the case with Palestine, every individual becomes a potential soldier in the path of "liberation." In this case, different leaderships try to recruit the population into their camp. Who is more successful is then measured in terms of their ability to mobilize the population towards their objectives. This process becomes especially important in legitimation of their leadership policies. As Kelman states, "[l]eaders need assurance that the public is prepared to accept the costs and risks that their policies will inevitably entail."[60] In this process the critical factor is the "population."[61]

Population as a political and economic resource is a fairly novel idea. In this aspect, population implies that people of a community become a major actor economic and political problem. Population also implies that people become conscious of their abilities and roles in the political and economic spheres of social life, and not simply subjects of a government.[62] As Foucault wrote, [t]his privileging of the population as a major actor and identity in the modern nation-state provides much of impetus and legitimation for conflict and war.[63] In other words, "citizens have to be encouraged to support the strategic understanding among competing states and be willing to mobilize for war (offer their bodies) and support that mobilization (offer their political acquiescence)."[64]

In order to get the support of their population, leaders use symbols that can evoke strong emotional reaction, and according to Kelman, the use of these symbols —which are developed in the early and continuing socialization process– "translates into automatic endorsement of the policies and actions that the leadership defines as necessary."[65] However, when there is not a single well-defined leadership but a number of groups that are competing for that position, this process becomes more complicated. All of these groups attempt to use various national or religious resources for symbols to evoke the emotions of their populations.

Looking at the internal politics of the Palestinian society, it is possible to see the competition of different groups to mobilize the Palestinian population towards their strategic and political narratives. In order to do that, these groups provide overall frames of meaning within the historical, cultural/religious context of the Palestinian society. Within this structure of meaning/culture, their narratives become effective thus, they constitute and reproduce systems of power and authority in which they coordinate the actions of the individuals. If this is the case, it becomes important to understand which of these groups are able to do what and why?

What is Hermeneutics?

For exactly this purpose, this work offers a theoretical approach, which is based on hermeneutics. Hermeneutics attempts to understand the interpretive processes of human interaction. The term hermeneutics comes from the Greek word "Hermeneutika" which means message analysis, things for interpreting. Hermeneutics was used in the ancient Greeks' study of literature. Christian scholars also used hermeneutics for ancient Biblical exegesis. Hermeneutics was rediscovered in the West during the Christian Reformation movement, when Luther argued that Bible must be read from the point of view that the texts are responses to historical or social situations rather than expressions of theological principles. Here, hermeneutics was used as a technique to penetrate into the text with the aim of finding a way to understand it. It was Dilthey and Schleiermacher that raised interpretation to a methodological principle in their attempt to create a general hermeneutics.[66] Schleiermaher argued that the temporal distance between the author and the interpreter blocks the true meaning of the texts and creates space for misunderstanding. This misunderstanding is a result of the historical context and prejudices of the interpreter. As a result, the message is not what it seems in the first instance, and the true meaning must be recovered by a systematic reconstruction of the historical period and the context in which it was produced.

Schleiermacher argued that interpretation is build upon understanding and has a grammatical as well as a psychological moment. The interpreter reconstructs and explicates the subject's' motives and implicit assumptions. Schleiermacher believed that the interpreter could understand the author almost better then the author himself, since interpretation highlights hidden motives and strategies. According to Schleiermacher, the aim of hermeneutics "is to rediscover the nodal point in the artist's mind that will render the significance of his work," and "historical knowledge opens the possibility of replacing what is lost." [67]

Dilthey, on the other hand, broadened Schleiermacher's approach and developed a philosophical method for history and human sciences. He believed that it was possible to produce objective knowledge and at the same time avoid the reductionist, mechanistic, ahistorical, and explanatory approach of the natural sciences. For him, natural and human sciences differed from each other and interpreting human interactions (the subject of human sciences) were similar to interpreting a poem or a discourse. He termed the desired comprehension of events and expressions "understanding" (*verstehen*), and distinguished it from the explanatory knowledge that was generated by the hypothetico-deductive method of the natural sciences. He emphasized that texts and actions were as much the products of their times as expressions of individuals, and their meanings were constantly constrained by both an orientation to values of their period and a place in the web of the author's plans and experiences. Thus, meanings are delineated by the author's worldview reflecting a historical period and social context.

Dilthey's "Understanding" approach is the basis of methodological hermeneutics, and involves tracing a circle from the text to the author's biography and immediate historical circumstances and back to the text again. Through interpretation or systemic application of understanding, the text reconstructs the world in which the text was produced. "Theological Hermeneutics, as Dilthey showed, developed from the reformers' defense of their own understanding of Scripture against the attack of the Tridentine theologians and their appeal to the indispensability of tradition; philological hermeneutics developed as instrumental to the humanist claim to revive classical literature."[68]

Nevertheless, the history of modern hermeneutics can be traced back to Husserl, who focused on what is immediate to experience and argued that every thing that is not immanent in consciousness must be excluded. His approach suggests that the meaning of the text has been fixed by the language and exists in an 'idealist' sense. Heidegger[69] reacted against Husserl's essentialist approach and rejected the notion of objective historical knowledge. He argued that man finds himself 'thrown into the world' in which language, culture and the institutions are givens. He insisted that it is not possible to "bracket-off" pre-understanding and to gain a transcendent, objective standpoint. Pure objectivity is never possible by the situated subject. He thus denied that there is a fixed meaning. For this reason, he developed his concept "*dasein*" (Being) which attempts to understand the situation from within, not outside of history. For Heidegger, interpretation is the "extrapolation of past understanding into the future."[70] Heidegger took hermeneutics from a theory of interpretation to a theory of existential understanding. With him understanding became embedded within the context of specific situations and a plan.

A student of Heidegger, Hans Gadamer moved beyond hermeneutics as a method of human sciences and gave it an ontological dimension by stating that understanding and interpretation is essential for a human's existence.[71] Gadamer started "with a critique of aesthetic consciousness in order to defend the experience of truth that comes to us though the work of art against the aesthetic theory that lets itself be restricted to a scientific conception of truth."[72] He took his work further and attempted to develop a conception of knowledge and of truth that corresponds to the whole of the human hermeneutic experience. However, he did not try to generate "a general theory of interpretation and a differential account of its methods." [73]His aim was rather to discover what is common to all modes of understanding, and to show that understanding is never a subjective relation to a given "object," but to the history of its effect. In other words, "understanding belongs to the being of that which is understood."[74]

For Gadamer, "the understanding and the interpretation of texts is not merely a concern of science, but obviously belongs to human experience of the world in general."[75] Understanding "is not concerned primarily with amassing verified knowledge, such as would satisfy the methodological ideal of science" but it is "also concerned with knowledge, and with truth."[76] He argues that sciences that deal with human beings are connected to modes of experience, in which a truth is communicated, and such a truth cannot be verified by methodological means proper to natural sciences.

Gadamer focused on historicity and argued that interpretation is an encounter between the researcher and a past that presents itself for interpretation. He, thus, introduced the historical object. He argued that a text is understood only if it is understood in a different way every time.[77] People read the texts differently at different ages because different questions, prejudices, and interests move them. The present situation of the interpreter, which is given and which can never be hold at a critical distance or be objectified, is what he calls "hermeneutical situation."[78] The historical, social and cultural context that the interpreting agent is situated within has an effect on the way the agent experiences the world and thus on the way he interprets the texts that he/she is engaged with. This context constitutes what he calls, "the horizon."[79] Therefore, "*Understanding is, essentially, a historically effected event*"[80] As a result, this means that "the text, whether law or gospel, if it is to be understood properly —i.e., according to the claim it makes—must be understood at every moment, in every concrete situation, in a new and different way"[81]He describes this process of understanding as "the fusion of horizons," where the horizons of past and present merge into one.[82]

According to Gadamer's definition, a horizon is the "range of vision that includes everything that can be seen from a particular vantage point."[83] There is a horizon of the present and the categories of understanding, which we cannot see beyond. The horizons of past and present overlap and fuse into one great horizon since one cannot disconnect him/herself from the past. For Gadamer, understanding is bound and embedded in history because understanding deploys the knower's effective-history, personal experience and cultural traditions to assimilate new experiences. Historically affected consciousness means that the very consciousness of the being is affected and determined by history. Gadamer's thesis is that "the element of effective history affects all understanding of tradition, even despite the adoption of the methodology of the modern historical sciences, which makes what has grown historically and has been transmitted historically an object to be established like an experimental finding-as if tradition were as alien, and from the human point of view as unintelligible, as an object of physics."[84]

In his "Universality of the Hermeneutical Problem"[85] Gadamer criticizes the ideal since Descartes that prejudice free objective knowledge is possible and asserts that this itself is a powerful prejudice. He further states that such a perspective ignores the temporality of the individual thus the temporality of interpretation. The initial structure of an effective-history constrains the range of possible interpretations, excluding some possibilities and calling forth others. This approach creates space for prejudices to be included. Interpretation is a subjective and continual process of interaction with and is conditioned by experience, particularly the experience of language, which shapes the individual in accordance with his/her linguistic traditions. It is sensitive to the impact of culture during the process of interpretation.

Gadamer's approach to understanding leads to the conclusion that a strict adherence to method is not sufficient to justify one's claims for truth, and it is not possible to determine which interpretation is 'true' because in the construction of an interpretation an individuality is always being pressed.[86] What the author intended to say in the text cannot be really known to the reader but has to go through the filter of the reader's horizons. It is through these horizons that the reader interprets the text and gives it a meaning. This allows competing interpretations of the same text to exist simultaneously.

This view of hermeneutics decentralizes the author. The interpreter does not attempt to understand the author historically but "*...intends to understand the text itself*"[87]

> ... this means that the interpreter's own thoughts too have gone into re-awakening the text's meaning. In this the interpreter's own horizon is decisive, yet not as a personal standpoint that he maintains or enforces, but more as an opinion and a possibility that one brings into play and puts at risk, and that helps one truly to make one's own what the text says. I have described this above as a "fusion of horizons.[88]

Gadamer's hermeneutical approach helps us to understand the process of interpretation and the existence of multiple interpretations. It gives clues to how individuals make sense of the world they live in and what influences the interpretive processes and what the possibilities of interpretation in a given "hermeneutical situation" are. It helps us, for example, to understand the existence of multiple interpretations within the Islamic discourse and how these interpretations are influenced by the effective histories of the interpreters within different time periods and under different circumstances. However, Gadamer's approach does not sufficiently answer one question: When does one particular interpretation become legitimized? It does not tell us, which, among different interpretations of war and peace within the Islamic discourse, becomes legitimated and why the populations' opinion in general tilts towards one narrative rather then the others. In order to answer this question, it is necessary to expand Gadamer's approach to include the power relations within the community, where the competition of interpretations takes place.

Power and Hermeneutics

The legitimization of narratives is about establishing a regime of truth. In this "struggle," truth is centered on a specific discourse/narrative and on the institutions that are linked in a circular relation with systems of power, which produces and sustains the regime of truth. Seligman makes a crucial distinction between authority, which is legitimate power, and power. Seligman[89] He argues that, for authority to exist, the legitimacy of its actions must be registered in the subjective experience and consciousness of the actors. This is what Weber called "the inner justification of dominion."[90] In contrast, according to Seligman, power rests solely on the coercion of the will.[91] This discussion takes us to the question, "what is power and how is it related to the legitimization of narratives?"[92]

Power and power relations are critical elements in constituting the legitimization of narratives, and thus, the "regimes of truth." "Truth" is a narrative and is communicated linguistically, so it can only be constituted through a discourse. In this process, power enables a certain narrative to be considered as "true." Foucault linked the establishment of regimes of "truth" to power relations:

> There can be no possible exercise of power without a certain economy of discourses of truth, which operates through and on the basis of this association. We are subjected to the production of truth through power and we cannot exercise power except through the production of truth.[93]

> Power never ceases its interrogation, its acquisition, and its registration of truth: it institutionalizes and rewards its pursuit.[94]

According to Foucault power is not contained only in the state, as the traditional theories of power assert, but is everywhere. The idea that the state is the sole possessor of power reduces individuals to subjects under state control without any effect. Rescuing the individual from its subjection to the state, Foucault argues that the origins of modern power lay in the micro-techniques and practices of early industrial workplaces, asylums, prisons, etc. It is at these micro-levels that power is initially found and constituted, and later incorporated and developed into larger institutionalized structures. Under this light, any study of power must first start from the micro-level, with its specific forms of exercise in different institutional sites. It is at these sites, where the manifold relations of power permeate, characterize and constitute the social body. Yet Foucault also states "these relations of power cannot themselves be established, consolidated nor implemented without the production, accumulation, circulation and functioning of a discourse."[95]

It is in these locales, or informal institutions, that narratives compete for legitimacy and insert themselves as regimes of truth. In this process power circulates in and through the production of these narratives. Power is not prior to discourses and practices but operates through them. Accordingly, this nexus between power/knowledge and discourse produces and establishes particular regimes of truth through normalization.[96] "Foucault's position," according to Peter Morgan "is that power circulates in and through the production of discourses in society where the nexus between power/knowledge and discourse produces and establishes, through normalization, particular regimes of truth."[97] This approach sees power as dispersed through actions, practices, and discourse. The relationship between power and discourse creates the conditions for particular regimes of truth to be established and legitimated.

However, narratives do not emerge in a void. They emerge in an already given field of possibilities, which they can realign or reconfigure. This field of possibilities constitutes what Gadamer would call horizons. Foucault also recognizes this given field of possibilities and states that discourses operate in an existing material world: against and in relation to prior and contemporary discourses; other discursive formations; and social, political and economic material forces (the non-discursive). This field of possibilities is what he calls a "field of strategic possibilities."[98] Foucault asserts that a discursive formation is constituted when there is a correlation and regularity among a number of discursive statements dealing with an object of discourse, operates by exclusion. According to Colebrook, this means:

> Discursive formations grant some statements a force, validity and truth effect which is achieved *inter alia* by the exclusion of other statements. Discursive formations include extra-linguistic phenomena such as institutions, practices and material sites of production for their legitimation.[99]

When this is the case, the examination of political struggles requires a close observation of the contest between different narratives for the discursive dominance over the object of struggle. In a struggle like this, it becomes important to understand how the political strategies of conflicting forces are deployed in discourse as well as how these discourses are articulated in relations to a chain of successive events.[100] In the course of this process, the non-discursive (informal and formal institutional) structures and inter-discursive (past and present narratives) must be taken into consideration. Different narratives/discourses are produced and reproduced at these institutional sites and compete for legitimacy and hegemony. It is through the systems of power operations and through these institutional sites that one narrative/discourse rather than others becomes legitimated and established as a regime of truth. Although in his works Michel Foucault investigated the emergence of new forms of power in the modern Western society by looking at the specific practices and techniques, such as disciplining apparatuses of the society, his conception of power can be meaningfully applied to the emergence of regimes of truth in other cultural contexts. Competing narratives can be meaningfully communicated within the historical, political, social, economic, and cultural/religious horizons and in relation to previous and existing narratives of a given society.

To put this into the present perspective, it is necessary to connect it to the Islamic narratives in Palestine. Islamic narratives of war and peace in the Palestinian Territories operate within the context of the conflict that has been going on for more then fifty years now. The historical experience with British imperialism and colonialism also has an influence on the way Palestinians perceive this conflict. Since the beginning of the conflict, Palestinians witnessed narratives of Pan-Arabism, Nationalism, Socialism, pan-Islamism, and finally Nationalized Islamism.[101] The support of Palestinian population fluctuates between these narratives due to internal and external developments (such as the defeat of Arab armies in the wars of 1948, 1967, 1973, collapse of Soviet Union thus the leftist movement, failure of the Oslo Process, claims of corruption, etc.). The critical events of the last two decades especially (such as *Intifada*, the Oslo Process, the collapse of the Oslo Process, and *al-Aqsa Intifada*) have provided opportunities for a shift in the discourse of peace and war in the region. The polls during the al Aqsa *Intifada*[102] showed that the Palestinian society was confused in terms of what narrative to believe in and who has the right and ability to represent it. Edward Said observed that during this period, Arafat and his Islamist opponents were getting somewhere between 40 and 45 percent, which he interpreted to mean "that a silent majority of Palestinians is neither for the Authority's misplaced trust in the Oslo Process (or for its lawless regime of corruption and repression) nor for Islamist violence."[103]

Death of Arafat in November 2004, once again, seems to have led to a shift in the Palestinian political arena. Mahmoud Abbas, successor of Arafat won the elections with 62% vote, signaling willingness of the Palestinian population for a new peace process.[104] Yet, Hamas made a strong showing at Palestinian local elections that took place at the end of 2004 and in the beginning of 2005 by taking the majority of seats both in Gaza and West Bank,[105] indicating the Palestinian population is still confused and undecided. These recent developments are calling the population for reconsidering the strategies adopted by the parties to end the conflict and to establish a democratic society in the region. It can be said that the Palestinian society is once again "*in between narratives*" and their choice will determine not only the future of the conflict and its resolution, but also their political, social, and economic future as Palestinian citizens.

Within this critical time period, different leaderships utilize cultural/religious and historical resources to meaningfully communicate with and move Palestinian population. Their narratives stem from the previous religious as well as secular and leftist liberation narratives[106] that have come to play an important role in the course of the conflict. And yet, it is within the existing formal and particularly informal institutions, such as medical centers, schools and universities, mosques, etc. that these narratives find a fertile soil to circulate. Within this context, narratives not only utilize pervious resources of power based on the relationship between traditional authority and domination, but also create new power relations. It is this complex and spiral[107] social context that different narratives compete with each other to insert themselves as regimes of truth.

The conflict between the Israeli and Palestinian communities, as many others, involves an intensive process of legitimation of narratives of war and conflict. In this process, religious (Judaism, Christianity and Islam) narratives play a crucial role. Both religious traditions incorporate narratives of just war, as well as narratives of peace in their systems. In order to undermine the narratives that justify war and violence, and to highlight those that promote peace and conflict resolution, scholars need to develop approaches that include an analysis of sources and forms of legitimacy and how these are operationalized in the conflict. Only then will it be possible to develop strategies that can counteract this process. This study attempts to expand in succinct formulation by looking at the process of legitimation of narratives among the Palestinian population in West Bank and Gaza. In particular, focuses on the different interpretations of war and peace derived from the Islamic tradition, and how understanding the process of legitimation can assist in resolving the conflict. For that reason it is necessary to understand the evolution of approaches to peace and war within the Islamic tradition over the course of its history.

Endnotes

1. See C. von Clausewitz. *On War* trans by. J.J. Graham (Routledge and Kegan Paul, London, 1966)

2. Vivienne Jabri, *Discourses On Violence- Conflict Analysis Reconsidered* (Manchester University Press, 1996), 22

3. The term "toolbox" is used here to refer to conflict resolution mechanisms such as mediation, problem-solving workshops, arbitration, etc.

4. The concept of "Western" is a problematic one, since it includes various different schools of thought and theories. It is a term that is ambiguous with many different connotations. A legalistic, positivist and quantitative perspective has been dominating the conflict resolution field since its emergence. Other theories and approaches that can be grouped under the general term "Western" include but not limited to Critical Theory, Postmodernism, Poststructuralism, Hermenuetics and Constructivism. Many of these schools deal with issues that are central to this work, and they largely inspire it. However,

recognizing these problems with the term, I employ "traditional Western" to refer to the dominant Anglo-American and continental European liberal perspective regarding the concepts of legitimacy and approaches to conflict resolution that is influential especially at policy and decision-making levels in the United States and Europe as a shorthand.

5. Some of these scholars include Johan Galtung, Jean Paul Lederach, Vivienne Jabri, Mohammad Abu-Nimer, Marc Gopin, Avruch, Kevin, Cynthia Sampson, among others. See also Oliver Richmond Maintaining Order, Making Peace (London: Palgrave, 2002) for grouping different conflict resolution approaches under three categories, namely first generation, second generation, and third generation approaches to conflict resolution.

6. Mohammed Abu-Nimer. "Conflict Resolution in an Islamic Context: Some Conceptual Questions" in Peace and Change (January, 1996): 22-40.

7. Another important aspect of this argument would be questioning 'reason.' However, since the conceptions of reason are tangent to the discussion of this book, and since it would unnecessarily expand the project, I will not go into that argument here. But for an informative discussion on different understandings of 'reason' in the Western conflict resolution literature see Jabri chapter 3.

8. Lederach 1997, 8.

9. Peter Wallensteen and Margareta Sollenberg. "After the Cold War: emerging Patterns of Armed Conflict, 1989-1994" *Journal of Peace Research.* (32: 3, 1996), 345-360.

10. For more detailed perspective see E Azar. "Management of Protracted Social Conflict in the Third World," paper prepared for the Fourth ICES Annual Lecture at Columbia University (unpublished) (New York, 10 June, 1986).

11. Kumar Rupesinghe. Civil Wars, Civil Peace: An Introduction to Conflict Resolution. (London: Pluto Press, 1988), 45

12. Edward Azar first drew attention to the special features of long-standing conflicts, and termed them protracted conflicts. See, Edward. Azar. "Protracted International Conflict: Ten Propositions" in Edward Azar and John W. Burton eds. *International Conflict Resolution* (London: Wheatsheaf Books 1986), 27-3 9. The concept of intractable conflict has been given considerable attention in recent studies. See Paul Diehl, Contiguity and Military Escalation in Major Power Rivalries. *Journal of Politics,* Vol. 47, No. 4, (1985), 1203-121 1; Goertz, Gary and Paul F. Diehl. The Empirical Importance of Enduring Rivalries. *International Interactions* Vol. 18, No. 1, (1992): 1-11; . Enduring Rivalries Theoretical Constructs and Empirical Patterns. *International Studies Quarterly* Vol. 37, No. 2, (1993): 147-171; Goertz, Gary and Paul F. Diehl.. The Initiation and Termination of Enduring Rivalries: The Impact of Political Shocks. *American Journal of Political Science.* Vol. 39, No. (1995): 30-52; Frank Wayman, W. 1982. Power Transitions, Rivalries and War. Paper presented at the Institute for the Study of Conflict and International Security. Urbana, Illinois; ;Charles Gochman, and Maoz Zeev. Militarized Interstate Disputes, 1816-1976 Procedures, Patterns, and Insights. *Journal of Conflict Resolution* Vol. 18, No. 4, (1984): 586-615; Jacob Bercovitch and S. Ayse Kadayifci "Conflict Management and Israeli-Palestinian Conflict: The Importance of Capturing the 'right Moment'" *Asia-Pacific Review* Vol. 9, No. 2 (2002): 113-129

13. Literature on Terrorism is a very rich one. Yet this project will not engage extensively in this literature in order not to expand its focus. However, sporadic references supported with footnotes will be incorporated into the project when it is considered essential. For a discussion on terrorist discourse see James Der Derian, *Antidiplomacy:*

Spies, Terror, Speed, and War (Cambridge and Oxford Blackwell, 1992) Chapters 4 and 5

14. Der Derian 1992, 7.
15. Der Derian 1992, 7.
16. Some of these scholars were mentioned in the previous chapter.
17. Lederach 1997, 75.
18. Lederach 1997, 75.
19. Lederach 1997., 43
20. J. Galtung. "Violence, Peace and Peace Research" in *Journal of Peace Research*. Vol.6 no.3 (1996): 167-191 Galtung has been among the first conflict resolution scholars since the 1960s and thus his cannot be considered as a new in terms of time. Yet, his approached developed over the couple of decades and his insights have come to play a much more significant role particularly in the 1990s in conjunction with the increase of intra-state conflicts.
21. J. Galtung. "Peace and Conflict Research in the Age of The Cholera: ten Pointers to the Future of Peace Studies." in *Peace and Conflict Studies* vol. 2 no. 1 (June, 1995), 11.
22. Rupesinghe 1988. 29.
23. C.G. Jacobsen. "Peacemaking as Realpolitik, Conflict Resolution and Oxymoron: the Record; the Challenge' in. *Search for Peace: Road to Transcend* Galtung and Jacobsen eds. (London: Pluto Press 2000), 15.
24. Jacobsen 2000.
25. Jacobsen 2000.
26. Jacobsen 2000., 4
27. Jabri 1996, 30.
28. Jens Steffek *The Power of Rational Discourse and the Legitimacy of International Governance.* Paper presented at the workshop "Analysis of Discourse and Ideas in European and International Affairs" (EUI, Florence, 12/13 May 2000), 4.
29. Weber, Max *Economy and Society*. Guenther Roth and Claus Wittich ed. (Berkeley: University of California Press. 1978), 31.
30. See Lederach 1997
31. Here, by "traditional" I mean the dominant approaches within the conflict resolution field that is influential especially at policy and decision-making levels, especially in the United States and Europe.
32. As mentioned earlier various scholars such as Laura Nader, Johan Galtung, and Jean Paul Lederach have implicitly focused on the concept of legitimacy. However, there has not been a study that expands on the importance of legitimacy in conflict resolution and connects it to conflict resolution theories directly.
33. Seligman, Adam B. *Modernity's Wager: Authority, the Self, and Transcendence.* (Princeton and Oxford: Princeton University Press, 2000), 4.
34. This work will utilize the 'Ideal-types' of legitimacy and legitimate authority as developed by Max Weber, since he is the most important scholar who dealt with this question in my opinion. Yet, I recognize that this does not exhaust the literature on legitimacy. Other scholars who dealt with legitimacy include David Beetham, *The Legitimation of Power*. (Houndmills: Macmillan 1991; Thomas Franck. "Legitimacy in the International System" in *American Journal of International Law*.82: (1988),705-759; Jurgen Habermas *Legitimation Crisis* (Oxford Polity Press, 1988; and J Rawls. *A Theory*

of Justice (Oxford: Oxford University Press, 1971). These scholars focus on the Western notion of legitimacy and do not explore different sources of legitimacy. Weber's influential Ideal-Types of legitimacy remain the major and most comprehensive work on legitimacy that includes different sources of legitimacy and connects them to authority and domination.

35. Weber, 1978, 33.
36. Weber, 1978
37. Weber, 1978.,34.
38. Weber, 1978.
39. Weber, 1978.36.
40. Weber, 1978.,37.
41. Weber, 1978.215.
42. Weber, 1978.
43. Weber, 1978.
44. Weber, 1978.
45. It is important to note that these categorizations, such as "sources of legitimacy," "authority," etc. do not necessarily represent the "real" world as it is. These categorizations are ideal types in Weberian terms. Before going further into analysis, it is important to say a few words on the way I utilize 'ideal types' in this study. Throughout the project I adopt "ideal types" as generic schemes that offer tools to make first observations. These first observations are later followed by more complex contextual and inter-textual analysis. Ideal types are not aimed at representing the "reality," or presenting 'essential' characteristics. They are deployed as conceptual categories that draw boundaries for the analysis and understanding of the social phenomena. It is with that understanding that various categorizations must be viewed in this project.
46. Seligman 2000, 4.
47. Weber 1978, 215.
48. Weber, 1978., 107
49. Weber, 1978.
50. See Weber 1978., 18-19
51. Simon Blackburn, *Oxford Dictionary of Philosophy* (New York: Oxford University Press, 1996), 107.
52. See Alec McHoul and Wendy Grace *A Foucault Premier: Discourse, Power and the Subject* (London: UCL Press) 1995 Chapter 2.
53. McHoul and Grace 1995. also see M. Foucault. "Appendix: The Discourse on Language) in *Archeology of Knowledge and Discourse on Language* Trans.A. M. Sheridan Smith (New York: Pantheon Books, 1972), 215-237.
54. Richard K Ashley. "Living on Borderlines: man, Poststructuralism, and War." In *International/Intertextual Relations: Postmodern Readings of World Politics.* In James Der Derian and Michael J. Shapiro eds. (New York Lexington Books, 1989), 263.
55. Ashley 1989.
56. Ashley 1989.
57. Ashley 1989.
58. Ashley 1989, 264.
59. Ashley 1989.

60. Kelman Herbert C. "Applying Human Needs Perspective to the Practice of Conflict Resolution: Israeli-Palestinian Case" in Burton eds. Conflict: Human Needs Theory New York: St. Martin's Press, 1990, 215.

61. Shapiro, Michael J. "Representing World Politics: The Sport/War Intertext" In James Der Derian and Michael J. Shapiro eds. 1989, 74.

62. Shapiro 1989.

63. Michel Foucault. *History of Sexuality: An Introduction, Volume I.* (New York: Vintage Books, 1978), 25.

64. Foucault 1978.

65. Kelman in Zartman and Rasmussen eds., 215.

66. See Gadamer, Hans-Georg. *Truth and Method.* Tans. Joel Weinsheimer and Donald G. Marshall. Second revised edition., New York: Crossroad, 1991), Part Two

67. Gadamer 1991. 166.

68. Gadamer 1991., 174.

69. See Martin Heidegger *Basic Writings*Edited by David Farrell Krell (San Fransisco: Harper and Row Publishers, 1977)

70. Lang, Chris. www.xenos.org/essays/litthry3.htm,2

71. Gadamer, 1991.

72. Gadamer, 1991., xxiii.

73. Gadamer, 1991., xxxi.

74. Gadamer, 1991.

75. Gadamer, 1991., xxi.

76. Gadamer, 1991.

77. Gadamer, 1991., 297.

78. Gadamer, 1991. 302

79. Gadamer, 1991. 302

80. Gadamer, 1991. 300 Italics in original

81. Gadamer, 1991. 309

82. Gadamer, 1991. 304-305

83. Gadamer, 1991., 302.

84. Gadamer, 1991., xxxiii-xxxiv.

85.Hans Gadamer. "Universality of the Hermeneutical Problem (1966)" in *Philosophical Hermeneutics: Hans Georg Gadamer* translated and ed. By David E. Linge. (Los Angeles: University of California Press, 1997), 3-17.

86. Gadamer 1991, 192.

87. Gadamer, 1991., 388.

88. Gadamer, 1991.

89. Seligman 2000

90. Max Weber. "Politics as a Vocation," in *From Max Weber: Essays on Sociology.* G.H. Gerth and C. W. Mills eds. (New York: Oxford University Press, 1976), 78.

91. Seligman 2000, 4.

92. Traditionally most literature in conflict resolution deals with power in the context of 'power asymmetry' in negotiation processes. This line of theorizing still considers power as being held by states as unitary actors who participate in the process of negotiation. These scholars include William Zartman "The Political Analysis of Negotiations: Who Gets What and When?" in *World Politics.*26:3 (1974); William Mark Habbeb, *Power and Tactics in International Negotiation; How Weak Nations Bargain With Strong*

Nations. (London: The John Hopkins University Press, 1988); A.J.R. Groom and Keith Webb "Injustice, Empowerment and Facilitation in Conflict" in *International Interactions*. 13: 3 (1987); and Keith Webb "Prediction in International Relations: The Role of Power, Interest and Trust" in *Kent Papers in International Relations*. Series I no. 11. (Canterbury Kent: University of Kent at Canterbury, 1992). On power see also Dougherty, James E. and Robert L. Pfaltzgraff, Jr. eds. *Contending Theories of International Relations: A Comprehensive Survey*. Fourth edition. (Longman, 1996), 66; Morgenthau, Hans J. *Politics Among Nations: The Struggle for Power and Peace*. Fifth edition. (New York: Alfred A. Knopf,1973); Waltz, Kenneth *Theory of International Politics*. (Reading, MA: Addison-Wesley, 1979); Holsti, K. J. *International Politics: A Framework for Analysis*.. (Eaglewood Cliffs, NJ.: Prentice-Hall, 1967); Kenneth E. Boulding. *Three Faces of Power* (London: Sage Publications, 1989).

93. Michel Foucault. Power/Knowledge: Selected Interviews and Other Writings 1972-1977. (London: Harvester Press, 1980), 93.

94. Foucault 1980.

95. Foucault 1980.

96. Morgan, Peter *Contested Native Forests: A Theoretical and Empirical Study* (Ph.D. dissertation, 1997), Mcmullan bros. at www.mcmullan.net/pmorgan/

97. Morgan, 1997

98. M. Foucault. *Archeology of Knowledge and Discourse on Language* (New York: Pantheon Books, 1972), 37.

99. Colebrook *New Literary Histories*, (Manchester: Manchester University Press, 1997), 67

100. Foucault 1972, 167.

101. By Nationalized Islamism, I refer to the narratives of groups like Hamas, and Islamic Jihad. After loosing faith in the commitment of Muslims around the world to aid them in their liberation and after realizing the impact of nationalism, these groups have come to form their Islamic narratives around the Palestinian national identity and limited their movement within the Palestinian Territories and Israel. Yet this does not mean that they do not believe in a Universal Islam. Rather the term here is used to refer to their strategy based on the belief that only an authentic Palestinian movement can bring about liberation.

102. Edward W. Said. "The Nation Feature Story" (February 4) http://www.thenation.com/doc.mhtml?I=3D20020204&s=3Dsaid 2002, 2.

103. E. Said 2002.

104. However, neither Hamas nor Marwan Barghouti, the jailed leader of the *al-Aqsa Intifada* run during this election. The polls that predicted that Abbas would win the elections also found that if Marwan Barghouti ran, "he would have beaten Abbas by a four-point margin." See Tony Karon "After the Palestinian Elections" *Time Monday January 10, 2005*

105. See John Ward Anderson and Molly Moore "Hamas Won Political Power in West Bank Vote" in *Washingtonpost* January 6, 2005

106. It is not uncommon to see Che Guevera posters hanging together with other religious figures (such as Sheikh Yassin) in the homes of many in the region.

107. I prefer using the term *spiral* instead of *circular* because circular implies a movement that comes to the same starting point, whereas spiral implies both a circular relation but also a movement that is beyond the initial starting point. I use the term to

indicate that the social context does not go back to the point of its start, but the incorporated new developments create a new point in this movement.

Chapter 3

The Text: Legitimacy in the Palestinian Context

Every discourse that attempts to establish a regime of truth bases its claims on the existing sources of legitimacy within the context of the society itself. Every discourse needs to establish and cultivate the belief in its legitimacy. Sources of legitimacy, in turn, will define the mode of authority, and the form of obedience to that authority. In the first part of this book I have introduced Weber's ideas on legitimacy as providing helpful typologies to differentiate between legitimacy's diverse sources. According to Weber, legitimacy of an order can be guaranteed in two principle ways: through purely subjective means or by the expectation of specific external effects, or interest situations.[1] The subjective sources of legitimacy could be affectual, value-rational, or religious. Furthermore, actors may ascribe legitimacy on the bases of tradition, emotional faith, value-rational faith, or legal factors.

If sources of legitimacy are based on rational grounds, that is, "resting on a belief in the legality of enacted rules and the right of those elevated to authority under such rules to issue commands,"[2] the type of authority is called "*legal authority*."[3] "*Traditional authority,*" in contrast, "[rests] on an established belief in the sanctity of immemorial traditions and the legitimacy of those exercising authority under them."[4] Finally Weber uses the term "*charismatic authority*" to describe the types of authority "resting on devotion to the exceptional sanctity, heroism, or exemplary character of an individual person, and of the normative patterns or order revealed or ordained by him."[5] Legal order calls for obedience to the legally established impersonal order. Traditional order calls for obedience to persons who hold the traditionally sanctioned position of authority, and are bound by this tradition. In the charismatic order, a charismatic leader is obeyed by virtue of the personal trust placed within him or her.

There are fundamental differences between the Western and Middle Eastern (Palestinian in this case) sources of legitimation. However, it must be noted beforehand that ideal types are not aimed at essentializing Muslims and the Islamic culture.[6] "Islamic culture is not a "thing" that can be reified into one objective or dimension;"[7] nor is it distributed uniformly among all Muslims or members of a Muslim community. Every individual reacts and interacts differently with his/her culture. Within the Palestinian context, every Muslim Palestinian interacts with the Islamic culture based on his/her experience, and is influenced by his/her specific circumstances. The Islamic discourse draws the borders of these interactions and enables the emergence of various narratives. These borders, however, are not necessarily static. They change over time due to external and internal factors. Observed from that angle, these ideal types serve as keys to analyze the possibilities and constraints of the emergence of "regimes of truth" and the establishment of certain forms of authority as legitimate.

In the Palestinian society, membership in the community is based on Islamic faith[8], and obedience to authority rests on the person's traditional status. In that line, the sources of legitimacy in the Palestinian Territories can be characterized as being based on subjective sources—mostly an ambiguous mixture of religion and custom—rather than external sources. One of the characteristics of the Palestinian community is *gerontocracy*. Weber applies the term gerontocracy to "a situation so far as rule over the group is organized at all in it is in the hands of the elders, [...] who are the most familiar with the sacred traditions."[9] Looking at the conflict resolution mechanisms such as *sulha*,[10] one sees the important role elderly people, who are believed to know the history of the community and the tradition well, play. An important attribute of gerontocracy and other traditional sources of legitimacy in general is that, authority is largely dependent upon the willingness of the members to comply with orders, since there is no personal mechanism to enforce them.[11]

Additionally, historically nomadism played a key role in the way that the society organizes it self in the Middle Easte in general, and in the Palestinian Territories in particular.[12] Nomadism tends to call for flexible and effective kin-based social organization. Evolved from this background, communal, religious, tribal and ethnic identity as well as patron-client relationships and patriarchal authority have influenced the sources of legitimacy in the Palestinian society.

Within this context, one of the major political groups in the Palestinian community, as well as other Middle Eastern societies, was the notables.[13] Three types of notables can be identified in the Palestinian context.[14] These were the "religious leaders" (*ulema*), who gained their legitimacy from the Islamic tradition and also controlling large religiously owned lands. The second group of notables was the "military leaders" who owed their status due to their arms and soldiers then commanded. Finally the third group consisted of "secular notables," who derived their wealth from land and trade. Kinship, lineage and tribal relations play a crucial role in the politics of notables.

Notables were especially important during the nineteenth and twentieth centuries because they acted as intermediaries between the Ottoman government in Istanbul and the Palestinian population. Notables remained as an important political group in Palestine as the ruling powers (Britain, Egypt, Jordan or Israel) continued to use them as intermediaries between them and the population. One of the often-used strategies was to co-opt the notables via distribution of resources to maintain social control in the territories. Even though social organization of the society has been going through a major transformation over the last decades and new leaders are emerging,[15] remnants of politics of notable is still present in the Palestinian community.

Religion also plays a crucial role as one of the sources of legitimacy in Palestine. As stated previously, Islam is the tradition that underscores the Palestinian community under investigation.[16] Islamic tradition derives its legitimacy in virtue of the sanctity of its roughly 1400-year-old rules and customs derived from the Holy Book, the Quran. These rules and customs call forth obedience to the persons who occupy a position of authority according to the Islamic tradition. These people include *imams* (religious clerics), *muftis* (jurists), *ulema* (Islamic scholars), *qadis* (judges), notables, and elderly people (such as members of *jaha*[17]) who are recognized for knowing the tradition well. The authority of these people is legitimated either in terms of the Islamic tradition within the limits of the Quran, the *Sunna* (Prophet's practices), the *Hadith* (Prophet's sayings), or in terms of those persons' discretion in that sphere which Islamic tradition leaves open to him or her.[18] Therefore, the person who is exercising the authority is not a superior, but rather a personal master; and the ruled are traditional comrades or subjects.

Although an Islamic legal system exists under the name of the *Shariah*, it differs from its Western counterpart significantly. A legal system in the Western sense is based on abstract rules that were normally intentionally established by agreement or by imposition, on grounds of expediency or value rationality, or both.[19] Sources of legitimacy in the West are external, based on interest situations. On the other hand, Islamic law derives its legitimacy from the Holy book of the Quran, along with sayings and examples of the Prophet. Concrete legal problems are resolved through an in-depth analysis of these sources by trained scholars, and a body of legal texts has come into life after this process. The *Shariah* (Islamic rules and regulations) is derived from these sacred sources. When faced with a challenge or a new problem, new rules can be legitimized by claiming that they have already been in the sacred Scripture, but were not yet brought to light. They become apparent only after the application of *ijtihad* (systematic intellectual reasoning), *qiyas* (analogy), or *ijma* (consensus) to principle sources of Islam in order to respond to the current problems.

Understanding the sources of legitimacy and legitimate authority becomes especially important when we look at the leaderships that attempt to establish their regimes of truth regarding the Israeli-Palestinian conflict. Various leaderships base the legitimacy of their authority on the Islamic tradition and their extensive knowledge of it. Leaders like Sheikh Yassin[20], based on their knowledge of the Quran, the *Hadith* and the *Sunna,* claim that their reading of the situation in Palestine is the correct one, and that their approach to the conflict is the one that is ordained by God. They construct their narratives of war and peace on their reading of various verses in the Quran and the Prophet's practices. While doing that they utilize the social and political space that emerges from the traditional ways the society organizes itself.[21] These traditional ways of organizing result from the relationship between authority and community. Therefore, in order to understand how these Islamic groups derive their legitimacy, it is necessary to look at the relationship between authority and community.

Political Authority and *Ummah*

Understanding the relationship between political authority, the *ulema* and the *Ummah* is the key to understanding the legitimation of narratives within the context of Muslim communities. This link becomes especially important to understand when war becomes legitimated, and who has the right to take the decision to wage war or sign a peace treaty on behalf of the Muslim community. This link is also crucial for understanding who has the right to interpret the Islamic sources, particularly concerning matters of war and peace. Without comprehending the link between the political authority, the Muslim community and the *ulema*, it would not be possible to understand the legitimation of narratives of war and peace within an Islamic context.

Relationship between the individual and community in the Middle East is derived from the 'traditional' sources of legitimacy. Social relationships in the Middle East can be characterized as 'communal,' based on the notion of *Ummah* (the community of believers). Weber classifies these social relations as 'communal' if the orientation of social action is based on a subjective feeling of the parties, whether affectual or traditional.[22]

The nature of society in the Middle East differs significantly from that of the Western countries. Western perspectives concentrate on the individual as the major unit of analysis, whereas in the Middle East emphasis is on the community (*Ummah).* The idea of the individual in Islamic society can be compared to the Greek idea that the individual is an integral part of the political process by which human-beings come to realize and actualize their potential. Religious, customary, and traditional values still play a defining role in these societies. For instance, absence of a state-proper in Palestine resulted in the revival of traditional institutions among the Palestinian population.[23]

Roots of these traditions date back to pre-Islamic times, given that after its establishment, Islam adopted some of the existing features of the pre-Islamic Arab customs. In this organization of society, a tribal model became the basis for the Islamic notion of *Ummah*. This concept prescribes that all people may be accepted into the Muslim community, regardless of ethnic origin, race, language, or tribe, through accepting that all men are descendents of Adam.

However, the importance of "tribe" in the Middle Eastern understanding of society can be detected even today. Daniel M. Varisco notes "the common denominator defining Islamic Arab society of the region is invariably a tribal origin, no matter how distant from the realities of present social life."[24] He adds that it was "the tribal connection that often legitimized political and social status, during the expansion of Islamic nations far from Arabia."[25] Like most other nomadic tribal organizations, Arab societies in this era lacked political unity. Social cohesion and order were highly dependent on the strict application of tribal customs and moral principles. These principles and customs underscored the unity and primacy of the tribe as a whole.

The crucial aspect of these customs, for the purpose of understanding the legitimation processes in the region, is that the legitimacy of the leadership was based on seniority, nobility, and reputed wisdom. Majid Khadduri states that the authority of the leader "rested more on the confidence and respect of his fellow-tribesmen than on the power of the loose machinery of his government."[26] Furthermore, Khadduri states that the most important feature of the leader in the pre-Islamic Arab society was to make decisions on the basis of custom, enforced by tribal public opinion, but that he had no authority to issue orders that exceeded the customary law, since he was only the executive and not the legislative head of the tribe.[27]

This primacy of custom and unity of the tribal community was adopted by Prophet Muhammad when he was implanting the seeds of the first Islamic community in Madina. Historically, a comprehensive legal and ethical framework of state was first constructed in the Madina era, under the leadership and guidance of the Prophet. A sense of community, with its institutions, aspirations and a sense of common history, was constructed by the time the revelation of the Quran was completed. This core community has become the ideal example for the Muslims. Today, the social construction of Madina (though many competing accounts exist) within the discourse of modern Islamic thinkers constitutes an important aspect of Muslim politics, as Peter Mandaville also stresses.[28] Later on, the pre-Islamic model of society continued to inform the way Islamic community organized itself. This Islamic community was called the *Ummah*.

Ummah in Islam, according to Mona Abul-Fadl "is a purposeful entity composed of a group, a *jama'a,* whose members, by virtue of a common faith, way of life and sense of destiny, have forged into a common historical consciousness."[29] Furthermore, she argues that the symbiosis of faith and community is the source of active social and political involvement for Muslims both as groups and as individuals. The concept of *Ummah* is the basis of an awareness of a common identity, allegiance, and purpose. This view is also supported by Serif Mardin, who states "a characteristic feature of *Ummah* is the license the community of believers arrogates to itself in taking a critical stand towards the authority of officials."[30]

According to Mandaville, the *Ummah* of Madina was initially "a 'defense pact' that united the city's clans to protect Muhammad and his followers," and included elements of religion, kinship relations, and territory, and preserved "a good deal of traditional practice with regard to the formation of alliances and kinship ties...with overtly 'religious' aspects of the community being confined largely to Mohammed's close followers."[31] Furthermore, he notes that the social solidarity of the *Ummah,* to a certain extent, was "still based on the traditional tribal idiom, albeit with a new focus of collectivity that could (and did) prevent a return to civic conflict and factionalism."[32]

Ummah brings with it a set of distinctive vocabulary, concepts, myths, social positions, and locations that are shared by Muslims in general. It creates its own discourse that enables Muslims to connect with one another. Thus, it becomes a resource for the mass mobilization and social organization of the community. Various Islamic institutions, where such a discourse is reinforced and activated, play an important role in this process. Analysis of these institutions will be dealt with in Chapter Seven.

Legitimation of the notion of *Ummah* can be found in the Quranic verses: "The believers are but a single Brotherhood..." (Q49: 10), "Verily this *Ummah* of yours is a single *Ummah*, and I am your Lord And Cherisher: therefore Serve Me (and no other)" (Q21: 92) and "Let there arise out of you a band of people (*Ummah*) Inviting to all that is good, Enjoying what is right, And forbidding what is wrong..." (Q3: 104). In various verses the Quran also gives guidelines on how Muslims should conduct their relations with each other, and with non-Muslims according to the Islamic notion of *Ummah.* These guidelines were interpreted and included in the development of the theories of society by the *ulema.* The Islamic notion of *Ummah* recognizes the existence of various different nations and tribes in order for human groups to get to know each other and compete in doing goodness. This reason is stated in the Quranic verse 49:13

> O mankind! We created You from a single (pair) Of a male and female, And made you into Nations and tribes, that Ye may know each other (Not that ye may despise Each other). Verily the most honoured of you In the sight of Allah is (he who is) the most righteous of you.

Theoretically, most of the personal and social life of the *Ummah* is regulated by *Shariah,* and is subject to an autonomous jurisdiction. Observance of a common code of life and submission to the Divine will have continued to structure the unity of *Ummah,* although various forms of government, culture and language separated the community. Abul-Fadl argues that the spread and perpetuation of the instruments of socialization together with the pervasiveness of the ethical-social code consistently sustained the sense of identity.[33]

Abul-Fadl also states that the community life in Islam is based on the idea that everyone is responsible for the others. This idea is based on the *Hadith* of the Prophet: "You are all, each and every one of you, entrusted with a charge and you are all, each and every one of you responsible for that charge."[34] Based on the nature of the issue, obligations and duties of Muslims are divided into two categories: collective and personal duties. Personal duties are those that every Muslim is ordained to follow and include pronouncing that there is no god but God and Muhammed is his Prophet, daily prayers, alms-giving, fasting, and going to Mecca if the physical and financial situation (of an adult Muslim) allows. Collective duties are those that are not compulsory for all Muslims. If there are enough Muslims to undertake these duties, they do it on behalf of all other Muslims. These duties include practicing *ijtihad* to understand what God wants humans to do, entailing education in medical and other sciences. On the issue of jihad there has been a disagreement between various Islamic groups. Khawarijs and fundamentalists argue that jihad is an individual duty, whereas the traditional Sunni approach takes jihad as a collective duty.[35] Yet, they all agree that commitment to justice is at the heart of the Muslim social consciousness and conscience.

At this point it is necessary to look at the concept of political authority as it developed in the Islamic world, because the concept of political authority is closely tied to legitimacy and the process of legitimation. Understanding political authority becomes especially important in order to understand the legitimation of war according to Islamic tradition. Sources of political theory in Islam include the Quran and the *Sunna*. According to Abul-Fadl the political expression of *Ummah* is the state. State in Islam has been founded on the basic principles that are stated in the Quran and the *Sunna*. Yet these sources do not prescribe a political theory that deals with every aspect of governance. For that reason, scholars of Islam over the centuries have resorted to *ijtihad* and *ijma* in order to develop a political theory of Islam. They observed the first state in Islam, which Mohammed established in Madina, and the conduct of four rightly caliphs[36] as their model.

The first and foremost principle of Islamic political theory states that all authority in the universe lies with God; therefore only God is to be obeyed. The second principle is based on the idea that Islamic Law is already legislated in the Quran and *Sunna*. Guidance was sent to human beings from time to time through various prophets, and Mohammed is the last prophet. In that respect, legitimacy of the authority is derived from the Quranic verse *an-Nisa* 59, which states that Muslims are commanded to obey God, the Prophet and those who are in authority as long as they are adhering to the orders and laws of God. The function of authority in Islam, therefore, is to protect the Islamic community, apply the Islamic Law and create conditions for a just social life. The system is expected to work for the success of the Muslim community in this world as well as to prepare it for the hereafter. And in order to realize these objectives, organization of the *Ummah* must be based on the principles of equality, solidarity, and freedom.

Three important features of the state, or the formal structure of the society, are important to understand the political authority in Islam. These are the Muslim community (*Ummah*), Islamic Law (*Shariah*), and the Sovereign (*Caliph*). In theory, the state in Islam belongs to God, and Muslims are his party (*Hizbullah*). There is an idea of a good and just life and happiness of people (*hayat taybiyya*), similar to the Greek idea of a good and ethical life of the citizens of the city. Major institutions of the state are based on the values of *Shura* (Council), *Ijtihad* (systematic intellectual effort), and *Ijma* (Consensus). The major and distinctive political institution is the caliphate, which represents the political unity of the community as a whole. In the Islamic political theory, the caliph is the head of the community, and although there is no clear procedure on how to appoint the caliph, the crucial aspect of it is that it must be confirmed by the *Ummah*, through a *bai'ah* (a symbolic way of rendering obedience). In that sense it is a social contract by which the community promises to obey the caliph, and the caliph promises to govern the community in conformity with the Islamic Law. The Islamic state has two major organs: the judiciary and the executive. Legislation is constitutionally undefined because the Quran and the *Sunna* already lay it down.

From this theory of the state, the supremacy of Islamic law is clear. In order to implement the Islamic law, it is necessary to have a directing head to execute it. This head is called the "caliph". But it is important to note that the caliph does not have an inherent power to legislate; his or her sole responsibility is to implement it. Observing from this point of view, scholars such as Tamara Sonn, Majid Khadduri argue that the Islamic form of state can be called a "nomocracy," rather than a "theocracy."[37] Their distinction is based on the argument that theocracy is a form of governance in which God is the governor, and those who are in authority claim to act on this divine authority. Conversely, nomocracy is a form of governance in which the state is governed by a system of codified laws. They argue that, in the case of Islam, the Islamic state is governed by *Shariah*, the Islamic Law, through its application by human beings who do not have divine authority, rather than being governed by God Himself.

Another important point is related to the question of how to nominate the caliph, since he is in charge of the application of the Islamic law. With regard to war, initially he was also in charge of determining when it is appropriate to declare war in the name of God, and to defend Islam and the community. In theory, Muslims are required to hand trust only to those who are the most competent, yet the procedure is clear neither in the Quran nor the *Sunna*. Looking at the appointment of four rightly guided caliphs, we see that there were different procedures. It was believed that the structures would evolve according to the wisdom and needs of the community, and are not permanent. It was assumed that different times and conditions would require different procedures, and that the real objective was to ensure that Shariah would govern the *Ummah*. Such a view displays sensitivity to temporality and historical conditions of changing societies and gives flexibility to the political processes. Such an attitude is also crucial in understanding how Muslim communities overcome various challenges that they are facing today, and in developing a model that is appropriate to the current needs and situation of the Muslim communities.

In order to understand the process of establishing political authority and how this process can contribute to developing procedures relevant to today, it is necessary to look at the period of four rightly guided caliphs. The common feature of these appointments is that an initial electoral college did the selection of the best man. This was followed by a private *bai'ah* and confirmation through a public *bai'ah*. After the death of the Prophet, distinct groups were formed with their respective leaders. After the first election, Umar proposed Abu Bekr, and the rest swore allegiance to him. This private *bai'ah* was followed by a public *bai'ah*. Abu Bekr nominated second caliph Umar and the community accepted his recommendation. Umar formed an electoral college before his death and his son was elected to have the deciding role if there was a tie. After consulting with the candidates and community, he voted in favor of Uthman. When Uthman was assassinated, Ali was nominated as the candidate. He refused to have a private *bai'ah* and accepted only the public *bai'ah*. From these different procedures, it is evident the consent of the people was crucial to the process.

Although the ideal political system in Islam is based on the system of caliphate, historical realities led to a proliferation of various forms of governmental rule, such as the sultanate. Later on, various rulers dominated various territories, and *Ummah* was divided into different political units, and "caliphate" for the whole *Ummah* existed in the name only. These rulers did not adopt the title of the caliphate, but titles such as sultan, *padishah*, or imam. They based the legitimacy of these titles on the silences in the Quran and argued the titles were mentioned in the Quran and were not opposed to anywhere in the Text. This is what Weber refers to as legitimizing one's authority in terms of discretion in the sphere that tradition leaves open to him or her.[38] Thus political power became diverse; yet a common arena of *Dar-al Islam* (lands ruled according to Islamic Law), based on a common sense of destiny and common practices, still existed and continued to inform the Muslim consciousness.

History records that the major change came with *Muawiyah* (whose legitimacy was questioned by some Muslim groups such as Khawarijs and Shi'as) who became the caliph after the fourth rightly guided Caliph Ali. His authority was accepted after a painful period of war and arbitration, which resulted in the polarization of Muslims into Sunnis and Shi'as. Followers and supporters of Ali argued that Muawiyah had acquired the title caliph unjustly due to a corrupted arbitration process, whereas others argued that since an allegiance was sworn to him, he was a legitimate caliph. Muawiyah's way of becoming a caliph was considered by some jurists as usurpation (*islita*), because it was obtained through coercion. Yet, usurpation is also considered one of the legitimate ways of obtaining caliphate by some of the jurists, as long as an allegiance was sworn to the caliph. It was also with Muawiyah that the institution of caliphate was transformed into a dynastic kingdom. He appointed his son as his successor and justified this act with the argument that this was the only way to prevent an internal discord (*fitna*) and, therefore, protect the unity of the *Ummah*.

Various Muslim thinkers hold the view that monarchy, which was slowly introduced, is also an acceptable form of state according to Islam, since Quran refers to the previous kingdoms. Among these thinkers, al- Farabi is the most prominent one. Influenced by Plato's idea of the Philosopher-king, he developed the idea of the Prophet-King, where Muhammad was the perfect example, and described the state of Madina as the ideal state. Monarchy and dynasties were justified by the claim that it was necessary in order to protect the internal order and integrity of the *Ummah* and to avoid *fitna* (internal disorder, or anarchy). This was based on the Quranic verse that stated "*fitna* is worse then killing" (Q2: 217). This development represented the rational justification of the formal and substantial departure from the ideal state due to the pressures of the current times. This doctrine of necessity was developed later on by al-Ghazzali, who argued that tyranny was better than chaos.

Nevertheless, various jurists still tried to justify the institution of caliphate. Al-Mawardi argued that the institution of caliphate was a result of the contract between the governor and the governed —the caliph and the *Ummah*—since it was chosen by an electoral body, and was the guardian of the *Shariah*, and was the chief administrator charged with the protection of the Muslim communal welfare.[39] Therefore he argued that as long as the sultans who held the actual power obeyed the *Shariah* and rendered loyalty to the caliph and considered their powers as delegated, they could be tolerated.

Al-Ghazzali argued that the caliph was a requirement of the *Shariah*, but considering the weakness, he saw him more as a spiritual leader and pointed out the necessity of obeying the persons who held military power.[40] Ibn Jama'a intended to bring back the caliphate; therefore he elaborated a theory on its aims, qualifications, and functions. But he concluded that the obedience was due to those Muslims who could install themselves in positions of political power provided that they implemented *Shariah* and preserved the integrity of the *Ummah*.[41] However, he added that an unjust ruler who did not obey the laws of God should not be obeyed. He also stated that the rule of sultans were valid due to the customs of the times, and it was the duty of the *ulema* (learned men of Islam) to serve as the guardians of the *Shariah*.

Ibn Taymiyya emphasized the strict adherence to the *Shariah* rather than reinstituting the caliph. He argued that after the four rightly guided caliphs, the *ulema* had become their heirs and the guardians of the Prophet's legacy. He insisted on going back to the Quran and the *Sunnah*, and how important it was to have pious sultans and *ulema* whose function was to see the justice of God prevail. For him the most important thing was the supremacy of the *Shariah* as the legal constitution of the state.[42]

Due to the transformation of political authority from a system of caliphate to the system of sultanate, *ulema* have become an important aspect of the society, with their role as interpreters of the Quran and the *Sunna*. We also observe that *fitna* (civil discord) has come to be seen as something unwanted. For that reason obedience to authority at the expense of justice, adherence to tradition and rituals are strongly emphasized. Political success of the Muslim community in this period against the "Superpowers" of the day—the Byzantine and Persian Empires—played a substantial role in the formulation of Muslim political ideals and the institutionalization of the caliphate, which lasted until the middle of the 13th century, when the Abbasid Caliphate collapsed and Baghdad was sacked by the Mongolians. Since then, there has not been an undisputed caliph, although there have been claimants to it.

This depiction of the theory of state in Islamic political theory points to the importance of the Islamic law in organizing life in Islamic community. Although many of the Islamic scholars such as al-Ghazzali, seem to justify obedience to political authority in order to avoid internal strife and chaos, the role of *Ummah* is very important for establishing social justice within the society. The role of *Ummah* in Islamic societies has become particularly important in the modern context as the role of 'population' is becoming more important due to fast transportation of ideas—i.e. democracy—which renders populations with more awareness about their social and political potentials.

The mission of the Muslim community is to create a moral social order. Government regulations, Islamic laws, and activities of religious police who monitor public behavior have all been justified as expressions of this total mission to command the good and prohibit evil.[43] The agents of state are chosen among the members of the *Ummah* as instruments of the collectivity, and are responsible for bringing about and implementing the just order that is prescribed by the Quran and the *Shariah*. The community bears an important responsibility for the establishment of this social justice by not obeying those who do not implement this just order. Thus *Ummah* becomes an instrument for the critical evaluation of the state policies.

As it is clear from the above analysis, the Quran, the *Sunna* and the *Hadith* constitute the bases of all claims to legitimacy in the context of Muslim communities. Any political authority must justify its actions and decisions based on these sources. Local leaders that practice peacemaking in the Palestinian community, also base their practices and their legitimacy on these sources. Islamic law, including Islamic Law of international relations, is derived from these sources. For that reason, understanding their nature and their role in an Islamic society becomes crucial. Therefore it is necessary to trace the development of Islamic law based on the interpretation of these main sources.

The Quran, *Hadith* and *Sunna*

Muslims believe that the Quran is the divine word of God literally revealed to Prophet Mohammed between 610-632 C.E., and accept it to be the most comprehensive guidance for human beings. For Muslims, the Quran is the unchangeable and direct word of Allah and it is the unchallenged source of Islamic beliefs, practices, and laws. The Quran is written in neither prose nor verse, yet has a powerful, captivating rhetoric which is read in a distinct, rather melodic way, and has a tremendous effect on Muslims when it is recited.

The word "Quran" is derived from the Arabic root "*qara'a*", which means 'he read".[44] The adjective form "*qarana*" means 'he gathered, he collected.'[45] Literally *al-quran* means "the reading", "the recitation" or "collection". Within the text of the Quran itself, the word is used to mean "reading" (Q17: 93), "a collection" (Q75: 17), and "recital" (Q75: 18). "The Quran more regularly refers to itself as a revealed discourse unfolding in response to the requirements of society over a period of twenty-three years (17:82; 17:106)"[46]

The Quran contains 114 *surahs* or chapters, which are divided into *ayats* or verses. *Surahs* differ in terms of their length: the longest *surah* contains 286 *ayats* and the shortest has only 3. The Quran is not revealed at once but over a 22-year period during which many developments took place and thus revelations include practical and political responses to the actual events of the day. Chapters are also divided according to two different periods of the Prophet's life, namely the Meccan period (610-622 C.E.) and the Madinan period (622-632 E.C.) Ninety-three chapters were revealed during the Meccan period while twenty-one chapters were revealed during the Madinan period.

After stating that the Quran is the most important source for Muslims, it is important to look at its contents. The Quran contains the dogma, a body of narratives, and moral and juridical injunctions.[47] Prophet Mohammed would recite the revealed verses of the Quran to His followers, who would then memorize and later record these verses. These portions of the Quran were collected and arranged after the death of the Prophet following an order of first Caliph Abu Bekr between 632 and 634 C.E. The third Caliph Uthman arranged the current day version of the Quran—his version is called the *Mushaf Uthman*.

The central dogma of Islam is the belief that "there is no god but God and Muhammad is His Apostle and the last Prophet." In addition to that, Muslims also believe in the previous prophets and their scriptures such as the Torah and the Bible. They also believe in the angels, in the Day of Judgement, predestination, and in Heaven and Hell. The six beliefs stated here are the main Islamic dogmas.

Beside these six main dogmas, Islam is based on five pillars—essential and obligatory practices, which are the core and common denominators of the faith. The first and most significant of these pillars is the profession of faith that is the *shahadah*, or witnessing that there is no god but the God [Allah] and holding that Muhammad is the messenger of God. The second pillar of Islam is the daily prayers. The third and fourth pillars are fasting during the month of Ramadan and almsgiving. And the fifth pillar is the Pilgrimage to Mecca if an adult Muslim is physically and financially able to do so.

Narratives that are stated in the Quran tell stories of former peoples, tribes, kings, prophets and saints. These narratives show how righteous people were awarded and God punished the wrongdoers. They provide guidance in terms of what is considered right and wrong, good or bad according to Islam and provide believers with codes of conduct. The central concern of the Quran is the conduct of men.[48] Together with moral and juridical injunctions, these narratives form the basis of examples and regulations concerning human conduct in this world.

The revelation of the Quran did not occur at once but gradually. This aspect of the Quranic revelation is the basis of the principle of *tadrij*. According to Farid Esack, *tadrij* acknowledges that gradual revelation "reflects the creative interaction between the will of God, realities on the ground and needs of the community being spoken to."[49] Esack argues that there were two main reasons for this gradual revelation. The first one is related to the fact that the Quran came as a day-to-day guidance. This aspect is explicit in the verse "We only gradually unfolded so that you may recite it to the people step-by-step and (therefore) We have revealed it only in pieces" (Q17: 106).[50] The second reason, states Esack, is that Islam came into life in the midst of a struggle and Muhammad needed the ongoing support and solace from his encounters with revelations.[51] This reason is derived from another Quranic verse that states "Thus that We may strengthen your heart thereby. We have arranged it well" (Q25: 32).[52]

Since the Quran is believed to be the direct word of God, and is eternal and applicable at all times, understanding the Quran "correctly" becomes the main endeavor for many Muslims in order to live by its rules. Nevertheless, the Quran does not provide direct answers to all the questions and problems that Muslims face. When a Muslim is faced with a problem that is not stated clearly in the Quran, *Hadith*, the Prophet's sayings, and the Prophet's conduct, *Sunna,* become important sources of guidance. Legitimacy of these sources are based on the Quranic verses "obey God and the Messenger…If you should quarrel over anything refer to God and the Messenger" (4:59) and "In God's messenger you have a fine model for anyone whose hope is in God and the Last Day" (33:21).

Based on this suggestion, after Mohammed's death his sayings were recorded by his companions. Yet, the proliferation of the *Hadith* and the *Sunna* called for criteria to distinguish authentic and fabricated *Hadith* and *Sunna*. With that aim, especially in the 9th and 10th centuries scholars attempted to collect traditions of *Hadith* and *Sunna* and the evaluation of tradition focused on the chain of narrators and the subject matter. The trustworthiness of the narrator was judged based on his moral character, intelligence, piety, and good memory. "Then a link by link examination of each of the narrators was conducted to trace the continuity of a tradition back to the Prophet."[53]

Secondary criteria involved the evaluation of the subject matter. This entailed "an examination to determine whether, for example, a tradition contradicted the Quran, an already verified tradition, or reason."[54] After this double evaluation, *Hadith* and *Sunna* were categorized according to the degree of their authenticity in terms of being sound, good, acceptable or weak. As a result of this enormous work collections of al-Bukhari and Muslim were recognized as the most authentic sources of *Hadith* and *Sunna*.

The Islamic legal system, or *Shariah,* is based on these three main sources. Moral and juridical injunctions in the Quran form the basis of *Shariah* or Islamic law. However, as Khadduri suggests, there is ample evidence to show that Islamic law evolved from Arab customary law and that after the expansion of the Islamic state, Islam absorbed local custom and practices of the conquered territories.[55] *Shariah* is a comprehensive legal system that governs all aspects of Muslims' life, both in private and public. "*Shariah* is a fundamental source of legislation rather then a temporal political authority".[56] It is believed that God is the sole sovereign ruler of the world and the sole legislator, and *Shariah* is God's law for entire Islamic community, indeed for all humankind. Therefore, *Shariah* is both the basis of law and the ethical system. Under the Islamic law, all acts are characterized, as obligatory, recommended, indifferent, reprehensible but not forbidden, or prohibited. Breaking the law is both a crime and a sin. Yet, *Shariah* does not provide constitutional or (independent) judicial restrains.[57] Therefore, although *Shariah* formed the main source of legitimacy, two complementary legal systems were developed within the course of Islamic history. These were *Shariah* courts that were increasingly restricted to family law and handling the religious endowments, and grievance courts, that dealt with public law, involving criminal, land, and commercial regulations.[58]

Traditional Mechanisms of Interpretation of The *Quran*, *Sunnah* and *Hadith*: *Ijtihad*, *Qiyas*, and *Ijma*

Although one may claim that God will enable true Muslims to understand the correct interpretation of the Quran, the existence of multiple interpretations concerning central issues in Islam poses the question, "how do we know which of these groups hold the key to the 'true' interpretation?" Since there is no single Islamic authority, which can claim such a position, it is upon the Muslim individuals to decide which groups they think represent the 'true' Islam. In this process, interpretation of, or understanding, the Divine Text becomes a crucial aspect of legitimation of various narratives within the Islamic tradition.

Legitimation of narratives, especially when it is based on a sacred text such as the Quran, always entails a process of interpretation. In this process of interpretation, every encounter invokes the experience of a tension between the text and the historical moment of interpretation. Texts are always understood within the effective history of the interpreter, *ulema* in the Islamic tradition. In this process, historical situatedness of the interpreting individual comes in contact with previous interpretations of the text, and acquires a new meaning. For that reason, in order to gain a better perspective of the emergence of different interpretations of a text one has to do both contextual as well as an inter-textual analysis of the hermeneutic situation.

Inter-textual analysis is based on the recognition that "texts" acquire meaning in relation to other texts. Interpreting a text, "understanding" its meaning or meanings requires tracing its relationship with other related texts. "Meaning becomes something which exists between a text and all other texts to which it refers and relates, moving out from the independent text into a network of textual relations."[59] Islamic texts, such as those relating to war and peace, are products of such inter-textual relations with other texts. They have evolved over the course of the Islamic history, influenced by various external developments. Furthermore, these texts have developed within specific historical, political, social, and cultural contexts. Therefore, these texts and the contexts from which they emerged cannot be separated. These texts present narratives that contain structures and struggles, expressed in the societies they were embedded in. Therefore, comprehending these inter-textual and contextual settings facilitates our understanding of why particular narratives have come to dominate Islamic discourse during different eras.

Such an analysis, applied to interpretation of the Quran regarding peace and war, must take into consideration the spatial/temporal moment in which Islam emerged. The Quran was revealed in the 7th century to a particular group of people faced with particular historical, social and ethical realities, and was written in a language that was relevant to the 7th century Arabia for it to be intelligible to the population there. Even Islamic scholars such as Mawdudi and Qutb, who are the founding fathers of Islamic fundamentalism, recognize this aspect of the Quranic message. As it is stated by Abul-A'la Mawdudi (d.1979 C.E.), Quranic contents are, "on the whole, vitally related to the taste and temperament, the environment and history and customs and usages of Arabia."[60] Sayyid Qutb, who contended that "Quran took it [society] by the hand step by step, as it stumbled and got up again, strayed and was righted, faltered and resisted, suffered and endured," also supported this position.[61]

Over the last 1400 years, Islam has expanded to different parts of the world with different cultural and linguistic traditions. These years have also brought with them significant socio-political and economic changes. Thus interpreting how God's guidelines would be applicable to a current situation has been a major field of inquiry in Islamic societies over the centuries. This becomes even more important in overcoming the major difficulties faced by the Muslims in the world today. This issue underscores one of the most important aspects of Islamic tradition.

As Mandaville notes, "Islam is 'a single discursive field'—a 'lifeworld' perhaps—yet one whose borders are constantly changing."[62] However, this "single Islam," as he adds, "does not necessarily have any direct correlation with the lived experience of being a Muslim, nor does it have to impart any essence or teleology to the religion."[63] Islamic discourse offers a set of meanings that are continually repeated and, based on this discursive field that operates as an "important bearer of social meaning within particular communities,"[64] Islam is narrated in various different forms to legitimize various socio-political projects. In this process of legitimization, "the coupling of history and Islam has an important discursive function related to the production of authority and authenticity."[65] Within this context, interpretation of the Scripture becomes crucial.

As stated above, the Quran is recognized as the direct, eternal, and universal word of God, and is thus applicable by Muslims at all times. However, individuals are temporal beings; therefore interpretation of the Quran is also temporal. The tension between the eternal and temporal aspects of the Text presents difficulties in interpretation. Societies change over the course of history, and new needs and problems emerge as a result of this change. Since the Quranic message is taken to be eternal, scholars of the Quran contend that a response to any societal change must have been incorporated within the Quran as well. Therefore answers to emerging new problems —it is believed— must be *hidden* in between the Quranic verses. It is the *duty* of Muslim scholars to unveil God's rules and regulations for Muslims, especially since Islam is a religion that penetrates into all aspects of the life of Muslims, from personal to social to political and economical. Therefore interpreting the Holy Text, and understanding God's will becomes of the utmost importance within the Islamic tradition.

Understanding what God ordains and expects from Muslims involves applying the Divine Scripture to the interpreter's present situation. At this point of application, there exists a tension between the fixed text, and the sense arrived at by applying it at the concrete moment of interpretation. The interpreter approaches the text with a particular question in mind. For instance, when a political authority under certain historical conditions attempts to wage war, the Muslim jurists try to determine whether this particular war is permissible according to Quran. Therefore they engage in questions regarding when war is permissible according to Islam and if the political authority in power has the legitimacy to do so. They search for the potential answers within the Text and also look into the practice of the Prophet to support their point of view.

Gadamer calls the various considerations of the interpreter the "horizon of questions."[66] These interpretations aim at concretizing both legal and theological validity of the answers the interpreters arrive at according to Islam. As Gadamer points out, this implies that the Text must be understood at every moment, in every concrete situation in a new and different way since the interpreter has different questions in mind.[67] Therefore, the historical situatedness of the Muslim scholars who attempt to understand what God's laws are regarding a particular problem (in the past and in the present) must be evaluated within their historical context and in relation to other texts they utilize.

Since interpretation plays a crucial role in Muslims societies, Islamic scholars have taken this process very seriously. These scholars developed various techniques to interpret the Islamic message and to unveil the Islamic law. In this development of Islamic law *reason* played a significant role: "A striking feature of Quranic discourse is the emphasis on the people's use of their innate intelligence in comprehending the revealed guidance which is accessible both in the Holy Book and in the Book of Nature."[68] Over the centuries, Muslims have developed sciences concerning the interpretation of the text, such as *ijtihad*.

Ijtihad comes from the Arabic word *jihad,* which means endeavor, or exerting effort. Scholars who practice *ijtihad* have been called *mujtahid*. The *Hadith* stated in the following quote constitutes the justification for *ijtihad* in Islamic tradition:

> In order to understand the Qur'aan [sic], you should first look to the Quran itself. If that does not help, then turn to the *Sunnah*. The Prophet (sallallaahu `alayhi wa sallam) sent Mu`aadh (radiyallaahu `anhu) to Yemen and asked him: "How will you judge the cases (that come to you)?" He replied: "I will judge according to the Book of Allaah". "But if you do not get anything there, what will you do?", the Prophet (sallallaahu `alayhi wa sallam) asked. He said: "I will refer to the *sunnah* of the Prophet (sallallaahu `alayhi wa sallam)". "But if you do not get it even there, what will you do?" the Prophet (sallallaahu `alayhi wa sallam) asked again. He replied: "I will exercise my judgment." Hearing this, the Prophet (sallallaahu `alayhi wa sallam) patted Mu`aadh (radiyallaahu `anhu) on the shoulder and said: "Praise be to Allaah who has guided the Messenger of His Messenger to what pleases His Messenger." This hadeeth has been reported in the Musnad and Sunan collections of hadeeth with a good isnaad. [Ahmad, Musnad V:230, 236, 242; al-Daarimee, Sunan, Muqaddimah, 30; al-Tirmidhee, Sunan, Ahkaam, 3; Abu Dawood, Sunan, Adhiyah, 11.][69]

However, the fact is that interpreters of the Divine Text are people, and people are not free from prejudice and error. This 'human' aspect of interpretation and the lack of certainty were recognized since the earliest Muslims. As Farid Esack states, during the Battle of Siffin (C.E. 657) supporters of Muawiyah demanded to resolve the conflict between him and Ali, the fourth rightly guided caliph, through *tahkim* based on Quranic principles.[70] Ali's dilemma, cited in al-Razi, reflected that of many Muslims':

> When Muawiyah invited me to the Quran for a decision, I could not turn my face away from the Book of Allah. The Mighty and Glorious Allah declared that 'if you dispute about anything, refer to Allah and His Apostle'. [However,] this is the Quran, written in straight lines, between two boards [of its binding]; it does not speak with a tongue; it needs interpreters and interpreters are people.[71]

Nevertheless, caliphs, judges, jurist or legal scholars had used intellectual reasoning and interpretation, when there is no clear, explicit revealed text, or the *Hadith* and the *Sunna*. "The use of reason (legal reasoning or interpretation) had taken a number of forms and been described by various terms; personal opinion, jurist preference, and analogical reasoning (*qiyas*)."[72] *Qiyas* refers to a practice, when a solution to a problem is not given in the Quran and *Hadith*, of drawing an analogy from a similar case stated in these sources by discovering the effective cause or reason behind a given rule. The reason behind that rule would lead to a general principle, which is then used to validate or deduce the new rule concerning the initial problem.[73]

Ijma, or consensus of the community, is another technique used by Islamic scholars to arrive at certain rules. Although in the beginning *ijma* was considered to include the *Ummah* in general, later on it became restricted to the learned scholars (*mujtahids*) who were trained in and also exercised *ijtihad* to arrive at certain judgments. The justification of *ijma* is based on the Quranic verse "...those who turn away from the Prophet and do not follow the way of the believers" (Q 4:115). In this verse, "the way of the believers" was taken to mean the *consensus* of the believers.[74] This view was also supported by the *Hadith* of the Prophet "my community will never unanimously agree on error."[75]

Another method used by Islamic scholars is abrogation (*naskh*). According to Ibn Manzur, *naskh* literally means 'the removal of something by something else [and] annulment.'[76] This term was used in Islamic interpretation of the Quran as the verification and elaboration of different modes of abrogation. Justification of *naskh* according to Islamic tradition is rooted in the Quranic verse "None of our revelations do we abrogate or cause to be forgotten, but we substitute something better or similar..." (Q2: 106) According to Esack, the modes of *naskh* can be classified as a) the Quranic abrogation of divine scriptures that preceded it; b) the repeal of some Quranic texts that are said to have been blotted out of existence; c) the abrogation of some earlier commandment of the Quran by the later revelations, while the text containing those commandments remained in the Quran; d) the abrogation of a prophetic practice by a Quranic injunction; and e) the abrogation of a Quranic injunction by the prophetic practice.[77]

Abrogation has caused much confusion within the circles of Islamic scholars. It has not been possible to reach a consensus on the abrogated verses, and almost all passages that were considered abrogated by one scholar were questioned by another scholar.[78] Furthermore, not every Islamic scholar favored *naskh*. Abu Muslim al-Isfahani (d. 1527 C.E.) denied the theory of *naskh* completely, while Muhammad Ibn Idris al-Shafi (d. 820 C.E.) and Fakhr al-Din al-Razi (d.1209 C.E.), contended that the possibility of abrogation does not mean that it occurred.[79] Reformists such as Sir Sayed Ahmad Khan (d.1898 C.E.) and Isma'il al-Faruqui (d.1986 C.E.) argued that "the revelations that came earlier in certain circumstances and which were modified or improved later, were not actually abrogated," but they were applicable to "conditions similar to those in which they were revealed."[80] As Esack notes, the debate concerning *naskh*, however, underlines what Fazlur Rahman calls 'the situational character of the Quran.'[81] Nevertheless, various Islamic groups use abrogation to justify their narratives concerning war and peace according to the Islamic tradition.[82]

During the interpretation of the Text in order to arrive at new rules, various principles are also invoked. One of these is to take into account the public or common welfare—what is good for the society in general—as the guiding principle for arriving at a rule. Another principle is the presumption that a state of affairs known to have existed in the past continues to exist unless proven otherwise.[83] An example of the application of this principle would be the presumption of the innocence of a person unless it is proven otherwise. Also customs and existing practices were taken into consideration in the process of arriving at new rules unless they explicitly contradicted the Scripture and the *Sunna* and the *Hadith* of the Prophet.

The practice of *ijtihad* led to different interpretations of the Text concerning various issues, and religious scholars started to group themselves around a leading scholar. This resulted in the development of diverse Islamic legal schools. Among these different legal schools, four of them emerged as the most prominent. These were: the Maliki school based on the works of jurist Malik Ibn Anas of Madina (718-795 C.E.); Hanefi school based on the works of Abu Hanifa from Kufa (699-767 C.E.); Shafi school based on the works of al Shafi'i (C.E. 767-820); and Hanbali school based on the works of Ahmad Ibn Hanbal (780-855 C.E.). All these schools agreed that the Quran and the *Sunna* were the main sources of the law but differed in their choice and emphasis on the particular techniques they preferred. The existence of different schools of law was not considered harmful to the Islamic tradition. On the contrary it was celebrated based on the *Hadith* "Differences of opinion among my community is a sign of Allah's mercy."[84]

Nevertheless, the above-mentioned four schools of law were accepted as the only legitimate legal schools by the tenth century, and Muslim scholars concluded that the work of legal interpretation was exhausted, and *Shariah* was completed. Therefore Islamic scholars after the tenth century dedicated themselves to the study of the works of these four jurists and writing commentaries about them.[85]

Modern Approaches to Interpretation of Islamic Texts

The decision to stop reaching at new laws was considered as the "closing of the gate of *ijtihad*." However, especially since the 19th century Muslim communities are faced with new challenges. These challenges included colonialism, imperialism, new economic and military distribution of power, new ideologies (such as nation-states, democracy, secularism, and Marxism among others) and new technological developments (such as television, the internet, and nuclear technology). Although first responses to modernity and West were of an Islamic nature, later on other ideologies came to the Muslim stage as a result of the political, social and economic developments of the times.

One of the most important developments that affected the Islamic political and social world was the emergence of the nation-state system. The transnational sense of community, based on the concept of *Ummah,* has been the focus of loyalty and source of identity for Muslims throughout the Islamic history. Voll states that "Tribal groupings, dynastic states, and other local organization had been of great importance, but they had not provided the framework for special ideological orientations as the local and regional groups had been viewed within the broader context of the Islamic faith and community."[86] But as nationalism and the idea of nation-states evolved in the Islamic world, the Islamic ideals regarding the community started to at times compete and at times complement these new notions.

In this process, regional heritages and ethno-linguistic differences formed the basis of a new kind of awareness and led to the development of the 'nation.' This new notion called for a political loyalty to the national community rather then to the transnational *Ummah* and the state emerged as the most effective locus of its operation. However, the boundaries of these new nation-states in the Muslim world were drawn by the imperial forces of the West and had little correspondence to the local realities. Nevertheless, "as the Muslim areas became independent, it was in the form of those new states, and the new state system incorporated older institutions in some cases and created new centers of loyalty in others."[87] While the international system considered states as legitimate political actors rather then religious or traditional communities, nations and states started providing group identity and ideological bases for social and political organizations as alternatives to *Ummah*.[88]

This new development was a traumatic experience for the Muslim community and created much confusion. The relatively sudden and imposed idea of the nation-state was coupled with feelings of backwardness and resentment under Western imperialism and domination. These feelings led to the emergence of various ideological movements that included nationalism coupled with nationalist (secular)-Westernization (as is the case with Turkey as the most significant example), Arab socialism (which was particularly influential in Egypt, Palestine, and the Iraqi and Syrian Baath Parties), and Islamic revivalism (which took different forms that will be discussed in the following paragraphs).

"The nationalist-Westerners were political activists but not often very radical in their social and economic programs."[89] Their perceived failure resulted in the emergence of an Arab socialism in the aftermath of WWII that advocated a more radical adaptationism through revolution. Although advocates of this ideology perceived religion as a personal matter, and called for separation of the old religious structures from politics, they employed a religious discourse to support radicalism. "Islam as a revolutionary faith could be cited as a support for contemporary revolutionary ideology, and Islam as part of a great heritage could provide support for national unity."[90] However, both nationalist Westerners and socialists followed a secular path in their political programs and tended to put religion in a subordinate position. As Voll states, the dominant ideological position in the 1960s was that of modernizing reformism, and there had been a transition from the nationalist-Westernizers to modernizing nationalist-socialists in many areas.[91]

During this period, conservative Islam played a less visible role, although Islam continued to guide the lives of Muslim individuals through habits, customs and symbols. As the political activism changed from an elite phenomenon to mass movements, these movements started to assume a more religious character. Nationalist and radical slogans and symbols, in this context, had a different significance on the populations than among the Western-educated elite[92] since religion continued to inform the meaning making processes of these populations. With the expansion of modern communication systems that enabled information to be transmitted faster and to wider circles of the society, especially after the 1970s, it became more difficult for the elites to control the process of mobilization. Thus by the mid 1970s, Voll argues that the style of Islam that was able to mobilize the religious stratum was the fundamentalist style.[93]

Islamic movements in the 20th century were effected by the developments stated above. The classical Islamic scholarship, based on established schools of law, were not furnished to respond to these developments. Hence, this situation led to some legal scholars of Muslim countries to formally declare the opening of the gate of *ijtihad* to deal with emerging problems. Among these scholars, Muhammed Iqbal (d. 1938 C.E.) argued that "closing the "door of ijtihad" is a pure fiction, suggested partly by the crystallization of legal thought in Islam, and partly by the intellectual laziness which in the period of spiritual decay turns great thinkers into idols,"[94] and suggested the "transfer of the power of *Ijtihad* from individual representatives of schools to a Muslim legislative assembly."[95] Khurshid Ahmad, vice president of the Jamat al-Islami, on the other hand, stated that God has revealed only broad principles and has endowed man with the freedom to apply them in every age in the way suited to the spirit and conditions of that age though *ijtihad*.[96]

Alas, this has been a painful process for many Muslims. The nostalgia of bright days of the successful "Islamic Empire" creates feelings of resentment among many Muslims today. This nostalgia, combined with an inferiority complex, led to the emergence of various approaches to cope with the problems of the modern world. Islamic scholar Sayyed Hossein Nasr observes that the current situation logically results in three attitudes.[97] The first attitude is that the current situation enforces the Islamic message and belief in the approaching end of the world. This attitude is based on recognizing that something has gone wrong with the world, as it is described by God himself in the Holy Book, and the current situation of Islam is itself a proof of God's message.[98] The second attitude suggests going back to the pure and original form of Islam since the current day problems are seen as a result of Muslims not following Islam properly.[99] Mostly Fundamentalist Islamists take this attitude. And the third attitude suggests that the Islamic message must be changed, modified, adapted or reformed to suit the modern conditions and be able to adapt itself to the modern world.[100] This attitude has resulted in various modernization approaches to Islam.

Taking Nasr's observation as a starting point, the modern day Islamic movements can be grouped under three categories, based on their perspective on the role and nature of *ijtihad* and their attitudes towards modernity. Drawing from the current literature on Islamic revivalism, I categorize these groups under the titles of Renewalist (*Tajdid)* movements, Reformist (*Islah*) movements, and Fundamentalist movements. The common denominator of these three movements is that they all are responding to the problems of the modern world and "social change," and they offer ways to deal with them. However, they differ significantly in terms of their conclusions and preferred solutions. Any attempt to understand the relationship between Islam and war and peace must take into consideration these general trends and the historical context that are influencing the minds of many Muslims. Therefore it is necessary to include a brief overview of these trends and how they impact the process of meaning-making within the modern Islamic scholarship and societies in general.[101]

It must be mentioned in advance that these movements did not emerge in a vacuum. *Tajdid* and *Islah* in particular are perceived to be rooted within the Islamic tradition and derive their legitimacy from various concepts and symbols embedded within this tradition. Based on this observation John Voll states, "the historical heritage provides at least some of the symbols and concepts available to Muslims,"[102] and in the absence of direct continuity, contemporary Muslim actions are influenced by the way they read the past experiences of Islamic world. Within that context both *Tajdid* and *Islah* are seen as reflecting "a continuing tradition of revitalization of Islamic faith and practice within the historic communities of Muslims."[103] Therefore, as Voll argues, both are perceived as "an authentic part of the working out of the Islamic revelation in history."[104] This belief in "continuity" assigns authenticity, and hence legitimacy to these movements.

The meaning, which the terms *Tajdid* and *Islah* embody, have changed over the course of Islamic history in accordance with the development of Islamic thought and are significantly influenced by the historical circumstances. Nevertheless, both terms represent the individual and communal effort to define Islam and the message of God based on the Quran, the *Hadith* and the *Sunna*.

The word *Islah* in Arabic suggests "a strong sense of moral righteousness" and "reshaping for the sake of improving effectiveness."[105] The justification of *Islah* can be found in the Quran when the story of Prophet Shu'aib is being told.

According to the Quranic story, Shu'aib tells his people "I only desire (your) betterment [*islah*] to the best of my power..."(Q11:88). The Quran also often praises those who work for *Islah*. Voll states, on the other hand, that *Tajdid* is a tradition from the Prophet Muhammed, although it has similar connotations. Justification of the tradition of *Tajdid* is based on the *Hadith* that records "God will send to his *Ummah* at the head of each century those who will renew its faith for it."[106] However, both terms do not depend on the Western notion of progress but are based on the "perfect model" that is depicted in the Quran and the organization of society in Madina. The aim of both *Tajdid* and *Islah* is to implement this ideal to existing conditions by being inspired by past experience. In order to empower the Islamic community, adherents of both movements call for strict application of the Quran, *Sunna* and *Hadith*, at the same time asserting the right of *ijtihad*.

Tajdid

Within this context, *Tajdid* (renewalism) is based on the argument that the current problems are a result of the corruption of the Islamic societies, which failed to live up to the ideals of Islam. In order to create modern Islamic societies the proponents of renewalism call for going back to the classical Islamic political theory, and to understand the workings of the ideal state of Madina. Renewalists aim to recreate the authentic Islamic lifestyle and traditions to keep the Islamic societies alive. They concentrate on grounding Islam within the community, and popularizing it. They contend that the ideal society can only come about through a renewal of religious identity, entailing a revival of religious rituals, norms and practices. They aim to restore justice and authentic values in order to reestablish continuity with the formative moments of Islamic history. In this process, social cohesion, mutual encouragement and cooperative endeavors are seen as central.

Renewalists are critical of the materialistic consumer oriented society, and aim to restore the society from within via education, combining scientific and technological advances of the West with traditional Islamic values and principles. In this effort, they favor a more literary interpretation of the Scripture, similar to that of Luther, and are less likely to utilize symbolic or esoteric interpretations. They insist going back to the original sources of Islam: they do not consider the later interpretations as binding, and often they reject these interpretations.

Renewalists can be viewed as sharing many similarities with Fundamentalists. In fact, many of the Fundamentalists, such as Mawdudi and Qutb, are seen as members of the Renewalist movement.[107] However, I share a similar view to that of Nasr and argue that 'fundamentalism' is a modern phenomenon that emerged as a unique response to the consequences of modernity, and there are no examples of a similar stance in the historical past. For that reason, in the Renewalist movement, I include those Islamic scholars and activists such as Muhammad Abduh, Rachid al-Ghannouchi, and Sheikh Yassin of Hamas, among others, who are both renewers and modernists.

In that respect these scholars and activists do not reject modernity but take certain aspects of it that are compatible with the Islamic values. Al-Ghannouchi's comments on "modernity" are a good example of this view:

> We want modernity, contrary to the ridiculous allegations made by those adversely inclined against political Islam, but only insofar as it means absolute intellectual freedom; scientific and technological progress; and promotion of democratic ideals. However, we will accept modernity only when we dictate the pace with which means it penetrates our society and not when French, British, or American interpretations impose upon us. It is our right to adopt modernity through methods equitable to our people and their heritage.[108]

Another example of their approach would be their attitude concerning the Islamic model of governance, especially their attitudes regarding democracy. Renewalists highlight the importance of participatory governance based on consultation, and consensus that are grounded in Islamic principles. For an appropriate model they look into the classical Islamic political theory and try to apply it to the current situation. For that reason, it can be said that they Islamicized modernity, by going back to classical sources such as the Quran, the *Sunna* and the *Shariah*.

Again, al-Ghannouchi, as well as Islamic Resistance Movement Hamas,[109] argues in favor of democracy, and even a free-market economy, as long as fair distribution is guaranteed. The following statement by al-Ghannouchi is a clear example of this view:

> When the compatibility of Islam and democracy is in question, some Westerners and Islamists maintain, as do the diligent opponents of political Islam, that the two platforms follow divergent paths.... This is done by segregating Islamic government and democracy to mean 'God's rule' and the 'people's rule' respectively.
>
> ....It is clear that 'God's rule' correlates to the rule of people or their representatives. Islamically, these are *ahl al-hall wal aqd,* an elective body of highly qualified and experienced scholarly individuals.
>
> ...there is no acceptable alternative other then democracy, one that is not exclusive, recognizing all perspectives. Stability will not occur unless we have a democracy of equality that embodies the people's right to control their civilian agendas without mandate; one that adheres stringently to the rotation of power; and one that strives for the fair distribution of wealth and establishment of a free-market economy.[110]

Islah

Although *Islah* and *Tajdid* share some similarities, there are significant differences, especially in their application of *ijtihad*. In that sense, I contend that *islah* (reformation) approaches the same problem—adaptation to change—from another angle. *Islah* comes from the word "*salaha*" which means to rectify, to return to the origin, to reform, and signifies a metaphor for going forward by going back to the origin, when things were in their right place. This origin is the state of Madina, which is the ideal state according to Islam. Yet the proponents of reform do not call for creating the conditions for bringing back the ideal state in the times that are past. On the contrary, they emphasize the essence of Islam. Valuing reason, they ask for the reopening of the gate of *ijtihad* that would allow reinterpretation of the sacred texts in accordance with the needs of the modern era.

Scholars within the *islahi* tradition emphasize ethical and moral responsibility of the individuals, universal principles, and enlightened adaptation, as well as progressive thinking. They do not reject cultural borrowing but argue that each cultural system can engage in a dialogue to learn from each other. The advocates of the *Islah* movement increasingly favor hermeneutical approaches in the modern sense, regarding the interpretation of the Sacred Texts. In their attempt to 'understand' the Text, in the context of modern world, they increasingly employ hermeneutical approaches.

Since the *islahi* approach and its proponents cannot be given justice here, I would like to focus only on Fazlur Rahman, Farid Esack, and Muhammed Arkoun who are some of the major key figures of the *Islah* movement. The reason for selecting these figures lies in their attempt to employ a hermeneutical approach similar to the modern sense of the term, introduced in Chapter Two. Although hermeneutics in the modern sense was not part of the Islamic tradition of *ijtihad*, these scholars mentioned above can be viewed as the pioneers of modern Islamic hermeneutics. Therefore they require special attention in the context of this project.

On the issue of Quranic hermeneutics, Fazlur Rahman, accepting the historical situatedness of the Quranic message, offers a process of interpretation that consists of a double movement, from the present situation to Quranic times, then back to the present. In his hermeneutical approach, Rahman suggests that "one must first understand the import of meaning of a given statement by studying the historical situation or problem to which it was the answer."[111] This step aims at understanding the Quranic message as a whole as well as in terms of the specific tenets that constitute responses to specific situations. The second step, on the other hand, consists of generalizing "those specific answers and enunciat[ing] them as statements of general moral-social objectives that can be "distilled" from specific texts in light of the socio-historical background and often-stated *rationes legis*."[112] These hermeneutical steps are based on his acknowledgement that the Quran as a whole incalculates a definite attitude towards life and has a concrete worldview, and contains no inner contradiction.[113]

Following this first movement that consists of the two steps mentioned here, comes the second movement. In this second movement, the general objectives must be applied to the concrete socio-historical context of the present. This step also requires a careful examination of the present conditions. After the assessment of these conditions, Rahman argues, "we can determine priorities afresh in order to implement the Quranic values afresh."[114] This second movement also serves as a correction of the results of the first movement, since "if the results of understanding fail in application to the current situation, then either there has been a failure to assess the present situation correctly or a failure in understanding the Quran."[115]

Rahman's approach to *ijtihad* suggests that hermeneutics as a method can be used to arrive at 'objective truths' concerning Quranic interpretation. Similar to the hermeneutical approach developed by Dilthey, he contends that it is possible to go beyond one's self and arrive at absolute "objective" meaning. He states that "the meaning of a past text or precedent, the present situation, and the intervening tradition can be fairly objectively brought under the judgement of the (normative) meaning of the past under whose impact the tradition arose."[116]

Situating himself within the "objective hermeneutical school," Rahman agrees with E. Betti that "the process of understanding is a "reversal" [his emphasis] of the original creative process: the forms that we try to understand and interpret now are to be led back to the creative mind whose original contents there were, not as isolated items but as a coherent whole, and made to live again in the mind of the understanding subject."[117] However, he adds that "this unity of forms cannot be attributed simply to the mind; one must also consider the situation to which it is a response."[118] He furthermore argues that, "every critique or modification of a tradition involves a consciousness of what is being criticized or rejected and hence to that extent, self-awareness."[119]

All conscious responses to the past involve two moments that must be distinguished. The first of these moments is the objective ascertaining of the past. This moment is possible in principle provided requisite evidence is available. The second moment consists of the response itself. And this necessarily involves, according to Rahman, values and is determined by the present situation of the interpreter, of which effective history is a part but of which the interpreter's conscious effort and self-aware activity also constitute an important part.[120] Hence, in his view, the interpreter has the capacity to be aware of his/her effective history and how that affects the process of understanding, and also s/he can self-consciously eliminate personal biases.

Muhammed Arkoun, in contrast, employs a different approach to interpretation of the Scripture. Arkoun, in his *Rethinking Islam Today,* rejects any links between his "modern perspective of radical thought applied to any subject… and *islahi* thinking"[121] However, when the Reformist approach is defined as modernizing Islam through a dialogue with West and modernity, based on human reason, and allowing reinterpretation of the sacred texts in accordance with the needs of the modern world, Arkoun's perspective can be meaningfully situated within the Reformist thinkers. Arkoun attempts to enrich the theological and philosophical approaches to religion by including the concrete historical and social conditions in which Islam always has been practiced.[122] His approach is influenced by the philosophical, linguistic and anthropological developments within the French intellectual circles in particular.

In his attempt to recapitulate Islamic knowledge and to confront it with contemporary knowledge, Arkoun notes that human beings emerge in societies through various changing "uses" (activity, experience, sensation, observation etc.).[123] Influenced by the French linguistic turn, he states that "each use is converted into a sign of this use [and] realities are expressed through languages as systems of signs,"[124] which emerges prior to any interpretation. Also the God's message itself is communicated through languages, which are systems of signs. Each sign is "a locus of convergent operations such as perception, expression, interpretation, translation, and communication. These convergent operations engage all of the relations between language and thought."[125] Acknowledgment of this has two major consequences according to Arkoun's perspective. First of all, the claim that Arabic language is sacred loses its validity. Secondly, the whole of Islamic thought is represented as a linguistic and semantic issue.[126]

Furthermore, Arkoun stresses that all signs and symbols are human products within the cultural, social, and historical situatedness of the subjects. Therefore, the Quran is also subject to historicity. After the establishment of this position, Arkoun asks:

> How can we deal with the sacred, the spiritual, the transcendent, the ontology, when we are obliged to recognize that all this vocabulary which is supposed to refer to stable, immaterial values, is submitted to the impact of history?[127]

Again, in his work *Rethinking Islam Today,* he states that "faith does not exist on its own," and adds that faith does not come from divine will or grace, but is "shaped, expressed and actualized in and through discourse."[128] Therefore, he challenges the classical Islamic theology and Islamic jurisprudence by arguing that the traditional system of legitimation and its vocabulary has no epistemological relevancy for the elaboration of knowledge today.[129] Moreover, he challenges the jurists and theologians for being too compromised by the ideological biases imposed on them by the "ruling class and its intellectual servants...[and] are authoritative only because they refuse to be engaged by the changing scientific environment."[130]

Arkoun's perspective is indeed radical observed from the point of view of the traditional Islamic approaches. His solution to the problem of interpretation starts with the assumption that the word of God is transcendent, infinite and unknown to humankind as a whole. Only various fragments of it have been revealed through various prophets. He continues to state that the word God was manifested in history by different prophets, and the argument that the Scriptures are worded by God, does not change the fact that the word itself has linguistic and historical aspects, since the word of God was transmitted through human languages, and was collected into a corpus under certain historical conditions.[131] And God's word is objectified as a written text, preserved in official canons, such as the *Mushaf* (written text) of Uthman.

Arkoun states that "the interpreting community is subject-actant of the whole terrestrial history represented, interpreted and used as a precarious stage to prepare the salvation according to the History of Salvation narrated by God as an educative part of revelation."[132] The socio-political context of the individual affects his/her relationship to the word of God. In his approach Arkoun argues that he does not put the transcendental beyond the parameters of "the true rationality" and he states that the "rationality" used at the theological stage of reason is more "related to the collective *imaginaire* then to the critical reason."[133]

Arkoun severely criticizes the traditional institutions where the interpretations of Islamic texts have been authorized. He argues that "reason" has established its authority outside of institutions and those experts (historians and/or linguists), who are trained "properly" will be able to access the true meaning of the texts.[134] Such a perspective ignores what texts come to mean for dealing with a particular situation, and what faith means for those who are not among the "experts," but practice their faith in everyday life. His perspective implies that knowledge is independent, and via correct methods it is possible to reach at "objective truths."

As the discussion above, point outs, no knowledge can be free of prejudice, or neutral, although it may be critical. It is the contention of this author that every reader approaches the text they are reading with his/her perspective, or horizon, with certain questions or expectations in his/her mind, or each reader is influenced by his/her experience. These perspectives or horizons impact the process of understanding, consciously or unconsciously. Therefore "objective knowledge" becomes questionable. Moreover, even if there is "objective knowledge," still, philosophers of knowledge have yet to develop tools to prove whose knowledge is objective, especially in social and theological sciences. For that reason, every truth claim, academic, theological, or etc. competes with other truth claims. In this process of establishing its regime of truth, every claim gets trapped within discourse/power politics.

The third scholar that I want to focus on is Farid Esack, who has been particularly influential on the way that I approach the process of interpretation. Following the Gadamerian perspective, Esack argues that there is a theological and historical basis for justifying a contextual approach to the Quran and the role of people elaborating its meaning.[135] Farid Esack, in his work *Quran, Liberation and Pluralism,* states that "One cannot escape from the personal or social experiences which make up the sum of one's existence."[136] And he adds that anyone who is reading a text or viewing a situation does so through the lenses of her or his experience.[137] For that reason it is not possible to claim that a given interpretation of the Quranic text is applicable to the whole world, since anyone who reads the Quran is influenced by his personal experience and within a particular context.[138] Since the formal statements concerning the texts are results of the intellectual effort of the *ulema*, they are accompanied by religio-political disputes "which inevitably impact upon theological developments and the way these statements are shaped."[139] In the final analysis, Farid Esack proposes that, within the context of today's world, Muslim scholars should ask: What is an 'authentic' appreciation of the Quranic message today? What makes and shapes "authenticity"? How legitimate is it to produce meaning, rather than extract meaning, from Quranic texts?[140] These questions are important for every Muslim scholar who attempts to understand the Quranic message for answering the problems of modern-day Muslim societies.

Writing from the South African context, Esack recognizes that the crucial aspect of interpreting the Quran, is the idea that one can get into the mind of the author, and understand what the author intended to mean. Since the Quran is regarded as the word of God, the issue of identifying with the "author" in order to get the real meaning behind the text, and "objective understanding" becomes problematic. Some traditional Islamic scholars, and Sufis in particular, have tended to focus on understanding God's message through the path of "inspiration-intuition."[141] Others have depended on how Muhammed understood the text. Esack criticizes these approaches by arguing that "the identification with the author" approach, in whatever form, does not take into account the differences in historical situations of the recipient of the text and the interpreter.[142] Furthermore, Esack adds:

> the essentialist and absolutist religio-political claims —God has inspired me or us with the correct interpretation'—which must follow any understanding so acquired are not consistent with the quest for pluralism," since the problem of 'purified minds' —one person's saint is invariably another's charlatan—and consequently conflicting monopolies over absolute truth, is a serious one with little or no space in any discourse on pluralism.[143]

Influenced by the Liberation Theology as it developed in South America, Esack looks at the role religion plays in political activism and attempts to understand "What led... Islamists regularly to invoke some "revolutionary texts" while quietly passing over other texts?" And asks, "How was Islam affected by its use as a means of liberation? What does this question of Islam being "affected" say about deeply held beliefs in the Muslim community of a faith which has a timeless essence and which transcends history?"[144] Deriving inspiration from the Quran and the struggles of all the prophets, Esack attempts to rescue religion from social, political and religious structures and ideas based on uncritical obedience and secure freedom of all people from all forms of injustice and exploitation including those of race, gender, class and religion.[145] He attempts to do that by adopting a Gadamerian hermeneutical approach and suggests the use of various hermeneutical keys to experience Islam as a liberative praxis.[146]

The first two keys he suggests are *taqwa* (an awareness of the presence of God) and *tawhid* (the unity of God). They are aimed at developing moral and 'doctrinal' criteria through which to examine other keys and the "theological glasses" with which to read the Quran in general, and more specifically the texts dealing with the issue at hand (in his case the religious Other). The other two keys, *al-nas* (the people) and the marginalized (*al-mutad'afun*) define the location of the interpretive activity. The last two keys he offer are justice (*adl* and *qist*) and struggle (jihad), reflecting the method and the ethos that produce and shape a contextual understanding of the word of God in an unjust society. Although he derives these keys from the particular context and issues involved in the South African context, these keys can be meaningfully applied to other areas, including the Israeli-Palestinian conflict. However, what is important to note in this study is his recognition of the situatedness of the interpreter and how it affects his/her interpretation, and the link he establishes between Islamic theory and its liberative praxis. Looking at the South African movement and how this liberative praxis has been put into practice is an inspiring and informative example of the way hermeneutical approach can be utilized in the Islamic world to bring peace and justice.

Fundamentalism:[147]

Fundamentalism, on the other hand is a movement that emerged as a response to the particular conditions that modernity created. Fundamentalism as a term has now come to be identified with Islamic movements in general, though originally the term was used to refer to a movement of alienated and culturally displaced White Protestants, who were concerned about the loss of their privileged status in the light of new immigration, urbanization, and industrialization.[148] In that sense, fundamentalism refers to a very narrow, specific group that is a product of modernism and rejects all forms of liberalism and elements of modern science (such as the theory of evolution). According to David Little:

> "Fundamentalist" originally appeared in a specific historical context to describe a very limited group of religious believers. The term gained currency in the 1920s in America in reference to some people best described as a militantly antimodern Protestant evangelicans. The movement grew out of an earlier concern among Protestant Christians to distinguish sharply among the saved and unsaved, between elect and unelect, by demanding adherence to certain theological fundamentals. The sect [adhered to] doctrines like a belief in the inerrancy of scripture and the virgin birth of Jesus Christ.[149]

Since fundamentalism was first referring to a particular movement in the United States, its cross-cultural applicability has raised questions. However, the Chicago Project undertaken by the American Academy of Arts and Sciences concluded that there are significant similarities among various fundamentalist religious movements across the world.[150] According to the Chicago project, the common aspects of these movements are that they are always reactionary, are concerned with basic "essences," or "fundamentals" of a religious tradition, with a devotion to absolute truth, and they see themselves as agents of the sacred power, person, or force which gives life to their group.[151] Deriving from the definition proposed by the Chicago Project, I take fundamentalism to refer to a specific group, within the Islamic movement in general, that reacts to the West, its institutions, concepts and scientific advancements, and calls for a return to the "fundamentals" of Islam.

Although fundamentalists have much in common with the *tajdid* movement, it also has significant differences. Voll states that "Islamic fundamentalism in the Arab East was more closely associated with concrete organizations then with general intellectual schools of thought, and two movements were the clearly dominant forces: the Saudi monarchy in association with the revived Wahhabi movement and the Muslim Brotherhood."[152] Looking at the impact of the encounter with the West and modernity on Muslim groups, Raphael Israeli argues that the diffusion of fundamentalist Islam in various countries can be accounted for by the convergence of the politically disaffected, the socio-economically disadvantaged and the spiritually frustrated, with a populist state of mind which purports to provide remedies outside the established order.[153]

Fundamentalists argue that the current decadence of the Islamic world is due to Muslims going astray and not practicing Islam properly. In order to change this condition, they argue that Muslims should go back to the formative years of Islam and create the conditions of the first Muslim community and state in Madina. They are in favor of reviving Islam in opposition to modernism and the Western civilization, which, they argue, served as the fertile soil in which modernism flourished.[154] They reject any cultural dialogue with the West, or the borrowing of Western cultural concepts that they believe are fraudulent. They call for strict application of the Quran and *Hadith* based on a strict literal interpretation. This leads to a rejection of *ijtihad* as binding and a rejection of any esoteric or symbolic reading of the Holy Scriptures. Fundamentalists hold the view that God asks Muslims to spread the Islamic way of life and law (*Shariah*) to all corners of the world with whatever means possible. This aim justifies practically any means, which includes offensive wars. In that respect they argue that jihad is the sixth pillar of Islam, that jihad must be undertaken by all Muslims, and that all Muslims must fight to establish God's way on earth.[155]

Among the advocates of fundamentalism, Islam Sayyid Qutb and Abul Ala Mawdudi have been the most influential figures. Since his execution in 1966 in

Cairo, Egypt, Qutb's writings have inspired many fundamentalist organizations and many young Muslims all over the Islamic world. As Yvonne Haddad states:

> His life experiences as well as his death became a perfect illustration of the one of the processes through which a revolutionary passes from enchantment with the West to the helplessness and marginality that it may inspire in those who find its values and norms not only foreign but inadequate, and finally the return to the roots where reintegration, conversion, and a new vibrant identity cohere and the human being becomes part of the revolutionary movement aimed at changing the world and bringing in a new ethical moral order based on freedom, brotherhood, and justice for all.[156]

Since Qutb employs a clear literary style that is didactic and homiletic, his interpretation of the Quran received wide popularity among Muslims. Qutb proposed Islamic ideology as an alternative to communism, capitalism, nationalism, liberalism, and secularism, and argued that his understanding of Islam has a powerful response to the current problems of the world, including uneven distribution of wealth, unemployment, unequal opportunity, corruption, among many others, and will free Muslims from subservience to either capitalism or communism.

Qutb maintains that *Shariah* is eternal and relevant at all times and all places, though he holds that Muslims can reinterpret it to apply it to their current circumstances. "The uniqueness of the Islamic vision," he contends, "is that it is fashioned by the *shariah* which created it, while other legal and social systems are a response to local, temporary needs."[157] Political institutions and ideologies, such as capitalism and communism that are emulated based on Western models are not only alien to Muslim people but also are fraudulent. Therefore, says Qutb, the process accepting modern Western culture and "Islamicizing" it must be rejected.[158] An Islamic approach on the other hand, he argues, is authentic, and for that reason will receive the support of the Muslim population. In order to have a moral and just society, he insists the ideology must be grounded in the Quran.

Writing during the Cold War era, Qutb criticizes both the capitalist bloc and the communist bloc for fighting to control the world and to manipulate it, and states that Islamic ideology constitutes a third direction and represents the only viable solution. As such, Qutb writes that Islam will not only bring justice but also provide a sense of dignity and of self-worth to the Muslim people. Qutb is severely critical of those Muslims who attempt to modernize Islam, or appropriate modernity to fit Islam by stating that they will harm both themselves and the whole of humanity. He states:

> Those who attempt to alter this [Islamic] vision either under the name of renewal, reform or progress, or under the guise of eradicating the

> remnants of the Medieval age or under any other slogan are our real enemies. They are the enemies of humankind.[159]

In regard to the governance of the society, Qutb argues that Islamic ideology is the only viable way, and states that Arab nationalism failed because they have just copied Western institutions. These Arab leaders, he claims, have been supported by professional religious men who were the enemies of Islamic government because they are aware that Islam has no professional clergy.[160] He states that an Islamic form of government must be based on the Shura (consultation). However, "the will of the people" in the Western sense is not compatible with the Islamic ideology since, according to Qutb, "popular sovereignty cannot be at the basis of legitimate authority because all sovereignty belongs to God," and people are only vice-regents of God on earth, executing his orders, and cannot be representatives of other men.[161] In that context the ruler receives his power and authority from "one source, the will of the governed", and his only role is to implement God's law. Based on the Quran, he states that anyone who does not govern by God's revelations is a *Kafir* (unbeliever) (Q5: 44), and must be disobeyed and fought by committed Muslims.

Like Qutb, Mawdudi, writing from the Indian context, also warned Muslims against the vices of modern Western forms of life and argued that Islamic form of life offered better solutions to the problems of his era. He believed that democracy is the kind of government in which the majority rules whether its views be right or wrong, and in which a minority may hope to have a voice in affairs only by transforming itself into the majority.[162] This, in his opinion, is the tyranny of the majority and does not guarantee rights and justice to all. Islam, on the other hand, will bring justice to all since it is based on the guidance revealed by God. Submission (Islam) brings earthly blessings and heavenly reward while rejecting it will only bring evil and eternal punishment. Mawdudi states that:

> ...the reforms which Islam wants to bring about cannot be carried out merely by sermons. Political power is essential for their achievement... the struggle for obtaining control over the organs of the state when motivated by the urge to establish the *din* (religion) and the Islamic *shariah* and to enforce the Islamic injunctions, is not only permissible but is positively desirable and as such obligatory.[163]

Both Qutb and Mawdudi had an enormous impact on modern Islamic movements all around the world. Although most Islamic groups have a different take on issues regarding modernity and relations with the West, as well as differing interpretations of jihad, the revolutionary call of Islamic fundamentalism represented in the writings of Qutb and Mawdudi has been received with great enthusiasm among young generations in particular. Islamic fundamentalism has been the most radical and vocal Islamic movement to express the frustrations and disappointments of the Muslims. The Taliban, who attempted to establish an

Islamic government based on a fundamentalist narrative, is the most well-known example of fundamentalist groups. Although fundametalist narrative favors an offensive interpretation of jihad, not all Islamic groups that justify violence and terrorist acts as legitimate forms of jihad are fundamentalist.

While Islam is a religion with a universal message, it is important to note that human beings live in different times, which entail different requirements. Classical political theory in Islam must be observed within its own context of time and space. It still has the potential to illuminate various issues and problems based on the way that Muslims have dealt with conflicts in history. It serves as a tool to understand how Muslims historically dealt with their conflicts and the problem of war. It serves as a starting point to understand and handle current problems. It serves as a window to understand how historical issues affected and influenced the way that Muslims interpreted the sacred texts, and legitimized the acts of those who were in authority.

Today, Muslim societies are still going through transition, where many of the classical political theory approaches are being rethought, and new approaches are emerging. Yet, there are still many more aspects of Islam to be discovered. Modern Islamic scholars are reinterpreting these texts within the context of our current times, in order to address the contemporary problems that the Muslim community faces today. Many of the Islamic leaders and scholars are influenced significantly by these developments and many of the modern Islamic narratives on peace and war are derived explicitly or implicitly out of the movements that are introduced in this chapter. Understanding the contextual nature of these theories and practices might enable us to understand the essentials of Islam and help us to develop theories that could serve as the basis of a peaceful and constructive approach to world peace and coexistence. With that in mind, the next chapter will look at the evolution of concepts of peace and war within the Islamic history, and will assess its implications for the Israeli-Palestinian conflict.

Endnotes

1. Weber 1978, 33.
2. Weber 1978., 215.
3. Weber 1978.
4. Weber 1978.
5. Weber 1978.
6. These ideal types are developed and employed as generic schemes to offer scholars and practitioners tools to make their first set of observations. Such initial observations should be followed by more complex contextual and inter-textual analyses of the societies under investigation. Ideal types are not developed to represent "reality," but to develop conceptual categories that draw boundaries for the analysis and understanding of sociological phenomena.
7. Abu Nimer 2003, 5.

8. I am aware that Middle Eastern societies also have and always had a sizable number of non-Muslims, especially Christians, and today Arab nationalism is an important element of identity as well as religious affiliation. However, this study focuses on the Islamic community and for that reason I refer to the membership of the community here within the Islamic faith.

9. Weber 1978, 231.

10. See Chapter Eight

11. Weber, 1978, 231.

12. Irani George E. and Nathan C. Funk. "Rituals of Reconciliation: Arab-Islamic Perspectives" in ASQ vol. 20 no.4 (Fall, 1998),60

13. See Albert Hourani. "Ottoman Reform and the Politics of Notables." In Beginnings of Modernization in the Middle East. William R. Polk and Richard L. Chambers eds. (Chicago: University of Chicago Press, 1968).

14. Hourani 1968.

15. See Chapter Seven

16. Although Christian Palestinian community is a critical and integral element of the Palestinian society, this study focuses only on the Palestinian Muslim community, which is the majority.

17. See Chapter Seven

18. An example would be the introduction of kingship under different titles such as sultan, padishah, malik, imam together with the system of caliphate.

19. Weber, 1978, 217.

20. Leader of the Islamic Resistance Movement (Hamas) in Palestine.

21. This will be analyzed further when I am looking at Hamas.

22. Weber 1978., 41.

23. See Chapter Seven

24. Daniel Martin Varisco. "Metaphors and Sacred History of the Genealogy of Muhammad and the Arab "Tribe"" in Anthropological Quarterly. (1995):.139-156, 139.

25. Varisco 1995.

26. Majid Khadduri. War and Peace in the Law of Islam. (Baltimore The John Hopkins Press, 1955.), 21.

27. Khadduri 1955.

28. Peter Mandaville. Transnational Muslim Politics: Reimagining the Umma.(London: Routledge, 2001), 73.

29. Abul-Fadl, Mona. "Community, Justice, and Jihad: Elements of the Muslim Historical Consciousness" in The American Journal of Islamic Social Sciences. Vol. 4 No. 1., 13-30. (1987), 14.

30. Mardin Serif. 1989. Religion and Social Change in Modern Turkey: The Case of Bediuzzaman Said Nursi (State University of New York Press), 162.

31. Mandaville 2001., 71.

32. Mandaville 2001.,72

33. Mona Abdul Fadl 1987, 17.

34. Quoted in Abdul Fadl 1987., 17.

35. For a detailed discussion on jihad see Chapter Four.

36. Four rightly guided caliphs are the first caliphs that were chosen by the Muslim community after the death of the Prophet. After the assassination of the fourth caliph Ali, the nature of the institution of caliphate changed, and their legitimacy was questioned by

various groups such as the Shi'as and Khawarijs. Shi'as in particular except only Ali as the rightful caliph. However, Sunni Muslims recognize the first four caliphs (Abu Bekr, Umar, Uthman, and Ali) as the rightly guided caliphs only.

37. Tamara Sonn,. "Political Authority in Classical Islamic Thought" in The American Journal of Islamic Social Sciences. Vol. 13. No. 3 (Fall, 1996) 309-324; See also Majid Khadduri 2000. "Theory of State" in Abdul Aziz Said et., 35-38 and Isma'il Raji al Faruqi Al Tawhid: Its Implications for Thought and Life (International Institute of Islamic Thought Herndon Virginia, 2000).92.

38. Weber 1978, 227.

39. Ralph, Salmi, Cesar Adib Majul and George K. Tanham.. Islam and Conflict Resolution: Theories and Practices. (New York: University Press of America, 1998), 40.

40. Salmi et al 1998., 41.

41. Salmi et al 1998

42. see Salmi et al 1998., 42.

43. John L. Esposito. Islam: The Straight Path. (Oxford: Oxford University Press, 1998) Third Edition, 29.

44. Farid Esack. Quran, Liberation, and Pluralism: An Islamic Perspective of Interreligious Solidarity Against Oppression. (Oxford: Oneworld, 1998), 52.

45. Esack 1998.

46. Esack 1998., 53.

47. Committee of Muslim Scholars (Assisted by Mahmud Y. Zayid). The Quran: An English Translation of the meaning of the Quran. (Lebanon: Dar al- Choura, 1980), XIII.

48. Fazlur Rahman. Islam and Modernity: Transformation of an Intellectual Tradition. (Chicago and London: University of Chicago Press, 1982), 14.

49. Esack. 1998, 54.

50. Esack. 1998., 54.

51. Esack. 1998., 55.

52. Esack. 1998.

53. Esposito 1998, 80.

54. Esposito 1998.

55. Khadduri 1955., 20.

56. Mahmoud el-Tigani, Mahgoub Dr. "Islamic Law, Human Rights and International Law: A Critique of Mahmoud Taha and An-Naim Part II" in Islamica. The Journal of The Islamic Society of The London School of Economics in Association with the Muslim Academic Trust. Vol. 2 No 4. Spring 1998, 62-71, 63.

57. Esposito, 1998, 100.

58. Esposito 1998.

59. Graham Allen. Inter-textuality. (London: Routledge, 2000), 1

60. cited in Esack 1998, 54.

61. Esack 1998.

62. Mandaville 2001, 56.

63. Mandaville 2001.

64. Mandaville 2001., 57.

65. Mandaville 2001., 58.

66. Gadamer 1991, 370.

67. Gadamer 1991., 309.

68. Abdul Aziz Said, Nathan C. Funk and S. Ayse Kadayifci .eds. Peace and Conflict Resolution in Islam:Precept and Practice (New York: University Press of America. 2001), 8.

69. Imam Ibn Taymiyyah "An Introduction to the Principles of Tafseer." How Tafseer is Performed? (1993) al-Hidaayah http://members.nbci.com/mazukiizani/quran.htm Here "good isnaad" means a good and trustable link, thus believed to be an authentic Hadith.

70. Esack. 1998., 49-50.

71. Esack 1998., 50.

72. Esposito 1998, 82.

73. An example would be: wine is explicitly prohibited in the Quran. The reason behind this rule is interpreted to be that intoxicants are prohibited in Islam, therefore other alcoholic beverages and narcotics are also prohibited.

74. Salmi et. al. 1998, 51.

75. Salmi et. Al 1998

76. Esack 1998, 57.

77. Esack 1998., 57-58.

78. Esack 1998., 58.

79. Esack 1998.

80. Esack 1998.

81. Esack 1998., 59.

82. I will return to this point in depth during the discussion of Offensive Islamic narratives on war and peace.

83. Esack 1998., 52.

84. Esack 1998., 56.

85. The Shi'a Islam has a different legal development with its own legal schools. And the gate of ijtihad is not considered closed in the Shi'a tradition. However, since the Palestinian Muslim community consists of Sunnis and 90 % of the world's Muslim population (this statistic is taken from Salmi et al., 4). and the majority of Palestian population, which is the subject matter of this dissertation, are Sunni, this section of the thesis focuses only on the Sunni legal theory.

86. John Obert Voll Islam: Continuity and Change in the Modern World (Westview Press. Boulder, Colorado, 1982), 149.

87. Voll 1982, 150.

88. Voll 1982., 151.

89. Voll 1982., 153.

90. Voll 1982., 154.

91. Voll 1982.

92. Voll 1982., 155.

93. Voll 1982.

94. Muhammed Iqbal. Six Lectures on the Reconstruction of Religious Thought in Islam, (Ashraf Lahore, 1986), 85-87,; cited in Abu Nimer, 2003, 85.

95. Abu-Nimer 2003..

96. Abu-Nimer 2003.

97. Sayyed Hossein Nasr. Traditional Islam in the Modern World. (London: KPI, 1987), 81

98. Nasr 1987.

99. Nasr 1987.
100. Nasr 1997.
101. However, an analysis of these movements is itself a theme for another project and cannot be dealt with in a just fashion here. For that reason, this section will introduce some of the general characteristics of these movements and outline briefly how they are related to the hermeneutical moment of modern history.
102. John O. Voll "Renewal and Reform in Islamic History: Tajdid and Islah" in Voices of Resurgent Islam. John L. Esposito eds. (Oxford University Press, 1983), 32-47, 32.
103. Voll 1983.
104. Voll 1983.
105. Voll 1983., 33.
106. Voll 1983.
107. Esposito., 1998.
108. Rachid al-Ghannouchi. "The Battle Against Islam," in Middle East Affairs Journal vol.1no.2 (winter 1993), 39.
109. See Chapter Six for Hamas' view on democracy.
110. Al-Ghannouchi 1992, 34-42.
111. Rahman 1984, 6.
112. Rahman 1984.
113. Rahman 1984.
114. Rahman 1984., 7.
115. Rahman 1984.
116. Rahman 1984., 8.
117. Rahman 1984.
118. Rahman 1984.
119. Rahman 1984., 10.
120. Rahman 1984.
121. Mohammed Arkoun. Rethinking Islam Today. (Washington. D. C: Center For Contemporary Arab Studies, 1987), 2.
122. Arkoun 1987., 3.
123. Esack 1998, 69.
124. Esack 1998.
125. Esack 1998.
126. Esack 1998.
127. Cited in Esack 1998, 69.
128. Arkoun 1987, 10.
129. Esack 1998, 70.
130. Esack 1998.
131. Arkoun 1987, 16.
132. Arkoun 1987.
133. Cited in Esack 1998 71.
134. Mohammed Arkoun. "The Concept of Authority in Islamic Thought: 'La Hukma illa lillah'" in Islam, State and Society K. Ferdinand and M Mozaffer eds. (London: Curzon Press, 1988) 53-73, 68.
135. Esack 1998, 49.
136. Esack 1998., 12.

137. Esack 1998.
138. Esack 1998.,12-13.
139. Esack 1998., 13.
140. Esack 1998.
141. Esack 1998., 74.
142. Esack 1998.
143. Esack 1998., 74-75.
144. Esack 1998., 9.
145. Esack 1998., 83.
146. Esack 1998., 86-87.
147. Since fundamentalist Islam has been the most studied field in the Western academic and popular literature I will not dwell much on its sources, reasons, and debates.. However, I will define it and evaluate its role and implications within the context of this work. For more information on fundamentalism see Israeli, Raphael. Muslim Fundamentalism In Israel. (London: Brassey's, 1993); Davidson, Lawrence. Islamic Fundamentalism. (Westport, Connecticut: Greenwood Press, 1998); Esposito, John. The Islamic Threat: Myth or Reality? (New York: Oxford University Press, 1992); Appleby, R. Scott ed. Spokesmen for the Despised: Fundamentalist Leaders of the Middle East. (Chicago: University of Chicago Press, 1997); Esposito, John. Islam and Politics. (Syracuse University Press, Syracuse. New York. 1991); 1983 The Straight Path, (New York: Oxford University Press, 1991); ed. Voices of Resurgent Islam (New York; Oxford University Press, 1983); Lapidus, Ira. Contemporary Islamic Movements in Historical Perspective. Center of International Studies. (Berkeley, ca.: University of California, 1983); Lazarus-Yafeh, Hava. "Contemporary Fundamentalism in Judaism, Christianity, Islam". in Jerusalem Quarterly. No. 47, (Summer, 1988), 27-39; Mitchell, Richard P. 1969. The Society of Muslim Brothers (London:. Oxford University Press, 1988).; Nasr, Sayyed Hossein. Islam and the Plight of Modern Man. (London: Longman, 1975); Shadid, M. "The Muslim brotherhood Movement in the West Bank and Gaza" in Third World Quarterly. Vol.10. No.2 (1988).
148. Timothy D. Sisk. Islam and Democracy: Religion, Politics, and Power in the Middle East (Special Middle East Program in Peacemaking and Conflict Resolution with the Jennings Randolph program for International Peace) (Washington D.C: United States Institute of Peace Press, 1992), 5.
149. Sisk 1992.
150. Sisk 1992., 6.
151. Sisk 1992. see also Martin E. Marty. "Fundamentalism as a Social Phenomenon." In Bulletin of the American Academy of Arts and Sciences. Vol. 42 (1988), 15-29.
152. Voll 1982. 172.
153. Israeli 1993 5.
154. Esposito ed.Voices of Resurgent Islam (New York: Oxford University Press., 1983), 34-42.
155. Their view on jihad will be dealt with in Chapter Six
156. Yvonne Y. Haddad "Sayyid Qutb: Ideologue of Islamic Revival" in Esposito 1983, 67.
157. Sayyid Qutb. Nahwa Mujtama Islami (Dar al-Shuruq, Beirut, 1975) 2nd printing, 47, 50,64. Cited in Haddad 1983., 71.
158. Haddad 1983.

159. Sayyid Qutb. Khassas al-Tassawwur al-Islami wa-muqawwamatuhu (Cairo: Issa la Babi al-Hilabi wa Shurakauhu, 1962), 105.

160. Qutb 1962

161. Andrea Nusse Muslim Palestine: The Ideology of Hamas (Australia: Hardwood Academic Publishers 1998, 75.

162. Charles Adams "Mawdudi and the Islamic State" in Esposito 1983, 103.

163. Khurshid Ahmad. Islamic Law and Constitution (Collection of Mawdudi's Speeches) (Lahore: Islamic Publications, 1967), 177.

Chapter 4

The Text: Islam, War, and Peace

Muslims, from fundamentalists to the adherents of strict nonviolence, agree that Islam is a religion of peace. In this perspective, the application of Islamic precepts will bring justice, harmony, order and thus, peace to the world. Muslims like to emphasize that the word *Islam* is derived from the word *salam/silm* (peace) suggesting peace through submission (*taslim*) to the will of God. Indeed like most other major religious traditions and secular systems, the Islamic discourse on peace is based on the claim that the goal of Islam is peace.

Islamic traditions of war and peace are based on Quranic verses. Since these verses refer to particular historical events, at times, they contradict one another. Therefore it has not been possible to develop a single Islamic tradition of war and peace. "Instead, there are a number of different traditions, each of which draws selectively on the Quran to establish legitimacy for its view of war and peace."[1] Many references to "peace" (*salam, silm, sulh)* in the Quranic discourse suggest that peace is a central theme in Islamic precepts. According to Quranic discourse, peace in Islam begins with God, since *as-Salam* (Peace) is one of the Most Beautiful of the ninety-nine names of God; "Allah is He [...] the source of Peace (and Perfection)" (Q 59:23). The Quran refers to peace as the greeting, language, and condition of Paradise (Q10:10, 14:23, 19; 61-63, 36:58). God calls believers to the "*abode of Peace*" by stating in the Quran that "But Allah doth call to the Home of Peace: He doth guide whom He pleaseth to a Way that is straight" (Q 10:25).

Various uses of the term "peace" in the Quranic discourse, suggests that the Islamic concept of peace is wider then the absence of war. These uses recommend that peace is a positive state of safety or security, which includes being at mend that peace is a positive state of safety or security, which includes being at peace with one-self, with fellow human beings, nature, and God. From fundamentalists to classical scholars and adherents of nonviolence in Islam, different individuals have associated peace with wide range of concepts. These concepts include, but are not limited to, justice and human development, "wholeness", salvation, perfection, and harmony.[2] "Justice" has been an integral aspect of the Islamic discourse of peace, since the Quran clearly states aim of religion is to bring justice: "We sent aforetime Our messengers with Clear Signs and sent down with them the Book and the Balance (of Right and Wrong), that men May stand forth in justice." Q 57:25). Without justice, there can be no peace. Therefore justice is the essential component of peace according to Quranic message.

Such interpretation of the Islamic understanding of peace suggests that justice is the overriding principle and it must transcend any consideration of religion, animosity, race, or creed. It is stated in the Quran that "O ye who believe! Stand out firmly For justice as witnesses To Allah even as against yourselves, your parents or your kin, and whether It be (against) the rich and poor..." (Q4: 135) and "...To fair dealing, and let not The hatred of others to you make you swerve to wrong and depart from justice. Be just for it is Next to Piety..." (Q5: 8). Jihad, which is often mistranslated as "holy war' against external forces, asks every Muslim to strive in the cause of God. In this context, to strive for the cause of God can be translated as striving for justice.

Thus, peace is the central tenet of Islam. Many verses of the Quran may be viewed as supporting this claim. Although there are verses in the Quran that permit war as a legitimate conduct to correct injustice and overthrow tyranny and oppression, various Quranic verses indicate that "there is a clearly articulated preference in Islam for nonviolence over violence, and for forgiveness (*afu*) over retribution."[3] The verse "the recompense of an injury the like thereof: but whosoever forgives and thereby brings about a reestablishment of harmony, his reward is with God; and God loves not the wrongdoers" (Q42: 40) advocates sincere forgiveness as the preferred option to establish God's harmony on earth. Hence, it can be argued that the Islamic notion of peace suggests a condition of internal and external order. In this context upholding peace is a responsibility of every Muslim.

The individual responsibility to uphold peace emerges out of the original constitution of human beings (*fitrah*) according to Islam, which is good and *muslim* in character.[4] According to this view every human being is created in accordance with the form and image of God and Divine Names or Qualities are manifested in their entirety in the human form.[5] Thus each individual is a representative of God on earth (*khilafat Allah fi l-Ard* Q2: 30), and responsible for the order thereof. This belief is based on the Quranic verse "verily, we have honored every human being" (Q 17: 70). It is also stated in the Quran that every human being is worth of respect because they are made "in the best of molds" (Q95: 4), and they possess the faculty of reason, which distinguishes them from the rest of the creation (Q2: 30-34). According to the Quranic tradition this faculty enables human beings to accept the "trust" of freedom of will, which no other creature is willing to accept (Q33: 72).

This quality of human form (*fitrah)* furnishes each individual with the prospect of being perfect (*insan-i kamil).* It is a question of choice for the individual to strive in that direction. Human *reason* or the individual *will* plays a crucial role in making this choice. Compared to the Western idea of free choice, the Islamic idea suggests that individuals can choose to follow the path of God as his stewardess on earth to bring justice, harmony and peace, thus perfect their humanity. Or the individuals can choose their egos, (*al-nafs)* and follow their own interests. Within this context, Suad al-Hakim argues that "the greater jihad (*jihad al-akbar*) in the Islamic tradition has always been the inner struggle to purify the self and behave in a manner which furthers rather then disrupts the divine harmony."[6]

Evolution of the Concepts of War and Peace in Islamic Tradition

The Quranic emphasis on peace is not an accident. Observing the geographical and temporal context in which Islam was revealed, it is possible to discern why peace was valued to such a great extent. This context also elucidates various verses of the Scripture that deal with "war" (*harb*) and "fighting" (*qital*). In addition, it is also important to note that the attitudes of Muslims regarding peace and war display differences over the course of Islamic history. There is no single doctrine of jihad that is accepted by Muslims. These attitudes towards peace and war evolved as a result of different cultural backgrounds, particular historical events, and distribution of power among political units. The juridical perspectives of war and peace that were generated in the course of history reflect these factors. An analysis of the context of Islam's emergence and a brief historical development of the Islamic tradition of jihad will serve to present the evolution of these concepts and how these elements contributed to the use of these concepts for the purpose of those authorities in power.

According to Fred M. Donner, the attitudes of the first generation of Muslims towards questions of war and peace were shaped by the cultural norms of pre-Islamic societies to which they had belonged, the attitudes toward war contained, implicitly or explicitly, in the Quran, and the dramatic events of their own times.[7] Islam came into life in Northern Arabia, where a nomadic and tribal social system was dominant. This nomadic and tribal system required mechanisms to provide the safety and security of its inhabitants, in which "group solidarity against the outsider and on the common assumption that an aggrieved group would try to apply the *lex talionis*—rally a threat or promise to get even rather than law."[8]

In this pre-Islamic Arab society, war was seen as a normal aspect of life, and a " state of war" was assumed to exist between one's own tribe and all others, unless a particular treaty or agreement had been reached with another tribe establishing amicable relations."[9] Although various conflict resolution mechanisms, such as *tahkim* and *sulha*[10] were developed during these periods, the communities were marked with turmoil. The arts of fighting were rewarded with the highest social respect, as well as the virtues of loyalty and generosity. As Donner states, the reality of war must have had a great impact on the way that the first Islamic community viewed war and shaped the popular attitudes towards it.[11] These were the eras where Justinian attempted to conquer the Roman West, Byzantium struggled with the Sassanian Persia, and Persia invaded most of Byzantium's Near Eastern provinces and Yemen (570 C.E.). Also a civil war between Heraclius and emperor Phocas (602-610 CE) and Samaritan revolt in Palestine in mid sixth century were among the major events in the region at the time of the emergence of Islam.

Mecca, where Prophet Muhammed was born and Islam first flourished, was a commercial and religious center amidst the Arabic tribes. This centrality of Mecca allowed for influences of the great states of Byzantium and Sassanian Iran. These imperial states contained a wide range of religious, cultural and linguistic traditions and had developed sophisticated political traditions and practices of warfare. Interactions with these states—military, commercial, or cultural—influenced the development of the Islamic ideas of war and peace.[12] Besides war being a reality of life in the region, these neighboring civilizations were also influential on the popular ideas and intellectual conceptualization of war in Islamic society in many ways. In this line, an additional observation stated in Donner is that, "another factor in the immediate intellectual background against which early Islam first appeared—in this case, one that had a profound influence especially on popular conceptions of war and peace—was apocalyptic thought."[13]

This worldview, greatly influenced by Christian and Judaic traditions, was resting on the belief that the world was near its end. The Day of Judgment was about to come with great catastrophes, and that the Kingdom of God would prevail and all evil will be overthrown.[14] In this scenario, although war was perceived as one of the major evils, a 'good war' to overcome the evil and the 'bad wars' played an important role. This apocalyptic conception of the world and the ideas of war embedded in this view were integrated by the Muslims into their vision of the world.[15]

Thus, Islam was born into this world, where war played a central role in the lives of the communities. As Muslims started to grow in numbers in Mecca they started facing resistance and persecution from the Meccans. However, during this time period Prophet Muhammad resorted to complete nonviolence. "In 615, in an effort to spare some of his followers from further persecution, Muhammad recommended that they seek haven in Abyssinia (Modern day Ethiopia)."[16] When the persecution of Muslims became unbearable, he chose to emigrate to

Yathrib (later on called Madina), a city in the north of Mecca, where he had secured the wellbeing of Muslims. In Madina, Muhammad lay the foundations of the first Islamic State, and entered into treaties with various Jewish clans. During his time in Madina, only when the Meccans laid siege to and attacked Madina in 627, he allowed fighting in self-defense. In 628 a truce was inked between the Muslims and the Meccans for duration of ten years. This treaty, known as the Treaty of *Hudaybiyah,* became the model for the Muslims in the future. Some of the Arab tribes of Mecca allied to break the treaty, which led to another war in 630 C.E.

Examining this historical context of the initial years of Islam as a political entity one sees "wars" as being permissible or just only for the defense of the religion and protection of the community. However, with the increasing power of the Islamic armies and establishment of territorial state, we observe that war was accepted not only for self-defense, but also as an aggressive tool for expanding Islam. Using the method of abrogation (*naskh*), many Quranic verses were reinterpreted to justify the offensive form of jihad, based on the argument that Islam is a universal message and therefore it was the *ummah's* duty to establish the order of God on earth. Therefore jihad was launched against all polytheists who were considered to be the enemies of Islam. The internal and external factors played a key role in the transformation of the dominant narrative of war and peace in this period.

As Islam expanded to different geographical regions people with different cultural and traditional practices embraced Islam. These groups included Turks, Mughuls, Indians, Africans, among others. With them, these different groups brought different attitudes towards war, and interpreted the Islamic legal doctrines on war in the light of their own traditional practices and personal experiences. Together with the introduction of these cultural and traditional practices, Crusades also played an important role in the evolution of the concept of war in the Islamic tradition. Although Crusades did not produce a "counter-Crusade,"[17] it resulted in the emergence of a "pseudo-*futuh*" literature, the literature, in a rather romantic way, deals with the early Islamic conquests. Even though this literature has very little documentary value for the early Islamic history,[18] it is still reflects how Muslims of this era idealized a nostalgic vision of successful jihad.

During the time period, when the Islamic political entity was strong in terms of its military, economic, and political capability, an offensive jihad doctrine dominated both the political discourse and the scholarly debates in the Islamic world. In this period, the expansion of the Islamic lands and calling non-Muslims to Islam were considered as the prime duties of the Islamic state. In this endeavor, offensive wars were considered as a necessity to expand the influence of Islam.

The evolution of Prophet's attitude was interpreted as supporting the evolution of the concept of jihad from nonviolent struggle to offensive wars. Jurist of this era held the position that in Mecca (around 10 years) and for a few months in Madina fighting was prohibited against oppressors of Muslims. During this period, Muhammad exhorted patience and indeed about seventy verses in the Quran are identified as illustrating this period. Later on the Muslims were allowed to fight their enemies only when attacked. This second stage, thus only allowed Muslims to fight in self-defense. The final stage suggests that Muslims are permitted to fight the enemies of Islam, against the polytheists, and idolaters absolutely and at all times.[19] Jihad was considered to be a collective duty incumbent upon all Muslims, first to defend then to expand the religion. To spread the message of Islam was seen as a duty by many jurists. The world was thus divided into *Dar al-Islam* and *Dar al-Harb.* Although such a distinction does not exist in the Quran, the jurists developed these categories due to their interpretation of jihad. According to the jurists of this era, *hudna* (truce) with *Dar al-Harb* was restricted only to 10 years, taking the example of *Hudaybiyah* treaty that Muhammed signed with the Meccans.

During the Abbasid period (750-1258 C.E.) the expansion of Islam ceased and at times receded.[20] There emerged an increasing gap between the "*Dar al-Harb/Dar al-Islam*" distinction and the turbulence of relationships between diverse power centers. The concept of *Saltanah* (sultanate) emerged and became associated with a centralized state. With the institutionalization of *Saltanah*, we also see the beginning of a state system with territoriality. This can be considered as the beginning of a new Islamic international system, in which the caliphate had to enter into non-belligerent relations with non-Muslim communities. With this development, a new division was introduced. This new division is called *Dar al-Ahd* or *Dar al-sulh* that means the land of treaty.

This new division signifies a new era, and the term, *Dar al-Ahd,* was first used by Shafi. It was designated to mean the lands that Islamic state had tributary relations with. These lands were allowed to be governed with their own rules and were not considered to be *Dar al-Harb*. Al- Mawardi considered these lands as *Dar al-Islam*. Yet, in the beginning these states were not considered to be equals of the Islamic State. In this period we see the beginning of a new era, which does not limit treaties to 10 years. An important development in this respect is the treaty between the Ottomans and the French in 1535 when the Sultan signed a treaty that was to last until the signatories died. Peace, in this new era acquired a new meaning, based on the power politics of the times.

The changing conceptions of jihad from nonviolent to defensive to offensive and again to defensive supports the claim that interpretation of the Scripture was closely influenced by the historical, socio-political context of the interpreters. Khadduri states that Islamic state went through 6 stages of evolution. According to his view, the period of the Madina state represents the city-state stage.[21] This was followed by the imperial state between 632 to 750 C.E. The universal stage lasted from 750 to 900 C.E. This was followed by the stage of decentralization until 1500 C.E. After 1500 C.E. came the fragmentation stage and lasted until 1918 C.E., and the final stage is the national stage. We also observe that attitudes towards peace and war have been directly influenced by the success and failures of the Islamic societies in history. Different stages displayed different attitudes towards other states, and was closely tied to the way that political theory was constructed. The lands where Muslims were in authority and where Muslims lived without fear of persecution was considered to be the land of peace (*Dar al-Islam*) whereas the lands where Muslims were not in authority was considered to be land of war (*Dar al-Harb*). Non-Islamic sovereigns were not recognized as equals.

As the conditions in which the Islamic entities interacted changed, so did the interpretation of the doctrine of jihad. Jurist's re-evaluated verses of the Quran regarding jihad, war, and peace in relation to the way they perceived the interest of the Islamic world. Their effective history had a direct impact on the way they understood these concepts. An important informative source on the doctrine of jihad and relations with non-Muslims is the *Siyar,* which is a compilation of rules and regulations on these issues, based on the Islamic jurisprudence.

Islamic Law of War and Peace: *Siyar*

Conduct of relations with other powers has been integral to the way that the Islamic states viewed the world. Therefore, how these relations should be administered was an important aspect of the Islamic law and jurisprudence. Shaybani developed the first rules and regulations, known as *siyar*, that were related to international relations in the 8th century. *Siyar* deals with the relations with the unbelievers in the enemy territory as well as with peoples with whom the Muslims entered into treaties, and *dhimmis* (non-Muslims living in the Islamic lands), and the rebels. These rules and regulations, called *siyar,* were based on the general provisions stated in the Quran regarding the initiation of hostilities, termination of war, and the general nature of treaties. Although these rules and regulations were considered to be a part of the Islamic *Shariah* in general, *siyar* acquired a distinct character and had become an analytical tool in the study and application of the *Shariah*. Quran, the *Sunna* and the *Hadith*, practices of the four rightly guided caliphs, practices of the later caliphs, opinions of the learned, treaties and agreements, official instructions to the military commanders and ambassadors, other state officials and customs are considered to be the sources of *siyar* (Islamic International Law). Juristic techniques, such as *ijtihad*, were utilized extensively to develop these rules.

The earlier works of *siyar* deals mostly with jihad, which had the juristic connotation of struggling for the cause of God by means of speech, property, wealth or life. However, it also was understood to exert effort to repel the enemy. Therefore, jihad came to be interpreted as applicable in three distinct ways. First it was interpreted to strive against a visible enemy. Second against the Devil. Finally, against ego or selfish interests. Ibn Taymiyya, for example, argued that jihad is achieved sometimes by the heart, sometimes by the tongue, and sometimes by the hand, and suggested two cardinal rules for jihad by the tongue and by the hand: Understanding and patience.[22]

The justification of these three interpretations came from the following three verses stated in the Quran:

> And strive for Allah with the endeavor which is His right.(Q22:78)
>
> Go forth, light armed or heavy armed, and strive with your wealth and your lives in the Way of Allah. (Q9:41)
>
> Lo! those who believed and left their homes and strove with their wealth and their lives for the cause of Allah, and those who took them in and helped them: these are protecting friends one of another. (Q8:72)

The *Hadith* that is narrated after returning from an expedition against the enemies of Muslims which states "We have returned from the minor jihad (war) to the major jihad (against the self)"[23] has been the basis of differentiating between these levels of jihad in the Islamic literature.

"War is considered as just whether commenced and prosecuted in accordance with the necessary formalities required under a certain system of law, or waged for justifiable reasons in accordance with the tenets of the religion or the mores of a certain society."[24] Like the Just War Theory of St. Augustine, Islamic doctrine of just war (*Jus ad bellum*) includes both a justifiable reason and the necessary formalities for prosecuting war. Islam commands that war can only be justified if it is in accordance with the sanction of religion and the implied orders of God. Since Islam aims at the radical transformation of human society into a social order governed by God, it demands willingness of Muslims to struggle (jihad) for this cause. Therefore Islam outlaws all war but the war that God permits; jihad.

Famous classical Islamic scholars adopted different approaches regarding jihad. Among these scholars al-Thawri and Abu-Hanifa argued that Islam only permits defensive wars. According to al-Thawri "Fighting against the associators (nonbelievers, i.e., those who associate others with God's divinity) is not an obligation unless they start the fight; then it is an obligation to fight back against them."[25] Abu-Hanifa states that "jihad is a duty on Muslims but they are not required to fight unless they are needed."[26] Al-Sarakhsi and al-Shafi, on the other hand, argue that Islam permits offensive wars. In that respect al-Sarakhsi says:

> To sum up, the command of *jihad* and fighting (to Muslims) had been revealed in stages....(the final stage being) the absolute order to fight (nonbelievers)... this means an obligation, but his obligation is meant to exalt religion (of Islam) and to subdue the associators.[27]

Al-Shafi, agrees with al-Sarakhsi and states that "Allah made the *Jihad* an obligation after it had been a matter of choice."[28]

Pondering on the reasons for different conclusions, lending support to the argument of this project, Ibn Rushd states that:

> The reason for their differences is the [apparent]contradiction between some author of the '*athar* (traditions) and the general meanings of [both] the book [Quran] and the sayings of the Prophet [PBUH].[29]

Although there has been a major controversy among the Muslim jurists themselves concerning when jihad is justified according to Islam, traditionally three reasons were accepted. The first reason suggests that jihad is justified to repel invasion or its threat. The second one suggests that jihad may be permitted to punish those who had violated the treaties. And third one suggests that jihad is allowed to guarantee freedom for the propagation of Islam. Fighting is also considered allowed against those who rebel, however there is some disagreement as to whether this sort of military action to be called jihad.[30]

Another important aspect of jihad is that, a legitimate authority must wage it. Since there is no distinction between the political and religious authority in Islam, it is agreed that the head of the Islamic community, the caliph, is the legitimate authority to wage war. Sunni theory of political authority does not question the legitimacy of the first four caliphs and recognizes their decision to wage jihad as legitimate. Donner summarizes classical Islamic conception of jihad as follows:

> The Islamic conception of legitimate war (*jihad*), once it is systematically developed is specially tied to the idea of the unity of Islamic state against all other non-Islamic states and the legitimacy of the caliph or *imam* as the single ruler of this Islamic state. It is only the state, headed by the legitimate caliph or *imam,* that can launch a *jihad,* so the Islamic conception of legitimate war in particular is inextricably tied to the notions of the unity of Muslim community and of its rulership. It is also connected to the idea of God-guidedness, which, like the idea of imperial unity, was forcefully projected in Byzantium propaganda, including the triumphs.[31]

However, the power of the caliph declined, as Islamic community came to be divided among multiple political entities, such as the sultanates. The decrease in the power of the caliph increased the importance of the *ulema* for justifying the political decisions of the leaders. The political authorities increasingly resorted to the legal decrees (*fatwa*), which would designate whether jihad that the leaders is about to undertake is legitimate, issued by the *ulema*. By the time of the Abbasid period, although the caliph would exercise political power, and would lead the jihad, the legitimacy of jihad and all religious duties come to be determined by the *ulema.*[32]

Another crucial point in understanding jihad is the "intention" (*niyyat*) behind it. Numerous *Hadiths* warn that fighting for the sake of material gains, conquest, or even honor in the eyes of fellow men, will earn no reward and is not allowed, since Islam forbids all wars but jihad. For that reason, jihad must be fought only with the intention of drawing nigh to God, and only for God. Although not all wars fought under the rubric of jihad by various Muslim rulers would fit into this category, all Muslim leaders attempted to justify their wars by stating that they fight for the sake of God alone.[33]

Siyar also laid down strict regulations regarding acts that were not allowed during war (*Jus im bello*). In that respect, Islam prohibits killing of non-combatants. Non-combatants include women, children, the blind, the old, monks and hermits, the insane or delirious, those who are physically incapable of actual fighting, and servants. Furthermore, torturing by fire, and burning of prisoners is strictly prohibited, as well as the execution of prisoners of war. Severing the heads of fallen enemies and sending them to higher authorities and mutilating the enemy and animals were also forbidden. Unnecessary devastation of the enemy lands and destruction of harvest and cutting trees, especially fruit trees were considered not allowed.

According to *siyar,* Islam also forbids adultery and fornication with female captives. Moreover, killing hostages as well as massacring innocent people are not allowed even if the enemy has resorted to such actions. *Siyar* also records that Islam forbids using enemy prisoners as shields or compelling them to fight their own army, and using poison arrows. Furthermore, according to *siyar* tradition, Islam does not allow violating agreements with the enemy on what they have mutually agreed to avoid in war, as well as retaliation against the enemy when they kill Muslim women, children, the aged and hostages, and for acts of mutilation.[34] Terry Nardin states that, the constraints on the conduct of war in Islam can be traced back to the pre-Islamic period of inter-tribal warfare, which also prohibited fighting during certain periods of time and condemned excessive destruction.[35] These tribal rules of warfare prohibited killing of children, the aged, prisoners, and women as codes of honor.

Whether or not all Muslim armies complied with these provisions is another question that will not be dealt here. It is suffice to say that these regulations during the war is based on various Quranic provisions as well as the conduct of the Prophet and four rightly guided caliphs, who are recorded to have followed these provisions strictly in battle.

The Islamic texts on war and peace, such as *siyar*, are products of the interaction between the Sacred Text Quran and the cultural context of the time of their emergence. By cultural context, I refer to the dominant narrative of the time, institutionally sanctioned structures and systems that make up the culture. The text and cultural context cannot be separated. As stated earlier, the emergent narratives of peace and war contain with them structures and struggles expressed in the society through discourses. These texts, such as *siyar*, do not present stable and clear meanings, but embody society's dialogical conflict over the meaning of words and concepts. Texts do not just utilize previous texts, such as the practices of the Prophet, his *Hadith*, or the practices of previous caliphs and commanders, and commentaries and interpretations of previous scholars on the issue of war and peace, but transform them for different purposes. Therefore the texts have a two-dimensional meaning. One is inside the text itself, and the other is the historical and social context of its emergence. This social context draws the boundaries of what can be said and what cannot be said it that given context.

As stated above, with the decline of political power of the caliph, *ulema* became crucial for unveiling the Islamic rules and regulations in every aspect of Muslim life. This included the regulations and rules of war as well. However, it was not easy for many Islamic scholars to produce ideas and reach at Quranic interpretations that did not comply with the expectations or the requirements of the political leadership. Politics of the day created conditions that limited the interpretations of the *ulema*, and created a system of dependency between the rulers and the learned-men of Islam. Sachedina supports this idea in the following paragraph:

> Regardless of different definition and interpretations of jihad that one can come up with in this discussion, the current religious meaning and interpretation of jihad as a Holy war has been influenced by the role of Muslim jurists throughout history, particularly in early periods, during which they justified offensive wars, and broadened the interpretation of Quranic jihad. Such interpretation can be explained by tangible political circumstances that forced the jurist to be pragmatic and realistic in their formulation of the jurisdiction for undertaking jihad, especially if the de facto rulers were willing to uphold the supremacy of Islamic law in a Muslim public order.[36]

Some of the current day Islamic intellectuals, from critical Muslim historians to moderate fundamentalist (with their varying conclusions), blame the decadence of Islamic societies in the world today onto this uncritical obedience of the *ulema* to the rulers and yielding to ruthlessness and injustice thereof. This obedience was carried into the 20th century. As a modern thinker puts it:

> Dependence is an ancient type of relationship, perhaps thousands of years old. Whatever its roots, suffice to say that contemporary Arab thought does not lead or inspire political power but is a tributary thereof. It does not initiate moves but follows the rules. The *sultan* orders and the *ulema* give their blessing, the *amir* sets the law and *qadis* judge accordingly— such a dependency is not only related to external constraints, e.g., censorship of the press and the electronic media, but is internalized and thus breeds a feeling of powerlessness, a lack of will and drive to launch a new intellectual initiative or to present a novel analysis of reality regardless of the directives of the people in power.[37]

This obedience of the *ulema*, and letting rulers intervene in the judicial system, levy illicit taxes, and introduce various innovations that were alien to Islam were criticized, for they were considered shirking their duty to set polity and society aright by various Muslim intellectuals all over the world, including Muslim Brethen Leader Hasan al Banna and Sayyid Qutb (father of present day radicalism). *Ulema* was also criticized for having rarely challenged unjust rulers, almost never having justified revolts against them, and never having developed a comprehensive political theory, and Islamic Law based on Islamic principles. "By the time some of them began to do so- very hesitantly, it is true- in the eleventh century, the realities of ruler-subject relations were so firmly lodged that they could hardly be rectified; not that the *ulema* actually tried: most political theorist contended themselves with justifying the status quo and adding an Islamic gloss."[38]

During the formative years of Islamic history, *ulema* was a small class of learned people which began to grow in numbers particularly after the 11th century, with the establishment of *madrasas* (religious schools) and *waqf* (religious endowments). These institutions provided new job opportunities, fellowships, and *ulema* that graduated from these *madrasas* were recruited into the bureaucratic system. By the 13th century, *ulema* became financially dependent upon the ruling classes. The new ruling class that came into power was alien to local culture and language, and was a military class, such as Memluks and Ottomans.

However, as Sivan points out, these new ruling classes provided a crucial service to the Muslim community,[39] as the Crusaders and Mongols invaded the Islamic lands. Besides, the internal struggle between Sunni and Shi'a Muslims were becoming more pronounced with its dire effects on the Muslim society. These new rulers, such as Memluks and Seljucks undertook to defend Islam against these enemies and created a new order within Islamic society. In the brink of such dangers, which could result in the annihilation of Islam, *ulema* accepted to collaborate with these rulers as long as they kept the lands in Muslim rule.

Additionally, Sivan argues that, when conflicts of interests emerged between the rulers and the *ulema*, which had jobs in the civil service, and lived off endowments controlled by the state, were reluctant to raise their criticisms with the fear of losing their livelihood.[40] They justified their compromise by arguing "one cannot exercise influence upon the state from within unless one becomes involved in the affairs of the state."[41] Nevertheless, as Sivan indicates, such an involvement "tied their hands and tongues, constraining their capacity to promote their ideals."[42]

Moreover, political leaderships did not hesitate to use jurists to justify their political ends, which also included territorial invasions and extension of their political and military power to other lands. Towards that end, they have favored those interpretations of jihad that justified and legitimized their actions and aggressive policies. Those jurists who did not comply with these requirements of political authority were punished severely. Looking at the bestowed fate of some of the influential scholars will serve to clarify this point.

Among these scholars, Abu Hanifa, who is the founding father of Hanefi legal school, was persecuted for refusing to work as a scholar or judge to the caliph. Imam Malik, who was one of the very first legal scholars and also the founder of Maliki school, was tortured for casting some doubt on the legitimacy of the political status quo under the caliph al-Mansur. Al Mawardi on the other hand did not want to publish his most famous work before his death out of fear; and Ibn Taymiyya died in prison for his critical opinions.[43] Under such conditions, it was a great challenge for many scholars to do independent legal reasoning that would go against the policies of political and military powers. Those leaders did not hesitate to punish or torture these scholars for their perceived interests, yet they still needed justification from the *ulema,* and for that reason they supported those who would legitimize their acts. At other times, they legitimated their authority by waging jihad.

Lending support to that observation, Donner states that the inconsistency between the juristic theory and political realities affected how Muslims viewed the legitimacy of waging war.[44] "What resulted in practice was an inversion of the juristic ideal: Muslim rulers did not consult the jurists to discover whether they were legitimate and therefore entitled to wage jihad, but rather by waging jihad they offered evidence of legitimacy of their claim to rule."[45] Donner presents the Ottoman tradition, where the sultans claimed the role of *ghazis* (warriors for the faith against the infidel) as a justification of their legitimacy, as an example of this phenomenon.[46]

Yet, this does not mean that those *ulema,* which contributed to the legitimation of jihad as an offensive tool, and justified the acts of political leaders, did so solely to pursue their self-interests. Many of these scholars sincerely engaged in the process of interpretation to find what is the true will of God. However, the historical and political conditions of their times influenced the way they understood the Text by creating the possibilities and constraints of interpretation. These conditions provided them with certain biases and prejudices in their reading of the Scripture. The specter of *fitna,* or internal strife among the Muslims themselves was considered the most important calamity for the Muslims society that it seems to have been used to justify almost anything. As Ibn Hanbal (d.855) stated:

> You should obey and not rebel against [illegitimate power]. If the ruler orders something, which implies sin against Allah, you should neither obey nor rebel. Do not support *fitna* (civil strife) neither with your hand nor by your tongue.[47]

Under these political and social conditions minor jihad doctrine (the doctrine of war) came to be the focal point in the political realm, whereas pursuing greater jihad was confined to social space under the supervision of *Sufis.* As the minor jihad became the dominant perspective, various contending narratives came to fore. In this framework, political leaders did not hesitate to suppress those interpretations that delegitimized their authority and right to wage war when they deemed necessary. Such an attitude on the part of the authorities contributed to the stagnation of Muslim communities in every aspect of their life.

As the European states were progressing, opening their 'door of *ijtihad'* wide, and developing critical approaches to call into question the religious dogmas, and advancing in sciences, the Muslim states and their societies were laying comfortably numb in their 'well-established' traditions, sinking deeper into political, social, economic, and ideological idleness. Although various sultans (such as Selim III and Mahmut II of Ottomans) attempted to introduce Western military and scientific achievements, realizing that the lands of Islam were in a state of decline, these attempts received great reactions from the traditional *ulema* and military institutions. When the European powers launched the campaign of colonialism and imperialism, the Muslim societies were surprised and unprepared, not realizing the discrepancy that emerged between the two worlds.

Contemporary Islamic Narratives of War and Peace

Due to the colonial experience, in the modern era (19th and 20th centuries), jihad took the form of resistance to Western invasion of Islamic lands. With this shift in emphasis, jihad has once again become mainly a doctrine of defense. Donner observes that the "jihad tradition" was effectively cut off by European colonialism during the nineteenth and twentieth centuries, as the Islamic empires such as the Ottomans were dismantled, and in many cases, European legal systems were introduced.[48] The 20th century Muslim history is marked by independence wars and emergence of nationalism, which found its expression in the nation-state system. During this period, Muslim world has been influenced not only by the discourse of nationalism, but also by communist, secularist, and liberalist discourses. Colonialism and exploitation became the main targets of revolutionary movements that were trying to establish the legitimacy of their rule. Yet, after the independence of Muslim nation-states there has been a growing demand for reinstituting some of the Islamic institutions and values.

In the process, the introduction and proliferation of print-media opened new avenues for the Muslim *Ummah* and brought new awareness to the potentials and the roles.[49] This new awareness created the locus for developing critical approaches that started to question the role of 'official' *ulema,* whose independence was called into question under the dictatorial regimes that governed the Muslim world. The increase of literacy level resulted in an increase of the number of people who had direct access to the Texts, without the mediation of traditional religious scholars. In this era, laypersons that did not receive the traditional religious education to become *ulema,* started interpreting the Quran, and questioning the interpretations of traditional scholars.

Among these, Sayyed Qutb, and Mawdudi (who are the founding fathers of Islamic fundamentalism) are among the most famous and influential. Again, in this time period, especially during the last past decades, Muslims became more aware of their role within the context of *Ummah*. This is particularly true for the Palestinians who, since mid 1970s, came to the conclusion that neither the Western nor the Arab countries, even their own leadership can resolve the Palestinian problem. But only the Palestinian people themselves, as a 'population' can bring about a change. The Islamic movement in Palestine was also effected by this mood and reflected this awareness in their program and narrative.[50]

All kinds of resistance movements against the West adopted jihad as an ideological framework, and a political rhetoric. In this context, the notion of jihad acquired a new momentum and some of the concepts of *Siyar* were rethought. The modern day interpretations of the Quran concerning war and peace can be grouped under three main trends in the Islamic world. I coin the first of these interpretations as "Offensive Islam", the second one I term "Defensive Islam", while I identify the third one as "Nonviolent Islam". All of these approaches operate within the Islamic discursive field, and take the Quran, *Hadith*, and *Sunna* as their sources. Sympathizers and followers of these trends read the same texts interpret them and come out with completely different conclusions. The roots of these narratives can be traced back to the formative years of Islam. As this chapter presented, different narratives gained dominance at different periods of Islamic history. The contemporary narratives of peace and war are responding to the current-day problems and can be situated within the Islamic movements stated in the previous chapter. Neither of these categories presented here are claimed to capture the 'pure' reality of the Islamic narratives within the Islamic discourse, but they too are ideal-types employed to distinguish certain characteristics of each groups. They do not necessarily correspond to the Islamic movements of fundamentalism, renewalism and reformism *per se* but carry certain elements from them. Nevertheless, for analytical purposes, the following pages will try to identify some important features of each of the narratives presented here.

Offensive Islamic Narrative of Peace and War

The offensive Islamic narrative of peace and war is based on the idea that Islam, as the only 'true path' to bring justice, freedom and peace, should be the religion that governs the world. Mostly, adherents of fundamentalism support this narrative hold that Islam is a religion that aims to expand its influence through offensive wars. Bessam Tibi notes "fundamentalism as a mass movement dates back to the 1970s, though its intellectual and organizational roots can be traced to 1928, when the Muslim Brotherhood (*al-ikhwan al-Muslimun*) was created in Egypt."[51] The leading figures of this movement are Hasan al-Banna, the founder of the Muslim Brotherhood, and Sayyed Qutb, the ideologue of the movement.

Fundamentalists are convinced that the current political, economic, and international system that dominates the world only breed oppression, injustice, and exploitation, therefore must be removed and replaced by God's governance. Freedom of choice (i.e. freedom of religion based on the Quranic verse: there is no compulsion in religion) can only come after these forces of oppression and tyranny, represented by the West and modernity, are eradicated, and where it is possible for people to adhere to and appreciate God's vision for humanity. Sayyid Qutb, who is one of the most influential figures support this idea, states this point clearly in the following paragraph:

> Truth and falsehood cannot coexist on earth. When Islam makes a general declaration to establish the lordship of God on earth and to liberate humanity from the worship of other creatures, those who have usurped God's sovereignty on earth contest it. They will never make peace. Then [Islam] goes forth destroying them to free humans from their power...this is the constant situation. The liberating struggle cf jihad does not cease until all religion belongs to God.[52]

In that regard, Qutb saw that there were serious obstructions in the way of the fulfillment of God's vision, and these obstructions must be eradicated "first by force that it may be possible to address the human heart and mind after being freed from chains."[53] In that process, Qutb asserted, jihad becomes crucial for the *dawah* (call to Islam). For this, he notes the precedent in the life of the Prophet, which he proposes as the prototype of the means of operating the *dawah* by stating that, while Muslims were restricted in their activities to preaching in Mecca, it became necessary for them to fight once they established the community in Madina.

> Islam is not a theological system that is realized when appropriated as an ideology... and then its mission ceases. Islam is a pragmatic activist system of life. It withstands other systems, which are based on power, and is supported by material power. For Islam to establish its divine system, it is inevitable that these material powers be destroyed and the powers that administer the systems that resist the divine way be annihilated.[54]

Advocates of this narrative argue that the Islamic narrative of jihad evolved from nonviolent to defensive because Muslims were not strong enough then. But after the revelation of the unconditional verse, Islam calls Muslims to spread God's rule on earth. They base their arguments mostly on the two verses that are coined "unconditional" (2:245 and 9:124), and also on "conditional" verses that they read of out their context. The proponents of this view have little, if any, tolerance for the members of other religions, including the "People of the Book." This attitude contradicts many verses of the Quran, where the rights of the People of the Book are clearly stated, especially the verse that states "Let there be no compulsion in religion" (2:256). Sayyid Qutb, who was the ideologue of the Brotherhood, enunciates the traditional argument that jihad is not for the sake of conversion, but to make the *Shariah* the law of the land, and thereby abolish oppressive political systems. In this line of argumentation jihad becomes justified not only for defense, but also for attack against any oppressor.

According to Qutb's interpretation of jihad, before declaring war, Muslims should invite people to join Islam, "the final religion", "the way of truth", and "the path of justice." If they refuse they are asked to pay poll tax as a symbol of cessation of hostilities and their affirmation of the freedom of Muslims to propagate their faith. If they refuse to pay the tax, then the Muslims are allowed to wage war. In order to remove the obstacles to establish the God's way on earth, Qutb justifies militancy and states that:

> Jihad works to realize the idea of universal revolution not aimed at rule, control or booty. In this revolution peace in all its aspects is realized: the peace of conscience, peace in the home and peace in the society... finally, the peace of humanity.[55]

> The dynamic spread of Islam assumes the form of jihad by the sword...not a defensive movement, as those defeatists imagine, who subjugate to the offensive pressure of Western orientalists...Islam is meant for the entire globe.[56]

In his defense of militancy, Qutb states that militancy is a necessary liberating force and argues "it has never been the intent of Islam to coerce people to believe in its ideology."[57] He adds, implying that 'the liberated people will not chose to re-establish the 'oppressive' regimes eliminated:

> ...Anyone who grasps the nature of this religion- as discussed above....understands the imperative for the dynamic movement of Islam by jihad with the sword –side by side-with the jihad through admonition- and would understand that it is not a defensive movement.[58]

In his book on *Islam and Peace in the World* Qutb argues that peace is the essential character of Islam, as he states: "Peace is the eternal principle; war is the exception which becomes a necessity when there is a deviation from the integration exemplified in the religion of the one God [resulting] in injustice, oppression, corruption and discord."[59] He does not, at the same time, hesitate to argue that jihad cannot be seen as a defensive war. In support of this argument he refers to the verse 22:39-40, which states:

> Permission to fight is given to those against whom war is made, because they are oppressed, and God is able to help them. These are the people who are expelled from their homes without cause because they said 'Our Lord is God.' Had God not checked one people by another, then surely synagogues and churches and oratories and mosques would have been pulled down, where the name of God is remembered often.[60]

According to Qutb, the Westernized modernists, who claim that Islam permits fighting only in defense, are "spiritually and intellectually defeated people," who search for moral justifications for jihad.[61] Rejecting that jihad is a defensive war in reaction to an attack on Islamic territory he argues that jihad is a permanent situation of armed struggle between two different consciousness. In this struggle, use of force against the unbelievers is a duty incumbent upon every Muslim, as the aim of Islam is to establish God's rule on earth and among the whole humanity. In that sense Islam rejects all forms of war (including wars of nationalism, racism, greed, economic expansion), except expanding God's rule on earth to bring justice and eliminate oppression and tyranny.

Qutb claims that fighting was not allowed during the Meccan period first by stating that "Freedom of preaching was assured in Mecca" where the Prophet had the opportunity to openly proclaim his message. Other scholars such as John O. Voll challenge this claim.[62] Voll states that the message Muhammed had a direct bearing on the personal and social condition of his time by rejecting polytheism (the religion of the Arab tribes then) and calling for a social responsibility toward the poor and underprivileged and warned of the coming Day of Judgement. For that reason, his message "aroused opposition in Mecca, since social obligations were being neglected by the wealthy merchants there", and also undermined the prestige and position of the local leaders.[63]

Qutb also contradicts himself when he is stating additional reasons for prohibition of fighting in this period. He states that "...this phase of the Islamic message was that of training and developing the potentialities in a particular environment for a particular nation under particular conditions."[64] In that sense, he argues that this training was to introduce Arabs to tolerate things, which they were not accustomed to.[65] He also suggests that the circumstances of the time rendered the peaceful means of propagating the message more effective, because fighting would 'generate feelings of revenge and motivate more blood-feuds' and also to avoid a civil war on a massive scale.[66] Finally, he also adds that the numbers of Muslims were limited in those times and under these circumstances, fighting would result in the annihilation of the Muslims.

Based on the same argument, and making a literal use of the Quran and *Hadith*, Hasan al-Banna states that jihad is an "obligation of every Muslim."[67] He begins his treatise by quoting from the second surah of the Quran, which states "Fighting is obligatory for you, much as you dislike it" (Q2: 216), and continues with the verse that states "if you should die or be slain in the cause of Allah, his mercy will surely be better than all the riches you amass" (Q3: 158). He also attempts to support this argument by quoting the verse "We shall richly reward them whether they die or conquer" (Q4: 74) and argue that Islam calls Muslims to fight for the cause of God, and to glorify martyrdom in war. While doing that he completely ignores the verses of the Quran that call for tolerance for others and patience, such as the verse that states: "you have your religion and I have mine" (Q109: 6). Instead, he prefers to cite the verse that states: "Fight against those who neither believe in Allah nor the Last Day... until they pay the *jizya*..." (Q9: 29) to expand the obligation of fighting even against the 'People of the Book.'[68] Al-Banna criticizes those who argue that *qital* (fighting) is of lesser value and states "The great reward for Muslims who fight is to kill and be killed for the sake of Allah."[69] "Al-Banna's treatise is in fact permeated with rhetoric glorifying death, which seems to legitimize the suicidal terrorist attacks often committed by Islamic fundamentalists"[70] and states that:

> Allah rewards the *ummah* which maters the art of death and which acknowledges the necessity of death in dignity.... Be sure, death is inevitable... if you do this for the path of Allah, you will be rewarded.[71]

In that line he had called for Jihad against the British arguing that it was incumbent upon all Muslims to repel the enemy, although the British invasion was over by the time he was writing, referring to the reports of *Hadiths*, and the Quran, and the Medieval jurists to defend that jihad is justified against all non-Muslims whether they fight against the Muslims or not.[72]

Abul A'la Mawdudi of India and the founder of Jamaati Islami, on the other hand, argued that Islam is a religion of revolution with a program to alter the social system of the whole world and rebuilt it in conformity with its tenets and ideals. In that sense, jihad refers to a revolutionary struggle and utmost exertion to achieve its goal.[73] These views of jihad hold the position that oppression should be fought against and is not in conformity with Islamic principles.

Fundamentalist groups such as Taliban and al-Qaeda are the most infamous representatives of this narrative of jihad in the modern day Islamic world. The media coverage gives the impression that the numbers of Muslims who are being drawn into this narrative are increasing. The Muslim rage in Pakistan, Indonesia, Iraq, among others, are pointed out as the proof of this fact, and the books on Islamic fundamentalism are the widest category of books published regarding Islam. However, contrary to the common belief, Islamic Fundamentalists consists of only a small minority of the Muslims in the world. Unfortunately, due to the sensational and horrifying acts that these fundamentalist groups have undertaken, the majority of the non-Muslim world has come to identify Islam with terrorism. The recent unbelievably tragic act of terrorism against the World Trade Center in New York and Pentagon in Washington D.C. seem to have taken this belief to its height.

Yet, not all Islamic terrorist groups fit into this category of offensive Islam. Various groups that argue that Islam permits war only for defensive reasons also justify the use of terror as a legitimate means to defend Islam. Therefore it becomes important to distinguish between those groups who purport offensive narratives of Islam that support terrorism and advocates of narratives of defensive Islam that support terrorism. This is the theme of the next sub-division.

Defensive Islam Islamic Narrative of Peace and War

The majority of Muslims within and outside of the Occupied Territories today agree that Islam permits use of violence only under certain circumstances and the most obvious one of these circumstances is 'self-defense.' Like most of the other nations, including United States of America, defensive war is considered a legitimate tool by most of the Muslims. As stated before, since the beginning of 20th century the notion of jihad has come to denote defensive war in response to Western colonialism and domination in particular. In this era, many modern Muslim scholars attempted to defend Islam against the Western charges that Islam is a violent religion, by claiming that jihad is only justified for self-defense. Among these scholars, Muhammad Asad of Pakistan and Muhammad Shaltut argue that jihad is purely defensive and Islam forbids aggression.[74] Also, Muhammad Abduh and Rashid Rida of Egypt argued that those verses that were considered unconditional commands to fight the unbelievers as conditional commands to fight only those who had broken their pledges, or had otherwise initiated aggression against the Muslim community.[75] Others, such as Ahmad Khan and Chiragh Ali of India even went further to argue that for defensive jihad to be permissible against the British, they would have to deny the Muslims freedom of worship, and since that has not been the case, jihad against the British is not permitted.[76] Still, most of the Muslims took a more militant stance against European imperialism during the colonial age, although they argued that Islam permits jihad on the defensive grounds.

In response to those, who claim that popular jihad for the purpose of proselytizing, exacting tribute, and exterminating the idolaters is one of the tenets of Islam, Chiragh Ali argues that: "All the defensive wars, and the verses of the Quran relating to the same, were strictly temporary and transitory in their nature."[77] In regards to those unconditional verses used by those, who adopt an offensive narrative of war and peace, Ali argues that "...the law of interpretation, the general scope and tenor of the Quran, and the context of the verses and parallel passages, all show that those few verse which are not conditional should be construed as conditional in conformity with other passages more clear, expressive, and conditional, and with the general laws of scriptural interpretation."[78]

Ali states that in the Quran there are only two verses (2:245 and 9:124) containing an absolute or non-conditional injunction for making war against unbelievers. However, he adds, neither these verses nor any other conditional verse, "by any rule of interpretation, show absolute injunction to wage war against the unbelievers without any provocation or limitation."[79] In support of this claim, the states:

> There is a rule in the exegesis of the Quran, as well as in other Scriptural interpretations, that when two commandments, one conditional, and the other general or absolute, are found on the same subject, the conditional is to be preferred, and the absolute should be construed as conditional because the latter is more expressive of the views of the author then the general, which is considered as vague in its expression.[80]

In order to defend this position, he delves into the classical Islamic theory of jihad and quotes those who claimed that jihad is an offensive means to spread Islam such as al- Sarakhsi, Ainee, ibn Hajar, and Halabi, and presents refutations of their arguments using the Quranic interpretation method by contextualizing the verses they refer to.[81] He uses the *Sunna* of the Prophet to prove that Islam is not aggressive. His work is extremely useful in presenting how different scholars in the Islamic scholarship interpreted jihad, as well as the Western scholarship. Furthermore, by identifying the verses used to justify aggressive jihad and refuting them by contextualizing them and employing a particular interpretive method becomes important to show how different approaches to jihad had developed.

The exponents of defensive Islamic approach to peace and war thus view jihad as a comprehensive effort in the path of God. This comprehensive effort requires "utilizing all the physical, mental, and spiritual faculties of human beings", and "of course, it also includes actual participation in war but only as a last resort, with those non-Muslims who actively oppose and hinder the *deen* [religion] of Allah and wish to subvert it."[82]

However, the question of defense is a complicated one. According to Muhammad Hamidullah what is considered a defensive war include punitive wars against the enemies of Islam, sympathetic wars in support of the struggle of oppressed Muslims in foreign lands, punitive wars against rebels within an Islamic state, and idealistic wars fought in order to command the good and prevent the commission of evil, together with fighting (*qital*) an enemy when attacked.[83] These attitudes are based on the verse (4: 74-76):

> Let those fight in the way of Allah who sell the little of this world for the other. Whose fighteth in way of Allah, be he slain or be he victorious, on him we shall bestow a vast reward.
>
> Those, who believe, do battle for the cause of Allah; and those who disbelieve do battle for the cause of idol. So fight the minions of the devil. Lo! The devil's strategy is ever weak.

The defenders of this interpretation of Islamic approaches to war and peace argue that Islam cannot be seen as a pacifist religion, because these verses, and similar others that deal with war (which at times justifies or even commands war), exist in the Quran. To support their view, these scholars, and lay people, who argue that jihad is permitted on the grounds of self defense, present various verses from the Quran and the Hadith, examples of the four rightly guided caliphs, various juridical rulings (*fatwa*) in Islamic history, like the defenders of both offensive and nonviolent Islamic approaches to war and peace. They argue that although Islam forbids wars of aggression, expansion, or prestige, Islam clearly permits wars for defense. Referring to the Quranic verse (2: 216):

> Fighting is prescribed for you, even though it be hateful to you: but it may well be that you hate something that is in fact good for you, and that you love a thing that is in fact bad for you: God knows, whereas you do not.

Basing his argument on the above-mentioned verse, Hashimi concludes "Islamic discourse on war and peace begins from the a priori assumption that some types of war are permissible —indeed required by God— and that all other forms of violence are, therefore forbidden."[84] Scholars such as Iftikhar H. Malik, recognize that "The Prophet would prefer peace over war, negotiation over confrontation and limited action over an outright plunder," but adds, Islamic 'Just War Theory' permits wars to defend *Dar al Islam*.[85] To buoy up his argument, he refers to the verse (8: 61) that states; " And if they incline to peace, incline thou also to it, and trust in God" and to the verse (47: 35) that states: " So do not falter, and invite to peace when you are the uppermost. And God is with you, and He will not grudge (the reward) of your actions," to say that peace must be granted even amidst a war in case the enemy asked for it.[86]

In order to support their ideas, defenders of the defensive narrative go back to classical Islamic scholars and state that Prophet did not resort to war against pagan Arabs until they persecuted the Muslims and violated their lives and properties. Similarly prophet declared war against the Byzantium and its Arab allies only when they killed the missionaries who were sent to peacefully summon people to Islam. As Louat Safi states:

> Islamic practice has clearly shown that the objective of war is not to propagate or spread Islam, nor is it to gain territory for the Islamic state. The aim is to fight any political authority that either prevents the Muslims from introducing the teachings of Islam to its subjects, or prevents its subjects from freely professing of practicing Islam. [87]

Exponents of defensive Islam are clear that, in the face of oppression and persecution, Islam calls Muslims to defend them selves, and to fight in order to establish justice and restore harmony. However, this narrative can further be divided into two sub-categories, based on their approach of conduct of war (*jus im bello*). The first subgroup argues that not only the ends but also the means of jihad must be based on ethical grounds, and state that, although war is permitted, it is also limited. Muqtedar Khan supports this view by interpreting the verse that states: "And fight them until persecution is no more, and religion is for Allah. But if they desist, then let there be no hostility except against wrongdoers" (2: 193). The second part of the verse, according to Khan, draws the limit retaliation against al! except those who are directly responsible for wrong-doing and also suggest that persecution could mean religious persecution.[88] Only those who actively persecute must be retaliated. He adds that also the verse (8:38), further reduces the scope for violent response by granting amnesty to those who stop persecution.[89]

The authoritative textbooks of Al-Azhar University (the oldest and most prestigious Islamic University) also adopt "defensive Islamic narratives of peace and war." The official narrative of al-Azhar suggests that offensive wars are not permitted, and in the modern age, communication networks offer a much better medium than armed conflict.[90] One of the most well recognized sheikhs, Sheikh Mahmut Schaltut argues that Islam allows pluralism and rejects the claim that Islam must resort to war to spread its beliefs by quoting the verse "Had Allah wanted, all people of the earth would have believed in Him, would you then dare force faith upon them" (10: 99), and also the verse "We have created you as peoples and tribes to make you know one another (49: 13). Interpreting the Quranic idea of war and peace in the light of these two verses, he concludes "war is an immoral situation," therefore it is not the right method.[91]

Sheikh Ali Jad al-Haqq's ideas are also in line with that of Schaltut. Al-Haqq states that jihad does not mean war, and if we want to refer to war we have to use the term "armed jihad" (*al-musallah*) to distinguish it from the everyday use of the term, such as jihad against ignorance, jihad against poverty, jihad against illness and disease, and search for knowledge is the highest level of jihad.[92] When jihad is defined as such, armed jihad becomes of minor importance and Islamic message can be spread without fighting. In support of this idea al-Haqq refers to the verses from the Meccan period where patience and nonviolent methods are preferred and states:

> In earlier ages sword was necessary for securing the path of *da'wa.* In our age, however, the sword lost its importance, although the resort to it is still important for the case of defense against those who do evil to Islam and its people. However, for dissemination of the *da'wa* there are now a variety of ways... those who focus on arms in our times are preoccupied with weak instruments.[93]

Upholders of this view call for strict application of rules of *siyar* and in particular, distinguish combatants and non-combatants. Therefore they conclude that, the Quran permits Muslims to fight to protect their faith, their freedom and their lands and property. Nevertheless, they add that the Quran insists that Muslims must be strong advocates of peace,[94] and if war is necessary, it must be fought as humanely as possible. Jamilah Jitmoud supports this argument referring to the *Hadith* the Prophet, after learning about it, criticizing the killing of an non-Muslim women and prohibiting the killing of women and children and the innocent people during wars, and stating that such strict regulations and restrictions rooted in the Quran and *Hadith* "keep it from becoming and act of violence."[95] Furthermore, if the non-Muslims are prepared to live with Muslims peacefully, then jihad would not be necessary, for Muslims have been urged to treat others with fairness.[96]

Another restriction concerning jihad they put forth is the requirement of *pacta sunt servanda*, honoring the treaties. According to this regulation, treaties contracted with non-Muslims need to be respected as long as the other party does not violate them, and the juridical source of this regulation lies in the verses (9: 1-2 and 9: 4) respectively:

> a declaration of immunity from God and His Messenger, to those of the pagans with whom you have contracted mutual alliance. So go about in the land for four months and know that you cannot frustrate God but that Allah will bring disgrace to the unbelievers;
>
> (but the treaties are) not dissolved with those pagans with whom you have entered into alliance and who have not subsequently failed you nor aided any one against you.

Also the following *hadith*, reported by al-Bukhari is put forth to defend this injunction:

> Whoever kills a person having a treaty with the Muslims shall not smell the smell of Paradise though its smell is perceived from a distance of forty years.[97]

However, the Islamic state can intervene militarily only when another political community threatens life and property of Muslims, and after all other means are exhausted, because the state is obliged to restore the rights of Muslims (2: 194).

The second subcategory includes those who argue that as Islam permits defensive wars, it also allows Muslims to utilize all the necessary means to win it. All the weapons of the opponent, which could also include nuclear weapons, and those weapons that cannot distinguish between combatants and noncombatants can be employed, as long as the opponent also employs them. This line of thinking is employed to justify terrorist attacks on civilians on the grounds that the adversary is also killing Muslim civilians. Many radical groups, such as Hamas, Hizbullah, and Islamic Jihad adopt this perspective to justify suicide attacks, or implanting explosives in social areas and non-military targets.[98] This sub-category of defensive Islamic narratives argue that under the current war system, where distinguishing between the civilian and military targets I increasingly difficult, Islam allows all that is "necessary," including suicide (or as they prefer to call "martyrdom") attacks to "defend" the Muslims against their enemies.

The supporters of this narrative recognize that in the Islamic tradition there is a clearly articulated regulation, both in the *Hadith*, and the practices of the four rightly guided caliphs as well as in the *siyar* tradition, concerning the ethical conduct during the battle. The Islamic tradition of *jus im bello* introduces two categories of restrictions. The first one concerns the permitted targets (e.g. civilian targets vs. military targets). The second category concerns the right methods and weapons that are permitted during the war (e.g. conventional weapons vs. mass destruction weapons including nuclear, chemical, and biological weapons). Those in this sub-category of defensive narrative of war and peace justify their position by arguing that under extreme conditions, some of these restrictions can be set aside.[99] They base their argument on the Islamic law precept that states, "necessity overrides the forbidden," which allows moral constraints to be overridden in emergencies, through the criteria for determining whether an emergency exists are vague.[100]

In this tradition, targeting women, children, the old and the weak is strictly forbidden, however, we see today that many Islamic groups, including those who employ defensive Islamic narrative, are increasingly using methods that do not respect these codes. Among these methods, suicide attacks are the most notorious and also the most controversial practices. Suicide attacks, which takes place in public areas such as shopping malls, restaurants, or hijacking planes and crashing into crowded buildings are clearly against the restrictions stated in the Quran, *Hadith*, the practices of the Prophet and his four rightly caliphs, as well as Shaybani's *siyar*. However, various *fatwas* (legal decrees issued by leading Islamic scholars) seem to justify these acts as martyrdom missions rather then defining them as suicide attacks.

As suicide or self destruction is one of the gravest sins according to Islamic tradition, based on the Quranic verse "give generously for the cause of Allah and do not with your own hands cast yourselves into destruction" (2: 195), this issue is a very sensitive one for Muslims. Therefore, presenting a solid justification becomes utmost important in legitimizing these attacks. This issue will be dealt in more depth when Islamic movements are discussed in the next chapter. However, it is important to note that for this group the end (defending and liberating the Islamic lands) justifies the necessary means. While doing that, they selectively read into Islamic history and quote *Hadiths* that point out to the rewards of fighting and dying for the cause of God and defending His religion and Muslims to justify these acts.

Especially in the context of the weakness of Muslim armies compared to that of United States, Israel, and other Western countries, the defenders of this position argue that there is no other way but to employ similar weapons or weapons such as suicide bombers to fight against those who invade Islamic lands, or attack Muslims. Suicide attacks undertaken by Palestinians against the Israeli occupation in particular, are seen as the "*only way*" to get the message across by increasing number of Muslims, when the Palestinian (non-existing) military power is compared to Israel -the military superpower of the region.[101] The rapid intensification of war in the region as both communities continue their stubborn policies of revenge and retaliation, it seems that this viscous cycle of violence and hatred will lead to the destruction of both peoples, unless an alternative narrative will emerge.

Nonviolent Islamic Narrative of Peace and War

The current representation of Islam in the Western media renders the term nonviolent Islamic narratives of peace and war almost an oxymoron. However, the reality proves otherwise. While the media questions Islamic violence, war as a means for self-defense is hardly questioned. Proponents of nonviolence are not the majority of the population when "national security" is perceived to be under threat in almost all societies in the world. One of the reasons for this weak support for nonviolence is that it is generally associated with pacifism, which is perceived as inaction or keeping silence at times of oppression and threat of violence.

Furthermore, on an ideological level, nonviolence is not a clearly defined concept. There exist a number of belief systems, which reject violence in principle, such as Buddhism and Gandhi's understanding of Hinduism. Gene Sharp distinguishes six principled nonviolence types, namely Nonresistance, Active Reconciliation, Moral Resistance, Selective Nonviolence, Satyagraha, and Nonviolent Revolution.[102] Martin Luther King identified the major principles of nonviolence as being physically non-aggressive, but spiritually dynamically aggressive; as not humiliating the opponent, but persuading the opponent and facilitating change through new understanding and awareness of moral shame to construct beloved communities; as directing its forces against the evil rather then against persons who are caught in these forces; as seeking to avoid both external physical and internal spiritual violence; and finally as being based on the conviction that the universe is on the side of justice.[103] Abu Nimer defines nonviolence as "a set of attitudes, actions, or behaviors intended to persuade the other side to change their opinions, perceptions and actions", and pacifism as "the overall principles that guide the application of nonviolent strategies."[104] In this sense, nonviolence means that the actors do not retaliate violently against their opponent, but absorb anger and damage as well as sending a message of patience and insistence in facing and correcting injustice.[105]

"From the nonviolence perspective, peace is defined as a process in which human beings can establish foundations for interacting with each other and with nature in harmony and to institute just social-economic structures, where human beings can flourish and fulfill their potentials."[106] Such a conceptualization of peace rests "on the acknowledgment of dignity and worth of each and every human being, the recognition of the needs and interests of all those involved and addressing social, political and economic injustices."[107] Therefore, "[n]onviolence implies an active commitment to social change that would ultimately result in a fair distribution of world resources, a more creative and democratic cooperation between peoples, and a common pursuit of those social, scientific, medical, and political achievements that serve to enhance the human enterprise and prevent warfare."[108] And, employing nonviolent active resistance becomes crucial for building peace that can be sustained.

Nonviolence as a means of affecting change and resolving conflict has been used in history successfully. Nonviolence approaches are based on the assumption that the exercise of power depends on the consent of the ruled, who by withdrawing that consent can control or destroy the power of the opponent.[109] When controlled and planned properly, nonviolent action can achieve significant social progress. Islam as a discourse incorporates values and principles that promote nonviolence and peaceful conflict resolution approaches. Moreover, Islamic history presents examples of how these values and principles can be successfully applied in conflict situations. Similar to the proponents of other narratives of peace and war, adherents of nonviolence in Islam base their narratives on the Quran, the *Hadith* and the *Sunna* of the Prophet, arguing that nonviolence is the preferred discourse. These Muslim scholars argue that although tradition and Islam incorporates different teachings and practices towards conflict and conflict resolution, there is a set of values, including, justice (*adl*), helping the poor (*ihsan*), wisdom (*hikmah*), forgiveness (*afu*), and compassion (*rahma*), if consistently and systematically applied, can transcend all levels of conflict.[110]

Islam incorporates values and principles that promote nonviolence, and its historical development provides examples of nonviolent practices. Thus, nonviolent narratives of peace and war can be perceived as authentic components of the Islamic discourse. Abu-Nimer argues that "uncovering and reconstructing nonviolent peace-building values and strategies will consciously assist in developing indigenous and local Muslim culture communities economically, socially, and politically."[111] Most of the scholars who are defenders of nonviolent narratives of jihad are situated within the *Islah* movement. In this sense, they contextualize the Quranic verses that deal with peace, war, and nonviolence, and argue that there is no theological reason for Muslims not to adopt nonviolence. In fact not to adopt nonviolence is antithetical to Islam.[112]

When articulating Islamic narratives on nonviolence scholars agree on some major points. One of the important arguments these scholars present is that the historical period has changed and new technology introduced weapons that cannot distinguish between the combatants and non-combatants. They assert that killing of non-combatants is clearly against the Islamic rules regarding *jus im bello* -based on *siyar*-, therefore violence cannot be permissible. Hence Muslims should adopt nonviolence. In support of this argument Jawdat Sa'id states:

> What is in the order of the world is that it has reached an extent that world problems can no longer be solved by violence (*bi-l- 'unf*). The evidence for this that the great powers themselves cannot use violence anymore to solve their conflicts. As for the weak and the oppressed (*al-mustad 'afun*) among small states, their violence will only turn in favor of the great powers whenever they attempt to solve their problems by such means.
>
> With the advent of the nuclear bomb, nonviolence has become an historical destiny— not just a choice as it was before. Those who do not accept this as true will only expose themselves to repeated suffering and losses. History does not change its course, people are the ones who adopt to it.[113]

The second justification they present for nonviolence in Islam is in relation to community. The status of the Muslim community in a global system and in local communities has changed and many Muslims live as minorities under non-Muslim rule. Their status and the relationship between Muslim governments and these non-Muslim governments are not same as it was centuries ago, for that reason new rules of engagement is necessary and Muslims should adopt nonviolence in this new global system.

The adherents of nonviolence also state that the use of violence as a means to address conflict was a minor element in the life of the prophet and in Scripture, and therefore, it should not occupy as much attention today. Islamic history, the Prophet's tradition, and Scripture itself are rich sources for developing nonviolent strategies to deal with current social and political problems. In order to justify their claims of nonviolence, these scholars and activists refer to Quranic verses such as:

> Whenever they kindle the fire of war, God extinguishes. They strive to create disorder on earth and God loves not those who create disorder (5:64);
>
> God commands you to treat (everyone) justly, generously and with kindness (16:90);
>
> Repel evil (not with evil) but something that is better (*Ahsan*) -that is with forgiveness and amnesty. (13: 22)

Among the scholars who explore role of Islam in nonviolent activism and in reconciliation, Chaiwat Satha Anand observes the tradition of the Prophet Mohammed. He states that jihad aims to put an end to "structural violence," but the means used are not independent of moral scrutiny.[114] On the basis of Quran and *Sunna*, he states that Islam forbids killing noncombatants and refers to the *Hadith,* which states; " Go in God's name trusting in God, and adhering to the religion of God's messenger. Do not kill a decrepit old men, or a young infant, or a women: do not be dishonest about booty, but collect your spoils, do right and act well, for God loves who do well."[115] To support the idea that Islam has strict rules concerning the battle-field he refers to a speech the first Caliph made before going to the battle that states:

> Stop, O, people, that I may give you ten rules for your guidance in the battlefield. Do not commit treachery or deviate from the right path. You must not mutilate dead bodies. Neither kill a child, or a women, or an aged man. Bring no harm to the trees, nor burn them with fire, especially those, which are fruitful. Slay not the enemy's flock, save for your food. You are likely to pass people who have devoted their lives to monastic services, leave them alone.[116]

Based on these strict Islamic rules, concerning the conduct of war and observing that the wars in the modern era cannot distinguish between combatants and noncombatants, and that weapons of mass destruction are not any ordinary weapons, but instruments of mass extermination, Anand concludes that the war under these conditions are not permitted according to Islam.[117] This argument is also supported by Inamullah Khan, who states that although at a minimal level Islam permits war, conduct of war must be as humane as possible.[118] In that respect Anand articulates eight theses on Muslim nonviolent action that are rooted in the original vision of Islam and 'true' meaning of peace thereof.[119]

The first thesis is that for Islam, the problem of violence is integral part of the Islamic moral sphere. Violence, if used by Muslims, must be governed by the rules prescribed in the Quran and the *Hadith*. If violence cannot discriminate between combatants and noncombatants, it is not acceptable according to Islam. Modern technology of destruction renders discrimination virtually impossible. Therefore Muslims cannot use violence in the modern world. Islam teaches Muslims to fight for justice with the understanding that human life is —as is all God's creation— has a purpose and is sacred. For that reason to be true to Islam requires Muslims to utilize nonviolent action as the mode of struggle. Moreover, Islam itself is a fertile soil for nonviolence because of its potential for disobedience, strong discipline, sharing and social responsibility, perseverance, self-sacrifice, the belief in the unity of the Muslim community, and the oneness of mankind.[120]

According to Maulana Wahiduddin Khan, who writes extensively on Islam and nonviolence, patience is the focus of about 200 verses of the Quran and referred to indirectly in many others. It is one of the core subjects of the Scriptures. For instance, one of the verses he refers to is one that states "And endure patiently whatever may befall thee." (31: 17) Patience (*sabr*) according to Wahiduddin Khan makes a person capable of finding a positive and successful solution to a problem. He states that patience is set above all other Islamic virtues with the exceptional promise of reward beyond measure (39: 10).[121] He furthermore states that the entire spirit of the Quran is in consonance with the concept of patience. Patience, he states, implies a peaceful response or reaction, whereas impatience implies a violent response. He continues, adding that the word *sabr* expresses the notion of nonviolence as it is understood in modern times.[122] In this context, "jihad" refers to nonviolent activism, while "*qital*" is violent activism. To support this view he invokes the Quranic verse "perform jihad with this (i.e. the word of the Quran) most strenuously." (25: 52). Since the Quran is not a sword or a gun, but a book of ideology, performing jihad could only mean an ideological struggle to conquer peoples' hearts and minds through Islam's superior philosophy.[123]

Wahududdin Khan also states that all of the great successes of Islam were achieved by nonviolent methods. His primary examples include the Prophet's life by stating that of the 23-year period of his prophethood, the initial 13 years, when Muhammed was in Mecca, the Prophet adopted nonviolence. When Meccans waged war against Him, the Prophet chose to immigrate to Madina, and this was also a nonviolent activism. When the Meccan unilaterally waged war against Him, the battles of *Badr* and *Uhud* took place but the Prophet made a 10-year treaty, called the *Sulh al-Hudaybiyah*, accepting all the conditions of his opponents. This peace treaty paved the way for peaceful constructive activities.

According to Wahiduddin Khan, these examples suggest that nonviolence is the preferred method in Islam. Although there are certain verses in the Quran that command *qital* (22: 39), they require crucial circumstances to be present. In that respect, Wahiduddin Khan states that aggression, launching an offensive war by the believers is totally forbidden. The Quran commands: "Fight for the sake of those that fight against you, but do not be aggressive (2: 190). Since initiating hostility is not allowed in Islam, only certain defensive wars can be permitted, "when they attack you" (9: 13) He states that according to Quran there was one form of war which was time-bound strictly in retaliation to its purpose, and this was to end *fitna,* since the Quran states: "Fight against them until *fitna* is no more" (2: 193). In contrast to the classical jihad literature and the offensive Islamic narratives, Wahiduddin Khan reads *fitna* to mean "that coercive system which had reached the extremes of religious persecution."[124] He also states that *fitna* refers to the ancient times when a political system dominated by coercion prevailed around the world, closing the doors to material and spiritual progress. Believers were urged to break this coercive system in order to usher freedom for material and spiritual progress.

He notes that there were only three real instances that Muslims entered a battle, referring to the Battles of *Badr*, *Uhud*, and *Hunayn*— undertaken by the Prophet, when it became absolutely inevitable. He also states that these battles lasted only for half a day, each beginning from noon and ending with the setting of the sun. Therefore, it is possible to say that the Prophet had actively engaged in war for a total of a day and half, and observed the principle of nonviolence throughout his 23-year prophetic career.[125] Thus, war takes a minimal role in Islam.

Wahiduddin Khan observes the greatest problem of the Muslim world is that they have forgotten the *Sunna* of nonviolence and resorted to violence. This resulted in losing what had been gained before. The contemporary realities require a return to the principle nonviolence of the Prophet, to rejuvenate the *Dawah,* the peaceful struggle for the propagation of Islam. However, Muslims today, he observes, are easily provoked and become violent at anything against their way of thinking, or even not to their liking.[126] Although not all Muslims are involved directly in violence, he states that according to Islam, keeping silent makes them indirectly responsible. He criticizes the modern *ulema*, intellectuals, and leaders of movements for adopting a violent narrative, and spreading this narrative among the young populations. And this violent mentality, he argues, is responsible for having alienated them from their neighbors, and the only way for them to change this situation is to 'return' to nonviolence. One crucial obstacle in the minds of many Muslims, he notes, is that peace does not guarantee them justice. However, he states that peace does not automatically produce justice. He gives the example of the *Hudaybiyah* treaty to illustrate that the Prophet made this peace not to exact justice, but to create opportunities. The treaty did give the Prophet the opportunity for *dawah* activities, and after that, the Prophet not only ensured justice but also set Islam upon a much more solid footing.[127]

Jawdat Sa'id, on the other hand, compares wars to the cruel practice of offering human sacrifices to Gods, stating that "today we continue the tradition of offering human sacrifices with the victim's willing consent-when we push people to go to war in the name of holy patriotism and heroism."[128] He adds, "we still have not understood that such a thing has changed into a mere sacrifice devoid of holiness or act of heroism."[129] Sa'id also asserts that armies and governments have lost their traditional role in protecting the populace; while people have resorted their role in protecting themselves.[130] This method (of war) no longer solves the problem, nor does it even bring the needed ease of conscience. Referring to Quranic verse, "God does not change the condition of a people until they change what is within themselves", he states that "as soon as we cease to place our trust in a Napoleon or a Hitler to make peace and unity, and as soon as we trust in ourselves being able to change what is within ourselves,"[131] we will be able to establish peace.

In that sense, the "sacred struggle," jihad, cannot mean violence and aggression, and the Quranic verse that reads: "God forbids you not respecting those who have not fought against you on account of your religion, and who have not driven you out from your homes, that you be kind to them and deal equitably with them" (60: 8), and "if they withdraw from you but fight you not, and (instead) send you (guarantees of) peace, then Allah hath opened no way for you (to war against them)" (4: 90). He states that the message of Islam goes further than this. Referring to the *Hadith* transmitted by the Prophet's companion Sa'd Ibn Abi Waqqas, Sa'id suggests that the message of Islam is "*Kun Ka- Ibni Adam*" (be as the son of Adam). With regard to fighting amongst Muslims, the Prophet is recorded to say to his companion Abu Dharr al-Ghifari, who asked him what to do, "stay in your house" when Abu Dharr asked "but what if someone entered into my home (to kill me), the Prophet replied: "if you fear to look upon the gleam of the sword (raised to strike you), then cover your face with your robe— this will he bear the sin of killing you as well as his own sin." [132] Furthermore Sa'id refers to the Prophet's statement that "whoever takes life by the sword, by the sword shall he perish."[133]

Sa'id argues that the true message of Islam is nonviolence and to support his view he highlights the story of Adam's sons Abel and Cain stated in the Quran, arguing that this story clearly illustrates God's preference for nonviolence. The story narrates that, Cain, jealous of his brother Abel because Abel's sacrifice was accepted by God and not his. When he attempted to kill Abel, Abel told him "if you stretch your hand to slay me, it is not me to stretch my hand against you to slay you for I fear Allah ..." (2: 28). The Quran goes on to say "if any one slew a person unless it be for Murder or for spreading Mischief in the land, it would be as if he slew the whole people. And if anyone saved a life it would be as if he saved the life of the whole people" (2: 32). In addition, responding violence with similar violence is to actually empower the position of the violent person.[134] Patience is the key to nonviolence in Islam since according to Sa'id, the Quran has all the Prophets speak: "And we shall surely bear with patience all the harm you do us." (14: 12-13) For that reason, he states that "it is obligatory upon us —people of understanding— and it is within our grasp, to continually maintain nonviolent peaceful contacts with other understanding people in the world, without waiting for the politicians."[135]

There is also a clear preference for forgiveness, especially when one repents. Sa'id argues that this is the basis of nonviolence in Islam. Building his argument on this basis, he insists that violence is illegitimate and forgiveness is the norm. To support his position, he refers to a famous Hadith that states:

> Whenever violence enters into something it disgraces it, whenever 'gentle-civility' enters something it graces it. Truly God bestows on account of gentle conduct what he does not bestow on account of violent conduct.[136]

Based on the same *Hadith*, Abdul Ghaffar Khan[137] stated that God grants to *rifq* (gentleness) what he does not grant to *unf* (violence).[138] Furthermore, he argued that the word *rifq* has been used in this *Hadith* as an antithesis to *unf* (which means violence). From here, he also argued that these terms convey exactly what violence and nonviolence mean in present times. This *Hadith* clearly indicates the superiority of the non-violent method. He also adds that according to the Quran, God does not love *fasad*, which is another word for violence. What is meant here by *fasad* is 'mischief' and this is clearly expressed in verse 205 of the second *Surah*. "When he turns his back, his aim everywhere is to spread mischief through the earth and destroy crops and progeny but Allah loveth not mischief." (2: 205) According to this verse, *fasad* is that action which results in disruption of the social system, causing huge losses in terms of lives and property. He interprets this verse as a proof that God loves non-violence. He abhors violent activity in human society, as a result of which, people have to pay the price with their possessions and lives. This is supported by other statements in the Quran. We are told in the Quran that peace is one of God's names (59: 23). Those who seek to please God are assured by the verse (16: 5) that they will be guided by Him to "the paths of peace." Paradise, which is the final destination of the society of God's choice, is referred to in the Quran as "the home of peace" (89: 30), etc.

Another important aspect of nonviolence in Islam is the concept of power. According to Rabia Terri Harris, power in Islamic understanding of nonviolence accumulates to people through the unarmed struggle and continues to reside there.[139] Armed struggle is only a branch, which dies if torn from its root- for it is only unarmed struggle that teaches reliance on God. This is based on the assumption that power in its essence is non-coercive. It is only dissipated, never generated through coercion. Observed from this point of view, power becomes an infinite spiritual resource, which infuses into those who abandon their own objectives for the objectives of their Creator.

Nonviolence in Islam is not simply a theoretical exercise to "feel-good," nor is it a modern hermeneutical extrapolation into a distant historical past. On the contrary, nonviolent interpretations of Islam base their narratives on various significant and successful nonviolent movements that took place in both pre-modern and modern history. Among these examples, the nonviolent movement of Pashtuns, led by Ghaffar Khan during the British colonial period in India, is a telling example.[140] Living in the North-West Frontier Province of British India, Pashtuns had the reputation of being extremely aggressive and violent. Their cultural norms emphasized vengeance and military arts. Johansen states that, "In selecting a case of nonviolent action from this cultural context, one is examining a difficult case in which the people and culture seemed unusually violent, in order to demonstrate that a militant group, displaying what today would be called "fundamentalist" tendencies bearing the fervor of religious nationalism (although led by a rare traditional leader), developed nonviolent strategies, pursued by a wide following, and achieved notable success."[141] However, it is from this context that Ghaffar Khan was able to articulate a nonviolent resistance movement to repel the British.

Ghaffar Khan, as a son of a religious chieftain, felt the personal religious calling to Serve God by uplifting his people through social reform and education. Ghaffar Khan was convinced that pervasive violence was responsible for the Pashtun society's inability to uplift itself.[142] Therefore he decided to create a nonviolent organization to bring social, economic, and political reforms. Based on this commitment, he established a nonviolent army, called *Khudai Khidmatgars* (servants of God), founded on Islamic principles. Consistent with the code of honor in the Pashtun society and Muslims beliefs, those who joined this army declared that they were willing to swear before God to give their lives for their people.

When Ghaffar Khan established his army (which also included women) they were drilled and disciplined with officers, cadres, uniforms, a flag, a drum and bagpipe corps. However, this army was completely nonviolent, and Khan told his followers that he was going to give them the most powerful weapon, the weapon of the Prophet, and this weapon was patience and righteousness, when standing against oppression. He stated:

> I am going to give you such a weapon that the police and the army will not be able to stand against it. It is the weapon of the Prophet, but you are not aware of it. That weapon is patience and righteousness. No power on earth can stand against it... when you go back to your villages, tell your brethren that there is an army of God, and its weapon is patience. Ask your brethren to join the army of God. Endure all hardships. If you exercise patience, victory will be yours.[143]

The basic teachings of this army were forgiveness, sacrifice, and nonviolence. Ghaffar Khan's interpretation extended the notion of *sabr* to mean renunciation of all forms of violence, thus became a key element in his religious teaching and practice. Joining the army required an oath to refrain from violence and from taking revenge, as well as to refrain from any antisocial customs and practices, and to devote at least two hours a day to social work. This oath was of great importance because Pashtun culture assumed that one's word could not be broken without losing one's integrity. The word must be honored with life.

Looking at the Ghaffar Khan's example, Johansen concludes that "Muslim religious teaching and discourse provided a basis for *enabling people to contest the meaning of their own tradition* in contemporary life," and Commitment to Islam "*sustained the determination and courage if the leadership* of the Khudai Khidmatgars movement"[144] As this case proves, faith not only created space within the minds of Muslims for employing nonviolence in unprecedented ways, but also reduced the moral space within which they considered violence to be legitimate.

Ghaffar Khan's example might strike readers as a unique and unprecedented in the light of current representation of Islam. However, it is not the only example. Islamic history is rich in such examples, and men were not the only figures who were successful in resolving conflicts nonviolently.[145] One of the important women figures concerning Islam and nonviolence is Lala Aziza from Morocco, who lived in the 14t[h] century.[146] According to the travel accounts of a religious scholar called Ibn Qunfudh, who met her in 1362, she had successfully reconciled a conflict between two groups peacefully. According to Ibn Qunfudh, al-Hinti, the governor of Marrakesh and the most powerful general in Morocco at the time was engaged in a battle to conquer all southern Morocco. His violence and aggression was well known to the habitants of the region. With his 6,000 men he came to Seksawa where Lala Aziza was living.

It was Aziza who met them near the mountains. Standing alone before the army and the general, she confronted them with her words and with his own faith. She spoke of the demands of the Creator on justice, the pull of the good, and wrong of harming God's creation. According to the accounts of the general, as recorded by Ibn Qunfudh, she answered him before he could ask anything. "She knew what was going on inside of him, his ideas, the way he was thinking, and he was unable to respond to her or to reject her requests."[147] With her words and argumentation, she was able to talk him out of the conquest. She also convinced him to leave the people unharmed. Her story has been told over the centuries as *the story of a woman who dared to stand up to a general and his army*. And her legacy has been an inspiration of the people of the region since then. During the colonial era, her sanctuary played an important role against oppression and violence. It is recorded that 8 men fled to her sanctuary when the colonial army conscripted them. They were protected. And the French official agreed to let them go.

These two examples of nonviolent action based on Islamic principles challenge the oversimplified caricaturization of Islam as a religion of violence that cannot or incorporate nonviolence. Systems of belief and action are not constant, but change as people contest their meaning. They also suggest that if the religious values are sensitively understood and implemented, they can contribute to peace, nonviolence, and coexistence. As Johansen also observes, every religious generation reconstructs its religious tradition to fit its perceptions of contemporary conditions.[148]

Every religious scripture is communicated through words, and the meaning of words may change over time. Therefore, although one might believe that God revealed guidelines to humanity, one must also realize that its meaning can only be communicated through words and symbols that are subject to human interpretation, in the face of ever-changing conditions. Furthermore, it is hard to claim, or at least convince others that one can understand God and know God. Then, it becomes crucial to realize that religious people have the duty and responsibility to reflect on their belief systems, contribute maximally to understanding the meaning of life, and to implement the highest values of their religion.[149]

To conclude, religion can be seen and abused as an obstacle to peace and to inflict violence. Samuel Huntington observes, "in the modern world, religion is a central, perhaps *the* central force that motivates and mobilizes people"(italics in original).[150] Indeed current conflicts suggest that this is the case. However, religious traditions also may be used to restrain violence and encourage people to transcend national even religious boundaries to express solidarity. As this chapter attempted to show, Islam, like all other religious traditions have been interpreted to contain contesting approaches towards peace and war and these interpretations have been employed by different groups to pursue different ends. The existence of multiple interpretations of a single religious tradition can be explained in various ways. It is important to remember that every religious scripture is communicated through words and has to go through human interpretation. "The meaning of words may change over time, new developments may require new concepts and new words, which are not in the scriptures. Therefore, although one might believe that God revealed guidelines to humanity, one must also realize that God's message can only be communicated through words and symbols that are subject to human interpretation, in the face of ever-changing conditions."[151] The next chapter will focus on Islamication of the Israeli-Palestinian conflict and the dominant narrative of peace and conflict. It will try to understand why this particular narrative, namely defensive Islamic narrative, has become the dominant approach.

Endnotes

1. Bassam Tibi. "War and Peace in Islam" in *The Ethics of War and Peace: Religious and Secular Perspectives* Terry Nardin eds. (New Jersey: Princeton University Press Princeton, 1996), 129.

2. See footnote Quran, 2512.

3. Abdul Aziz Said et. al. 2001, 8.

4. Abdul Aziz Said et. al. 2001., 7.

5. Suad Al Hakim. "Islam and Peace" Paper presented at the Symposium *Islam and Peace in the 21st Century.* February. Translated by Tara Aziz and Karim Crow (1998), 5.

6. Abdul Aziz Said et. al. 2001, 7.

7. Fred M. Donner.. "The Sources of Islamic Conceptions of War" in *Just War and Jihad: Historical and Theoretical Perspectives on War and Peace in Western and Islamic Traditions* John Kelsay and James Turner Johnson eds. (New York: Greenwood Press, 1991), 31-69, 33-34.

8. Donner 1991. 34.

9. Donner 1991.

10. See Chapter Eight

11. Donner 1991., 42.

12. For a detailed study of influences of Byzantium and Sassanian Iran see Donner 1991.

13. Donner 1991., 43

14. Donner 1991.

15. Donner 1991, 45. Donner supports this argument by looking at one of the earliest dated Arabic inscription (64 A.H./ 683-684 C.E.) which reveals an apocalyptic outlook by mentioning Israfil, the angel who in Muslim eschatology sounds the trumpet of doom on the Day of Judgement, and also looking at the Hadiths of the Prophet . See Donner 1991.

16. Salmi et al. 1998, 23.

17. Donner 1991, 53.

18. Donner 1991.

19. Muhammad Talaat al-Ghunaimi, *The Muslim Conception of International Law and the Western Approach.* (The Haugue: Martinus Nijhoff, 1968), 147.

20. See Esposito 1998.

21. Khadduri, Majid. "The Islamic Theory of International Relations and Its Contemporary Relevance," in *Islam and International Relations.* J. Harris eds. (Frederick A. Preager Inc., 1965), 24-39, 30.

22. Zaiuddin Sardar, "The Other Jihad: Muslim Intellectuals and Their Responsibilities" in *Inquiry* (London) Vol. 2 no. 10 (October 1985), 40.

23. Muhammad Abdul Lateef al Sobki, "Al Jihad in Islam" *The Fourth Conference of the Academy of Islamic Research* (Cairo Al Azhar Academy of Islamic Research, 1968), 158. Cited in Salmi et. al. 1998, 67.

24. Khadduri 1955, 57.

25. Cited in AbdulHamid A. AbuSulayman *"Islamic Jurisprudence and Modern Needs: The Challenge of Renewal"* in Abdul Aziz Said et. al. 2001, 66.

26. AbuSulayman 2001.

27. AbuSulayman 2001.

28. AbuSulayman 200

29. AbuSulayman 2001., 68.

30. Mehdi Abedi, and Gary Legenhausen.. "Introduction" in *Jihad and Shahadat: Struggle and Martyrdom in Islam*. Mehdi Abedi, and Gary Legenhausen eds. (The Institute for Research and Islamic Studies (IRIS), 1986), 10.

31. Donner 1991, 37.

32. Donner 1991., 17.

33. See the *fatwa* issued by the Ottoman sultan during the WWI, calling the Muslims to jihad in Said et. al. 2001

34. These prohibitions are taken from Salmi et al. 1998, 124-125.

35. Terry Nardin. *Peace: the Ethics of War and Peace: Religious and Secular Perspectives*. (Princeton University Press, 1996), 259.

36. Abdulaziz A. Sachedina, "Justification for Violence in Islam." *War and Its Discontents: Pacifism and Quietism in the Abrahamic Traditions. J.P. Burn Ed. (Washington DC: Georgetown University Press* 1996), 129.

37. H. Hanefi. "Arab Nationalist Thought in the Balance," *Qadaya Arabiyya*, (March-April, 1978), 21 Cf. Fu'ad Zakariya interview with *al-Thaqafa* (Amman) April 1983. Cited in Emmanuel Sivan,. *Interpretations of Islam: Past and Present*.. (Jew Jersey: The Darwin Press, Princeton, 1985), 107-108.

38. Emmanuel Sivan. *Interpretations of Islam: Past and Present*. (Princeton Jew Jersey: The Darwin Press, 1985), 109.

39. Sivan 1985., 110-111.

40. Sivan 1985., 123.

41. Sivan 1985.

42. Sivan 1985., 123-124.

43. Husam el-Khatib, "The Jurisdiction of Classical Islam" in *Islamica* vol. 3 no. 1 (Summer, 1999), 79-88, 81.

44. Donner, 1991 51.

45. Donner 1991.

46. Donner 1991., 57-58.

47. Ibn Asakir. *Ta'rikh Madinat Dimashq* (Damascus.): 182; Abu Yusuf 1969. *Kitab al-Kharaj* trans. Ben Shemesh, (London, 1977): 43; Ibn Hanbal.. *Kitab al Sunna* (Cairo, no date): 35 cited in Sivan, 129.

48. Donner 1991, 58.

49. See Mandaville 2001.

50. See Chapter Six, also Appendix I.

51. Bessam Tibi 1996, 137.

52. Cited in Haddad 1983, 82.

53. Haddad 1983.

54. Haddad 1983.

55. Haddad 1983., 83.

56. Sayyid Qutb. *Ma'alim fi al tariq* 13th legal ed. Dar al Shuruq, (Cairo, 1989), 72 cited in Bessam Tibi, 1997 139.

57. Tibi 1996., 82.

58. Tibi 1996, 83.

59. Tibi 1996.

60. See Sayyid Qutb. "War, Peace and Islamic Jihad" in *Contemporary Debates in Islam: An Anthology of Modernist and Fundamentalist Thought*.Mansoor Moaddel and Kamran Talattof eds. (New York: St. Martin's Press, 2000), 223-245, 235. Note that Muslims who defend religious pluralism use this verse and defensive Islam to support the

idea that Islam recognizes other religious traditions and protects their place of worship. Whereas Qutb interprets this verse to support wars against oppression and corruption in general.

61. Sayyid Qutb Ma'alim fi al Tariq: 72, 82 cited in Nusse 1998: 71 See also Qutb 2000, 227.

62. John Voll 1982, 9.

63. Voll 1983.

64. Qutb 2000, 236.

65. Qutb 2000.

66. Qutb 2000. .

67. Hasan al Banna *Majmu'at Rasa'l al-Imam al-Shahid Hasan al-Banna*_new legal ed. (Cairo: Dar al Da'wa, 1990), 275 cited in Bessam Tibi 1996, 137.

68. Bessam Tibi 1996, 138.

69. Tibi 1996.

70. Tibi 1996.

71. al Banna, 289 cited in Tibi 1996, 138.

72. Hasan al-Banna. *Five Tracts of Hasan al-Banna (1906-1949)*_Charles Wendell tr., (Berkeley: University of California Press, 1978), 142 ff.

73. S. Abul A'la Maududi *Jihad in Islam.* (Lahore: Islamic Publications, 1980), 5.

74. Muhammad. Asad,. *The Principles of State and Governance in Islam.* (Berkeley: University of California Press, 1961).

75. Rudolph Peters. *Islam and Colonialism: The Doctrine of Jihad in Modern History* (The Hague: Mouton, 1979), 129.

76. See Mehdi Abedi at. al., 13 see also Moulavi Chiragh Ali *"War and Peace: Popular Jihad"* in Moaddel and Talattof eds. 2000, 71-94, 72.

77. Ali 2000., 72.

78. Ali 2000., 73.

79. Ali 2000.

80. Ali 2000.

81. Ali 2000., 77-82.

82. M.M. Qurashi. *"The Concept of Islamic Jehad"* in *Islamic Thought and Scientific Creativity,* Vol. 2, No. 1 (1991), 57-71, 58.

83. Muhammad Hamidullah, *Muslim Conduct of State* Lahore: Sh. Muhammad Ashraf, 3rd ed. (1953), 164-65, 166-69.

84. Sohail Hashimi.. *"Interpreting the Islamic Ethics of War and Peace."* In *Ethics of War and Peace: Religious and Secular Perspectives.*_Terry Nardin eds. (Princeton: Princeton University Press, 1996), 151.

85. Malik, Iftikhar H.. *"Islamic Discourse on Jihad, War and Violence"* in *Journal of South Asian and Middle Eastern Studies*_vol. 21, no. 4 (Summer, 1998), 47-78, 59.

86. Iftikhar 1998.

87. M Safi Louay "Islam and Peace' in Islamic Horizons (September/October, 1996): 42-43, 43.

88. Khan, Mohammed A. Muqtedar. *"Peace and Change in the Islamic World"* paper presented at the conference *Islam and Peace in the 15/20th century.* Washington DC. (February, 1997), 2.

89. Muqtedar Khan 1997., 3.

90. Tibi 1996, 137.

91. Tibi 1996., 136.

92. Tibi 1996.

93. Jad al- Haqq. *Bayan ila al-nas* (Cairo Al-Azhar, 1984-88) 2 vols. 1:277, 278-79 cited in ibid.

94. Muqtedar Khan 1997, 5.

95. Jamilah Jitmoud. " Principles of Jihad in the Quran and Sunnah" in *State Politics and Islam* Mumtaz Ahmad ed. (American Trust Publications 1986),133-146, 140.

96. Jitmoud 1986. 142.

97. See Jitmoud 1986., 141.

98. See next Chapter.

99. Tibi 1996, 133.

100. Tibi 1996.

101. For an analysis, see next Chapter.

102. Gene Sharp *Politics of Nonviolent Action* (Boston: Sargent, 1973) vol. III.

103. Martin Luther King, Jr. "Nonviolence and Racial Justice" in *Christian Century.* (February 6, 1957), 165-167.

104. Abu-Nimer 2003, 14. Update information

105. Abu-Nimer 2003.

106. Kadayifci-Orellana, Ayse S. "Religion, Violence and The Islamic Tradition of Nonviolence" in *The Turkish Yearbook of International Relations* No. 34, 2003; 23-62, 38.

107. Kadayifci-Orellana 2003.

108. Daniel L Smith-Christopher. *Subverting Hatred: The Challenge of Nonviolence in Religious Tradition"* (Cambridge, MA: The Boston Research Center for the 21st Century, 1998), 10.

109. Said, Abdul Aziz; Lecture notes, (November 11, 1997)

110. Abu-Nimer 2003, 37

111. Abu-Nimer, 2003, 21.

112. See Abdul Aziz Said et. al. 2001, Abu-Nimer, 1996, Abu-Nimer, forthcoming; 1998; Eknath Easwaran, *A Man to Match His Mountains: Badshah Khan: Nonviolent Soldier of Islam* 1984; Khalid Kishtani, *Towards Nonviolence* (Amman: Dar al Karmil, 1984); Rabia Terri Harris "Nonviolence in Islam" in *Subverting Hatred: The Challenge of Nonviolence in Religious Traditions* Daniel L. Smith-Christopher ed. (Cambidge, MA: Boston Research Center for the 21st Century, 1998)95-113, Jawdat Said, *The Doctrine of the First Son of Adan: The Problem of Violence in Islamic Practice.* 5th edition (Damascus: Dar al Fikr, 1993), Chaiwat Satha-Anand, "Core Values for Peacemaking in Islam: The Prophet's Practice as Paradigm". in Elise Boulding eds. *Building Peace in the Middle East: Challenges for the States and Civil Society.* (Boulder Co: Lynne Reinner Publishers. 1993); Maulana Wahiduddin Khan, "Non-Violence and Islam" Paper prepared for the Symposium: *Islam and Peace in the 21st Century*. Washington D.C. (February 6-7, 1998).

113. Jawdat Sa'id. *"Peace- or Nonviolence- in History and with the Prophets"* Paper written for Conference on *Islamic Values for Change* trans. By Dr. Abduhu Hammud al-Sharif, revised with notes by Dr. Karim Crow. (Syria: Bi'r Ajam, Qunaytra, April 3, 1997), 1.

114. Chaiwat Satha-Anand "The Nonviolent Crescent: Eight Thesis on Muslim Nonviolent Action" in Abdul Aziz Said. Et. al., 2001 198.

115. Satha-Anand 2001.

116. Satha-Anand 2001., 199.

117. Satha-Anand 2001., 201-202.

118. See Inamullah Khan "Nuclear War and the Defense of Peace: The Muslim View," in *International Peace Research Newsletter*. Vol. 23, no. 2 (April 1985), 9-11.

119. Satha-Anand 2001, 209.

120. Satha Anand 2001.

121. Maulana Wahiduddin Khan. "Non-Violence and Islam" Paper prepared for the Symposium: *Islam and Peace in the 21st Century*. (Washington D.C. February 6-7, 1998), 1.

122. Wahiduddin Khan 1998.

123. Wahiduddin Khan 1998., 2.

124. Wahiduddin Khan 1998., 5.

125. Wahiduddin Khan 1998., 6.

126. Wahiduddin Khan 1998., 11.

127. Wahiduddin Khan 1998., 13.

128. Jawdat Sa'id 1997, 3

129. Jawdat Sa'id 1997..

130. Jawdat Sa'id 1997., 4.

131. Jawdat Sa'id 1997.

132. Jawdat Sa'id 1997., 7. This Hadith is found in Abu Dawud' Sunan, "Bab al fitan", see *madhab Ibn Adam al-Awwal,* 79-80.

133. Jawdat Sa'id 1997.

134. Jawdat Sa'id 1997., 6.

135. Jawdat Sa'id 1997., 8.

136. Cited in Abu-Nimer 2003, 43.

137. See below.

138. Sunan, Abu Dawood, 4/255.

139. Rabia Terry Harris, "Nonviolence in Islam: The Alternative Community" in Daniel L. Smith-Christopher eds. *Subverting Hatred: The Challenge of Nonviolence in Religious Traditions.* (Boston: Boston Research Center for the 21st Century, 1998), 95-113, 108.

140. This example becomes striking in contrast to the current situation in Afghanistan today, since Pashtuns are an ethnic group mainly living in contemporary Afghanistan. This movement dissolved after the establishment of Pakistan (Ghaffar Khan was opposed to separation of Pakistan as a distinct state and believed that Hindus and Muslims should stay together and coexist peacefully), and many of its member became citizens of Pakistan, although some remained in India. However, considering the violent tendencies of the Muslims in this part of the world make the example of Ghaffar Khan even more interesting of a case study.

141. Robert C. Johansen, "Radical Islam and Nonviolence: A Case Study of Religious Empowerment and Constraint Among Pashtuns" in *Journal of Peace Research* vol. 34, no.1 (1997), 53-71, 57.

142. Johansen 1997, 58.

143. Cited in Johansen 1997.

144. Johansen 1997, 66-67. Emphasis in the original.

145. Since the scope of this study does not allow me to present all the important cases of nonviolence in Islam, I will refrain my self to two examples presented here. Selection of these examples have been subjective, though, I believe they have important relevance to current issues in the Muslim world today. The first example is chosen be-

cause it is relatively a modern example, and a very interesting case. See footnote 142. The aim of the second example is to show that even during the years when Islam was stronger, nonviolence was used as a method of conflict resolution, and it was not confined to men only.

146. M. Elaine Combs-Schilling. "Sacred Refuge: the Power of a Muslim Female Saint" in *Fellowship* Vol. 60 no. 5-6 (May/ June, 1994).

147. Combs-Schilling 1994.

148. Johansen 1997 55.

149. In support of this idea see Ibid., 56, and Esack, chapters 2 and 3 in particular.

150. Samuel Huntington. "If Not Civilization, What?" in *Foreign Affairs*. Vol. 72, no.5 (December-November, 1993), 186-194,192.

151. Kadayifci-Orellana 2003, 61

Chapter 5

Context: History of Effect

The last two chapters introduced texts that make up the discursive space in Islam—the Quran, the *Hadith*, and the *Sunna*—interpretive traditions in the classical and modern Islamic periods and three narratives of peace and war—offensive, defensive, and nonviolent—within this discursive space. This Chapter will discuss the Islamication of conflict in the Palestinian Territories by looking at how and why the Islamic overtones have come to play a central role. This Chapter will also introduce the emerging Islamic narrative within the context of the conflict and assess the reasons behind its emergence.[1]

The previous two chapters will be the points of reference for the following chapters since they were intended to construct the textual background on how the Islamic movements within the Palestinian Territories articulate their narratives. This Chapter will also look at the meaning making processes and show how the religio-cultural, historical, social, and political context effects the interpretation of these texts in the Palestinian case. In this process I will particularly look at how the effective history and the experience of occupation, within the context of transformation of Islamic world in general, limits and also creates the possibilities of what can be claimed as "truth."

The aim here is to show how the contextual factors, such as the religio-cultural traits of the society, and particular historical events have contributed to the meaning making processes of the Palestinian society and how, in return, these meaning making process molded the way the events were interpreted. The underlying assumption here is that, cultural objects (e.g. religious narratives, nationalist-secular or Marxist-leftist ideologies) may be used by various actors to form lines of action (e.g. suicide attacks, demonstrations, etc.), or may enable actors to define certain issues, beliefs, and forms of action as legitimate and others as illegitimate, thus reproducing or challenging social structures and relations of power.[2]

According to this perspective the construction and reconstruction of meaning occurs at the nexus of event and cultural object (e.g. religious values) since there is an interdependent influence of culture and action on social change.[3] There is a co-constructive relationship between events and narratives. The events affect the narratives and narratives affect the way events are perceived or rendered meaningful. As Sahlins and Sewell argue, although events are shaped by some set of ideas, beliefs, or rules embodied in ritual, symbol or speech (such as calling those, who died during clashes with Israelis, martyrs), they also transform these same cultural objects and social structures.[4] Sahlin observe that events disrupt the operative systems of ideas, beliefs, values, roles, and institutional practices in a given society.[5] And in return, the events change the way in which social actors think about the meaning and importance they assign to modes of actions and the rules that govern interaction, groups and their discourses, symbols, and rituals.[6] This perspective is in line with the Gadamerian understanding of how the effective history of the situated actor influences the interpretation process.

Historical events that influence the experience and interpretive process of the individuals (e.g. wars, upheavals, peace agreement, etc.) may generate attention on a particular problem, win credibility for a movements frame (e.g. liberation of the land), encourage new organizations to join a movement (e.g. Hamas and Islamic Jihad), or serve as a model of success that foments expectations among constituents of future movement victories.[7] Therefore we need to ask why narratives change under certain circumstances. How does the effective history, the experience of the affected individuals, or particular historical events change the frames of meaning or undermine various narratives?

Individuals, who are recognized as having legitimacy to narrate, craft new arguments and adopt preexisting ones (such as the narrative of jihad in the classical Islamic tradition), then arrange these arguments in various combinations to pursue their ends. These ends or expected outcomes, might include alternative conceptions of what the debate is about (e.g. liberation, and struggle against Israeli occupation), what the potential consequences are, contesting ideologies (e.g. contesting nationalism, secularism, or Marxism) or the meaning of categories that underline different narratives (e.g. jihad, martyrdom, etc.), challenging or reinforcing collective beliefs, and discrediting rival speakers' arguments by aligning them with illegitimate ideologies or social groups or constructing rivals as public enemies (e.g. Yassin discrediting Arafat's argument on nationalism and secularism as being atheist in a predominantly Muslim society and arguing that they are serving the interests of the Israelis and the USA, thus, are traitors).

These narrators might reject solutions (e.g. the Oslo Peace Process), change goals (e.g. acceptance of possibility of a truce with Israelis), or rework their arguments when they contradict or fail to resonate with their audiences (e.g. nationalization of Islam after realizing that the Palestinian population has lost faith in ideologies such as pan-Arabism or Pan-Islamism and came to the conclusion that only Palestinians themselves can liberate their country).[8] Failure to do so may undermine the legitimacy of their position or impair their capacity to mobilize their audiences.[9]

Therefore, the meaning making process is not a static one but a dynamic one in which the narrators compete with other narrators in the same discursive field for legitimacy. As stated by Ellingson, "[m]eaning is thus constructed through the ongoing process of contestation within a discursive field as speakers jockey to gain legitimacy for their position, the support of targeted audiences, and the opportunity to implement their solutions."[10] In this process when the expected outcomes are not reached, and new events occur, when the solutions fail (e.g failure of the Peace Process) the audiences (e.g. Palestinian population) may alter their interests and beliefs, change the meaning of various actions and identify new ways to achieve their goals and look for ways to achieve them (e.g. increasing support for Islamic solution represented by Hamas, or Islamic Jihad). As Ellingson states, under these conditions:

> [a]s the horizons change, some solutions may be rejected and some diagnoses judged incorrect, while others are accorded greater authority. Speakers respond to the event and altered horizons by reworking their discourses—jettisoning arguments that are untenable, adopting those of their rivals, or crafting new ones that incorporate the event... as the ground from which to asses the viability and legitimacy of old and new arguments— to make them more resonant with their audiences' new horizons of expectations and to help speakers compete more effectively within the field of debate.[11]

As Muslims are struggling to adjust to the "modern" world, they are considering alternative political avenues. Different groups in the Middle East and in the Palestinian Territories in particular are increasingly adopting religious narratives to gain the support of the populations and to come into power. In that respect they attempt to reinstate the *Shariah* into the social and political system. But Islam and *Shariah* mean different things to different people. The disagreement on and vagueness of how to interpret Islamic texts creates a discursive space in which different narratives compete with each other, and also gives the opportunity to different groups to interpret Islam towards their constructed ends. This phenomenon is stated by A. Elizabeth Meyers as follows:

> In many areas, what reinstating the *shariah* might involve in practice is often left vague by the proponents of Islamication when they are seeking popular support. This vagueness is also politically useful, since it allows Muslims who favor Islamication in the abstract to read into shariah [sic] the content they would like them to have.... Governments that adopt programs of Islamication naturally propose ideological formulation that serve to consolidate their power while oppo-

> sition groups appeal to ideological conception of Islamic requirements that justify campaigns to unseat those in power.[12]

Moreover, this struggle for legitimacy is carried to institutional sites where their arguments are introduced to and disseminated among the population. Universities, health institutions, religious sites such as mosques and endowments, various cultural and religious rituals such as prayers, fasting, among others become sites for the actual competition in the society. The rise of Islamic narratives in Palestine gives us the unprecedented opportunity to study how religion (Islam in this particular case) is used to justify policies and action of various groups regarding the Israeli-Palestinian conflict and its resolution, and which one of these narratives is becoming legitimated among the population in the Palestinian Territories. The following chapters, thus, will attempt to show how particular events have shaped the discursive space in Palestine and what events have let to the emergence of Hamas's narrative on peace and war as a powerful challenge to the nationalist one represented by the Palestinian Authority.

Islamication of Israeli-Palestinian Conflict

The Islamic movement in Palestine became an important dimension of Palestinian politics, especially after the mid-70s. As stated eariler, in the beginning of the 20th century, the Muslim world encountered new concepts such as nationalism, democracy, etc. In the Middle East, discourse about nationalism, pan-Arabism, and pan-Islamism came to compete for political legitimacy and power. The remains of this unresolved competition can be seen in many Middle Eastern countries today. The colonial experience and the failed modernization movements seem to have tipped the scale towards an "Islamic solution." Today, Islamic symbols, slogans, and ideology have become important features of Muslim politics. Both governments and opposition groups do not hesitate to resort to Islam to legitimize their discourses and to recruit followers. Appropriation of Islam for their constructed ends resulted in contesting claims over the religion itself.

The emergence of the Israeli state has religious roots, which go back several millennia. According to Jewish tradition, God gave the land of Israel to the Jews. The term Eretz Israel signifies the relationship between Judaism and the land of Israel. And the term "Israelis", which has been used since 1948, invokes biblical references to the ancient Israelis.[13] However, this land has been considered sacred by three religions, namely Judaism, Christianity, and Islam. For the Jews, Jerusalem is the location of the first and second Temples, and the remaining wall of the second temple, called the Western Wall or the Wailing Wall, is the holiest place according to Jewish tradition. Jerusalem is important for Christians, because it is where Jesus Christ is believed to have been first crucified and later resurrected. The path, which he walked before the crucifixion, called "Via Dolorosa" has tremendous meaning for Christians around the world. Jerusalem is also the third most holy place for the Muslims, since it is the first direction to which Muslims were asked to turn to while praying. It is also believed that the Prophet Mohammed made his journey to Heaven from there. Masjid Al-Aqsa and the Dome of the Rock, built at the location where it is believed this journey took place, stands on the same location where Jews believe the Temple of David once was. Not only Jerusalem, but also cities like Bethlehem, Hebron, and Nazareth, among others, have great significance for all Jewish, Christian, and Muslim traditions. Such a small piece of land filled with tremendous meaning for zealots of these religions make this conflict a particularly difficult one.

The roots of the modern conflict, which earned itself a central place in world politics in 1948, can be traced back to the 19th century, to the emergence of Zionist ideology in Europe, and to the first immigration of Jews to the land in the 1880s. The Zionists, invoking the slogan, "A land without people to a people without land," issued the Balfour Declaration in 1917 in England. Jewish immigration increased, particularly during the British mandate. This flow of Jewish immigrants to the region transformed regional politics and gave birth to various movements, one of which was the Arab revolt of 1936-1939.

These first Islamic movements were mostly organized at the grass-roots level, and involved both violent and nonviolent activities. In 1937, a partition plan suggesting a "two state formulation" was proposed but rejected by the Palestinians and Arabs. In 1948 the UN proposed another partition plan but this, too, was rejected. This was followed by violence that became a full-fledged war, which resulted in the establishment of the state of Israel in 1948.

Other significant events of this conflict include the Wars of 1967 and 1973. In 1967 Israel occupied the West Bank, Gaza, the Sinai, and the Golan Heights. Although Israel returned Sinai and Golan Heights, it retained the others. This was a turning point in the history and consciousness of Palestinians. The war of 1973, ending with the victory of Israel, was another traumatic event in Palestinian and Arab history, and had a deep impact, particularly at the societal level, contributing to the proliferation of Islamic alternatives in the Arab/Muslim world. Another crucial point in the history of the conflict was Israel's invasion of Lebanon in 1982, which was received with severe criticism, especially within Israel.

During all this time, the Western media, in particular, reflected these wars as defensive wars for Israel and represented Palestinians, especially PLO, as terrorists, determined to destroy the Jews, who had suffered a great deal, especially during the holocaust. This perception was to change with the Palestinian uprising (*Intifada*) of 1987, which was initially a nonviolent resistance movement. The success of the movement (at least during the first part of it) restored the self-esteem and self-reliance of the Palestinians to a great extent.

Although the Gulf war had a negative impact on Israeli-Palestinian relations, with the involvement of USA, an intense and systematic diplomacy started to resolve the conflict in October 1991. Combined with back channel Oslo meetings, Arafat and Rabin were to shake hands in 1993 in Washington, D.C. This was a crucial step in the eyes of the many, since it symbolized a situation in which both parties recognized each other and gave the impression that they were ready to negotiate. Unfortunately, these hopes did not last too long; Rabin was assassinated and Islamic groups such as Hamas launched terrorist attacks.

The nature of the conflict has shifted over the course of its history. Once a terrorist, Arafat came to be recognized as the "legitimate" leader/representative of the Palestinian people and has been asked to cooperate with Israelis to eliminate the new threat to Israel, "Islamic fundamentalism" or the "Islamic resistance movement." Today, "Islamic fundamentalism," in the form of "terrorism" is recognized as one of the major threats to Israel, both from its Arab citizens and from residents of the Occupied Territories. Therefore, any understanding of Israeli discourses and the Arab-Israeli peace process requires an appreciation of the depth of Israel's concern about the "Islamic fundamentalist" determination to destroy it and the role of Jewish religious parties in the movement to create settlements in the Occupied Territories.[14]

Another important factor to keep in mind is that the main opposition to the PLO and the peace accord comes from the Palestinian Islamic groups such as Islamic Jihad and Hamas.[15] Considered from this perspective, religion becomes an important factor for understanding this particular conflict. The situation of Palestinians after the establishment of the state of Israel and the expansion of Israel into other regions have resulted in a call for Jihad, holy war against "infidels," by numerous Muslim countries, and especially by various Palestinian groups. This shift also has (or should have) a grave impact on the conflict resolution approaches in the region.

In addition to understanding the rise of Islamic movements during the last decades in particular, it is also important to remember that since the establishment of state of Israel has religious roots, the reaction and resistance to it also has had a religious dimension from its very inception. As Musa Budeiri states, the "Islamic movement in Palestine was instrumental from the very beginning of the British Mandate in assimilating a nationalist discourse."[16] The plight of Palestinians after the establishment of the state of Israel in 1948 and the expansion of Israel into other regions in 1967, and 1973, have resulted in the proliferation of various religious groups that base the legitimacy of their actions and policies in the traditions of Islam. However, these religious groups were neither unified amongst themselves, nor were they the only discourse out there. They had to compete with one another, and also with nationalist-secular, Pan-Arabist-Nasserist, and Marxist-communist discourses to earn the support of the masses for legitimacy. The feverish interaction, at times in the form of competition, and at times in the form of cooperation has shaped the development of a unique Palestinian political arena where emancipation of the land has been key to all these narratives.

The first response to Zionism and British occupation dates back to the establishment of Muslim/Christian societies in the summer of 1918, and their first congress in 1919. Although the religious aspect of the conflict was not yet at the center of these meetings and these first responses, the fact that they were led by religious figures indicates the importance of the leader having a religious affiliation. This point becomes clearer if we remember that the first well-known leaders (Izz ad-Din al-Qassam and Hajj Amin al-Husayni) of the Palestinian community had religious backgrounds and gained their legitimacy through their religious affiliation in particular. This is, in itself, enough to illustrate the significant role Islam played in the Palestinian society since the initial years of the conflict (1917-1948).

The current day Islamic movements (which date back to the mid-1970) in the Occupied Territories in large part parallel these earlier Islamic movements.[17] First of all, the current day Islamic movements refer to the examples and heroic figures of the previous movements, and are largely inspired by them. This influence can be seen in Hamas leaflets, which refer to the earlier events and heroes to encourage young Palestinians to join their resistance movement. An example of this is presented in Beverly Milton-Edward's work:[18]

> Our people, on the 19th November 1935, fighter of the jihad, a scholar, a professor and al-Azharite, Sheikh Izz al-Din Qassam wrote a new page in the history of heroism when he fell martyr while fighting the British... al-Qassam was the spark for the revolution of 1936.

In both eras the Islamic movements have not been a unified whole but have consisted of various branches and have been organized around various individuals. The Islamic movements of the 1930s also influence the nature and themes of current day protests and narratives as both sets of movements are organized around the idea that the Palestinians should reassert their Islamic identity and transform it into a struggle against the occupation of their land.[19] There are also significant similarities between the responses of both British and Israeli forces, which react through detention, imprisonment without trial and deportation, and implementing similar emergency regulations.[20]

Although the Palestinian Islamic movement is connected to and related to Islamic revivalist movements responding to colonialism and modernity at the end of the 19th and the beginning of the 20th centuries, the particular circumstances of the Palestinian population contributed to the movements' distinct character.[21] Understanding this relationship is important, since it constitutes one of the major horizons in which the current day Islamic narratives are articulated. The intellectual climate instigated by people like Muhammed Abduh and Rashid Rida have been influential in the transformation of Muslim consciousness, especially in the Middle Eastern context.

Approaches of both Rida and Abduh can be situated within the *Islah* movement that was described in Chapter Three, since they were committed to going back to Islamic principles to find answers to the problems posed by modernity. They wanted to modernize Islam in order to advance the Islamic civilization to where it once was. In that direction, Abduh wanted to combine eastern and western sciences to reform the Muslim world. He stated that Oriental nations have no ambitions, little hope of life, and are willing to accept inferiority, "while the Western nations have the highest and noblest objectives."[22] Rida also believed that the Islamic world needed to adjust to modern times by reviving Islam and the Prophet's tradition, and calling for the unity of the Arabs. In that context he stressed that borrowing from European science and civilization was necessary.

The influence of this first generation of Islamic reformists was not distributed uniformly among the Muslims of the world. Notwithstanding the transformation of their own perspective on how to reform Islam (Rida's ideas, especially, became more conservative in response to the political developments in Egypt during his lifetime), different groups and individuals emphasized different aspects of reformist thought. For example, Hasan al-Banna[23] took a perspective that was to become fundamentalist, while different Palestinian leaders developed other strategies based on the same messages.[24]

Islamic revivalism (especially the ideas of Abduh and Rida) that was taking place in the Muslim world had a deep impact on the Islamic scholars in Palestine and played a crucial role in the evolution of the intellectual horizon of the Palestinian Islamic leadership. This influence was juxtaposed with the effect of Zionist immigration supported by the British mandate based on the Balfour Declaration (1917). Zionist immigration backed by the British led the Arab community and its leaders to articulate various responses. According to Edwards, the response came "through the emergence of Palestinian-Arab nationalism, with its demands for self-determination, as well as political and physical control over the land," and also "through the emergence of a radical modernist Islamic movement championed by Sheikh Izz ad-Din al-Qassam."[25] She states that eventually "a marriage of convenience took place between the forces of *ulema*-based institutional Islam and the emerging nationalism of the region's traditional notable families."[26]

The social organization of Palestinian society at the end of the 19th Century and also at the beginning of 20th Century was based on "traditional community" as described in Chapter Three. In this social organization, Islam played a significant role together with tribal norms that underscored the legitimacy of local authorities. There was a strong tradition of *ulema* and *a'yan* (notables). Within this context, notables, who played a critical political role between the Ottomans and the people within certain limits, emerged as a powerful and influential class. Hourani states that "notables —apart from the *qadis*, in Palestine came from leading wealthy and influential Palestinian families, who controlled the most important political and religious posts in Jerusalem and played critical role as intermediaries between the population and Ottomans."[27] Their importance increased in the 19th century, as the Ottomans introduced new rules and taxes as a part of the Ottoman Reformation (*Tanzimat*), because the local population was in need of the intermediaries, whose cooperation and knowledge was more crucial than before. As Mattar states,

> religious notables, such as *muftis* (Muslim experts who give non-binding legal opinion [*fatwa*] on the Sacred law [*Shariah*] and *naqibs* (doyens of the descendents of the Prophet), generally derive their influence not only from the positions they held, but also from their family's religious reputation, the connection of the local '*ulema*' (Muslim religious experts) with the palace, family wealth (usually based on the custody of waqfs or religious endowments), or a traditional connection with the commercial class.[28]

There were also notables without any religious affiliation who derived their power from a political or military tradition, from the memory of a particular ancestor, or from the control of agricultural production through the possession of a *malikane* (hereditary tax farm).[29]

The politics of notables was present in its purest form in holy cities such as Jerusalem, since Ottoman authority there had to be real because "its legitimacy in the eyes of the Muslim world was bound up with its control of the Holy Cities and pilgrim routes."[30] And in these cities the notables were members of an ancient aristocracy, some of whom were heirs to a long religious and learned tradition.[31] Building coalitions with other notable families, the *ulema*, leaders of the armed forces, as well as organizations in the general population, such as the guilds was a common political behavior in the region.[32] Although this political position of the notables was undermined and narrowed by the British during the colonial period, these notables retained their dominant social and economic status.

Arab nationalism found its fertile soil among the Palestinian notables during the mandate era. As the notables were increasingly being educated in Western-style institutions, were connected to Western intellectual circles, and were reading the developments in Europe, they adopted a more secular and nationalist discourse, although Islamic vocabulary and symbols were still used to communicate their ideas. The idea of nationalism was much less developed among the masses in Palestine. The masses were mostly illiterate and were not affected by the Western cultural and intellectual influence. During the Palestinian revolt of 1936-1939, the leadership, comprised of notables, failed to harness "the idea of nation-state to the demands of the rural masses and channel it into an effective demand for rights from the British authorities."[33] This failure of the notables to achieve legitimacy created the space for religious leaders to gain support.

Another important reason for the Islamic discourse to gain support in this period is that Islamic vocabulary and concepts were familiar to the Palestinian population, and no other vocabulary would be comprehensible to the rural inhabitants of the country. Islam was one of the main constituents of the "horizon" of the Palestinian people, who could make sense of their current situation through the lenses of their religio-cultural language and symbols. Islam was the medium through which this message was made comprehensible to the population, since this language and its symbols were cultural categories familiar to the society. *Imams* (preachers) and clerics became channels for disseminating the ideas of resistance and organizing mass social action as a religious duty via their sermons, especially during Friday prayers. Islam served to mold the ideology of resistance and the experience of first British Mandate and Zionist immigration, then Israeli occupation. In return "Islam" was molded by the experience of the Mandate, immigration, and occupation, as together they constituted the horizons in which the religious texts and doctrines were interpreted.

Since Islamic terminology was the most familiar and comprehensible language for the population, both secularist-nationalist and communist Marxist groups adopted Islamic language when articulating their discourses and mobilizing the masses. They often resorted to religious concepts such as jihad, *Shahid* (martyr), *Fedayeen* (fighter), and *al ard al-Muqaddasa* (holy land) in their rhetoric.[34] The Crusades and the eventual Muslim victory over them became a major symbol of the situation in Palestine. This view is also sported by Budeiri, who states that the Palestinian struggle "against the Jewish colonization was perceived in religious terms and this was their only recognizable *Weltanschauung*."[35]

The First Islamic Leaders in Palestine

Sheikh Izz ad-Din al Qassam

The first Palestinian leaders in the 20th century derived their legitimacy from their religious positions. Within this context, Sheikh Izz ad-Din al Qassam (1882- 1935), who is recognized as the first Palestinian modernist Islamic leader, emerged as a prominent figure, as he was able to empower the peasants through Islamic discourse.[36] In his understanding of Islam he was greatly influenced by the Islamic modernist movement of Muhammed Abduh and Rashid Rida, and believed that the only way for the Muslims to rise again would come through a revival of Islam. Born and raised in a Sufi family in Syria, Al-Qassam harshly criticized the institutional *ulema* for the regression of the Muslim world. He also argued that the *fatwas* issued and appeals raised by them were ineffective strategies to deal with the problems of the Palestinian people, which included colonialism and Zionist immigration

As an alternative strategy, Al-Qassam introduced the idea of armed struggle through jihad to modern Palestinian politics. The Palestinian population perceived itself to be entrapped by Zionist immigration, as the people were dispossessed of their lands which were sold to the Zionists by absentee landowners. However, as a result of the conflict of interest and competition for power among the rival families, Palestinians were unable to form a mass movement to stop these developments. Furthermore, the religious authorities, including the *ulema* and the *muftis*, were "engaged in their own power struggles which they linked to emerging secular-nationalist aspirations."[37]

Al-Qassam, who, as a preacher, traveled to rural Palestinian areas, was able to preach his modernist Islamic message. He was able to empower the much-neglected peasant and the newly emerging urban classes, many of whom were illiterate and dispossessed of their lands. In his unique political and military organization he was able to encourage the participation of the poor, dispossessed, and illiterate. During his activism he introduced Islamic political vocabulary, "with which large numbers were familiar."[38] By doing that he gained popularity among the Palestinian rural population. He also started working with the young Palestinian Muslims at the Muslim Youth Association, and introduced his ideas on responding to colonialism by defending Islam through jihad.

This message was received with favor by the Palestinian youth, whose lives were already marked with increasing violence. In that respect, Edwards cites Police Commissioner Tegard, who notes:

> His interpretation of the parts of the Quran which sanction the use of physical violence, was unorthodox...but his policy of selecting from amongst the poor, ignorant and more violently disposed of the pious, he was able ...to obtain a small following.[39]

Al- Qassam's message was mostly appealing to people who were very poor and frustrated. According to the confession of a member of his group, as reported by the British reports:

> He joined the gang voluntarily, in order to escape from his miserable existence and he spent about a week with them [al-Qassam and his men] in the caves of Jenin hills. The Jews and English eat meat with rice, but we poor people have to be satisfied with a few olives, declared the prisoner at the end of his statement.[40]

By the 1930's al-Qassam had obtained a *fatwa* from a well-recognized Damascus Sheikh that declared that jihad against the British and the Jews was permissible according to Islam. He took this *fatwa* to the mosques and private meetings. Based on the reception of the *fatwa* by the population, he "organized small, secret groups of supporters, who in turn recruited others, many of whom undertook weapons-training."[41] The current day Islamic movements such as Hamas and Islamic Jihad still resort to the same procedure of recruiting supporters, especially into their military wings.

With the hope of putting an end to Islamic activism, the British, killed al-Qassam in an ambush on November 20, 1935. His death ignited such reaction among the Palestinians that British authorities were astounded. Thousands of people, not including the nationalist-secularist camp, were gathered at al-Qassam's funeral. The public was confident that the Palestinian leadership, including the institutional *ulema* was selling land secretly, and it was al-Qassam, who was the "friend of the peasants" who had taught them the "powerful political and religious message to combat these forces of evil."[42]

This outrage alarmed the leaders of the nationalist-secularist movement led by Palestinian notables and created fear in their hearts that their influence over Palestine was waning in the shadow of al-Qassam's death. A year after his death, al-Qassam's message gained renewed popularity, and his death was linked to the demands of different groups within the Palestinian leadership, in an effort to draw the popular support into their own camps. Even the nationalist-secularist movement used al-Qassam's death as a powerful symbol of the struggle for liberation in their nationalist discourses. Budeiri states that "posthumously his martyrdom served to transform Islam being a part of *a'yan* politics to becoming a means of mobilizing popular participation in the struggle for independence."[43] During this period, while even the nationalist secularists were holding memorials for al-Qassam, his own followers went underground and started a series of assassinations of the mandate police and Palestinians accused of selling lands to the Zionists or helping them in any other way. Today, al-Qassam is recognized as one of the first and main heroes of Palestinian liberation struggle. He is considered an inspiration for the Islamic groups, and the Military wing of the Islamic Resistance Movement: Hamas is named after him.[44]

Hajj Amin al-Husayni

Al-Qassam was not the only Islamic leader who adopted an Islamic narrative in response to colonialism and Zionism. Another Islamic leader was Hajj Amin al-Husayni, who was the Mufti of Jerusalem, the most important religious post in Palestine under the mandate system. In contrast to the military orientation of al-Qassam, the Mufti tried to find a political solution to the Palestinian problem without resorting to violence. However, as the riots between 1936 and 1939 spiraled out of control, the Mufti failed to succeed in his attempts.

The Mufti of Jerusalem had been a minor official in Palestine until modern times when the increased status of Jerusalem and of the urban Mufti in general enhanced his importance."[45] During the Ottoman period, the Mufti of Jerusalem was subordinated to the Sheikh al-Islam[46] in Istanbul, and thus restricted in jurisdiction until the British occupation (1917-1918). The High Commissioner during British rule replaced Sheikh al-Islam. The post of Mufti became an important position after this period. The importance of this position came from controlling the *Shariah* courts and the *waqfs*.

Based on the tribal system enhanced by the sources of legitimacy derived from Islam, which gave a special status to the *ulema*, "Muhammed Amin al Husayni was a product of the political and economic environment of the traditional Jerusalem elite."[47] Amin became an important Palestinian leader in the 1920s, which was a result of the way he was able to utilize various traditional mechanisms, together with his good organizational skills and his message, which combined religious and nationalist narratives. Mattar states that "[in Palestine] there was a tradition going back to pre-Islamic Arabia in which a leader was chosen for his descent and ability."[48] Putting this tradition into action, Amin claimed to be a descendant of Arab aristocracy and claimed lineage back to the Prophet. And with a few exceptions, Amin's family, the Husaynis, had held the position of Mufti since the 17th century. His lineage and family tradition of holding the position of Mufti for such a long time formed the basis of Amin's religious and political legitimacy.

Rashid Rida, who was one of the leaders of the movement when Amin was still a student, introduced him to the Islamic revival movement. Rida was a follower of Jamal ad-Din Afghani and Muhammad Abduh, and he would stay with the Husayni family when he visited Jerusalem. Like al-Qassam, Amin was influenced by modernist ideas, however, their strategies differed significantly. Edwards states that the difference between al-Qassam's and Amin's understanding of modernist Islam was a result of the close relations Amin had with Rida, who later on adopted an increasingly conservative approach.[49] Although Amin did not accept many of the modernist ideas, and was not appreciative of the technological and scientific gap between the Zionists and the Palestinians, he believed that the role of Islam was inseparable from politics and that religious symbols should be used to unite the Arabs.

Amin's personal position as a Mufti was strengthened because he established a Muslim orphanage, a museum and a library within the *Haram al-Sharif*, supported schools, planted trees on the *waqf* land, expanded welfare and health clinics, and renovated two important mosques of the *Haram*. He also raised funds from other countries, including Saudi Arabia, Kuwait, Bahrain, India, and Egypt. These actions gave him the opportunity to establish relations with other Muslim leaders in the region, and as a result, he was also recognized among the other Muslims as a leader of the Palestinian people and as a Muslim figure.[50] The establishment of the Supreme Muslim Council (SMC) in 1921, and the appointment of Amin as its president increased Amin's power even more in Palestine, giving him complete control over Muslim affairs. Thus the SMC became an important political and religious institution in Palestinian politics. However, the conflict over power between the notables of Palestine made it impossible for the SMC to function effectively, hindering any unity among the Arabs.

Although Amin was the most powerful Palestinian man in Palestine due to his position as the Mufti, the British ultimately controlled this power. The British bestowed religious (therefore political power) on the al-Husayni family. This was a part of their strategy to build up alliances among the indigenous landowners.[51] Still, due to the power of his religious position and strong extended family, Amin was able to get support, especially until the 1930s.

By the1930s the peasants were increasingly becoming dispossessed, and the Mufti had to find a way to satisfy their demands without creating problem with the British authorities. In an effort to do that, Amin organized a meeting in 1935 where 500 religious notables gathered to discusses issues. This, according to

Edwards, was the first and last attempt by institutional Islam to respond to the political situation in Palestine.[52] One of the reasons for this was that the *ulema* and clerics of institutionalized Islam were losing legitimacy in the eyes of the population as the *ulema* and notables, including Amin's own family, continued to sell land to the Zionists.

The *fatwa* issued after the meeting that "declared brokers of land were enemies of Islam and the Prophet, and they would not be accorded religious rights of burial in Muslim cemeteries, and that they should be neglected and humiliated"[53] went unheeded. Furthermore, in the eyes of the population, institutional Islam also failed to take the lead in the revolts and protests during the period of 1936-1939. Subsequently, institutional Islam, represented particularly by the Mufti, started losing its legitimacy.

According to Budeiri, "Islam was a mobilizing force that the Mufti utilized to highlight the threat to Muslim hegemony in Palestine."[54] Although Islamic vocabulary and symbolism, as cultural resources, were crucial and central for mobilizing the population for resistance, the Islamic movement was not successful in holding the torch of resistance. The Islamic movement, by the end of 1948, had failed to articulate a unified position with a coherent program to lead the resistance. The 1936 revolts led the British to pressure Palestinian institutions. Although the Palestinian masses were critical of his poor work for the Palestinian cause, the British concluded that Amin, as the most powerful man in Palestine, was working against British interests. Amin lost his post by the end of 1937, and by 1948 the leadership of both institutional Islam and revolutionary Islam were all in exile, leaving the Muslim community without leaders. In this vacuum, the Muslim Brotherhood started taking among the Palestinians.

Islamic Movements and Wars Against Israel

War of 1948

According to the 1947 UN partition plan (resolution 181) the British government was to relinquish control of Palestine on May 15, 1948 and Palestine would be partitioned into Arab and Jewish States. This partition plan gave 55 percent of the historic Palestine to the Jews who, at the time, were only 31 percent of the population.[55] Bethlehem and Jerusalem were considered to be separate bodies under international auspices. Palestinians and Arabs rejected the UN offer. Hostilities were soon to turn into a war, in which Jewish forces had the upper hand as they had been organizing an army since 1942, while the Palestinians had been disarmed by the British authorities.[56]

In April 1948, Haganah, together with Irgun and Stern[57] and international Zionist volunteers, launched major operations in Palestine and destroyed Palestinian villages, killing many Palestinian civilians. As a result of these attacks and terrorism, thousands of Palestinians became refugees as their homes were destroyed and they were expelled. The League of Arab States was founded partly to create an Arab policy on Palestine and aid Palestinians in their struggle. Arab armies were sent to combat the Jewish forces; however, the Arab armies did not have the numbers and equipment to fight. Also King Abdullah colluded with the Zionists hoping to annex Transjordan.[58] Eventually, the Arabs and Palestinians lost the war, and the Israeli State was established on May 14, 1948.

The war and the Arab defeat in 1948 were humiliating for the Arab armies. The destruction of Palestinian society, and the dispossession, dispersal, and destitution of Palestinians is called *al-Naqba* (The Catastrophe). The plight of refugees after the *Naqba* caused major trauma in the Palestinian consciousness. 750,000 to 800,000 Palestinians (out of 900,000)[59] in the areas occupied by Israel in 1947-1948 became refugees and fled their homes at the end of the war heading into the West Bank, Gaza and other Arab countries. In the aftermath of *al-Naqba*, the concept of nationalism as it had developed has been instrumental in keeping a sense of Palestinianhood alive, shaping the identity of Palestinians through their culture, historical heritage, and common roots. The miserable conditions of the refugees increased the despair and frustration of the Palestinian community and contributed to more militant attitudes among them.

The war of 1948 also had a devastating impact on the Islamic movement. Its leaders were in exile, the SMC was abolished, and Jordan received the control of the holy sites. At the end of the war Gaza came to be controlled by the Egyptians, and the West Bank came under Jordanian control. Egypt and Jordan had competing interests, and Palestinian territories became an arena for their competition. This led to different evolutions of the Islamic movement in the West Bank and Gaza. Within this context, the Palestinian identity kept the Palestinians united. After the collapse of the Islamic movement led by al-Qassam and Amin, the Muslim Brotherhood became the most important voice for Muslims in Palestine.

The Muslim Brotherhood Society was founded by Hasan al-Banna in March 1928 in Egypt with the goal of building an Islamic society based on *Shariah*. The Brotherhood was concerned about the Palestinian problem since Palestine was considered the third most holy place according to Islam. Influenced by renewalist and fundamentalist tendencies, the Brotherhood was convinced that the current situation in Palestine was a direct result of Muslims abandoning their faith. The political program of the Brotherhood stressed the importance of reviving Islam, going back to its "fundamentals" to save Palestine and to redeem the Muslim world in general. It contended that an Islamic state based on *Shariah* and with the resurrection of the caliphate, must be established, and to do that jihad was a necessary tool. This jihad was not only limited to armed struggle, but included eliminating poverty and illiteracy and constructing a civilization according to Islamic principles.[60]

In 1935 Hasan al-Banna's brother, Abd-al-Rahman al-Banna, met with the Mufti of Jerusalem in Palestine, and in 1936, the Muslim Brotherhood Society carried out propaganda activities on behalf of the Palestinians during the revolts. The society became popular after the Second World War, when it sent representatives to call people to Islam, opposed Zionism, and assisted in the training of Palestinian scouts. Many Muslim Brotherhood Society members joined the Palestinians during the war of 1948. According to Abu-Amr, by 1947 there were about 25 Brotherhood branches in Palestine, and the Mufti of Jerusalem, Hajj Amin al-Husayni was designated as the local Brotherhood leader in Palestine, which also helped its influence spread.[61]

The Brotherhood had played and active role during the 1948 war, although it failed to challenge the Zionist forces and never produced an army. This involvement aided the Brotherhood in becoming popular among the Muslim youth, especially in the refugee camps. By concentrating its activities in the refugee camps, the Brotherhood was able to build a strong base of local and popular support, "harnessing the energy of the young refugees and directing it to an Islamic agenda."[62]

According to the Brotherhood, Palestine is a Muslim land and Israel has no right to occupy any part of it. The Brotherhood also believes that Muslims have a fixed historical and religious right, derived from Islam, which cannot be removed. It also believes that Muslims have this right under the international human rights regime and modern international law. Any political arrangement that leaves Israel intact is considered treason. The Brotherhood rejects recognizing Israel and argues that any recognition as such will legitimize conquering a Muslim land. Establishment of an independent Palestinian state is also rejected on the same grounds. Furthermore, any political or diplomatic solution is also rejected together with the idea of holding an international peace conference, conducting negotiations, and any Israeli-Palestinian dialogue, including contacts with progressive Jews or democratic forces in Israel.[63]

The Brotherhood holds a pan-Islamic perspective and rejects the concept of nationalism, since it implies geographic boundaries, and argues that commitment to land alone is a mistake, thus the question of Palestine must be seen as a religious matter. The issue of Palestine is linked to the wider Muslim community, and the Brotherhood sees itself as part of a world movement. The contention is that Islam provides the Palestinians with the necessary ideological, spiritual and psychological means to resist occupation and defeat Israel.[64] Any Muslim's silence regarding the Palestinian issue is considered to be a grave sin, because the Brotherhood holds that Islam calls for defense when an injustice is done to the Muslims and when a Muslim land is occupied.

Coming from this perspective, the Brotherhood offered an alternative strategy based on the establishment of an Islamic state, society, and regime in one of the neighboring countries. This Islamic entity would serve as the base for the Islamic movement in Palestine. Furthermore, the Brotherhood had more access to financial resources than any other group at the time, and thus had more leverage in the region. The Brotherhood in Gaza, especially, was receiving support from the mother branch in Egypt. Members or sympathizers that were working in Saudi Arabia and the Gulf countries were also sending donations. This added to the strength of the organization after 1948.[65]

The development of the influence of the Muslim Brotherhood Society followed two different routes in the West Bank and Gaza. This was the result of the two different political histories in these regions.

The Tale of Two Palestinian Territories

The Tale of The Gaza Strip:
In the Gaza Strip, the Brotherhood was popular because of its participation in the 1948 war. It was one of the largest organizations. In the 1950s, many politically active people saw the Brotherhood as an important and primary stepping stone, since it represented shared values and ideals.[66] Most of the members were students in the refugee camps. The League of Palestinian Students was formed in Cairo, and was controlled by students who were members of or sympathized with the Brotherhood. According to Abu-Amr, Yasir Arafat was among these sympathizers. [67]

The coup d'état of Nasser in Egypt and his policy of secularization and pan-Arabism impacted the Brotherhood as it generated alternative avenues of political action. Edwards states that Nasser's narrative was received with much excitement among the Palestinians, who believed that the unified Arab forces would deliver their land back.[68] However, Nasser's regime crippled the Brotherhood's activities and pushed it underground. In this period the Brotherhood's leadership in Egypt opposed the endorsement of the Evacuation Treaty of 1954 between Egypt and Britain. This was followed by an attempt on Nasser's life, and the Brotherhood was accused of being an accomplice. This resulted the Brotherhood being banned in both Egypt and Gaza, and hence its activities became more secretive.

This did not stop political activities of the Brotherhood. The Brotherhood participated in mass demonstrations protesting a proposed plan to resettle Palestinian refugees from the Gaza Strip in the Sinai Desert in 1955. In 1956, it participated in the opposition to the Israeli occupation of Gaza, and in 1957, it took part in the nationalist demonstration rejecting a plan to internationalize the Gaza Strip. But difficulties in conducting underground activities resulted in the decrease of its influence. When Israel occupied the Gaza Strip for the first time, acting on the support of France and Britain during the Suez crisis from October 31, 1956 to March 17, 1957, Palestinians resorted to passive resistance and civil disobedience. Strikes and mass demonstrations asking for the withdrawal of the Israelis were organized. The Muslim Brotherhood joined the resistance through leaflets, but rejected armed resistance. The Brotherhood did not have much ability to mobilize activities among the refugees and local populations and had to conduct their activities from underground cells since Nasser had weakened it.[69]

In addition to the difficulties of being an underground organization, the founding of the Fatah movement also undermined The Brotherhood's success. The founders, organizers, and leaders of Fatah were Gaza Strip university activists studying in Egypt. Fatah became an important factor, especially after the Arab defeat in 1967.[70] Al-Fatah, the inverse Arabic acronym for Harakat al-Tahrir al-Watani al-Filistin (the Palestine National Liberation Movement), also means conquest, and refers to the "opening" or Islamication and Arabization of the Middle East.[71]

Fatah differed from the Brotherhood with its emphasis on Palestine, believing that only the Palestinians themselves could resolve the Palestinian problem. This reversed both the pan-Islamist and pan-Arabist discourses. Many of the well-known Palestinian figures who started out in the Brotherhood later joined this new movement and Fatah became the main challenge to the Brotherhood. The establishment of the Palestinian Liberation Organization (PLO) by Nasser in 1964 was the final blow for the Brotherhood as the PLO was now the main organization in Palestinian politics. By 1967 the Brotherhood had become ineffective, and thus the Islamic movement went silent.

The Tale of The West Bank:

The Brotherhood had a much different story in the West Bank. The West Bank was annexed to Jordan in 1950. Here, the Brotherhood was permitted to pursue its activities relatively freely. These activities included the publication and distribution of Islamic literature and the conduct of social activities. Leaders of the Brotherhood in Jordan were critical of the ties between the West and Jordan, yet they gave their support to the Jordanian king in confrontations with other local political forces.

In the West Bank the notables retained their important position, and the competition between them extended to Muslim institutions that were under Jordanian control, and undermining Palestinian unity in the face of colonialism and Zionism. Institutional Islam underwent a major transformation, as all religious institutions were placed under the Ministry of Religious Affairs in Jordan. The Jordanians appointed a new Mufti. And the Muslim and waqf authorities were no longer unified, as they were divided among Egypt, Jordan, and Israel. This made institutional Islam function inadequately.

Under these circumstances, the Muslim Brotherhood in the West Bank flourished, as it did not challenge the Jordanian monarchy. The Brotherhood distanced itself from the nationalist agenda, and adopted an anti-imperialist and pro-*Shariah* narrative that was compatible with Jordanian rule. It focused on education and preaching to redeem the Muslim community, and concentrated on the internal renewal of Palestinian society through Islam.

The Brotherhood also did not support an armed struggle to liberate Palestine. Call for an armed jihad was postponed until the Islamic transformation of Palestinian society was completed. The Brotherhood's inaction was seen as a failure. This failure to challenge the Israeli occupation has been subject to various criticisms.[72]

The Brotherhood objected to armed struggle on two grounds. First, the Brotherhood had been preoccupied with preparing a new generation capable of fighting the enemy. Secondly, the public endorsement of armed struggle would give Israeli authorities a pretext to strike at the Brotherhood prematurely. Nevertheless, the pressure resulted in a gradual change in the Brotherhood's position on occupation. In this period, anti-nationalist and pan-Islamic sentiments were not attractive to Palestinians who were feeling oppressed by the Jordanian authorities. Slogans had become more militant and contained less religious appeals and references.[73] Although nationalism was rejected on the basis of primacy of religious affiliation, this development shows that a combination of religion and nationalism seemed to be more appealing.

War of 1967

The Six Day war in June 1967 is another turning point in modern Palestinian history as following the war Israel occupied the West Bank, Gaza, the Sinai and the Golan Heights. Although Israel has returned the Sinai and the Golan Heights, it continues to occupy the West Bank and Gaza to this day, despite UN Resolution 242, adopted on November 22, 1967. This was the beginning of the end for pan-Arabism and other secular ideologies in the Arab world. The defeat of 1967 may have led to the rise of Islamic movements in Arab/Muslim countries, but it resulted in the emergence of nationalist and leftist-Marxist narratives among the Palestinians.

For Arab states Palestine was important as a way of achieving legitimacy in the region and as a way of controlling the PLO and its potential threat to their own systems. The 1967 defeat was a blow to the Arab regimes and undermined their legitimacy in the eyes of their populations. This legitimacy crisis gave Islamic groups in the Arab countries other then Palestine the opportunity to raise their voices and gain more legitimacy.

In response to the defeat, Islamists in other Arab countries looked for solace in Islam and pressed the slogan "Islam is the solution." Islamic movements perceived this as the defeat of the secular, nationalist, and socialist ideas. This defeat allowed an increase in the influence of the conservatives, who had an Islamic orientation. This defeat was considered to be a "divine revenge" by the Brotherhood, because the struggle was missing the religious commitment, and had failed to follow divine laws. During the conflict Islamic leaders from other countries called for support from outside Palestine.

The war of 1967 was colored by Islamic sentimentality from the beginning. The Sheikh of al Azhar University in Egypt issued a *fatwa* in the wake of the war, calling for jihad to liberate usurped Palestine. Such an Islamicated atmosphere drove the political leaders towards adopting a more religious rhetoric. For example, even the King of Saudi Arabia called out "To jihad citizens! Nation of Muhammed and Islamic peoples."[74] However, the voices of external Islamic actors faded soon after the end of the war, since Jerusalem, and thus Muslim holy places, were not only occupied, but *de facto* annexed by the Zionist entity. The defeat was hard to swallow and the shock was to stay with Muslims for a long time. To develop a policy on Palestine and Muslim holy places, in particular, the World Islamic Conference convened in Amman in September 1967, and called to "save" the holy places. However, once again, its members failed to unite, and while the call for jihad was made to all Muslim states, no one rushed to volunteer another confrontation with Israel.

The defeat had different consequences for the Palestinians than their Arab brothers. The defeat of the 1967 war resulted in the Palestinians losing faith in the Arabs and focusing on national struggle and on clandestine military organizations. It accelerated the development of the Palestinian national movement independent from the Arab governments' control. In Palestine, nationalism rather than Islam became the dominant narrative. The Palestinian left and groups promoting a secular Marxist ideology called for armed struggle gained support. These groups were in favor of separating politics and religion, and this presented a cultural dilemma for the Palestinians. One thing was clear for the Palestinians: Israel's overwhelming military power could not be defeated by conventional war. They had to find an alternative way to combat the enemy.

Palestinians were not only disappointed in the Arab regimes but also the PLO, which was founded in 1964 and was recognized by the Arab League. A popular armed struggle was not part of the PLO's political program. Instead it had assembled and stationed a conventionally trained and equipped army in Egypt, Syria, and Iraq.[75] During the war the PLO failed to match its verbal extremism with military success. The Palestinian social and political fabric was weak and divided, the local elites were not able to resolve their internal conflict and power struggles, and the Arab world was ideologically and organizationally fragmented. Struggle for legitimacy and recognition as the true representatives of the people was paramount, as various commando groups had to compete with local leaders in the Occupied Territories. The political attitude that emerged within this chaotic political atmosphere of clashes and competitions reflected the social divisions and fragmented authority in Palestinian society.

Together with other groups, Islamic groups were affected by this unstable political arena and had to adopt strategies to adjust to the realities on the ground. The obstacles in the pre-1967 war had weakened the organizational base in Gaza, and the policies that accommodated Jordanian rule undermined the popular support in the West Bank. Furthermore, the Muslim Brotherhood failed to participate in the war. Yet, the defeat opened new avenues for addressing the Palestinian struggle for self-determination. The option of armed struggle based on *fedayeen* fighting assumed significant legitimacy and there was a rapid rise in the status of the national movement.[76] In the aftermath of the 1967 war, the liberation struggle in Palestine increasingly took a secular position and was influenced by Marxist ideologies and liberation movements in places like Latin America, among others. However, Islam had not totally disappeared.

Within the context of the post-1967 war period, Fatah emerged as the most popular Palestinian group. Some of the reasons for this were its broad nationalist appeal that could encompass supporters and recruits from nearly all ideological perspectives, and the simplicity of its political goals. Fatah insisted that the liberation of Palestine was primarily a Palestinian affair and no other state could be entrusted with it. At best, other Arab regimes could provide aid and protection, and if necessary, conventional armies.

Although Fatah does not claim to be an Islamic movement, and in fact, is secular, nearly all of Fatah's leaders are Sunni Muslim Palestinians. The language of Fatah is filled with Islamic images and vocabulary and some of its most influential leaders are deeply religious. The Islamic language and symbolism not only appeal to the majority of Palestinians, who are Muslims, but also to the sensibilities of Fatah's religiously oriented supporters, such as the rulers of Saudi Arabia and Kuwait.[77]

Islamic Movement after 1967

The grave impact of the occupation was felt in every aspect of life in the Palestinian Territories. It had an impact not only on the political, but also on the economic, social, and cultural aspects of life, as employment shifted from the agricultural realm to the Israeli labor market. The Islamic movement had to come to terms with this new reality on the ground. However, it was unable to respond initially as the occupation and the changes it brought to Palestinian society outraged the movement. Now the holy places, such as the Dome of the Rock and al-Aqsa mosque, were under the control of the Israelis. The Israeli authorities now curtailed Islamic activities. The borders were closed therefore it was harder for Islamic organizations to keep contact with their bases outside the Territories.

In this period, Sheikh Hamed as-Saqeh, who was the president of the *Shariah* court and chief *qadi* in Jerusalem, initiated a Palestinian Islamic protest. He gathered various notables to discuss how to respond to the annexation and the occupation. The *fatwa* issued after this meeting was perceived as furthering only the Jordanian interests rather than the Palestinians. After this meeting, the Muslim population hostile to Jordanian interests moved towards supporting radical secular nationalists. The leadership of the Islamic movement of as-Saqeh, based on the old notable system, aligned with the Jordanians failed, to get the support of the Palestinian population.

These developments rendered Palestinization of the Islamic movement inevitable in Palestine. Occupation led to new interpretations of various chapters of the Quran that dealt with Jewish enmity during the time of the Prophet and reignited the Crusades and pseudo-*futuh* literature.[78] Thus, occupation of Palestinian lands was not seen as just a military or political act, but as a continuation of a religious conflict between the Jewish and Muslim peoples. Therefore, the religious character of this conflict was emphasized in a new manner. As Edwards states, this conflict, "illustrated in the chapters of the Quran and the stories of the *Hadith* (sayings of the Prophet), took on a fresh perspective in the light of perceived defeat as the Jews occupied the Islamic holy places."[79] This transformation of the narrative led to the emergence of a specific Islamic interpretation of the conflict. In support of this view, Edwards cites Dr. Ali Sharabat, who states:

> The war was a point of breakthrough where most Palestinians Muslims were concerned. It signified an end to the slogans, ideologies and end to the Arab regimes. Also with the 1967 war and the occupation of Jerusalem and al-Aqsa an awakening from this took place. Eventually a new strategy arose, an understanding which was completely different from the past thoughts and actions… Muslims realized after 1967 that they could no longer rely on others to provide solutions.[80]

Palestinian *fedayeen* (those who sacrifice themselves and die for the national cause) forces emerged in Gaza. These militants took possession of the ammunition left behind as the Egyptian armies left Gaza and started using it against the Israelis. The Gazan *fedayeen* were modern revolutionary fighters for national liberation, rather than religious salvation.[81] They included both male and female figures, which were celebrated as heroes in Palestinian society. The *fedayeen* were inspired heavily by the guerilla movements in Vietnam, China, and Latin America.[82]

The Islamic movement was quick to adopt these *fedayeen,* and glorify their acts as heroic, and call those who died in the process "martyrs" thus attributing a religious character and legitimacy, although the movement was unable to offer them an alternative path. However, the Israel launched military attacks on the *fedayeen* and transferred hundreds of thousands of them to detention camps. All political activity was restricted and the Israelis took control of municipal services. Thus, the Palestinian national struggle was crushed. The political vacuum created by the deportation of the nationalist movement created the needed space for the Islamic movement to reemerge. This reemergence began in 1973-74, after the next war with Israel.

War of 1973

In 1973 Egyptian and Syrian armies launched a successful attack on Israel and Israel was able to turn things around only after a massive airlift of advanced military equipment from the United States.[83] Even though it was victorious at the end, this war was costly for Israel and shattered its illusion that the Israeli military was invincible. The war of 1973 was particularly important for the Islamic movement in Palestine, as it had added to the strength of the religious camp. The initial victory in the war quickly acquired a religious meaning. The victory was attributed to the faith of the troops and the power of Islamic doctrine. A religious sentiment was strongly emphasized. Various religious symbols were used to highlight the power of Islam. One of these was the month that the war took place. The war took place during Ramadan, the Islamic holy month. The code name given to the war was *Badr*, which referred to the victorious *Battle of Badr* that was led by the Prophet Muhammad.

The year 1973 was also the year when the oil revolution took place in the Arab world that increased the wealth of the region. The Islamic movements were able to benefit from this wealth. By that time, various militant groups had been founded and had become active. This increased the awareness of religious issues among the public. With this impetus, the Islamic movement was able to reorganize itself in the mid-1970s.

In 1974, the Arab summit in Rabat recognized the PLO as the only legitimate representative of the Palestinian people. Although the PLO was a secular movement, the dominant political faction within the PLO, as stated previously, was Fatah, "which attracted the largest number of Palestinians into its ranks" and had a markedly Islamic political discourse.[84] As Budeiri suggests, one can argue that this was what enabled Fatah to draw support from every sector of the community as it continued to engage in a popular narrative that was filled with religious imagery and well-entrenched within the framework of an Islamic-oriented value system.[85]

In this period, two major Islamic movements with distinct focuses and strategies emerged. These were the *Mujama* and the *Islamic Jihad* groups. The charismatic leadership of Sheikh Yassin headed the Mujama in Gaza. Unlike the previous two Islamic leaders –Amin and al Qassam, who both studied at al Azhar University in Egypt and came from families with a religious tradition Yassin did not have formal religious training. Furthermore, he lived in a small, conservative and religious village as a refugee. He did not preach the role of Islam in politics. Instead, he chose to involve himself with the society he lived in and used the dynamic of the spoken word in the mosque and in the sermon.[86] He emphasized serving the community rather then claiming political status, and in 1973 he formed a small welfare and charity-based society called Mujama (Islamic Congress).

Mujama began its operations in institutions that were neglected by the nationalist movement and thus, did not challenge the nationalists. It began to organize a network of welfare and education services, established small medical and dental clinics in the refugee camps, and began running kindergartens and classes on the Quran and the *Hadith* in the mosques. Mujama adopted some of the reformist and gradualist principles of the Muslim Brotherhood movement. However, Mujama did not distinguish itself through its anti-occupational activity, and its political energies were devoted to defeating the enemy within, the PLO, and emphasizing that the only way to liberation was through establishing an Islamic state.[87] Furthermore Palestinian society had become increasingly secular and nationalist, especially in the West Bank in the 1970s and the beginning of the 1980s.

The Israeli authorities supported the Mujama as a way to counteract the nationalist movement, borrowing from the British the policy of "divide and rule." "By nurturing the conservative and traditional trend, the Israeli authorities hoped to diminish the progressive and radical appeal of the movement for national liberation."[88] However, in about a decade, the Islamic movement in Palestine was to become the major challenge and the biggest threat to Israeli security. One of the contributing factors to this was Israel's invasion of Lebanon and ousting of the PLO leaders in 1982, and the massacres of Sabra and Shatilla, which brought the end of the nationalist movement.

The failed experience of pan-Islamism, pan-Arabism and the appeal of self-reliance affected the Islamic movement that emerged in the 1970s. The Palestinian population was not impressed by these grand ideologies anymore and was convinced that the Palestinians themselves could only resolve the Palestinian problem. Thus, they preferred to direct their political energies to ending the Israeli occupation, rather than to re-Islamicating their own societies. For that reason the new Islamic movement had to incorporate Islamic values with nationalist elements. This led to the transformation of Islamic movement.

In the early 1980s, the Palestinian Islamic Jihad (consisting of a number of different organizations)[89] put forth the notion of an Islamic movement committed to the waging of jihad against the Israelis. The founding of the Islamic Jihad movement was led by Fathi Shiqaqi, who was a member of the Brotherhood, in the late 1970s. By this time, Shiqaqi had concluded that the Brotherhood was "suffering from a serious crisis reflected primarily in its neglect of the national question, its failure to offer alternative priorities, and its evasion of the real concerns and central challenges facing the nation."[90] In addition to that, the Brotherhood was lacking a methodology in their approach to Islam. Furthermore, Shiqaqi also stated that "most of the Palestinian national forces kept Islam (as culture, identity, and ideology) at a distance from the conflict and did not give it any place in their program for struggle and their daily life."[91]

The Islamic Jihad was thus founded as a solution to the problematic of religion and the homeland, of Arabism and Islam. As Shallah states, this problematic was about "nationalists (*wataniyyun*) without Islam and Islamists without Palestine."[92] In order to change this situation, Islamic Jihad offered a revolutionary Islamic response to the question of Palestine with the slogan "Islam, Jihad, and Palestine —Islam as the point of departure, jihad as the means, and Palestine as the object of liberation."[93] This politicized the conflict in a way not seen since the days of al-Qassam.[94]

The novel approach of this Islamic movement was to put Palestine first in the debate about political Islam in the Occupied Territories. Contrary to the previous Islamic movements, including the Mujama, ending the occupation was perceived to be the prerequisite for the transformation of society and rise of Islam. Thus, it was a revolutionary and anti-establishment movement aimed at putting an end to Israeli rule. Its leaders were Islamic intellectuals (who were influenced by al-Afghani, Abduh, Rida, al-Banna, Qutb, Khomeini, Ali Shariati, Mawdudi, and later Turabi, and Ghannouchi, al-Qardawi, among others), who appropriated nationalistic sentiments and used them to support their political call for liberation. They held the view that:

> It is futile for the Islamists to dream of complete independence or a comprehensive civilisational revival, while the center of colonial operation remains fully entrenched, fully fortified and fully equipped in Palestine to do what pleases in our land, and hell-bent on imposing 'the Israel era' in our region.[95]

Although Palestine was the primary issue for the Islamic Jihad movement, its connection to the wider Islamic world was strongly emphasized, as liberation of Palestine was viewed as a test for the Muslim community in general. They used mosques, schools, and universities to gain popular support and mobilize the population by stressing the mobilizational sides of Islamic worship and rites. Similar to the previous movements, the Islamic Jihad movement held the position that Palestine was an Islamic land usurped by infidel rulers. To ignore the Palestinian problem was to ignore the call to jihad as a religious obligation, emphasizing the pivotal place of Palestine in the greater liberation struggle of Islam in the modern era. To the members of Islamic Jihad, the Palestine question and struggle were questions of "right and wrong."[96] Therefore they stated that:

> What is now taking place in the Holy land is not just a battle for the Palestinian people alone. It is the battle for Islam, a battle for the future of the entire *Ummah*. It is a battle against the forces of arrogance— against the colonial hegemony over our world.[97]

Other significant events that took place in the Islamic world at the end of the 1970, and the beginning of the 1980s were also influential in the articulation of the new Islamic movement in Palestine and provided the movement with moral, psychological, and political support. One of these significant events was the Iranian revolution of 1979. The Islamic Jihad movement embraced the Iranian revolution as a model for Palestinian liberation, and the revolution became a symbol for the possibility of overthrowing strong regimes with the support of the population. Iran, similar to Israel, was receiving large amounts of American aid and was a close ally of the United States. If the Iranian Shah could be overthrown, maybe Israel could be next. However, other Islamic groups, such as Mujama, did not accept the Iranian model because of its Shi'a character. Shallah argues that although the confrontation between Islamic Jihad and other Islamic groups such as the Brotherhood and Mujama seemed to focus on support of the Islamic Revolution in Iran, the real issue underlying it was the armed struggle.[98]

Other significant events of this era that affected the Islamic movement include the rise of Islamic influence in various countries such as Sudan, Tunisia, and Algeria. Also the PLO was now in exile in Tunisia, disconnected from the realities and developments in the Occupied Territories. The failure of the PLO to deliver its promised objectives, the expulsion of PLO forces from Lebanon in 1982, the frequent changes of its political positions, and the corruption and inefficiency attributed to its institutions and leaders affected the image of the PLO. This gave the political space for other groups to emerge. The loss of PLO bases in Jordan and Lebanon increased the visibility of the Islamic movement in the Occupied Territories. Internal disputes within the PLO were also undermining the authority and legitimacy of the movement, especially Fatah. Taking advantage of this unstable political atmosphere, various groups were trying to establish alliances with others. For example the Muslim Brotherhood established an alliance with Fatah, and this maneuver gave them the opportunity to disseminate the Islamic message to wider audiences, particularly in the universities.

The rise of Islamic resistance in southern Lebanon and Islamic militant groups, such as Hizbullah, following Israel's invasion in 1982, also was an influential factor in the emergence of the Islamic movement in Palestine. Another crucial factor in the rise of the influence of Islamic movements in the Occupied Territories is that the movements have been able to rely on the support of broad segments of the society. Israel, as a foreign and unjust occupier is seen as a threat both to the Arab identity and to its Islamic character. Islamic Jihad, in particular, was able to manipulate these sentiments and use the political vacuum created by the collapse of the nationalist movement to instigate a movement that was to become Israel's biggest headache.

First Intifada

Although the Islamic Movement has grown steadily since the mid-seventies, it was with *Intifada* (literally meaning "shaking off") in December 1987 that it gained significant importance and became a major force in the balance of power in the Palestinian society. The outbreak of *Intifada* came as a surprise to everyone. "Yet in addition to reflecting a basic and instinctive rejection of Israeli military rule, the *Intifada* reflected a complex rubric of changing attitudes towards the prevailing potential order outside as well as within Israeli occupied territories."[99] The initial two years of the *Intifada* were based on predominantly nonviolent strategies that included demonstrations, obstruction of Israeli settlement policy, refusal to cooperate, psychological annoyance and irritation of Israelis, boycotts, strikes, solidarity and support, developing alternative institutions, and civil disobedience. Also during these initial years, children would take the streets and throw stones.

In December 1987, triggered after a traffic accident in which an Israeli vehicle killed Gazan laborers, hundreds of thousands of Palestinians took to the streets in Gaza and soon were joined by the Palestinians in the West Bank. However, the seeds of *Intifada* were sown several years before its December date. In the aftermath of the invasion of South Lebanon (1982) by Israel, both Israelis and Palestinians realized that the military option was not effective. Besides, the accord of 1985 between Arafat and King Hussein of Jordan did not produce any new hope in regards to resolving the conflict and ending the Israeli occupation. At the Arab Summit, held in Amman in 1987, the Palestinian problem was given very low priority, and Arafat was not received with a Head of State status.[100] In fact, Arafat was not even invited to the Summit by King Hussein. The feeling that only Palestinians could resolve their problems was strengthened once more.

The frustration of the Palestinian society is best reflected by Rashad al-Shawwa in an interview broadcast on Israeli radio on December 10, 1987 (the third day of *Intifada*):

> One must expect these things after twenty years of debilitating occupation. People have lost hope. They are frustrated and don't know what to do. They have given up hoping that Israel will give them their rights. The Arab states are unable to do anything, and they feel that the PLO, which is their representative, also has failed.[101]

In addition to these developments, a strong popular movement emerged in the 1970s with the involvement of all Palestinian political factions and with the creation of many institutions and organizations working on health, women, agriculture, and other professions.[102] Alternative structures of charitable societies, professional associations, and mass organizations were developing since mid-1970s; and these organizations formed the basis for organizing the *Intifada*. These institutions and organizations mobilized all sectors of Palestinian society and cultivated values of solidarity, service and resistance.[103]

Various organizations, including the Center for the Study of Nonviolence in Jerusalem, started by a Palestinian American named Mubarak Awad, and the Committee Against the Iron Fist Policy led by both Palestinian and Israeli activist were training and organizing the Palestinian population and disseminating the ideas of scholars and activists of nonviolence such as Gene Sharp, Gandhi, and Martin Luther King, Jr.. However, not only nonviolent organization for the *Intifada* precipitated the uprising. Military operations undertaken by Islamic Jihad also served to pave the road to it.[104]

Eighteen months before the *Intifada*, Islamic Jihad launched a series of daring attacks on Jewish targets, first in Gaza later on in the West Bank. This was a crucial move on the part of Islamic Jihad since until then it had not yet gained wide support from the population and was competing with other groups, especially with Mujama, for popularity.

These military operations were strongly felt in Israel, and the Israeli authorities promptly reacted by arresting more than fifty members of Islamic Jihad. But six of the arrested Jihad members were astonishingly able to escape from Israeli prisons. This escape not only astounded the Israelis but also indicated the level of sophistication and organizational skills of Islamic Jihad.[105] It was believed that the population protected the escapees, as Israeli authorities were never able to recapture them.

These attacks and the spectacular escape invigorated incredible popular support among the Palestinians, instigated legends of valor, set off pride, courage, and of spirit of self-sacrifice. Of particular novelty, Islamic Jihad promoted sacrificing one's own life for "the cause of Palestine, thus Islam" and encouraged to take significant risks without any fear. The attacks and the targets they chose reflected the religious nature of the conflict, strong belief in jihad, the history of hostility, and the kindled the specter of al Qassam. Like those, who died before the *Intifada*, those who died in these operations during the *Intifada* were immediately declared martyrs.

Within weeks, a massive coordination effort produced an organized underground and a unified leadership that steered the entire community to nonviolent actions through weekly or biweekly fliers and communiqués for the next two years. The national movement, including groups like Fatah, PFLP (Popular Front for Liberation of Palestine, and DFLP (Democratic Front for the Liberation of Palestine, and CP (The Communist Party) was quick to organize under the United National Leadership of the Uprising (UNLU), which was backed by the PLO. A coherent Islamic response came later and Islamic influence was rather unclear in the beginning of the uprising, although both Islamic Jihad and Hamas claimed the credit. Indeed, since religion was an integral aspect of the Palestinian society, demonstrations had a religious dimension. Funerals, filled with religious sentiment, played an important role in the uprising.

In the first few months of the uprising, Islamic Jihad co-operated with nationalist groups to mobilize the people and organize the mass movement. Israeli authorities responded by deporting the leaders of Islamic Jihad and the nationalists. This gave the opportunity for the Islamic Resistant Movement (*Harakat al-Muqawama al-Islamiyya*) also known as Hamas, to emerge as the greatest challenge to both Israeli occupation and to the hegemony of the secular-nationalist movement. Hamas was run by the same leadership of the Mujama and emerged as an activist Islamic organization that publicly challenged the authority of the national movement to win popular support.

Mosques played an important role in organizing and directing the *Intifada* and mobilizing the people. Journalists and policy makers rushed to conclude that *Intifada* was an Islamic revolution.[106] Israeli authorities started cutting the wires of mosque speakers and arresting local preachers; other cases of disregard for traditional Islamic practice were also recorded.[107] However, the Islamic political structure was far from being united. Different political actors attempted to seize this opportunity to capitalize on the unprecedented internal political changes.

These attempts reflected the power struggles within Palestinian society, the need for internal democratization, an increase in the acknowledgment of the populist sentiment, and the decline of the elitist approach to politics.[108]

Islam played a significant role during the *Intifada*, including the nonviolent phase of the movement. [109] During the initial years of the *Intifada*, various Islamic structures, symbols, customs, rituals and attitudes were utilized by a predominantly Muslim society. Indeed, Islam both as a religion and a cultural trait plays an important role in the Palestinian society. For instance, mosques provided actual and symbolic focal points, being the only natural community gathering places in most Muslim villages and towns. The mosque was also used as a symbol of religious unity among Muslims.[110] Besides giving inner strength to Palestinians to resist, the Islamic emphasis on sacrifice, sharing resources and helping each other have characterized the *Intifada*. As Abu-Nimer states, some Palestinians viewed *Intifada* as an extension of Ramadan (the holy month of Islam where the Muslims are required to fast). Furthermore, *shahid*, the witness or martyr, derived from Islam, became one of the central symbols, and most Palestinians regardless of their religious creed adopted the term *shahid* for those who were killed during the *Intifada*.[111] Abu-Nimer argues that one of the reasons the *Intifada* functioned successfully was its Islamicate context.[112] Observing that the Palestinian society incorporates Islamic values into the processes of consensus in local and family leadership and in dispute settlement, he argues that the leadership of the *Intifada* can be seen as an extension and development of this popular tendency in Islamicate societies.[113] He states that it was this network of leadership that enabled to organize the complex resistance movement. In addition to these structural and institutional contributions of Islam, various Islamic values and principles have also underlined *Intifada*. Some of these values include forgiveness, steadfastness, commitment and discipline, unity and solidarity.[114]

Revival of Islamic values during the *Intifada* did not mean, however, that support for Hamas and Islamic Jihad also increased. On the contrary, these Islamic groups seized that opportunity. The Hamas leadership recognized the political significance of directing strikes and started arranging localized actions via publishing leaflets. Hamas strategy was to undermine the PLO's credibility, claiming to be the sole legitimate representative of the Palestinian people. This created conflict between Hamas and UNLU, but UNLU was careful to avoid any internal confrontation and conflict, and sought to contain rather then confront opposition. In the final resort, the strength of the *Intifada* was its ability to unite all Palestinians around one issue: to end the occupation.

Intifada was costly not only for the Israelis but also for the Palestinians. More then 1,100 Palestinians were killed; more then 100,000 wounded; 15,000 were held in detention without charge or trial for at least 6 months; 300 Palestinian homes were demolished and 2,000 people were left homeless as a result.[115] By 1990, Israeli repression led to the transformation of the nonviolent tone of the movement. Especially Islamic Jihad and Hamas started advocating a limited return to violence and conducted a number of attacks on Israelis. The internal political conflict and power-struggles made it impossible for the leadership to control the Palestinians. The lack of effective international response, especially after PLO's perceived support for Saddam Hussein, also undermined the non-violent strategies of the movement.

Nevertheless, *Intifada* did have a significant impact. It not only restored the self-esteem to the Palestinians, but also managed to make the Israelis more aware of the consequences of occupation. The *Intifada* also mobilized international support, and Israeli left wing political activists and peace activists, to take action against the Israeli occupation in West Bank and Gaza. *Intifada* was an attack against the Israeli consciousness, by reversing the victim-aggressor perceptions. Until then Palestinians were depicted as aggressors, as terrorists, determined to eliminate Jews. The obvious power disparity between the Israeli army and the dispossessed Palestinians living under miserable conditions not only unnerved the international community, but also the Israelis. But this was not enough to end the Israeli military occupation, as Israel limited its exposure by rotating its soldiers and legitimized violence by nurturing the negative image of the "Palestinian" as a backward, uncivilized terrorist, enemy of the Jews. To maintain the dehumanization of the "other/Palestinian," Israel limited contacts between the Israeli citizens and Palestinians.

Hamas found support form a wide range of groups in the Palestinian society. These included young Islamist activists, those who were disillusioned with the PLO, many people from the refugee camps, middle classes, professional and white-collar workers. "Of the young men who flocked to its ranks, many had refugee backgrounds and saw an opportunity for self-identity and esteem *vis-à-vis* the rest of society through their association with this religious organization which put a mark of holiness on them."[116]

Hamas was able to act relatively freely, especially in the first months of the uprising. This was facilitated by continuing close relations between the Israeli authorities and major Islamic leaders of Hamas, former members of Mujama, who enjoyed the support of Israeli authorities in their attempt to undermine the PLO. Ironically, Hamas was viewed as "partner-for-discussion"[117] to eliminate the threat of the PLO. Lisa Taraki records that Israeli Television's Arabic Service, for example, has studiously avoided interviewing or giving prominence to Palestinian nationalist figures; still, it broadcasted a wide-ranging interview with Sheikh Yassin, describing him as the "spiritual leader" of the Islamic movement in the Occupied Territories.[118] This was followed by another interview with Sheikh Bassam Jarrar, associated with Hamas. Further, Israeli and foreign media took the lead in publicizing the distribution of the Hamas Charter.

Israel perceived Hamas as a "moderate" Islamic organization for social reform rather then a revolutionary organization with the goal of jihad to end the occupation of all Palestine. Israelis had extended legitimacy and status to Hamas in order to marginalize the PLO. No Hamas leader or member was imprisoned. Israeli authorities had turned a blind eye to the Hamas meetings and large amounts of financial aid coming in for Hamas. Hamas had a welfare network, and was receiving *zakat* from all over the Muslim world. Thus Hamas was able to extend financial aid to needy Palestinians. Hamas' financial situation, especially compared to the PLO, strengthened after the Gulf war in 1990.[119] In May 1991 it was reported that the US$ 28 million a month that Saudi Arabia had given the PLO before Gulf Crises was now going to Hamas.[120]

The relationship between Hamas and Israel was to change dramatically in 1989. The close relation between Hamas and Israel was not unnoticed by the Palestinian population. If Hamas was to consolidate its position among the Palestinians, as the only legitimate representative of the Palestinian people, it had to resolve this uncanny relationship with Israel. In mid-1989 Hamas adopted the techniques of Islamic Jihad and UNLU and targeted Israeli military personal killing two Israeli soldiers. Edwards argues that the incident of killing two Israeli soldiers "was a calculated and dramatic bid for popular Palestinian opinion at a time when support for the uprising appeared to be flagging."[121]

Following this event, Israel started to arrest and deport the Hamas leadership and its members, including charismatic leader Yassin. In 1990s, Hamas adopted a more public position to gain international legitimacy and replace the PLO. Hamas adopted an even more militant attitude after the massacre of seventeen Palestinian Muslims during prayers in the Al-Aqsa mosque by Israeli police in October 1990. They initiated attacks against the Israeli soldiers and settlers and declared that every soldier and settler in Palestine was a target.

The Rise and Fall of the Peace Process

The Oslo Peace Process, initiated in Norway in 1990, opened another new era in the Palestinian history. This process, however, experienced significant problems from the very beginning. The Islamic movement in Palestine, and Hamas in particular, rejected any negotiations with Israelis and Americans, under the conditions dictated to the Palestinians. Since the beginning of the negotiation process they insisted that under the current conditions it was not possible to reach a just and favorable solution. This view was reflected in Hamas supported journal *Filastin al-Muslima* (FM) January 1990, which stated that "certain Palestinian leaders" (no doubt referring to Yasser Arafat) were exploiting the gains of the *Intifada*, by making concessions to the American and Zionist claims, therefore, the establishment of Hamas, was a "true" blessing (*kutwa mubaraka*) since they were the only ones defending the "real aspirations" (*tatallu al-haqiqiyya*) of the Palestinian people.[122]

Following the announcement of the Madrid Conference, Hamas called for a strike to protest the conference and the PLO. Going even further, Hamas also issued a *fatwa* condemning the Palestinian Delegation. It increased its attacks on Israeli targets and also on the Palestinian collaborators, considering these attacks as a religious duty to protect the religion against Israel. In December 1992

Hamas kidnapped an Israeli officer and asked Israel to release Yassin from prison. Israel responded by launching a war against the Islamic movement and expelled over 400 of its members.

The expulsion was viewed by the Palestinian community as a part of a larger plan to expel all Palestinians from the Occupied Territories, and many took to the streets in Gaza. Political violence against the Israeli targets increased, and support for Hamas grew. The international community also condemned the expulsion policy. The expulsion also invigorated a feverish debate on the place of the Islamists in the Palestinian political life. The PLO could not ignore the public outrage and the popular support Hamas enjoyed. In order to maintain its legitimacy in the eyes of the public, the PLO had to side with Hamas and halt the talks until the pressure for the PLO to return to the table mounted. The PLO was experiencing its worst crisis in thirty years and Arafat had to resign from his post as the chairman. Nevertheless, secret second track negotiations in Norway had started in the same period, and ended with the surprising handshake of Arafat and Rubin in Washington DC.

The Declaration of Principles signed on September 13, 1993 as a part of Oslo Accords turned the tide against Hamas. The Oslo Accords were based on a form of limited autonomy for the Palestinians in parts of the West Bank and Gaza. A five-year interim period, during which the final status negotiations would be held on issues concerning the status of Jerusalem, settlements, rights of refugees, among others, was initiated.[123] In this period Israeli troops were to withdraw and Israeli civil administration would relinquish its powers to the Palestinians, who were to deploy their own civil administration to maintain public order, and take responsibility for taxation, welfare, health, education, and tourism. The Oslo Accords also stipulated elections for a Palestinian legislative council with limited powers.

In return, the Palestinian delegation agreed to recognize the right of Israel to exist, to cease claiming sovereignty over pre-1948 borders, and to stop the violence by nationalist groups against Israel. Both sides believed that they made incredible concessions and gained a lot, but it was not easy to persuade their constituencies of the benefit of the deal. The PLO was faced with challenges coming from within and from communist groups such as PFLP, DFLP, and others, as well as the Islamists. The Islamic movement was completely excluded from this crucial historical event. Despite its popular support, Hamas failed to gain legitimacy as a partner for peace in the eyes of the Israelis and the International community.

Hamas denounced the Oslo Accords and all the negotiations and agreements that followed it. The Oslo Accords were viewed as a betrayal to the Palestinian liberation struggle. Both Israel and the PLO were turned against the Islamic movement and Hamas in particular. To respond to these new developments, Hamas joined nine other rejectionist groups, including communist groups such as PFLP and others, and formed the Palestinian Forces Alliance (PFA).[124]

During the peace process Hamas represented itself as the champion of resistance to Arafat's "sell-out" of Palestine through jihad and reiterated calls to resume *Intifada*. However, the optimistic atmosphere in Palestine regarding the Peace Process led Hamas to adopt a gradualist policy. In 1993, Sheikh Yassin wrote a letter from prison in which he raised the possibility of *hudna* (truce) with Israel if Israel withdrew from the Occupied Territories. Also, based on Yassin's suggestions, Hamas adopted a more moderate stand. Hamas even announced that, although it rejected and renounced the Oslo Accords, it would not work to undermine the PNA or threaten national unity.[125] The popular pressure in its own ranks moved Hamas to adopt a cautious policy against open or direct confrontation with the PLO. Hamas recognized that under these circumstances, it was enough to maintain public support and resist the rise of secular rule through political opposition, and thus chose to commit itself coexist with the nationalists.

Both Hamas and Jihad strictly maintained their political opposition until the spring of 1994. The massacre of February 25, 1994, where a Jewish settler from Hebron killed more than 25 Palestinian worshippers while they were praying in the Ibrahimi Mosque in Hebron was a turning point in Hamas strategy. Hamas issued a leaflet that stated that "The settlers will pay for the massacre with the blood of their hearts," and launched a new strategy based on "a life for a life."[126]. After that point, Hamas declared that the violence was now directed significantly —not at military, but at civilian targets inside Israel's Green Line. These declarations were followed by five suicide attacks, killing 35 people and wounding 135. However, even after the suicide attacks, Hamas did not abandon the possibility of a truce with Israel if Israel withdrew and dismantled the settlements.

These suicide attacks and continuing violence towards the Israelis created a conflict between the Palestinian Authority and Hamas. This conflict took a more serious direction when the Palestinian police lost control in November 1994 at Gaza's Palestine Mosque and killed 14 people and wounded 270. Hamas, in an effort to avoid a civil war, restrained its followers. This stance was abused by Arafat, who turned the conflict into a factional one between Fatah and Hamas, hoping to undermine the popularity of Hamas. However, Hamas was not deterred; on the contrary it increased its suicide attacks.

The gap between Hamas and the Palestinian Authority became more obvious during the legislative council elections of January 20, 1996. Initially, Hamas was debating whether to participate in the elections for the Palestinian legislative council. The Palestinian Authority was eager for Hamas to participate in the elections in order to involve the Islamic movement in the Oslo process and to increase its own legitimacy.[127] According to some Hamas members, participating in the elections would mean recognizing Israel, while others, over came this obstacle, developing an ingenious solution deriving from Islamic tradition of *hudna*. Yassin, the ideologue of Hamas interpreted the tradition of *hudna* in a way to accommodate the present day realities, taking into account the expectations and frustrations of the Palestinians.

In order to participate in the elections Hamas put forth certain conditions, which included a temporary cease-fire (*hudna*), agreed trough the consensus of opinion of religious leaders (*ijma*), with the Zionist enemy. This *hudna* would allow Palestinians to address other issues within the society and would not mean opening a dialogue or negotiations with the enemy. During the *hudna* period, it would be possible for Hamas to participate in the elections.

Not all Hamas members agreed to participate in the legislative elections of 1995. Some members of the movement believed that participation in the elections would give legitimacy to Israel and the PLO, and this was in no form or shape acceptable. This view is reflected in the question that Gaza Islamist Mohammad Hindi asked: "Can the jihad continue when there is an Islamic political party, when the basic rights of Palestinians are ignored by their own representatives and no one is sure of the rules of the game?"[128] Eventually, Hamas rejected participating in the elections.

As the hopes for peace —albeit still distant—a had arisen from the horizon, optimism among the Palestinian people was high. The PLO seemed to have reasserted its legitimacy as the sole representative of the Palestinian people. According to Kristianasen, the 1994 establishment of the Palestinian Authority and the introduction of "autonomy" in Gaza and Jericho were unassailable, and according to opinion polls, Palestinians inside the Occupied Territories —in sharp contrast to the diaspora—collectively endorsed the peace process and, despite deep disappointments, largely continued to see no alternative to Oslo.[129] Edwards states that by the end of September 1992, 73 percent of the Palestinians living in the Occupied Territories favored continuation of negotiations with Israel, with 60 percent supporting the leadership of PLO.[130] In this atmosphere, Arafat was elected as the President, despite all criticisms. According to Farsoun and Zacharia, the elections showed that Arafat was still "the symbol of Palestinian Nationalism, at least for the majority of the West Bank and Gaza Strip Palestinians."[131]

The Islamic movement, on the other hand, started loosing blood, as the polls showed that Hamas had only 17 percent support (the other groups had 22 percent support).[132] Nevertheless, Hamas did not end its activities among the population. The Palestinian Authority asked Hamas to stop the violence against Israeli targets in and from the areas of self-rule. Hamas also had to take into account the public mood. Although Hamas adopted a policy of tying military operations to Israeli outrages, the effects of collective punishment could overshadow mass anger at Israel.[133] They had to find a way to restrain the fervor of a young generation of Palestinian that had grown up during the *Intifada*, nurtured on the idea of armed struggle.

In addition to disputing with the PLO, supporters of the Islamic movement continued to operate their social institutions, in which they were able to keep in touch with the people. In 1993, Hamas was reinforced by a new generation of professionals better able to engage with the outside world in its own language and to reflect the movement's enhanced status within the Palestinian arena, although the original leadership —mainly sheikhs and religious leaders— still played an important role.[134]

Election of Israeli Prime Minister Netanyahu and a new hard-line Likud-led coalition in May 1996 undermined the peace process further. During the election campaign, Netanyahu had been critical of many aspects of the Declaration of Principles and interim agreements, and had voiced opposition to any future establishment of Palestinian sovereignty. After the elections, these attitudes were reflected in the new Israeli government's policies, including its support to additional Israeli settlement activity in the Occupied Territories. These policies had a detrimental effect on the peace process and Palestinians' hope in a future peace was shattered. As the support for peace process faded, terrorist attacks by extremist Islamist groups intensified. The March 1997 suicide attack in Tel Aviv was followed by other suicide attacks in Jerusalem in July and September of that year. In retaliation, Israel imposed comprehensive closures and suspended revenue transfers to the PNA. Furthermore, Netanyahu declared that settlement activities would not stop and he would not be bound by the Oslo Agreement to withdraw from additional territories unless the Palestinian Authority met Israeli security demands. In October Israel's attempt to assassinate a Hamas official in Jordan failed, but this attempt contributed to the deterioration of the situation.

The Netanyahu's government was replaced by Barak led Labor party on May 17, 1999. The new Israeli government signaled its intent to continue with the peace process. The Palestinian Authority responded in kind; the two sides met at Sharm al- Sheikh, Egypt in September 1999. However, the challenges confronting the peace process were still formidable and the pace of the peace process was not successful in restoring Palestinians' hope of a just peace.

Return of the Intifada

.As the economic situation worsened and the number of settlements increased, and as the Peace Process failed making progress on the sensitive issues concerning the borders of the state of Palestine, right of return, and the status of Jerusalem, the Palestinian population lost faith in the process and began to think that the Islamic leaders were right in their suspicion. The core of Oslo agreements was seen as the preservation of Israel's security, not regaining Palestinian lands. As Kristianasen notes, "as long as there is no progress towards a settlement that meets Palestinian aspiration, it [Hamas] will remain the only credible opposition voice within the Palestinian arena."[135]

By the time of the Camp David Summit in July 2000, Palestinians' belief in peace and the Israeli interest in a "real" peace were completely shattered. Islamic movement in general, and my interviewees (both secular and Islamist) shared the feeling that Palestinians were betrayed not only by Muslims and Arabs in general, but also by their own leadership, the PLO. On the eve of Camp David Summit, neither the Islamists nor the secularist had any faith in the summit and all the groups were convinced that this meeting would fail to produce a just agreement for the Palestinians.

At Camp David Summit, both the Israeli and Palestinian Delegations failed to reach a final settlement. Israel claimed that it made the most generous offer that it could make, whereas the Palestinians argued that Israel's offer did not restore justice nor meet the Palestinians basic demands. In September 28, 2000, the head of the right-wing Likud Party, then in the opposition, Ariel Sharon visited the Al-Aqsa Mosque—Islam's third holiest place and one of the most sensitive issues regarding the conflict—surrounded by Israeli guards. This visit was perceived by the Palestinians as Sharon's claim to sovereignty and was followed by demonstrations, which soon turned into violent riots, sparking what is now known as the second *Intifada*, or *Al-Aqsa Intifada*. Soon the street fighting and riots spread out to the Occupied Territories.

After the spark, a new wave of "retaliatory" violence took hold of the region. In an effort to stop the violence, Palestinian leader Arafat, Israeli Prime Minister Barak, U.S President Clinton, Egyptian President Mubarak, King of Jordan, Abdullah, U.N Secretary Annan, and E.U. foreign policy chief Solana met in Sharm al-Sheikh, Egypt. The leaders at the meeting agreed to establish an international fact finding commission led by former U.S. Senator George Mitchell, and reached a cease-fire. "On 23 December 2000 President Clinton offered his "parameters," which formed the basis of subsequent negotiations that took place in Taba, Egypt, and which were accepted, with reservations, by both sides."[136] In the closing communiqué of the Taba negotiations on 27 January 2001, "the sides declared that they have never been closer to reaching an agreement and it is thus our shared belief that the remaining gaps could be bridged with the resumption of negotiations following the Israeli election."[137] However, this "official," top-down cease-fire failed to stop the violence on the ground. Further meetings and attempts to end violence were undertaken by the leaders, headed by President Clinton, but, they too would fail.

The violence and escalation of the conflict could not be halted. After hardline Likud leader Sharon took office in the first half of year 2001, he initiated a strategy to isolate violent areas of the Occupied Territories, imposing blockades on various Palestinian cities and raiding Palestinian areas with gunships, sophisticated tanks and war planes. The Palestinians responded with more suicide attacks orchestrated by various groups including Islamic Jihad, Hamas, and Al-Aqsa Brigade associated with Fatah. On March 31, 2002, Israel declared that now it was at war and called Arafat "the enemy of Israel and the entire free world."[138] In support of this policy, Sharon argued that war against Palestinian Terrorism was based on the same values and principles of the "War Against Terrorism" launched by U.S. President Bush after the September 11, 2001 attack to the World Trade Center in New York and the Pentagon in Washington D.C.

During the first two years of the Al-Aqsa *Intifada*, the death toll had already exceeded the death toll of first *Intifada,* which lasted 7 years. This number unfortunately is very likely to increase before the violence is over. During this time, Israel held Arafat responsible for the violence and escalation of the conflict, although most of the suicide attacks and bombings have been claimed by Islamic Jihad and Hamas, who have opposed Arafat's policies and peace agreements.

As the peace process ultimately proved to be fruitless, both the Palestinians and the Israelis were disappointed and lost faith in a peace agreement. This disillusionment, combined with the corrupt, autocratic, and undemocratic rule of Arafat's Palestinian Authority drove the population away from further legitimizing the Palestinian Authority. One of the indicators of growing dissatisfaction and resentment towards Arafat was seen in the reaction of the Jenin Refugee camp inhabitants, who protested Arafat's visit following his release from his Ramallah compound in May 2002. For fear of his life, Arafat was not able to land his helicopter into the camp. Once again, Islamic groups seized this opportunity to shape discourse on peace and war in the region.

The world community failed to intervene and pressure Israel to stop its attacks on Palestinian civilians during the recent Israeli attacks on various Palestinian towns and refugee camps, including the siege of church of Nativity in Bethlehem in April, 2001. Thus, the feeling that only Palestinians themselves can change their condition by resisting occupation, prevailed once again. In this atmosphere, the Hamas' views started gaining more credibility once again.

As violence increased over the last years Israel re-occupied almost all of the West Bank, confined Arafat to his compound, and initiated the construction of the internationally criticized Wall of Separation, to prevent Palestinian Terrorists entering Israel. Furthermore, Israel undertook relentless targeted attacks on militants, destroying houses and killing civilians, including many children in the process. During these targeted attacks Sheikh Yassin, the spiritual leader of Hamas, and Abdel Aziz al Rantisi, one of the prominent leaders of the organization was assassinated, creating uproar among the Palestinians. However, death of Arafat in November 2004 created an opportunity to end the deadlock in the region, as first elections for over nine years took place and as Mahmoud Abbas (or Abu Mazen) succeeded Arafat as the new head of the Palestinian Authority. In the meantime, changing its long-term policy, Hamas decided to run in local elections and won almost two thirds of the seats both in Gaza and West Bank. Moreover, Abbas was able to negotiate a truce with the militants and to convince them to stop military operations against Israel, as long as it was mutual. At the same time, Israel agreed to release gradually 900 prisoners, and withdraw from various settlements in Gaza. In September 2005, Israel, completing its unilateral disengagement plan, removed Jewish settlements, and military equipment from the Gaza Strip but retained control over the airspace, borders and ports, which created confusion within both Israeli and Palestinian communities. Additionally, Israel's attack on Lebanon in July 2006, which failed to achieve its goals that included rescuing abducted Israeli soldiers and undermining Hizbullah's power, despite destroying the main infrastructure of the Lebanese society, and killed over 1200 Lebanese, mostly children and women, split the Israeli society. Hizbullah emerged with a military and political victory.[139]

The landslide victory of Hamas in the Palestinian Legislative elections in January 2006 opened a new chapter in the conflict as many international entities, such as the US, EU, among others, cut off aid with the newly formed Hamas government, leading Palestinian community further into financial and social hardship. Violent conflict between Hamas and Israel continued to take lives of Palestinian and Israeli civilians, furthering mistrust and animosity. In the meantime, political competition between Hamas and Fatah has turned into violent clashes at ministries, universities and the streets. Although an agreement was reached at Mecca, chosen for its religious symbolic value and forming of a new coalition government is underway, it is not clear how long this agreement will last and how it will impact the Peace Process in general.

These developments add to the desperation of Palestinians. There is mutual distrust and suspicion on both communities and at this very delicate historical moment it is crucial that we learn from past mistakes and understand the social, political, cultural and religious dynamics that have an impact on this conflict. For that reason, the next Chapter will look at the rise of Islamic movement, particularly Hamas among the Palestinian population.

Endnotes

1. An exhaustive study of Islamic narratives in the Palestinian society would necessarily have to address in detail every major group. Due to financial and time constraints, this work mentions the main features of the principal voices in the making of Islamic and secular narratives, however, it focuses in certain detail on the narrative of Hamas. A comparative approach that covered different narratives in other Islamic, secular, and lefitst groups is the natural extension of areas for further research.

2. See. Stephen Ellingson. "Understanding the Dialectic of Discourse and Collective Action: Public Debate and Rioting in Antebellum Cincinnati," in Dough McAdam and David A. Snow eds. *Social Movements: Readings on Their Emergence, Mobilization and Dynamics.* (Los Angeles, CA. Roxbury Publishing Company, 1997) 269; Pierre Bourdieu,. *Language and Symbolic Power.* (Cambridge, Mass: Harvard University Press, 1991).

3. Ellingson 1997.

4. Sahlins, M. "The Return of the Event, Again: With Reflections on the Beginnings of the Great Fijian War of 1843 to 1855 between the Kingdoms of Bau and Rewa." (37-100) Aletta Biersack eds. in *Clio in Oceania: Toward a Historical Anthology.* (Washington D.C: Smithsonian, 1991); Sewell, W.R.. "Three Temporalities: Toward an Eventful Sociology," T. J. McDonald eds. *The Historic Turn in the Human Sciences.* (Ann Arbor: University of Michigan Press, 1996) and Ellingson.

5. Sahlins 1991, 44.

6. Ellingson 1997.

7. See Klandermans, Bert. "The Social Construction of Protest and Multiorganizational Fields (77-103) A.D. Morris and C.McClurg eds. *Frontiers of Social Movement Theory*. (New Haven. Conn.: Yale University Press, 1992),92-93; and "The Formation and Mobilization of Consensus," (77-92) Bert Klandermans, H. Kreisi and S. Tarrow eds. *International Social Movement Research*, vol. I (Greenwich, Conn.: JAI Press, 1988), 185.

8. See next Chapter.

9. Ellingson 1997, 272.

10. Ellingson 1997.

11. Ellingson 1997, 272-273.

12. Ann Elizabeth Meyer, "The Fundamentalist Impact on Law, Politics, and Constitutions in Iran, Pakistan, and the Sudan." In *Fundamentalism and the State: Remaking Polities, Economies and Militancy*. Martin Marty and Scott Appleby, eds.(Chicago: Chicago University Press, 1992), 110.

13. Simona Sharoni and Mohammed Abu-Nimer, "The Israeli-Palestinian Conflict." in *Understanding the Contemporary Middle East*. Deborah J. Gerner eds.(London: Lynn Reinner Publishers, 2000), 166.

14. Barry Rubin. "Religion and International Affairs" in *Religion, The Missing Dimension of Statecraft* Douglas Johnston and Cynthia Sampson Eds. (New York: Oxford University Press, 1994), 29

15. Rubin 1994.

16. Musa Budeiri, "The Palestinians: Tensions Between Nationalist and Religious Identities." In *Rethinking Nationalism in the Arab Middle East*. James Jankowski and Israel Gershoni eds. (New York: Columbia University Press, 1997), 195.

17. This idea is supported by Beverly Milton-Edwards *Islamic Politics in Palestine*. (London: Tauris Academic Studies, 1996), 12.

18. Edwards 1996, 11 cited from Hamas leaflet *"The Martyr al-Qassam: No to the Balfour Promise, Yes to the Uprising"* 27 October 1988.

19. Edwards 1996., 12.

20. Edwards 1996.

21. Edwards 1996, 7-8.

22. Muhammad Abduh "The Necessity of Religious Reform" in Moaddel and Talattof eds. 2000, 48.

23. Hasan al-Banna is the founder of the Muslim Brotherhood .

24. Although it would be interesting to compare and contrast the narratives of various different groups across the Muslim world and influential intellectual leaders of these groups (such as al-Banna), this sork will limit itself mostly to the Hamas narrative.

25. Edwards 1996., 10.

26. Edwards 1996.

27. Albert Hourani. *Arabic Thought in the Liberal Age, 1798-1939* Rev. ed. (London: Oxford University Press 1971) 47-48.

28. Philip Mattar. *Mufti of Jerusalem : Al-Hajj Amin Al-Husayni and the Palestinian National Movement*. (New York: Columbia University Press, 1988), 3.

. See also Albert Hourani. 1971, 45.

29. Mattar 1988 ., 3.

30. Hourani 1971, 9.

31. Hourani 1971

32. Hourani 1971., 3.
33. Edwards 1996, 10.
34. See Budeiri, 1997 196.
35. Budeiri 1997.
36. Edwards support this idea Edwards 1996., 11.
37. Edwards 1996, 15.
38. Edwards 1996, 13.
39. Edwards 1996, 17.
40. Cited in Edwards 1996. Frustration and resentment expressed by this person is not different than those of most Palestinians after fifty years. In addition to these, Palestinians today also have to deal with humiliation of defeat and oppression under occupation.
41. Edwards 1996., 18.
42. See Edwards 1996., 19.
43. Budeiri 1997, 197.
44. See Hamas website for more information on Hamas's views of al-Qassam at http://www.hamasonline.com/indexx.php?page=Qassam/Izz%20al-Qassam
45. Mattar 1988, 22.
46. The highest Islamic authority under the Ottoman system.
47. Mattar 1988, 1.
48. Mattar 1988., 24.
49. Edwards 1996, 24.
50. Mattar 1988, 30.
51. Mattar 1988., 25.
52. Edwards 1996, 27.
53. Edwards 1996., 28.
54. Budeiri 1997, 197. The numbers according to Sharoni and Abu-Nimer are: the Jewish state was to receive 57 percent of Palestine, including the fertile coastal region and the Jews represented only 33 percent of the whole population. See Sharoni and Abu-Nimer 2000, 170-171.
55. Samih K. Farsoun and Christina E. Zacharia. *Palestine and the Palestinians.* (Boulder, Colo.: Westview Press, 1997), 111.
56. For a detailed account on 1948 war see Farsoun and Zacharia 1997.
57. Jewish underground guerrilla organizations and terrorist groups established to attack and terrorize Palestinians. Counterparts of Hamas and Islamic Jihad in Israel.
58. Edwards 1996.
59. Numbers from Farsoun and Zacharia 1997, 123.
60. See Edwards, Farsoun and Zacharia, Voll, 1982 and Nusse 1998.
61. Ziad Abu-Amr *Islamic Fundamentalism in the West Bank and Gaza.*(Bloomington and Indianapolis Indiana University Press, 1994).
62. Edwards 1996, 44.
63. For more information on Muslim Brotherhood's ideology and history see Abu Amr 1994 and Edwards 1996.
64. See Edwards 1996., 25.
65. See Abu Amr 1994 for more detail.
66. Abu Amr 1994., 45.
67. See Abu Amr 1994.

68. Edwards 1996,. 46.
69. Edwards 1996., 52.
70. Farsoun and Zacharia 1997, 176.
71. See Farsoun and Zacharia 1997.
72. See Farsoun and Zacharia 1997, 226. Also see Abu Amr and Edwards.
73. Farsoun and Zacharia 1997., 37.
74. Cited in Edwards 1996, 77.
75. William B. Quandt, Fuad Jabber, Ann Mosely Lesch. *The Politics of Palestinian Nationalism*. (Berkeley, Los Angeles; University of California Press, 1973), 50.
76. Edwards 1996, 78.
77. See Quandt et. al. 1973, 89.
78. See Chapter Four.
79. Edwards 1996., 87.
80. Edwards 1996. 87.
81. Edwards 1996., 94
82. This influence was still alive while I was in the West Bank. At the homes of many refugees that I visited, there were framed posters of Che Guevara next to the photos of family members who had fallen during clashes with Israelis. Children as young as six were singing a song in Spanish for Che Guevara, who was their hero model. The song said: "Che camino, patria o muerte tu destino" which can be translated as "Che's way fatherland, or death is your destiny."
83. Sharoni and Abu-Nimer 2000, 174.
84. Budeiri, 1997, 201.
85. Budeiri 1997.
86. Edwards 1996, 101.
87. Edwards 1996. 104.
88. Edwards 1996.
89. These organizations included Islamic Jihad (Shaqaqi-Auda faction), Islamic Jihad Jerusalem Brigade, Islamic Jihad Battalions, and Islamic Jihad Palestine (Amar faction).
90. Interview with Ramadan Abdallah Shallah (the secretary general of the Movement of Islamic Jihad) by Khalid al-Ayid in Damascus December 1998. This interview was published under the title of "The Movement of Islamic Jihad and the Oslo Process" in *Journal of Palestinian Studies* XXVIII, no 4 (Summer 1999), (61-73), 61.
91. Shallah 1999.
92. Shallah 1999., 62.
93. Shallah 1999.
94. Edwards 1996, 116.
95. Leaflet published in the name of the Islamic Jihad movement in occupied Palestine, 8 March, 1988, 2 cited in Edwards 1996, 118.
96. Interview with Shallah, 66.
97. Interview with Sheikh Abd al-Aziz Auda, one of the founders of the Islamic Jihad movement, "The Wound in Palestine is a Wound to the Heart,' *al Fajr*, 23 August 1987 Cited in Edwards, 118.
98. Interview with Shallah, 62.
99. Edwards 1996, 144.

100. See also Khaled Hroub, *Hamas: Political Thought and Practice* Washington D.C: Institute for Palestine Studies, 2000), 36.

101. Quoted in Aryeh Shalev, *The Intifada: Causes and Effects.* (Tel Aviv and London: Westview Press, 1991), 13.

102. Abu-Nimer 2003, 166.

103. Abu-Nimer 2003., 167.

104. See Edwards 1996, 121-123.

105. Edwards 1996. 122.

106. Edwards 1996., 145.

107. Edwards 1996.

108. Edwards 1996.

109. For the Islamic roots of nonviolent intifada see Abu-Nimer 2003

110. See Abu-Nimer 2003, 230.

111. Abu-Nimer 2003., 235.

112. Abu Nimer 2003., 239.

113. Abu-Nimer 2003.

114. For a detailed discussion see Abu-Nimer 2003., 242-249.

115. Abu-Nimer 2003., 172.

116. Edwards 1996, 147.

117. Edwards 1996., 151.

118. Lisa Taraki "The Islamic Resistance Movement in the Palestinian Uprising" *Middle East Report* January-February 1989 (30-32), 30.

119. PLO's Support for Saddam Hussein undermined its relations with especially Gulf countries. On the other hand, Hamas leaflet 64 had called Saddam Hussein to withdraw its troops, to maintain support from its Gulf funders.

120. Edwards 1996, 155.

121. Edwards 1996., 152.

122. *Filastin al Muslima* (FM) January 1990; 7 cited in Andrea Nusse. *Muslim Palestine: The Ideology of Hamas* (Australia: Harwood Academic Publishers, 1998).

123. See Geoffrey Watson, *The Oslo Accords: International Law and the Israeli-Palestinian Peace Agreements* (Oxford: Oxford University Press, 2000).

124. Edwards 1996, 162.

125. Edwards 1996, 175.

126. Wendy Kristianasen. "Challenge and Counterchallenge: Hamas's Response to Oslo" in *Journal of Palestine Studies.* XXVIII, no 3 (Spring 1999) (19-35), 23.

127. Kristiansen 1999., 27.

128. Quoted in Edwards 1996, 165.

129. Kristianasen 1999, 22. Kristianasen states that the Jerusalem Media and Communication's Center's Poll no. 7 of June 1995 on Palestinian attitudes toward a year of autonomy showed that 69.7 percent of Gazans and West Bankers supported it, 74.9 percent supported the extension to the West Bank, and 57.9 percent were optimistic for the Future. See Kristianasen footnote 6.

130. Edwards 1996, 163.

131. Farsoun and Zacharia,1997, 285. Arafat received 87.1 percent of the vote according to Farsoun and Zacharia.

132. Edwards 1996.

133. Edwards 1996., 22.

134. Kristianasen 1999, 21.

135. Kristiansen 1999., 33.

136. International Crisis Group *A Time to Lead: The International Community and the Israeli-Palestinian Conflict* Middle East Report no.1 (Amman/Brussels, 10 April, 2002), 6.

137. Cited in International Crisis Group 2002 . See ibid. footnote 8.

138. Washington Post 31 March, 2001

139. "Hizbullah's Shallow Victory" *The Economist* 19 August 2006

Chapter 6

The Context: Legitimating the Narrative of Peace and War in Palestine

In the previous Chapter, I revisited the history of the Israeli-Palestinian conflict, with a focus on the Islamic movements within the Palestinian society and highlighted the role of effective history: e.g. the experiences of the Palestinian community with the British Mandate, Jewish immigration, establishment of the "Zionist" State, and the wars that took place between the Arabs and the State of Israel. I also looked at the impact of First and Second *Intifada* and the Oslo Peace Process. The previous Chapter also briefly examined the impact of disputes and "power politics," on the emergence of Palestinian narratives, both in the Arab world in general and within the Palestinian society in particular. With this version of the (hi)story, I attempted to introduce some of the factors that constrained—but at the same time enabled—the emergence of a particular Palestinian Islamic narrative regarding the conflict.

In Chapter Six I will look at the emerging Islamic narrative of peace and war in this context, mostly focusing on the Islamic organization/movement of Hamas. I will look at the interaction between the events and the narrative of Hamas and will try to understand the dynamic relationship between them. In this Chapter I will also analyze Hamas' narrative of "justified war" and "justified methods of war." My arguments will rest on the interviews that were conducted during the Summer of 2000 in the West Bank and East Jerusalem, on Hamas leaflets and Charter, as well as on published interviews with different groups of Palestinians. Here, I will also explore the social, political and psychological dynamics that allows Hamas' narrative to become legitimized among the Palestinian population.

Since my interviews were conducted before the outbreak of Al- Aqsa *Intifada*, mood was one of frustration and disappointment. The Palestinians that were interviewed for this study had very low expectations in regard to the Camp David Summit and the peace process in general. In this atmosphere, there was less emphasis on peace than war. The following pages reflect the frustration and disappointment of the Palestinian people. As a result, the focus is more on war than peace. Since the beginning of the second uprising, new voices on nonviolence and peace have emerged, such as International Solidarity Movement[1] and Grass-roots International Protection for the Palestinian People[2]. But it was not possible to find funding for a second trip to the region because of the dangers it presented. Additionally, although there is has been moments of renewed hope in the region, such as the cease-fire agreement between Israel and Palestine in January 2005, many of these short lived cease-fires, continuation of violence, increasing unemployment and destruction of Palestinian infrastructures only intensifies the frustration among the Palestinian people. In order effectively grasp windows of opportunities it is important to address roots of disappointment and to learn from these previous mistakes and failures. It is also critical that we understand what contextual elements led to the acceptance of a particular interpretation of the religious texts in the first place.

Contextual developments in the Israeli-Palestinian conflict have had a significant impact on the fluctuation of narratives of war and peace. These contextual developments have a direct bearing on the individual and communal experiences, and shape the way individuals view their conflict, the way they perceive their enemies, and their options regarding the resolution of the conflict. These experiences, their effective history, form their horizon in the search for religious/cultural values and texts to make sense of their lives, their sufferings and ways to deal with them. It is from the perspective of their lived experience that people approach their religious texts and draw conclusions on how they should act under certain circumstances. They interpret these texts with their fears and with specific questions, concerns, and frustrations in the back of their minds.

After fifty years of conflict, the Palestinian people feel that they have tried various methods to resist occupation, ranging from war to nonviolence. However, they are still under occupation, deprived of their rights to economic, social, and political development. Perhaps for those reasons, they state that this is an existential war and that they will resist and fight for their rights and their homeland until they perish or get them. They are disappointed and frustrated with the peace process and their living conditions. Within this context, Islamic narratives offer them an alternative avenue. As a result, nationalized Islamic narratives have become an important alternative to those narratives (such as Pan-Arabic, leftist and secular narratives) that have dominated the Palestinian political discourse over the last few decades. In support of this argument, one of my interviewees argued that:

> Islamic movement is unifying and many schools are converting to their approach because now many Palestinians have come to the conclusion that the only way to defeat Israel and protect Palestine is to resort to Islam as a whole way of life, because then, God will give them the strength and motivation and aspiration to succeed. [Sura Baqara states that] if you believe in God, he will give you victory against the enemy. People are frustrated with secular ideologies.[3]

When asked about the use of force in Islam, or in general, most of my interviewees stated that:

> How come the Palestinian resistance against unjust occupiers and oppressors, who invaded our land and persecuted us from our homes, is seen as a form of terrorism or illegal violence, while the liberation wars of other countries are considered just and heroic acts of self-defense?
>
> Does the world expect us to stay mute and docile and do what ever they want us to do, while Israeli armies are killing us, taking our land and resources and establishing settlements on our soil? Are we expected to watch these things happen in silence and accept them? Why do we not have the right to defend our rights, and ourselves while everybody else has them? And under these conditions, Islam allows fighting for self-defense.[4]

These words represent the views of the many Muslims, particularly in the Occupied Territories. One of my interviewees, who defined himself as a secular stated:

> During the seven years that followed Oslo we saw nothing happened. There is no right of return, prisoners are not freed, Jerusalem and water are still issues, houses are still being demolished, Palestinians are still being killed. We want peace to stop all these, but since Oslo nothing changed... We have to wait and watch to see what happens with the negotiations [Camp David Summit]....I used to believe in peace but not anymore. Peace should encourage...[5]

Another interviewee also expressed his discontent with the Oslo Process by stating that:

> I am not living in peace ... I cannot go to Nablus or to Jerusalem to theAqsa mosque for "security" reasons. What kind of peace is this? But we will stay here as long as possible. I prefer to die than to live like this... Leaving now would mean to forget my country.[6]

Furthermore, Palestinians added that both international law and the Universal Declaration of Human Rights affirm the legitimacy of self-defense to resist an occupying army. For example one of my interviewees stated:

> They [different political groups within Palestinian Territories] all agree on taking back the rights [of the Palestinian people] and defending themselves. ...International law is also supportive of this as well and different religious groups that operate here also share the same ideas. If there is an occupation, fighting becomes self-defense and international law supports this.[7]

Currently three groups, each having distinct identifiable narratives, can be observed within the Palestinian context. The first group is the secular-nationalist affiliated with the PLO, which consists of those who support the PNA and the peace process. This group consists of various different sub-groups. Among these sub-groups, Fatah, headed by Arafat since the late 1960s until his death in November 2004, has been the largest group and historically dominated the political scene. Some of the Fatah members are known for being pious Muslims and have conservative Islamic views, although they do not support Hamas and Jihad. However, by incorporating various groups under the motto of liberating Palestine, Fatah was able to draw support form all segments of society. Fatah's experience since 1960s and the international legitimacy it received during the peace process added to its strength within the society. A great majority of the Fatah leadership supported Palestinian participation at the Madrid Conference and the peace process, agreeing on a two-state solution and land-for-security arrangements with the Israelis. Before the Oslo Agreement, however, the leadership of PLO, and thus Fatah, were in exile, first in South Lebanon and after that in Tunisia. Living outside the Occupied Territories for a prolonged time resulted in its disconnection from the realities and the developments on the ground, particularly in its inability to directly participate in the uprising. Besides, the emergence of autonomous leaderships during PLO's period in exile posed a threat to its leadership position.

Immediately after the Oslo Process the PLO, now the Palestinian National Authority (PNA or PA –Palestinian Authority), consolidated its status as the legitimate representative of the Palestinian people. The eventual failure of the peace process, coupled with the Palestinian Authority's alleged corruption and its failure to establish strong infrastructure, all combined to undermine this status. Those leaders who emerged during the first *Intifada* criticized the PNA for selling out the gains of the uprising for individual benefits. The PNA adopted harsh measures against these opposition groups and many leaders and scholars were executed. The autonomous leaders that emerged during the *Intifada* considered themselves insiders (led by Marwan Barghouti), whereas the PLO leadership and aids of Arafat were considered outsiders.[8] Barghouti formulated a unified leadership that included all factions, including the Islamic groups such as

Hamas and Jihad.[9] According to Khalid, the struggle is now between the insiders and the outsiders, and added, "the insiders lead the Al-Aqsa *Intifada* now, and outsiders are not able to stop them."[10]

The second group in Palestine consists of the leftist-Marxist groups that are influenced by revolutionary movements around the world, prominently from Latin America. These groups include the Popular Front for the Liberation of Palestine (PFLP), the Democratic Front for the Liberation of Palestine (DFLP), Palestinian Democratic Union (FIDA), and Palestinian People's Party (PPP), which was formerly the Palestinian Communist Party (PCP). According to one of my interviewees, Nidal, this group was the strongest during the Cold War, since the Eastern European Countries, Communist parties around the world, and also the Soviet Union supported it.[11] These countries not only supported the leftist groups in terms of funding but also by providing medical and educational help, convening conferences, and so on. These groups have been extremely active in terms of politicizing the population, providing services through committees and at student blocs, before and during the *Intifada*. By and large, they were the first to organize and mobilize the population. However, the fall of the Communist bloc had a negative impact on these groups as they lost their sources of financial and technical support.

Furthermore the Oslo Process undermined the solidarity among these leftist groups. Various Palestinians argued that Oslo was the main reason for the lack of unity among the Palestinian groups. In support of this idea, my interviewee, Basam stated, "Oslo is the main reason for the separation between Palestinians."[12] "Oslo Among the leftist groups, the FIDA and PPP supported the peace process, while PFLP and DFLP opposed the process and retained their position for getting all of Palestine back (in that sense they agree with the Islamic groups). This debate further divided and weakened the Left. Subsequently, those groups that rejected the peace process came together in an alliance called Palestinian Forces Alliance (PFA), together with Hamas. Many of the members and supporters of these leftist groups are currently in the process of deciding which path to follow. Leftist groups appreciate the Islamic groups' willingness to die for the country and their sacrifices. The main division between the Islamist and Leftist today revolves around the issue of democracy. Leftist groups are in favor of a strictly democratic state, and they criticize the Islamic groups for not being democratic enough.[13]

The third important group in Palestine is the Islamic bloc, consisting of groups such as Hamas, Islamic Jihad, and Hizb-u Tahrir. Under the current circumstances Islamic groups such as Hamas and Islamic Jihad emerge with their alternative narratives and claims of legitimacy. Basing these claims of legitimacy on religious grounds in a community where religion still plays a predominant role in social and cultural life, these groups attempt to establish their regimes of truth as the *only* truth out there. The primary inspiration of these groups' positions on key topics, such as the image and treatment of Jews, acceptability of a truce or peace agreement, or methods of war, is drawn from the Quran and *Hadith*. These sources, together with classical theological, juridical, philosophical and spiritual literature and contemporary works and statements of the *ulema*, are handled and re-appropriated from a scripturalist or literary perspective to answer current problems of state and society. The Islamic groups stress the "timeless truths of perceived religious knowledge, and resort extensively to the tradition of *naskh* (abrogation) in order to neutralize the effect of verses that would challenge their interpretation of these texts. The following paragraphs will expand on the views of Hamas and on how they respond to the conflict and interpret Islamic texts within the current context.

After the Oslo Process, the Palestinian Population has taken refuge in the Islamic message. As stated above, the Islamic movement is increasingly viewed as a unifying force, as they come to the conclusion that "the only way to defeat Israel is to resort to Islam as a whole way of life; because then God will give them the strength and motivation and aspiration to succeed."[14] This Islamic narrative seduces a population frustrated with secular ideologies.[15] This Islamicated mood led the insider leader Marwan Barghouti to include Islamic groups into his new unified leadership, as he recognized the strong influence of Islam in the region, as well as the need to include Islamic groups to establish a strong coalition against Arafat's bloc.

Hamas Narrating

Islamic groups such as Hamas and Islamic Jihad, by restricting the notion of jihad to self defense, find a fertile soil in the hearts of many Muslims who have come to believe that the only way to emancipate Palestine from oppression and occupation is through a war of liberation. Ideologically, both Hamas and Islamic Jihad adopt Sunni Islamic perspective, since the majority of Muslims in Israel and Palestinian Territories are Sunni Muslims. This interpretation of Sunni ideology in Palestine combines the anti-colonial and anti-secular perspective of the Islamists in other parts of the world with an anti-Zionist and anti-Jewish perspective.[16]

Ideology of Hamas and Islamic Jihad, especially the anti-Zionist and anti-Jewish sentiments of the Palestinian movement, were shaped by the Islamic doctrine drawn from the Quran and *Sunnah*, and evolved according to the necessity, expediency, and realpolitik in response to the changing political circumstances and the effective history of the Palestinians since the first immigration of Jews into the region in 1881. Edwards argues that Hamas ideology was initially rooted in a modernist-reformist Islamic approach to political change based on the works of scholars such as al-Afghani, Abduh, Rida, al-Banna, and Qutb, in an attempt to make sense of a foreign occupation, military subjugation, and the Western domination of ideas of daily life.[17] However, lumping these scholars together without paying attention to the differences in their approaches to interpretation of Islamic sources or to their attitudes towards the West and its institutions over-simplifies the evolution of the Islamic intellectual arena and blurs their differences.

As detailed in Chapter Three, the Islamic responses to modernity can be categorized under three groups, namely renewalists (*tajdid*), reformists (*islah*), and fundamentalists. Although there has always been intensive interaction between these groups, they differ significantly in terms of their attitudes towards the non-Islamic world and their solutions to the problems faced by Muslims today. These differences become especially important for understanding the approaches of different groups towards war and peace. An analysis that fails to differentiate between these groups will risk misguided conclusions.

Although most of the modern media and scholarship represent both Hamas and Islamic Jihad as fundamentalist Islamic groups, they differ significantly from fundamentalist groups such as Taliban and al-Qaeda. As stated before, this study makes the distinction between fundamentalist and renewalist movements, according to their approaches to modernization, interpretation of the texts and their concept of jihad.

Fundamentalist movements deny merit to any Western idea or development (i.e. democracy) and argue that the only way to restore the Islamic community is to go back to the formative years of Islam, by creating similar conditions of the 7th century Arabia. They reject Western technology and science, like Taliban who prohibited TV and listening to music. They press for the complete seclusion of women and do not allow women to receive education. They call for strict application of the Quran and Hadith, based on a strict literal interpretation and reject *ijtihad* and any esoteric or symbolic reading of these texts.

Another important characteristic of fundamentalist movements is their belief in God's ordain on all Muslims to spread the way of God (*Shariah*) on earth by all means, including offensive wars. Similarly to the Khawarij perspective, they argue that jihad is the sixth pillar of Islam, a duty incumbent upon every Muslim to fight to establish God's justice and way (*shariah*). Both Hamas and Islamic Jihad, on the other hand, do not share the same views on Jihad, *Ijtihad*, or the *shariah*. Therefore, although these Islamic groups in Palestine are extremist groups, they are not fundamentalist groups as defined in this study.

Another example that highlights the difference between these groups and fundamentalists is the debate over democracy. Hamas in particular argues in favor of democracy and states that democracy is not a Western phenomenon, but that Islam incorporates democratic principles through Islamic principles such as *shura* (consultation), *ijma* (consensus), and calls for free elections to express the will of people. Indeed one of the main criticisms these groups have towards PLO is that PLO and its institutions are undemocratic and autocratic. So they call for democratization, and representation of the will of the people. Both in their handout[18] and FM of September 1990, Hamas states that the "real nature" (*al-*

huwiyya al-haqiqiyya) of the Muslim people is the longing for a democratic form of rule. For that matter, they criticize the oppressive and dictatorial Arab governments and declare that the "will of people" should govern the state. Although Hamas argued for the establishment of a democratic regime in the Palestinian Territories and the democratization of the Palestinian institutions, it had refused to participate in previous elections in order not to legitimize the Oslo peace process. However, due to the changing political and social climate after the death of Arafat Hamas recently stated that it is ready to participate in the parliamentary and municipal elections of February 2005[19] and finally came to political power as a result of democratic elections held in January 2006.

Nusse argues that "the will of people" is understood as a monolithic bloc and that as Hamas is convinced that their understanding is the only possible one, there cannot be disagreement between the true believers.[20] Even though it might be possible to question the sincerity of their belief in democracy, the fact that Islamic groups in Palestine argue that Islam incorporates values that promote democracy evinces one of the major differences between them and the fundamentalists. This idea of "the will of the people" is not compatible with the fundamentalist idea, defended by Sayyid Qutb, "popular sovereignty cannot be at the basis of legitimate authority because all sovereignty belongs to God."[21] Qutb's perspective leads to the conclusion that people are only the vice-regents of God on earth, executing his orders, and cannot be representatives of other men.[22] Nevertheless, developments to follow the election of Hamas will illustrate how sincerely Hamas is committed to democracy.

Another major difference between fundamentalists and Hamas is the issue of non-Muslims. Muslims in Palestinian Territories in general and Hamas in particular, have a more tolerant attitude regarding the non-Muslims than that of fundamentalists. After the long experience of coexistence between Palestinian Muslims and non-Muslims, such as Christians, Jews, and Druze, and after sharing the same experience of occupation and humiliation, Palestinian Muslims pay more heed to the Quranic verse that states "no compulsion in religion." In that respect, they seem to have a more tolerant and pluralistic view compared to the fundamentalists, who seem to have very little, if any tolerance towards non-Muslims, including "the people of the Book." Within this context, many Palestinians refer to the rule of Salah ad-Din Ayyubi as an example of just conduct. In this vein, in the context of understanding the relationship between Muslims and non-Muslims, Sheikh Alami stated:

> Look at Salah ad-Din Ayyubi! He was known as a very just sultan, who treated his Christian and Jewish citizens with justice and equality so that the Christians gave him the key to their holy places. Whereas the Crusaders slaughtered more then 100,000 people, Muslim and Jewish alike.[23]

All my interviewees, including various influential religious figures strongly emphasized that Islam forbids forcing others to accept Islam, since spreading the word of God might make people say that they are Muslim but will not bring Islam to their hearts. Therefore, they all added, it is not permitted (also useless) to wage offensive wars to spread Islam. They contended that Islam only permits defensive wars. They stated that self-defense becomes legitimate when Muslims are persecuted from their homes, oppressed, treated unjustly, or not allowed to practice their religion, or attacked and killed. In that line, an interviewee stated that:

> One of the duties of a Muslim is to share that peace, which God bestowed upon them and filled their hearts, with others. This means that a Muslim must deal with non-Muslims in a peaceful manner, on the condition that they do not harm the others.[24]

This view was also supported by the Imam of Abraham Mosque in Hebron, who stated:

> Islam is a very peaceful religion and Islam comes from the word "salam," which means peace. Islam wants to bring peace. There is no compulsion in Islam...[25]

The relationship between Muslims and non-Muslims, particularly Christians is a crucial issue for the Muslim leadership in the Palestinian Territories because Palestinian community consists of an important Christian community. Because Palestine and especially Jerusalem is the holiest place according to Christian tradition, there has been an important Christian community in the region for centuries. This community has become an integral aspect of Palestinian society. One of my interviewees articulated this perspective as follows:

> Christians are part of the culture and Palestine is a part of Arab culture. They [Christians] are targeted too in places like Beit Jala and Beit Sahour. They are not afraid of Islam because that is protection for them. There is no conflict between religions.[26]

Another interviewee added:

> Christians are 2 percent of the Palestinian population. They are in fact a part of the struggle ... There is an understanding that Palestine is unified against Israel. Some [some Christians] are sided with Arafat because Arafat's wife is Christian, but they are not the majority.[27]

The Christian community in the Palestinian Territories has been suffering under the Israeli occupation as much as the Muslims and has been part of the resistant movement as vehemently. Their support has been crucial for the success of any resistance movement. Thus, they have played an important role in resisting the occupation. For that reason, it has been critical for the Islamic leadership not to alienate the Palestinian Christians.[28]

Still, Hamas and Islamic Jihad do share with the fundamentalist certain views that Muslims have deviated from the "right path" and that is the reason for the current decadence of the Islamic civilization. As stated in the Charter of Hamas[29] and often emphasized in various (unofficial Hamas) journals such as *Filastin al-Muslima* and *Mithaq*,[30] victory is with those who believe in God and obey God's commands. The failure of the Muslim world in the 20th century must be related to the Muslims deviating from the right path (*sirat al-mustaqim*). Therefore the liberation of Palestine becomes a test for Muslims in general, because "this jihad" can be won only by adhering to "God's commands" strictly, under the banner of Allah.[31] In order to prove "the truth" of their argument, they often refer to Muslim victories in history against the non-Muslims. In that respect, the example of Salah ad-Din Ayyubi's recapturing Jerusalem from the Crusaders becomes and important narrative for Hamas.[32] In their construction of myths they resort to those stories that have been narrated within the communities for centuries and have thereby become part of social consciousness. For example, according to Nayef, people in Hebron believe they are the children and supporters of Abraham (Ibrahim according to Isiam); thus they are the protectors of the Holy Land.[33] He added that:

> When the Holy Land was captured by the Crusaders it was Salah ad-Din Ayyubi who restored it to Islam and many people came to the region with him: he is the Great ruler of the region. He is known for his justice and courage. Many people are still waiting for another Salah ad-Din Ayyubi to come and rescue them.[34]

Their analyses and accounts of these past wars and victories enter the interpretive struggles through which the history of a people is constructed. By locating these wars in the Palestinian people's recollection they engage them into a politics of interpretation. By fixing stories of past victories they shape spaces (Palestine) and events that constitute the bases of being a Muslim. These stories create the imaginative boundaries that contain the identity of the people. They influence self-interpretations and modes of inclusion and exclusion. These stories or narratives provide contexts for action, such as "defending the nation" through war or suicide attacks. These narratives reconfigure the imagination of the population within which actions have meaning.

Islamic groups in Palestine, including Hamas and Islamic Jihad, also agree with the fundamentalists that the original *Ummah* in Medina under the direct guidance of the Prophet was the perfect society and the perfect political model. These groups steer the imagination of the populations towards their idealized version of the society of Medina. However, their imagination is constrained by the world they are living in and with their experience of being in this world.

Therefore, their interpretive imagination differs from that of fundamentalists on the total rejection of the Western success and merit. On the contrary, they argue that change is an integral aspect of life, and that the Islamic message has foreseen these changes and modernity, which can in turn be Islamicized by applying "true" Islamic principles and values. For that reason, they emphasize the importance of education of men and women in Muslim societies.

One of the crucial aspects of Hamas' narrative regarding the Israeli-Palestinian conflict is the way they view the conflict. Hamas refers to the current conflict in an entirely religious perspective and argues that the State of Israel is a religious, Jewish state, which discriminates on religious grounds against its non-Jewish citizens. Hamas also insists that religious doctrine has considerable weight in Israeli decision-making, and that therefore the conflict between Jews and Muslims must be seen as the continuation of conflict between two religious traditions.

In order to support this view, Hamas extensively borrows from Quranic tales and sagas, and interprets the Quran and Hadith with this perspective in mind. Hamas interprets Islamic history and sources from the perspective of turbulent relations of today and extrapolates conclusions that support their interpretation. For example, based on their interpretation of the Texts, they promise their followers "the Zionist enemy will be defeated" and indicate this as a Quranic fact.[35] For example they use the Quranic verse 17:4-8.

> And we decreed for the Children of Israel in the Scripture, that indeed you would do mischief on the earth twice and you will become tyrants and extremely arrogant! So, when the promise came for the first of the two, We sent against you slaves of Ours given to terrible warfare. They entered the very innermost parts of your homes. And it was a promise (completely) fulfilled. Then We gave you once again, a return of victory over them. And We helped you with wealth and children and made you more numerous in manpower. (And We said): "If you do good, you do good for your ownselves, and if you do evil (you do it) against yourselves". Then, when the second promise came to pass, (We permitted your enemies) to make your faces sorrowful and to enter the mosque (of Jerusalem) as they had entered it before, and to destroy with utter destruction all that fell in their hands. [And We Said in the Taurat (Torah)]: "It may be that your Lord may show mercy unto you, but if you return (to sins), We shall return (to Our Punishment). And We have made Hell a prison for the disbelievers

Reading this verse in the light of the current they events they argue that the Zionist Jews have "returned to sins" by turning away from God and by persecuting the Palestinians from their homes, and that they will be punished again as it is stated in the Quran.

In the context of the conflict, their view of the Jews is the Jews that the Prophet challenges in the 7th century Arabia,[36] rather then the Jews with whom that the Prophet made a contract and established a state in Medina. They read and understand the verses of the Quran from the raucous relations of today. In that respect, they refer to the *Surah Touba* (Repentance; Chapter 9), which deals with the 'hypocrites', among other things. The Hamas Charter, article 9 quotes verses 75 to 77 from this *Surah*, which reads:

> Amongst them are men who made a covenant with Allah that if he bestowed on them of His bounty; they would give (largely) in charity, and be truly amongst those who are righteous. But when He did bestow of His bounty, they became misers, and turned their back (from their covenant), averse (from its fulfillment. So he hath put, as a consequence, hypocrisy into their hearts ...

Here, Hamas ideologues interpreted 'amongst them are men' to mean that the Jews are hypocrites and cannot be trusted. As Edwards observes, the same *surah* (9:90) also refers to the Bedouins (or the Desert Arabs), exactly in the same way together with other pagan groups, but Hamas excludes those verses and does not call to arms against the Bedouins.[37] Instead, it focuses on the Jews to claim that the current war is a continuation of the conflict in the formative years of Islam.

In their interpretation of Islamic history, Hamas also refers to the Battle of *Khaybar* between some Jewish tribes and the Prophet. On the other hand, they rarely mention the non-conflictual relationship between Jews and Muslims (historically there are only a few conflicts between Jews and Muslims), when they do, they argue that in this relationship the Muslims protected the Jews since Islam enshrines the principle of protection of minorities. In their attempts to renounce Jews, Hamas even refers to various Christian anti-Semitic publications in the West, such as *The Protocols of the Elders of Zion*.[38]

However, over the years, Hamas' definition of who is the "enemy" has also changed. Hamas Charter presents the traditional stereotype of a Crusader-style world Jewish conspiracy against Islam.[39] The Charter defines the "enemy" as general as possible.[40] This language starts to become less visible later on. According to Hroub, this transformation of language is a result of the experiences of the Hamas leadership outside of Palestinian Territories.[41] Hroub argues that "a number of leading personalities who have lived abroad and been exposed to wider experiences than their counterparts in Gaza Strip (who formulated the Hamas Charter) have re-oriented Hamas' political thinking and influenced the formulation of its discourse."[42] Since then, Hamas established relationships with Western states and international bodies such as United Nations.[43]

The transformation of the language also incorporated a more sophisticated conceptualization of the "enemy." For instance, in an interview published in FM, April 1990, one of the Hamas leaders made a distinction between the "Jew" and the "Zionist":

> The non-Zionst Jew is one who belongs to the Jewish faith, whether as a believer or due to an accident of birth, but does not relate to the above ideas and takes no part in aggressive actions against our land and our *umma* [sic]. The Zionist, on the other hand, is one who embraces the aggressive Jewish ideology and becomes an instrument for the realization of those ideas on our land and against our *umma* [sic]. On this basis, Hamas will not adopt a hostile position in practice against anyone because of his ideas or his creed but will adopt such position if those ideas and creed are translated into hostile or damaging actions against our *umma* and our nation.[44]

My interviewees supported this distinction between the Jew and the Zionist. In that line, the Mufti of Jerusalem stated, "I do not hate the Jew, I hate what he does."[45] Sheikh Huseyn also stated that:

> There are no problems with Jews, yet there are problems with Zionism, which wants to get rid of all the Palestinians.[46]

Still the negative image of Jews is common among the Palestinian Muslim population due to the turbulent relations with the state of Israel and its Jewish citizens. For example, an interviewee drew links between the Israelis and the crusaders by stating that "the presence of Israel is like the presence of the Crusaders and they will not stay too long."[47] The same interviewee also referred to the Quran and argued that:

> Quran tells us about the nature of Jews. They are a group of people who did not give others (Goyim/gentiles/non-Jews) their rights. We do not expect any good things from them. They will not give any thing unless take more. [48]

In a lecture presented to Christian seminarians in Hebron, one of the sheikhs referred to the Bible to support the negative image of the Jews. In his lecture he state that:

> Concerning the Jew and the current situation here, we can still go back to Injeel [Bible] and see what it says about the Jews. Isaiah states that Jews are hypocrites and cannot be trusted. In Matthew also there are statements to support this one. They have killed the Prophets [referring specifically to Jesus] and did not follow the word of God [referring to Bible][49]

Jihad a la Hamas

Although Hamas documents constantly refer to jihad and its importance, Hamas officials insist that jihad is a form of self-defense and that all forms of resistance adopted by the movement stem from the same justification upon which the national Palestinian resistance movement based its struggle. Hamas views jihad as a defensive act against aggressive oppressors occupying their land, that is, a war of last resort, justified by self-defense. Hamas argues that when there is no government, the people have to turn to acts of aggression as a means of defending the Muslims of Palestine from a foreign occupation.[50]

The narrative of self-defense seemed to be the most appealing narrative in Palestinian Territories during the phase (Summer of 2000) this research was conducted. The emphasis was on "self-defense" rather than "peace." Going back to the Islamic conception of *peace as presence of justice*, most of my interviewees connected peace in Islam to justice (*Adl*) and rights (*haqq*). In that line, many argued that when there is injustice, persecution, oppression and occupation, Islam, like the United Nations Charter, and other international documents, allows for self-defense. For example, Sheikh Huseyn stated that:

> There are rules in Islam for peace making. These rules call for justice and rights. [These rules] aim to provide safely and to protect lives of people. When these conditions are met, Islam calls to make peace with every one. Today, negotiation between Israel and Palestine does not reflect justice. Negotiations are not going in the direction that satisfies the condition of justice and give back the rights of Palestinians.[51]

The imam of Abraham Mosque in Hebron also supported this view: "Islam is just and wants to bring justice to all."[52] He also argued that, when there is no justice, Islam allows fighting in self-defense and stated: "Islam requires peaceful relations with every body, but acknowledges self-defense for protection of their lives and their land. The Quranic verses support these ideas."[53] Sheikh Alami, who stated, supported this argument:

> For peace in Palestine I want to speak about the right, because God is the *Haqq* [right]. Before I can speak of peace I must have my rights back ...
>
> According to Islam, when two parties have a conflict you have to deal with it in a just manner and you have to identify who has rights. Justice is very important according to Islam and you have to do what is just.[54]

Within this context, Palestinian resistance against Israel was seen as self-defense, thus considered permitted according to Islamic understanding of war and peace. For example, the Mufti of Jerusalem stated that:

> Today, there is injustice, there is occupation [in Palestine]. According to Islam, when the Islamic lands are occupied, it is a duty upon every Muslim—young or old, women or men—to take up jihad/struggle, any way they can defend themselves and their lands. The condition of jihad is the occupation by foreign powers.[55]

At the time, nonviolent approaches to the conflict were received with suspicion, and were not favored. When asked about nonviolence (*la unf*) in Islam one of my interviewees, a supporter of Islamic Jihad, stated that:

> In terms of *la unf* there are different schools in Islam and there is flexibility under the limits that Islam sets. You can choose between different options...under the current conditions here it is very difficult to apply *la unf*.[56]

Osman, who is a supporter of Hamas, offered a different view:

> All the time world persecuted the victims and listened to the winner, it is [nonviolence] the propaganda of Israel....we cannot do as Ghaffar Khan. British were colonial but settlements are here to stay. We cannot do the same as Hizbullah; they have open borders and can get weapons. We are weak.[57]

In support of that argument, Sheikh Abdus-Salam stated that:

> Wave of nonviolence serves the criminals today more then the victims. And victims are in need of a more practical ideology to release themselves from their current positions and earn them equal rights. Nonviolence has become an umbrella waved by the *zalimun* (tyrants) to appease the victims so that they do not oppose and do not defend their rights. They like to have the victims goody-goody. They talk about human rights etc. but do not use it when it is due. Strength of the weak is in its weakness, if they have concrete aims to achieve...[58]

On that note, the Mufti of Jerusalem stated that:

> [In Islam] the basic idea is peace, yet Islam allows fighting for self-defense. When we look at the world we see that all states have armies. There has always been war and war is accepted as a social necessity today. And the fact that all states have armies proves this point. Also fighting injustice is a duty upon every Muslim. When a country is weak no one supports her. A proof of this is the USA-Vietnam war. Vietnam wanted peace but no one listened to it, until the USA wanted it. In South Lebanon Hizbullah have been fighting against Israel. So force works.[59]

Within the context and mood presented above, Hamas' interpretation of jihad as a self-defense mechanism, become attractive to many Palestinian Muslims. Hamas seeks inspiration from Islamic values in its mobilization efforts and in compensating for the huge differences in material resources between the Palestinian people and their supporters on one hand and Israel and its supporters on the other. According to Sheikh Yassin, Hamas is struggling against Israel because "it is the aggressing, usurping and oppressing State that hoists the rifle in the face of Palestinians."[60] He insists that the only language Israel understands is the language of force, and therefore, they will use the same weapon of Israel in their defense, until the entire land of Palestine is liberated.[61] Furthermore, Hamas officials also use various verses in the Quran and *Hadith* to assure that those who fight for a just cause, following the way of God, will be rewarded in the afterlife, especially if they fall martyrs on the path of liberation of their land and religion. For instance, they quote Quran (4: 75), which reads: "whosoever fights in the way of God and is slain or conquers, We shall bring him a mighty wage."

Hamas reassures that the Quranic promise for those who have fallen in this struggle is rich in reward "and besides these shall be two gardens-green pastures, therein two fountains gushing water, there in fruits and palm-trees and pomegranates, therein maidens good and comely." (Quran 55: 65). Because of its mobilizing and motivating effect, secular and leftist groups use this narrative as well. For example, the PLO leader Arafat in 1982, following the Israeli invasion of Lebanon, referred to Jihad and martyrdom,[62] Nevertheless, Islamic groups can use this narrative more convincingly and have more legitimacy because they are led by imams or sheikhs, who are believed to have a better understanding of the texts, can claim that they have access to the "true" meaning of the religious texts, and make this promise of paradise. Their religious position gives them the legitimate authority to talk about who can and who cannot go to heaven. Therefore they can make use of this narrative more effectively.

Hamas also claims that when a Muslim land is invaded, it becomes a duty upon every Muslim to defend the Muslim land. Deriving justification of armed resistance from Islam, the movement further states in its Charter "the day that the enemies usurp a Muslim land, jihad becomes *fard-ul-ayn* (compulsory) upon every single Muslim." Therefore, to confront the Jews, who have usurped Palestine, the banner of jihad must be hoisted. After the Oslo process failed, Hamas stressed that the only real means to liberation is the armed struggle, and no one within the Palestinian camp claimed that armed struggle was illegal, including those who signed Oslo.

This view also finds support among many Palestinians. For example, Sheikh Abu Tayyib stated:

> Today 2/3 of the land of Palestine is considered to be *dar ul harb* [the land of war] according to Islamic law, since the rules of Islamic law is not implemented here and there is kufr [heresy]. Muslims are op-

> pressed here. For that, Muslims all over the world must finish the case of war and return Palestine to its real owner and to remove oppression above them. It is a duty for all Muslims. It is well known that if any part of Muslim land is occupied, jihad is obligatory until they are free from the enemy. All Muslims will sin otherwise.[63]

Contrary to the experience of other Palestinian groups, Hamas restricts the armed struggle to Palestine and considers Palestinian territories (including inside Israel) the only legitimate battlefield. By insisting on limiting the armed struggle to Palestine, Hamas averted any attempts to carry the struggle outside Palestine. Thus, Hamas was able to keep its image as a national liberation movement, whose military effort is directed against the occupiers.[64] This strategy also reflects the defensive character of Hamas' understanding of jihad.

Hamas' notion of jihad is closely connected to the way Hamas views the international system. Ironically, Hamas' perspective on international system is similar to the perspective of Realist International Relations theorists. According to FM June 1990,[65] and FM January 1990,[66] Hamas sees the modern world divided into peoples, nations, states, communities, and schools of thought, the main actors being states (*duwal*) and people (*shu'ub*). Each one of them fights to gain influence and dominion within this system. The states are engaged in a permanent struggle for domination of the system militarily and economically. Strong states struggle for the preservation of the status quo, while the weaker states are struggling to bridge the gap between them and the richer and stronger ones. Thus, the international system only understands the *logic of power* (emphasis added). The most powerful imposes his own interests, while nobody protects the oppressed and the weak. Hamas further contends that, within this system, Western states support the dictatorships in the Arab world, and oppose democratization and development of their own forces.

Hamas is convinced that the international organizations are also a product of this international system and that they reflect the power politics of the state system. Due to this fact, Hamas officials claim that the decisions of these organizations cannot be considered objective or just, and hence, binding. They serve the interests of the mighty states and are dominated by the West, and by the USA in particular, who they assert, proved to be hostile to Islam and are allies of Israel against the Palestinian people. As stated in Hamas Charter, "[i]nitiatives, and so-called peaceful solutions and international conferences are in contradiction to the principles of the Islamic Resistance Movement.[67] Regarding the Madrid conference, Hamas Charter states that "[k]nowing the parties constituting the conference, their past and present attitudes towards Moslem [sic] problems, the Islamic Resistance Movement does not consider these conferences capable of realizing the demands, restoring the rights or doing justice to the oppressed."[68] They add, "[t]hese conferences are only ways of settling the infidels in the lands of the Moslems [sic] as arbitrators," and conclude that,"[t]here is no solution for the Palestinian question except through Jihad."[69]

Workings of the United Nations (UN) are perceived, by the majority of Palestinians, to support the Hamas view, as many of them observe that the UN and other international organizations fail to support the Palestinians. All the Palestinians I interviewed indicated that "although the UN might have passed some resolutions, power politics of the international system, dictated by the USA, have prevented their application." Hamas embodies this complaint and argues "UN never implemented any resolution on Palestine, while they were immediately ready to enforce the resolutions on Kuwait."[70] Furthermore, Hamas, based on the example of the UN resolution concerning the massacre at Mount Temple on October 8, 1990, states that "it took five days for UN to pass a weak resolution, however, any decision against the Islamic world is passed immediately.[71]

Nevertheless, Hamas does not deny dialogue with other nations through international organizations, nor does it advocate an end to participating in the international system. For example introductory memorandum of Hamas stated that Hamas "respects resolution issued by international organization and bodies unless they usurp or contradict the legitimate rights of our people to their homeland, their property, and their right to jihad until they are free and enjoy self-determination." [72]Also, Hamas does not exclude the possibility of creating a new international organization to work on justice and to protect the oppressed. Indeed, in their communiqué printed in FM November 1990,[73] Hamas calls for a new organization based on justice (*adl*) and equality of opportunity (*takafu al-furas*). In addition, as a matter of religious duty, Hamas calls the leaders of the Arab States to take a more active role in the international system and to defend the rights and interests of the Muslim *Ummah* more assertively.

Nevertheless, Hamas is also aware that the solidarity among the Muslim *Ummah* is weak, and that the Muslim community is fragmented. Their Muslim brothers across other regions have abandoned the Palestinians, failing to join their forces to combat the Israeli forces to support the fight of Palestinians against the oppressive occupiers. This condition is manipulated and furthered by the Western powers, predominantly Israel and USA.[74] For that reason Hamas calls for the unification of the Islamic *Ummah* to defend the rights and interests of Muslims, with the Palestinian struggle serving as the ultimate test. However, based on their feeling of being abandoned by both the Arab and Muslim world, Hamas Charter article 12 states that Islamic Resistance Movement is a nationalist movement, while article 7 indicates that "[a]s a result of the fact that those Moslems [sic] adhere to the ways of the Islamic Resistance Movement spread all over the world, rally support for it and its strands, strive towards enhancing its struggle, the Movement is a universal one."

Contrary to various previous Islamic narratives, Hamas does not despise nationalism but recognize its importance in the consciousness of the modern populations. Thus, Hamas incorporates a nationalist narrative into its discourse by asserting that nationalism is a religious creed. Furthermore, Hamas advocates nationalism by stressing that, "if other nationalist movements are connected with materialistic, human or regional causes, nationalism of the Islamic Resistance

Movement has all these elements as well as the more important elements that give it soul and life [connected to the source of spirit and granter of life-God]."[75] Therefore ideologues of Hamas, following the Islamic Jihad, have appropriated Islamic discourse to include nationalism and nationalized Islam. In order to not to distort Islamic universalism, which emphasizes piety rather than racial, cultural, or ethnic origin, Hamas stresses that nationalism is only one aspect of the liberation struggle of Palestine. According to the Hamas Charter, Palestinian liberation has three circles. These are: the Palestinian (nationalist-*wataniyya*), Arab (regionalist- *kawmiyya*) and Muslim (universal- *ummah*) circles with each of them having their role in the struggle against Zionism.[76]

Intifada, which was considered an authentic Palestinian movement, has become an important symbol for Hamas, as well as for other groups. Hamas views *Intifada* as a form of jihad, for it reflected the "will of people;" this view has been revived during the al-Aqsa *Intifada*. Hamas believed that *Intifada* resulted in making the Jews think more and argued that 'the *Intifada* was a curse laying upon [the Jews] until the Day of Judgement, and that their end would come through the hands of the *Shabab* (youth) of Palestinian people."[77]

It is important to note that, although both Hamas and Islamic Jihad called for return to violence, they participated in the nonviolent phase of *Intifada* and utilized various many of the nonviolent techniques in mobilizing and recruiting supporters, as well as in planning and participating in many nonviolent actions.[78] The social acceptance and application of nonviolence made it very hard for these groups to launch violent attacks, as they were greatly concerned with the legitimacy and acceptability of their actions. In that sense, they were extremely responsive to the popular mood that favored nonviolence.

In their evaluation of the *Intifada,* Hamas claims that success was due to return of the Islamic principles of social solidarity and self-sacrifice, as opposed to individualism, greed, self-interest, and lack of tradition, which were harmful inclinations connected with the occupation and the Oslo process. Hamas argued that these "Western" norms and values were breaking down the solidarity among the *Ummah* and threatening the traditional way of life by promoting fragmentation, and were thus harmful for resistance against the occupation. As Bassam stated, this phenomenon is referred to as the "culture of Oslo" (*thakafah Oslo)* in the Occupied Territories.[79] In order to prevent the fragmentation and disputation brought about by the Western inclinations, Islamic movements called the population to return to the tradition and Islamic values and emphasized the importance of education as an integral part of jihad.

One of the important characteristics of Hamas is that "its vision of the struggle assigns popular participation the most important role ..."[80] As opposed to the elitist politics of the pre-1980s, Hamas adopted a more populist approach, recognizing the role *population* plays in having access to power and consolidating its regime of truth. In this respect, Hamas stated:

> ...Truthfully, the bright pages of our struggle in the land of Palestine is part of the history of Arab and Islamic peoples; it is not the history of governments and regimes. While the *umma* [sic]can be considered the strategic depth of the Palestinian cause and of Hamas as a movement, the popular forces within the *umma* [sic]are the core of that depth. They are the real reservoir of strength of our movement in its long struggle with the Zionist enemy. For this reason, Hamas believes it is imperative to consolidate its ties with popular forces and institutions in the Islamic Arab *umma* [sic] and t appeal to their goodness, pride, and generosity ...[81]

In a context like the Palestinian Territories, where multiple groups compete for legitimacy and power, and where every individual is a potential soldier, population becomes a critical force in the balance of narratives. Who is successful in establishing his/her regime of truth is, thus measured by the popular support it receives. For this reason, it has been imperative for the groups in the Palestinian Territories to adopt narratives that will seduce the population and attract them into their camps. Familiar myths, and vocabulary, religious sagas and images play an important role in this process. By linking past, present and future through these cultural objects, various groups engage the population in the meaning making process. As much as narratives are influenced by events, narratives also render events meaningful by engaging the population through activating popular myths, sagas and symbolism.

Hamas derives legitimacy of its narrative from the respected status of its members in the society. This respect is based on the belief in their knowledge of Islam, and their status as people of religion, in a society where sources of legitimacy are based on tradition and religion. Often, most Muslims are not educated enough on the Islamic positions regarding key issues. Therefore, the general population is lacking the necessary background to engage in convoluted debates on crucial issues. Islamic leaders, in such contexts, often simplify various religious texts, and reduce them to lowest common denominators.

This trend of simplification can be clearly seen in Hamas' narrative and in the way Hamas uses myths and other cultural objects to dehistoricize Quranic verses. By doing so, Hamas constructs a story in which all time, place and difference are cast part of a grand project. For example, according to Hamas, the liberation of Palestine is not only about the persecution of a people out of their homes, and nor is it just political or national. It is rather "a religious problem, and should be dealt on this basis" since it contains Islamic holy sites such as the al-Aqsa Mosque, "which is bound to the great Mosque in Mecca in an inseparable bond as long as heaven and earth speak of *Isra* (Mohammed's midnight journey to the seven heavens) and *Mi'raj* (Mohammed's ascension to the seven heavens from Jerusalem).[82] In that direction they utilize various religious myths to justify their narrative, provide exemplar models for action, connect people, spaces and time.

One of the popular myths concerning the Israeli-Palestinian conflict they utilize extensively states "the stability will not prevail until Jesus comes and Yejjuj and Mejjuj[83] go to war."[84] The myth has it that this battle will take place in Palestine. Sheikh Tayyib stated that the Jewish tradition refers to the same event as *Har Majiddo* (Mount of Majiddo)[85] "and there exists a big prison for Palestinians in Majiddo now."[86] By connecting this myth with the prison where the Palestinian prisoners are held, they engage the population in the politics of presence. Such myths are woven into the Friday sermons or in informal gatherings to show how the Quran has it all written down and proves the "truth" of their narratives. These popular myths and symbols are powerful vehicles to construct images of the enemy and incite emotional and religious reactions among the public. They are used to mobilize the population to undertake various acts such as suicide operations, demonstration, etc.

As stated earlier, Hamas understanding of jihad is wider than simply war or fighting. In the Hamas Charter, article 15 states that "in the face of the Jews' usurpation of Palestine, it is compulsory that the banner of Jihad be raised," and continues, "to do this requires the diffusion of Islamic consciousness among the masses, both on the regional, Arab and Islamic levels." In this struggle, every one has their duty and way of struggling. Hamas Charter adds that "it is necessary that scientists, educators, and teachers, information and media people, as well as the educated masses, especially youth and sheikhs of the Islamic movements, should take part in the operation of awakening (the masses).

Hamas believes that bringing people back to the mosques, to the ritual of prayer, to fasting and to the giving of alms will revive the Islamic society and will give the moral, spiritual, and psychological strength to defeat the Israeli occupation. In that line, Hamas undertakes various social services, such as providing emotional and financial support to the families of those who died in combat, establishing kindergartens, religious schools, and providing medical and dental care through its clinics. Therefore, it can be concluded that Hamas' notion of jihad is wider than fighting (*qital*) and includes economic, social, and educational aspects of the struggle (jihad) as well. This view is also supported by Husam al-Nasir, who states that:

> This jihad [Hamas' understanding of jihad]... should be understood in the broad sense of encompassing.... armed struggle, operations and combat, social science, the triumph of truth ad social justice, the achievement of unity, etc. There should be a broad understanding of the changes desired in all fields, as there are all necessary for a multi-dimensional and multi-goal-oriented military, political, ideological and social jihad in the service of the common goals of liberating the *umma* [sic], and its heart, Palestine, and of achieving the unity and resistance of *umma* [sic].[87]

Still, Hamas' understanding of jihad justifies armed struggle as a legitimate reaction of Israeli aggression as a form of self-defense. In that respect, the Islamic movement in Palestine shares the fundamentalist idea that jihad is the individual duty (*fard-ul ayn*) of every Muslim. However, while the fundamentalist perspective argues that jihad is the sixth pillar in Islam and must be conducted until the God's way prevails on every corner of the world, Islamic movement argues that jihad is permitted and becomes a duty upon every individual Muslim both men and women, only when the Muslim lands are invaded and Muslims are persecuted.

Suicide (Martyrdom) Attacks

Hamas adopts various methods for struggling against the Israeli occupation. As mentioned above, these methods range from social services to armed fighting. Among the methods that Islamic groups such as Hamas and Islamic Jihad (increasingly also Fatah) employ in response to occupation, suicide attacks are the most controversial and discussed. Hamas claims to use suicide attacks to rebalance the asymmetric balance of power between Palestinians and Israelis. According to the *USA-Today* article by Jack Kelley, suicide attacks, "which have spread fear and despair among Israelis, have proved to be the deadliest weapon in the Palestinian arsenal during the current [al-Aqsa] *Intifada*, or uprising.[88] Indeed suicide bombers came on the scene as the ultimate weapon of asymmetric warfare, one that could penetrate even to the democratic core of American society, as another article, printed in *Newsweek,* notes.[89]

In their interpretation of jihad Hamas adopts a "retaliatory" attitude towards the Israelis. Following the principle of reciprocity and retaliation, suicide attacks, especially targeting the Israeli civilians inside the Israeli Green Line, became an important military tactic for Hamas after the Hebron Massacre of February 25, 1994. Following that massacre Hamas declared "The settlers will pay for the massacre with the blood of their hearts," and launched a new strategy based on "a life for a life."[90]

Since suicide attacks are a controversial issue not only in terms of international law, but also according to the Islamic law, finding a strong basis for these attacks has been an important aspect of the narrative of the Islamic movement.[91] In respect to the suicide attacks, Sheikh Yassin, in an interview with Kristianasen,[92] recognizes that both Islamic law and international law prohibit attacks on civilians. However, he also stresses that Israel had been "the first to violate these laws" and that since Palestinians are the victims, he states,

> It is our right to treat them in the same way that they treat us. So I am asking the whole world to call on Israel to stop attacking our civilians, and if they do, we'll reciprocate. It is their decision.[93]

This "principle of retaliation" invokes the way that the "doctrine of necessity" is interpreted by Hamas to justify and legitimize those acts that are considered illegal under Islamic law. Within this context, Hamas believes that the doctrine of necessity nullifies those restrictions that concern the distinction between civilian and military targets. This view finds great support among the members and sympathizers of Islamic groups such as Hamas and Islamic Jihad. In an interview, 24-year old Gazan member of Izz ad-Din al Qassam Brigade Abu al-Abed reflects this justification as a response to Israeli attack; he states, "I support the suicide operations inside Israel. We never initiate the violence. Our operations are always in response to a particular crime committed against us."[94] He adds:

> People say that we are killing Israeli civilians, and I respond to that there are Palestinian children being killed while trying to get food for their families or going to school. The Koran says 'He who commits aggression against you, you may commit aggression against him in the same manner." So this is our right. We respond in kind.[95]

Hamas officials insist these operations "represent an exception necessitated by the Israeli insistence on targeting Palestinian civilians and by Israel's refusal to an understanding prohibiting the killing of civilians on both sides, an understanding comparable to the one reached between Hizbullah in southern Lebanon."[96] Yassin argues that Hamas does not endorse the killing of civilians, but that there is no other option to respond to the murdering of Palestinian civilians. During my interview with Sheikh Abu Tayyib, in reference to killings of civilians, he stated:

> Islam prohibits killing civilians and especially women and children. Sometimes Muslims are forced to kill innocent people, not because of Islam but because of circumstances. In Ramle 3,000 people were ordered to be killed by Rabin. And the massacre of Hebron. So your way becomes the way they use against you. Threatening them by their own way.[97]

Suicide attacks, "the only consistently effective military weapon in the Palestinian armory against Israel,"[98] instigated much debate, not only in the Western media, but also among Islamic intellectual circles all around the world. The debate concerning suicide attacks in the Islamic world first started in 1980s, when the Shi'a militants adopted it as a strategy. Nevertheless, the validity of this tradition from an Islamic point of view was strongly questioned by the leading Shi'a scholar Sheikh Muhammad Husein Fadlallah.[99] Eventually, such tactics were abandoned by Hizbullah by the end of 1980s. Ironically though, we see that the Islamic Jihad published a long *fatwa* (legal opinion) legitimizing what they call "martyrdom attacks." However, no Islamic scholar had signed the *fatwa*, and suicide attacks were not considered part of the liberation movement until 1993, when Hamas launched the first Palestinian suicide attack.[100] In order to legitimize suicide attacks, Islamic leaders lacking formal Islamic training issued self-proclaimed *fatwas.*

Increasingly, the official *ulema,* including those in other Arab countries, are supporting suicide attacks. The amplification of social pressure makes it hard for those scholars who offer an alternative view. Religious leaders who have not received proper Islamic education criticize official *ulema* for being "servants of autocratic states," supported by the USA, thus pay lip service to those authorities that appointed them, especially if they are against suicide attacks. For example, when the Grand Mufti (the highest religious authority) in Saudi Arabia, Sheikh Abd al-Aziz bin Abdallah Aal al-Sheikh declared on April 21, 2001 that Islam forbids suicide attacks, he was severely criticized, not only by some of the prominent Islamic scholars, but also by various secular personalities in the Arab world. Al-Sheikh commented to a London-based and Saudi owned newspaper al Sharq al Awsat:

> What you call suicide bombings in my view they are illegitimate and have nothing to do with jihad in the cause of God. I am afraid it is another form of killing oneself.[101]

This comment triggered much criticism. Abdel Aziz al-Rantisi, a leading Hamas figure from Gaza rebuffed Al-Sheikh's comment by stating that "suicide bombers do not kill them selves because they are bored with life. They die as a means of killing their enemy, even if they kill themselves in the process."[102] In April, 2002 the new Mufti of Egypt, in the semi-official *al-Ahram* newspaper referred to the suicide bombings carried out by Palestinians against Israeli settlers in the West Bank and Gaza as "one of the highest levels of martyrdom."[103] Sheikh of Al-Azhar, Mohammed Sayed Tantawi was also quoted saying, "the actions of martyrdom undertaken by the Palestinians are in self-defense and are a sort of martyrdom as long as they are intended to kill fighters, not women and children."[104]

Although not all Palestinians support the suicide attacks, these attacks do enjoy a great deal of support from the majority of the population living in the Occupied Territories. There is a great social acceptance and legitimacy of the suicide attacks as heroic and holy acts of resistance among the Palestinians. This support for suicide attacks increased dramatically since the first suicide attack undertaken by Hamas. According to Christopher Dickey, the support for suicide attacks was 20 percent in 1995-1996. Whereas another poll conducted during the *al Aqsa Intifada* indicated that the support had risen to 80 percent.[105] As the principal of an elementary school in Gaza, Muhammad Abu Rukbah observes that children see "images on TV, the posters in the streets, the honor of the martyrs' families, for they want that kind of honor for themselves, for their families."[106]

The suicide attacks are made possible through Hamas's interpretation of the martyrdom myth.[107] Islam holds that God will reward those individuals who die for the cause of God. In various verses the Quran refers to those who die in the path of God as martyrs and state that:

> Indeed Allah has traded with the believers their lives and wealth in return for paradise if they fight for the cause of Allah whether they are martyred or victorious and this is a promise from Allah which he has made a duty upon himself clearly recorded in the Torah, the Bible and the Qur'an. And who is more faithful in his promise than Allah; so enjoy this good news for your allegiance and loyalty to your Lord for this is the greatest achievement... (9: 111)

The myth of martyrdom and the symbol of "the martyr" represent the utmost act of devotion to God. As a powerful mythic construct, it gives meaning to not only one's existence, but more importantly, to one's death.[108] Substantiated by the myth of martyrdom, suicide attacks invoke the myth of ultimate form of sacrifice for God, for justice, and for one's own people. Such devotion to their cause, and not fearing death makes Palestinians feel superior in terms of their resolve, determination and faith. Suicide bombers remind the outside world that this is an unfair fight. After being humiliated by Arab defeats in the previous wars with Israel, living under the occupation with no recognized rights and lacking self-determination, the symbolism of martyrdom empowers the Palestinians to face their "almighty" enemy with courage. Suicide attacks endow Palestinians with the sense that they are not powerless or subservient, but can do something about the situation, and sap the Israeli morale, thus obliterate their psychology. These operations also aim to create a sense of insecurity and fear among Israelis, which the Palestinians constantly feel. Besides, by lending meaning and dignity to these actions, the myth of martyrdom provides comfort and paramount means of coping with suffering and loss, especially to the families of these individuals who undertake suicide actions.

Therefore, disparagement of suicide attacks emasculates the psychological, existential, and conscientious needs operative in the meaning making process, which the religious narrative fulfills. Attempts to delegitimize suicide attacks render the deaths of those young Palestinian men (and women) meaningless, a criminal act, and a sin. Such attempts undermine the myth of martyrdom, which mobilizes Palestinians to become human bombs as opposed to the nuclear bombs and other military technology Israel has in this asymmetric warfare. These claims create a lacuna of meaning in the process of making sense of life and death, and a meaningful and empowering justification of their "most effective strategy", or so they perceive. Such claims not only defame suicide bombers, but also make it harder to cope with loss and suffering.

In an attempt to understand why and how an individual would explode him/herself, most of the Western media and many Western scholars focus on the narrative of the "72 virgins" and "unlimited sex" in Heaven waiting for the martyrs as the incentive for young people to undertake suicide attacks.[109] Although killing civilians should not be accepted in any way or form under any condition, in any society, the focus of these "analyzes" are on "how can one blow up him/herself," rather than on killing of civilians. These journalists and pundits, similarly to the selective readings and interpretations of any religious texts to pursue their ends, focus on the "virgins of heaven" as the basis of suicide attacks. Such caricaturization not only attempts to ridicule and delegitimize Islam (rather than challenging the killing of civilians as a result of suicide attacks), but also aims at representing the Palestinian and Islamic culture as obsessed with sex. More than journalism, this approach is instrumental to the dehumanization of the enemy, which ultimately serves to justify violence and destruction.

This analysis fails to account for those who sacrifice their lives for their countries in the militaries all over the world, recognizing the risk of being killed in a combat with the "enemy." Furthermore, this analysis does not account for the suicide attacks undertaken by non-Islamic groups such as PKK in Turkey and Tamil Tigers in Sri Lanka, among others. Rather the why and how of suicide attacks must be sought in more sober, and but not less "passionate," aspects of zealotry and frustration and humiliation under a foreign occupation. As the Israeli terrorism expert Shaked states:

> Most of the bombers don't sign up for martyrdom for the promise of unlimited sex. They join because of their absolute devotion to God and their desire to die with Jewish blood on their hands. It is not a heroic thing, it is a holy thing.[110]

Ely Karmon of the Counterterrorism Institute, on the other hand, argues that "neither Freud nor Allah is the primary motivator here; the dream of 'Palestine' is."[111] Furthermore, these bombers know that their families will be financially compensated, their pictures will be posted in schools and mosques, and they will earn a special place in Heaven for having fought to defend Islam and justice. It is usually the case that after a bombing, an activist approaches the father of the bomber with an envelope containing $10,000. According to Abu Shanab, this money is a form of reparation to help the family rebound from their loss, but Israeli authorities argue that this financial aid provides one of the main incentives for the bombers.[112]

The social and economic conditions make financial support critical in the context of Palestinian society. Islamic groups, such as Hamas take advantage of this situation. When a Palestinian dies (regardless of them being suicide attackers or not) members of Hamas visit the family of the dead and offer their help economically and socially. Nayef, one of my interviewees supported this argument by stating:

> ... since the economic situation is very difficult for many people, it is these religious groups that help them economically and socially. For example, if anyone gets killed they [religious groups] are the first ones to go and visit his family and comfort them by saying that they have a secure place in heaven since they are martyrs. They also build hospitals ad give food to people. And many people, whose living conditions are worse than bad, feel like they have nothing to loose and it is better to secure a place in Heaven than to live under these conditions and under the oppressive occupation of Israeli forces. For that reason, their solution and offer becomes appealing to many people in the region.[113]

In his analysis Dickey states that: "There is nothing natural about killing yourself in any culture," and adds that:

> In those who have waged suicide-war, the strongest motivations is protection of home and heart, Japan's kamikaze pilots saw themselves as the last line of defense for their families in World War II. Sri Lanka's Tamil Tigers, who have carried out more than 170 suicide attacks in the last 25 years, are fighting at the behest of a charismatic leader to secure their homeland. Lebanon's Hizbullah has a radical Islamic ideology, but it was created and grew as a response to Israel's 1982 invasion of their country. Although martyrdom is revered in Islam, the Quran recognizes the martyrdom only of those who fight to defend their faith and their land. Suicide, as a means to escape from this life, is regarded as a sin.[114]

In order to stop suicide attacks, Israel is adopting extremely harsh measures, which include collective punishment strategies such as bombing the houses of the families of suicide attackers.[115] Israel also attacks Palestinian cities, and refugee camps with F-16s and other high-tech weapons, bulldozing buildings without discrimination, closing down hospitals, preventing ambulances to take the wounded to hospitals, enforcing curfews, destroying all forms of infrastructure that a society needs to function. However, as Kristianasen notes, this does not prevent attacks by elements driven underground, since the region is awash with arms, and there is no shortage of young people ready for sacrifice.[116]

Most Palestinians who support suicide operations view them as the only effective weapon against an all-powerful enemy in an asymmetric war. In this asymmetric conflict Palestinians state that they have no weapons to defend themselves against one of the strongest armies of the world and certainly the strongest army in the region. Moreover, Israel receives military and financial support from the USA, and the USA is the only superpower in the global system currently. Palestinians feel that under these circumstances, when there is no one protecting their rights and standing up for justice, they have a right to use any weapons and any means that is available to them. Shallan notes the effectiveness of this method and states:

> In the spring of 1996, following a series of martyrdom operations carried out by Hamas and MIJ [Movement of Islamic Jihad] —operation that sent the leaders of international arrogance rushing to the Sharm al Sheikh Summit—we saw the Zionist masses on television screens screaming that they are in the wrong place. This is the first time in the history of Zionist entity that martyrdom actions forced the Zionist mind to question the usefulness of establishing a Jewish state on usurped land, on the ruins of a people who will chase them back with resistance and Jihad until the end of time.[117]

Palestinians who support suicide operations insist that they have chosen this path because they had no other choice, and that Islam allows for exceptional measures under extreme conditions, such as civilian casualties when there is no other way to defend them. As one of the members of Izz ad-Din al-Qassam Brigade (the military wing of Hamas), Abu al-Abed states:

> Every human being who has his land invaded, all he possesses taken and his rights denied has a right to resist. He has a right to do this by any means he has. The military operations we undertake do not lead immediately to the freedom of Palestine, but are a step in that direction.[118]

He also adds:

> If you had your house invaded and the invaders moved into your house, would you not accept anything less than removing them from your home? [119]

> My family supports me in this. Let me make this clear we are more ready to accept death than the life we lead. And this goes to all Palestinians. We have no security. The word suicide is not important. We do not see it as suicide. It is resistance.[120]

The Palestinians perceive the Oslo Process as a sham, because it only had the intention of providing security to the Israelis, and neglected the Palestinian demands. Shallah states this perception in his interview with Khalid al-Ayid;

> The core of the Oslo agreement is the preservation of Israel's security, not regaining Palestinian lands. The Wye River Memorandum linked the so-called redeployment of the Israeli army from any portion of the land to the achievement of full security for Israel.[121]

In support of this view, one of my interviewees stated that:

> During the seven years that followed Oslo we saw nothing happened. There is no right of return, prisoners are not freed, Jerusalem and water is still an issue, houses are still being demolished, Palestinians are still being killed. We want a peace that will stop all these, but since Oslo nothings changed...[122]

Furthermore, many Palestinians are convinced that the Israeli society cannot be considered a civilian society in the traditional sense. This view is supported by some of my interviewees, such as Sheikh Abu Tayyib, who stated that:

> The Islamic information is still my base but all the Israeli society becomes soldiers at the age of 10, and every year for three months they are called to the army until they are 35 years old. During the *Intifada*, Israelis killed many children, women, and pregnant women. We told them that we will not kill civilians if you stop killing civilians.[123]

Another interviewee, Dr. Azzam, on the other hand stated that:

> Islam rejects hurting the civilians yet in our context it becomes very difficult to determine who is a civilian and who is not. For instance the massacres of 1990 and 1994 were results of attacks by the civilian Jews to the civilian Palestinians. The anger and rage today is a reflection of those now. Besides in Israeli military there are women and every body is a soldier. Settlers walk around with machine guns, and are more dangerous to Palestinian civilians then soldier. All the Israeli society is soldiers so Islam is very strict about civilians but definition of civilians is not the same in Israel...my grandfather was killed carrying tea. His houses is taken by Israelis no ...they [Israelis] have guns and bombs and live in our houses ...[124]

This view is also supported by Abu al Abed who states that:

> Israeli society is a militarized society, not a civilian one. From very young age, 12 or 13-years-old they start the military training. At the age of 17 they go to the army. This is both for men and women.[125]

Although Hamas justifies jihad as a self-defense mechanism, its officials are confident that the jihad in the form of an arm struggle will continue until its conditions are accepted. According to Sheikh Yassin these conditions include establishment of a Palestinian state following the withdrawal of Israel from all the Palestinian lands it has occupied since 1967, dismantling all the settlements, the release of all Palestinian and Arab prisoners, and noninterference in Palestinian national affairs.[126]

Following his release from the Israeli prison, Yassin offered a cease-fire agreement to Israel, in the form of a truce that would last for a period of 10 years, following the example of the *Hudaybiyah Treaty*, and would not entail recognition of the State of Israel. Israel would agree to withdraw all its troops from the 1967 Occupied Territories and to dismantle all Jewish settlements erected on Palestinian soil since 1967. In addition to these, Israel would free all Palestinian prisoners in its detention centers. In return, Hamas would agree to stop all military operations against Israeli targets during the 10 years of the cease-fire. Israel, however, did not respond to Yassin's offer.[127]

Majority of Hamas members supported Yassin's offer. Abdul Aziz al-Rantizi, a Hamas leader inside the Occupied Territories indicated his support for the essence of Sheikh Yassin's idea as follows:

> With respect to the armistice as an interim solution, we are not opposed to the idea, because it safeguards the right of the Palestinians to demand their homeland be returned to them. An armistice in this context means not recognizing Israel. Sheihk Yassin set a time limit on it, namely ten years, which is consistent with the Hudaihbah [sic] truce and is not inconsistent with religious law[128]

Another Hamas leader, Abu Marzouq, also supported this view:

> As a resistance movement, it is our opinion that if the enemy's government wishes to extricate itself from this impasse, it should not seek to impose surrender on the Palestinian people. There could be a peace treaty or an armistice that would provide an exit from the complicated situation in the region and allow disengagement from the crisis.[129]

According to Hamas, the main difference between a peace treaty and an armistice is that the latter is not of limited duration but is open-ended.[130] A treaty would "involve capitulation of Palestinian rights and acceptance of the usurpation of those rights by Israel," but an armistice "puts a freeze on the situation as far as rights are concerned."[131] Although an armistice is limited in duration, there is a possibility of "renewal." Yassin explained his perspective on an armistice in an interview with *Maariv* Newspaper:

> One can envision an agreement for a limited period, let us say 15 years, but not forever... I cannot commit future generations to that course of action. They will have to decide for them selves.[132]

Although members and supporters of both Hamas and Islamic Jihad consider the possibility of a truce, they are stern not to recognize the State of Israel. As Abu al Abed states:

> We would accept a transnational agreement or initiative under which there is a cease-fire between us and an Israeli entity, but we do not accept a two state solution as the basis for lasting peace. As a combatant, I would accept a cease-fire in return for Israel giving up Gaza,

> the West Bank and East Jerusalem, but we can never recognize the state of Israel.[133]

To conclude, when we observe the interpretation of Islamic texts concerning war and peace by Islamic groups such as Hamas and Islamic Jihad, we see that their horizons of past and present overlap into one great horizon, since they cannot disconnect themselves from the past. Their understanding is bound and embedded in their effective history, which is molded by their experience and cultural traditions. The social, religious, and national context—itself a result of the complex interaction of historical, economical, socio-political and cultural factors—lies behind the development of contemporary Islamic narratives in Palestinian Territories.

These contextual factors strongly impact the way that texts are interpreted and related to each other, as they determine which texts, other then the primary sources, will be used to support particular interpretations. (An example of this would be to use the doctrine of Jihad interpreted by Ghazzali, or Shafi, rather then Shaybani and Hanefi, which support a more extremist approach). Utilizing previous texts and myths to support particular narratives forms the inter-textual (the relationship between various texts) aspect of the analysis.

In most cases, most Muslims are not well acquainted with Islamic positions on key topics. This is partly due to the communication gap between educated religious authorities and local urban or village religious leaders. In addition, many of the traditions of Islamic reasoning (*ijtihad*) are "often simplified and reduced by local religious leaders into lowest common denominators –ignoring minority views, nuanced exceptions for specific circumstances, or sophisticated methods of juridical reasoning."[134] These local religious leaders, such as Sheikh Yassin, do not generally have knowledge of the classical and modern debates on these issues, and this lack of knowledge lends additional weight to the discourse of the most conservative of Islamist positions, especially on issues carrying great emotional and symbolic weight.[135] This can be clearly seen in Palestine in regard to sensitive issues such as the extent of force and violence sanctioned by Islam. The analysis of the emerging narratives in Palestine shows how discussion on these issues—particular at the popular level—is reduced to their simplest forms, dogmatic statements, and slogans. This simplistic, even reductionist approach capitalizes on emotional and psychological factors such as popular anger, frustration, depravation, hate and revenge.

The challenge in analyzing this subject is to grasp the narratives in the exact specificity of their occurrence, determine their conditions of existence, try to identify their limits, and establish their correlation with other narratives that may be connected with them, and show what other forms of narratives they exclude. This study shows that the inter-textual and contextual aspects of the meaning-making process creates a discursive space in which various narratives—such as secular-nationalist; Marxist-leftist; nonviolent, defensive, or offensive Islamic narratives of peace and war—compete with each other for legitimacy and dominance. These contextual and inter-textual elements draw the limits of that which can be included in the narrative. In this case, Hamas re-interpreted the notion of jihad to include nationalistic elements, by utilizing Islamic texts, myths, and symbols within a context of weakening pan-Arabic and pan-Islamist ideologies and increasing awareness that only the Palestinians can liberate their homeland.

Additionally, scholars must also take into account "who" is narrating. It is important to determine who has the right or legitimacy to narrate, and who derives from the narrative his/her own special quality or prestige, and claims that what s/he is saying is the "truth." In that respect, we have to look at the status of the individuals—such as Sheikh Yassin or Yasser Arafat—within their religio-cultural, social, and political context to proffer such a narrative. In the Palestinian context, individuals with strong family or kinship ties and/or military, political or religious backgrounds enjoy greater credibility within the society[136]

In terms of religious narratives, only religious experts are sanctioned by religious law and tradition with legitimacy in the eyes of Palestinian Muslims to proffer narratives concerning jihad and martyrdom. In that sense, only religious experts, (institutional *ulema* or local sheikhs,) are believed to be competent and to possess the necessary religious knowledge and tradition. As I have noted, neither PLO nor other secular nor leftist groups are legitimized to promise salvation through martyrdom, although they have also occasionally referred to the jihad and *shahadah* in their narratives.

Another crucial point to remember is that the legitimacy of these individuals is also defined by their position within in relation various domains or groups are also defined on the basis of situations at hand. For example, the specific conditions described in Chapter Five allowed Arafat to emerge as the legitimate representative of the Palestinian people, as the leader of PLO. After a crisis of legitimacy following the Israeli invasion of Lebanon, the Peace process and the hope for ending the conflict renewed Arafat's legitimacy among the Palestinian population. However, the collapse of the Oslo process and his perceived weakness and inability to change the living conditions of the Palestinian population drained his legitimacy once again, until he was held as a prisoner in his own compound till his death.

A new chapter in Palestinian social and political history was instigated when Hamas won the majority of the local elections in 2005. Hamas victory during the January 2006 elections further reflects a shift in the 'balance of narratives' However, competition between narratives is far from over. On the contrary, current chaos and violence in the Palestinian social and political embodies the severe competition of narratives and authority. Once again, multiple, competing narratives are clashing; they are incompatible, but are based on the same conditions of emergence. These narratives are alternative in the sense that they cannot be true at the same time. For instance an offensive and nonviolent interpretation of jihad competes for dominance. In effect, not all possible alternatives can be realized or established as the dominant regime of truth. Therefore, not only what can be said, or who says it, but also how these groups reach out to the society becomes crucial in the process of legitimization. In that respect, the institutional sites, such as mosques, educational institutions, or health centers, are yet other arenas where these narratives clash.

In the modern era, especially since the 1970s, Islamic groups have been actively providing social services, including financial and emotional support, as well as medical and educational services to the Palestinians, especially to the families of those killed by the Israelis. Therefore, to understand how these groups derive their legitimacy, it is critical to examine the institutional sites that provide the forum for these social services and for the dissemination of narratives. In the context of the current situation, the success of local religious leaders and of Islamic organizations in general, depends, to a large extent, on their success in these institutional sites. The next Chapter will focus on the institutional sites, where alternative narratives compete for legitimacy.

Endnotes

1. For more information on International Solidarity Movement (ISM) see http://www.palsolidarity.org/
2. For more information on see http://www.pngo.net/GIPP/
3. Interview with Khalid, Washington D.C. December 10, 2001.
4. Interviews with Bassam, Isa, Osman, and Sami.
5. Interview with Bassam, Bethlehem, July 18, 2000.
6. Interview with Sheikh Abu Tayyib, Bethlehem, July 22, 2000. Interviewee emphasized the word "security."
7. Interview with Dr. Azzam, Hebron July 20, 2000.
8. Interview with Khalid, Washington D.C December 10, 2001.
9. Interview with Khalid.
10. Interview with Khalid.
11. Interview with Nidal, Dheisheh Refugee Camp, Bethlehem June 30, 2000.
12. Interview with Bassam, Bethlehem, July 18, 2000.
13. Interview with Nidal, Dheisheh Refugee Camp, Bethlehem June 30, 2000.
14. Interview with Khalid, Washington D.C December 10, 2001.
15. Interview with Khalid.
16. See, Khaled Hroub. *Hamas: Political Thought and Practice (*Washington, D.C.: Institute for Palestine Studies, 2000), 45.
17. Edwards 1996, 182.
18. *Bayan Hamas* no. 62, 13. 8. 1990 cited in Nusse 1998, 75.
19. Reported by Alan Johnston BBC news January 25, 2005. See also http://:bbcnews.com
20. Nusse 1998., 78.
21. Nusse 1998., 75.
22. Nusse 1998.
23. Interview with Sheikh Alami Jerusalem, July 5, 2000.
24. Interview with Sheikh Alami.

25. Interview with the Ibrahimi (Abraham) Mosque, Hebron July 6, 2000.

26. Interview with Mahmoud Washington D.C. December 10, 2001.

27. Interview with Khalid, Washington D.C. December 10, 2001.

28. Exploring the role of Christians in Palestinian resistance to Israeli occupation and their relationship with the Islamic groups would be a very interesting area of study. However, this dissertation will not cover this important area of study.

29. See Appendix I introduction and article 9.

30. All the citations from these journals in this work are taken from Andrea Nusse. Here, the references to *Filastin al-Muslima* (FM) and *Mithaq* will be followed by the date and the page number stated in Nusse 1998.

31. Nusse 1998., 52.

32. Hamas Charter article 35.

33. Interview with Nayef Al-Watan Center Hebron July 19, 2000.

34. Interview with Nayef.

35. Shaykh Abu al-Waleed al-Ansari *The Termination of the Zionist entity; A Qur'anic Fact* By Translated by Abu al-Waleed al-Hamawi at http://www.hamasonline.com/indexx.php?page=Qassam/termination_zonist_entity

36. Edwards 1996, 186.

37. Edwards 1996. See verse 90 of the same Surah for reference to Desert Arabs, or Beduins.

38. See Edwards 1996, 188-189. See also Hamas website, which has a link to *The Protocols of the Elders of Zion*, at www.hamasonline.com

39. Hroub 2000, 49.

40. See Appendix.

41. See Hroub 2000, 50-52.

42. Hroub 2000., 50.

43. Hroub 2000.

44. Cited in Hroub 2000., 51.

45. Interview with the Mufti of Jerusalem, al-Aqsa mosque, June 26, 2000.

46. Interview with Sheikh Husayn, Aqsa Mosque, Jerusalem, June 25, 2000.

47. Interview with Sheikh Abu Tayyib, Bethlehem, July 22, 2000.

48. Interview with Sheikh Abu Tayyib.

49. Lecture given by Dr. Hafiz at the Islamic University of Hebron on War and Peace in Islam on July 20, 2000.

50. Dr. Hafiz 2000., 191.

51. Interview with Sheikh Huseyn, Aqsa Mosque Jerusalem, June 25, 2000.

52. Interview with the imam of Ibrahimi Mosque, Hebron, July 6, 2000.

53. Interview Ibrahimi Mosque 2000.

54. Interview with Shaikh Alami Hebron, July 5, 2000.

55. Interview with the Mufti of Jerusalem, al- Aqsa Mosque, June 26, 2000.

56. Interview with Isa and his three friends, University of Bethlehem, July 19, 2000.

57. Interview with Osman and his four friends, University of Bethlehem July 19, 2000.

58. Interview with Sheikh Abdus-Salam, Hebron July 21, 2000.

59. Interview with the Mufti of Jerusalem, Jerusalem July 23, 2000.

60. Azzam Tamimi. "The Legitimacy of Palestinian Resistance: An Islamic Perspective" paper presented at the *7th Annual Conference of the Center for Policy Analysis on Palestine*, Washington, D.C. 11 September, 1998.

61. Tamimi 1998.

62. Arafat stated: "It was us that gave jihad a meaning in the present time after it has been absent for so long. In the siege of Beirut we lost 72,000 dead and wounded. We advance for martyrdom and ask whoever wants to follow. And I ask you, did I prevent anyone from using whatever method he chose to liberate Palestine?" cited in Edwards, 202.

63. Interview with Sheikh Abu Tayyib Bethlehem, July 22, 2000.

64. Hroub 2000, 64.

65. FM June 1990, 26.

66. FM January, 1990, 3.

67. See Hamas Charter article 13.

68. Hamas Charter.

69. Hamas Charter.

70. FM September 1990, 7 cited in ibid, 60.

71. FM November 1990, 7, Ibid., 52.

72. Cited in Hroub 2000, 51.

73. FM November, 1990, 52.

74. Hamas Charter article 32.

75. Hamas Charter . article 12.

76. Hamas Charter article 14.

77. FM January 1990, 1.

78. Abu-Nimer 2003, 228.

79. Interview with Bassam, Bethlehem, July 18, 2000.

80. Hroub 2000, 66.

81. Cited in Hroub 2000, 66 footnote, 52.

82. Hamas Charter article 15.

83. Muslims believe that Jesus was ascended to heaven and will return to earth before the doomsday. The doomsday will start with an all-encompassing war (similar to Armageddon) between two parties referred to as Yejjuj and Mejjuj in the Quran. There is no clear indication of who these parties are.

84. Interview with Sheikh Abu Tayyib Bethlehem July 22, 2000.

85. Also known as Armageddon.

86. Interview with Sheikh Abu Tayyib Bethlehem July 22, 2000.

87. Husam al-Nasir *Harakat al-muqawama al-Islamiyya (Hamas): Al-intilaq wa mu'adalat al-sira* [Islamic Resistance Movement (Hamas): The launching and plan of struggle] (London: Muslim Palestine Publications, 1990) 18-22. cited in Hroub, 47; footnote 15.

88. Jack Kelley. "Devotion, Desire Drive Youths to 'Martyrdom'" *USA TODAY* 07/05/2001.

89. Christopher Dickey. 2002 "Inside Suicide, Inc." *Newsweek* at http://www.msnbc.com/news/735266.asp, 2.

90. Kristianasen 1999, 23.

91. Two Hamas webpages attempt to show the Islamic basis of these attacks. See http://www.hamasonline.com/indexx.php?page=Qassam/martyrdom%20operations and also http://www.hamasonline.com/indexx.php?page=Qassam/martyrdom_not_suicide

92. Hamas website., 31 Interview with Sheikh Yassin, Gaza City, 20, November 1997.

93. Hamas website.

94. Interview with Abu al Abed "Voices from the Conflict." *BBC News* at http://news.bbc.co.uk/hi/english/static/in_depth/middle_east/2002/voices/abu.stm.

95. BBC News 2002, 3.

96. Tamimi.

97. Interview with Sheikh Abu Tayyib July 22, 2000 Hebron.

98. James Drummond. 2002. "Martyrdom Debate Points to Harder Islamic Line" *The Muslim News* 04/04/2002 at http://.muslimnews.co.uk/news/news.php?article=2134.

99. Reuven Paz, "Saudi Fatwah against Suicide Terrorism. [sic]" *Peace Watch*, The Washington Institute's Special Reports on the Arab-Israeli Peace Process, Number 323, May 2, 2001.

100. Paz 2001.

101. Paz 2001.

102. Nadia Abou El-Magd 2001. "Politics of Fatwa" in Al-Ahram Weekly On-line 3 - 9 May Issue No.532.

103. Newsweek 2002, 1.

104. Newsweek 2002

105. Newsweek 2002, 5.

106. Newsweek 2002., 2.

107. See http://www.hamasonline.com/indexx.php?page=Qassam/martyrdom%20operations and http://www.hamasonline.com/indexx.php?page=Qassam/martyrdom_not_suicide

108. Gopin, Marc, *Holy War Holy Peace* (Oxford University Press, 2002), 31-32.

109. USA Today 2001, 2-4; Newsweek 2002, 4.

110. USA Today 2001, 4.

111. Newsweek 2002, 5.

112. Newsweek 2002., 6.

113. Interview with Nayef Hebron, July 19, 2000.

114. Newsweek 2002, 8.

115. Milliyet May 12, 2002 (Turkish Newspaper) www.milliyet.com.tr.

116. Kristianasen 1999, 33.

117. Shallah 1999, 70.

118. BBC News 2002, 1.

119. BBC News 2002, 3.

120. BBC News 2002., 2.

121. Shallah 1999, 67

122. Interview with Palestinian student Bassam. July 18, 2000. Bethlehem.

123. Interview with Sheikh Abu Tayyib. July 22, 2000 Hebron.

124. Interview with Dr. Azzam July 6, 2000. Hebron.

125. Interview with Abu al Abed in *BBC News,* 2.

126. Kristianasen 1999, 31.

127. See Hroub 2000, 81.

128. Quoted in *Al-Sabeel* (Jordan), 10 November 1993 and cited in Khaled Hroub *Hamas: Politcal Thought and Practice* (Washington D.C.: Institute for Palestine Studies, 2000), 82.

129. Quoted in *Al-Sabeel* (Jordan), 19 April, 1994 and cited in Hroub 2000.

130. Hroub 2000.,81.

131. Hroub 2000.

132. Cited in Hroub 2000., 85.

133. BBC News 2002, 3.

134. Crow, Karim. "Divided Discourse: Muslim Discussion On Islam And Peace," *Nonviolence International,* unpublished paper. (Washington D.C, July, 1997), 4.

135. Crow 1997.

136. See Chapters Five and Seven.

Chapter 7

Non-Text: In Between Narratives

Developments since the Hamas victory in 2006 elections signal that the Palestinian society is on the verge of a major internal competition for authority and power between Hamas and Fatah. This competition has cost the lives of many Palestinians until the Mecca Agreement was reached in February 2007. It is not yet clear how enduring this agreement will be for it is now being tested as the fractions try to rein in their fighters while the politicians are trying to finalize the creation of a power-sharing government.[1] Such internal fragmentation and chaos further distances any possibility for peace in the region. However, violent clashes between the two factions are not new. Violent clashes have occurred between two groups periodically as they competed for the control of various Palestinian institutions. Competition of control over these institutions is closely tied to the competition of narratives between these groups.

Previous two Chapters introduced the contextual factors, which constitute the effective history of the Palestinians and influence the way various Islamic groups interpret Islamic texts. These Chapters identified various narratives that have been competing with each other in the Palestinian context. I have particularly focused on the narrative of Hamas and tried to show reasons behind its emergence. This Chapter will focus on institutional sites where this "struggle" or competition for legitimacy takes place. As discussed in Chapter Two, legitimization of narratives involves establishment of "a regime of truth." I argue here that in this struggle truth is centered on a specific discourse/narrative and on the institutions that are linked in a circular relation with systems of power that produce and sustain the regime of truth. Implicit in my analysis, I utilize Foucault's conceptualization of power to show how these narratives compete for legitimacy within institutional sites in society. Institutions are relatively enduring and stable set of relationships between different people, and between people and objects. These institutions have a physical presence (e.g. classrooms, mosques, churches, synagogues, or clinics), but more importantly, they are also constituted by relationships (e.g. teacher-student, cleric-believer, and doctor-patient). Institutions can be found in a variety of fields, such as religion, education, the law, government, culture, and the family. Institutions can be private or public. Private institutions operate at the private sphere of social life, such as family and personal concerns. Public institutions operate at the public sphere, such as work, economic realm, government, or education.

Public institutions can be further separated into two groups. I define the first group as "formal institutions. Formal institutions are those institutions, which are directly related to the state, constitute parts of the state, or through which the state realizes, perpetuates or reinforces its policies, ideology or its authority. I define the second group as "informal institutions." Informal public institutions are those institutions, which are not directly related to, controlled or directed by the state. This means that these institutions are mostly independent of financial, ideological or political pressures of the state, and have a relative freedom in terms of the content of their workings. Churches, mosques, local organizations, regional associations, the sports clubs, among others, are some examples of such institutions. Informal institutions present an intermediary level between the state and the individual. Public institutions draw their authority from their capacity to speak the "truth" about some situation. Although public institutions authorize their activities by claiming to be speaking the "truth" these truth claims are dependent on power/narrative apparatuses. It is in these locales that narratives compete for legitimacy and insert themselves.

Institutions present themselves as agencies of regulation, arbitration, and demarcation, as a way of introducing order.[2] Institutions are the sites where different discourses/narratives are produced, reproduced, and in which they struggle for legitimacy and hegemony. In this struggle, power and power relations are critical elements of legitimization of narratives. In that sense power becomes a set of forces, which establishes positions and ways of behaving that influence people. In this understanding of power, as observed by Foucault, power is not held by any particular group or individual within a society, but is exercised from innumerable points, "in the interplay of nonegalitarian and mobile relations."[3] Power flows from one place to another very quickly and thus is mobile. Relations of power are not in a position of exteriority with respect to other types of relationships such as economic process, knowledge relationships, etc., but are immanent in them.[4] Power is not imposed from above but comes from below. Power circulates and operates through discourse and practices and power is first found and constituted at micro level and later incorporated and developed into larger institutional structures. These micro levels are these institutional sites examined in this study, such as prisons, educational centers, work places, and medical institutions. Manifold relationships of force that take shape and come in the machinery of production, in families, limited groups, and institutions, are the basis for wide-ranging effects of cleavage that run through the social body as a whole.[5] A network of power relations eventually forms a dense web passing through apparata and institutions, without becoming localized in them.[6] Knowledge and truth are produced out of power struggles and they are used to authorize and legitimate the workings of power.

Many different forms of power exist in societies. These include legal, administrative, economic, religious, and military among others. "What they have in common is a shared reliance on certain techniques or methods of application."[7] These techniques of power allow for the exercise of power and the production of knowledge. There are no universal forms in which power is exercised. Power relations are derived from the way the society organizes itself, Power functions through various techniques, utilizing the sources of legitimacy of a particular society. It is through various training procedures and techniques that power "disciplines"[8] and establishes regimes of truth.

Another important point is that, there are connections between the "techniques of power and the forms of knowledge that developed alongside them."[9] Thus, "knowledge gained on the basis of disciplinary power is formulated according to 'norms' of behavior."[10] These norms of behavior and knowledge are historically and culturally situated, but are not static. Techniques of power have the capacity to change, produce, or reproduce cultural forms and social stratification.

Understanding power from this perspective becomes especially important in the current world system, where a variety of authorized narratives exist, rather than a homogenous discourse. More people and institutions have access to "truths," and no individual or institution can claim undisputed access to "truth." Therefore individuals and institutions compete with others for legitimacy, negotiating their positions when necessary (e.g. nationalization of Islam) and gain support. This is particularly due to the emergence of "people" as a critical force in the balance of narratives.[11]

Narratives do not emerge in a void, but rather develop from a pre-existing field of possibilities, which new narratives can realign and reconfigure. This field of possibilities is constituted by various horizons (such as the textual, contextual and non-textual domains,[12] in which the past, the present and an image of a future is constructed). These narratives operate in a material world, against and in relation to prior and contemporary narratives, other discursive formations, and social, political, and economic material forces. In this process, power moves around and through different groups (e.g. the PLO, the Marxist-Leftist groups, or Islamic groups), events, institutions, and individuals. Furthermore, the way people understand the world, develop values and aspirations and the way they react to events are constituted out of various technologies of power. Individuals are strongly influenced/ affected by the workings of power through institutions such as universities, mosques/churches/synagogues, or medical agencies.

In these institutions, the workings of power/narrative place certain individuals in authority, thus who is speaking becomes important. For example, religious institutions grant religious leaders, such as imams, or religious scholars to legitimately talk about religious issues. It is through these institutional sites that the narrators disseminate their narratives and from these sites they derive legitimacy and point of application (its specific object and instruments of verification). As it is stated by Foucault:

> ...in our societies (and no doubt in many others) the property of discourse- in the sense of the right to speak, ability to understand, licit and immediate access to the corpus of already formulated statements, and the capacity to invest in this discourse in decision, institutions, or practices- if in fact confined (sometimes with the addition of legal sanction) to a particular group of individuals.[13]

Furthermore, the position of the narrator is also defined by the situation that is available for him to occupy in relation to various groups of objects. Thus these institutional sites become crucial to understand how the political strategies of conflicting forces are deployed in discourse and how they are articulated in relations to a chain of events.

As stated before, Islamic narratives of war and peace in Palestine operate within the context of Palestinian experience with the British Mandate, Egyptian and Jordanian rules, Israeli occupation, the wars of 1948, 1956, 1967, 1973, and the invasion of South Lebanon in 1982, the *Intifada*, the Oslo process and second *Intifada*. Furthermore their experience with pan-Arabism, Pan-Islamism, and fall of Communism are also important aspects of the Palestinian horizon. Palestine becomes a particularly interesting case because there is no formal state, and still considers itself be a social liberation movement. This situation creates particular problems for the Palestinian people, which will be discussed below. In this study the PNA and instruments that are tied into its policies will be considered as formal institutions, such as the prisons, police forces, etc., whereas institutions that base their operation in the grassroots movements will be considered as informal institutions, such as NGOs, religious institutions, or associations. Although the distinction is somewhat blurry in this particular case, understanding the role of these institutions is very important to grasp social organization of the society under occupation.

This chapter will mention various institutional sites (e.g. mosques, Sufi lodges, charitable societies, etc.) and will look at two clashes that took place at medical and educational institutional sites. Both medical and educational (especially universities) institutional sites have played a crucial role in the struggle for legitimating various narratives within the Palestinian society. Universities, for example, seem like the most "natural" locales for the emergence of new ideas and dissemination. As Foucault states:

> Education may well be, as of right, the instrument whereby everyday individual, in a society, like our own, can gain access to any kind of discourse. But we well know that in its distribution, in what it permits and in what it prevents, it follows the well-trodden battle-lines of social conflict. Every education system is a political means of maintaining or of modifying the appropriation of discourse, with the knowledge and the powers it carries with it."[14]

On the other hand, the medical/health institutions are interesting examples to show how various narratives compete in institutions, which deal with seemingly more basic/biological aspect of human lives, namely health issues. The examples presented here aim to show how these health care institutions were politicized and became sites for competing narratives. This section will not undertake a textual analysis of the narratives that competed for legitimacy. Nor will it delve into a deep analysis of techniques and methods of power used at these sights by these groups for not to expand this volume further. Nevertheless, it will focus on these sites as the locales of struggle for these groups in their attempts to legitimize their narratives.

The Nature of Institutional Sites in Palestine

Institutional sites reflect the power relations of the society in which they are operative and are influenced by them. These institutions derive their legitimacy from their social, political, religio/cultural and discursive context and in turn they affect this context through their workings. Institutions play an important role in the Palestinian society. They reaffirm Palestinian identity, contribute significantly to the development of political consciousness; they serve as bases for building a national solidarity movement and mobilization of the population. They also provide crucial social services in the fields of health, education and agriculture. Therefore they alleviate suffering of the people in the absence of a proper state, which would normally provide these services to its population. Accordingly, they play a key role in the Palestinian society.

Since there has been no Palestinian state and a Palestinian government, the Palestinian society lacks formal public institutions, which provides key services to the public. Consequently, informal public institutions that were created or rejuvenated to serve these critical social needs were based on the pre-1948 institutions. These institutions derived their legitimacy from religion, tradition, and their long history. Familiarity of the population with these institutions enabled these institutions function under the difficult conditions created by occupation.

In order to understand the workings of the institutional sites in Palestine, it is necessary to go back to the social organization of the society. One of the crucial aspects of Palestinian social institutions is the influence of religion and culture. As stated in Chapter Three, the impact of nomadism has a deep imprint in most of the Middle Eastern culture, society and politics[15]. Flexible and effective kin-based communities, lineage, and tribe relations are still influential in these societies. Communal, religious, tribal and ethnic identity remains strong forces in social life, as do patron-client relationships and patterns of patriarchal authority. As opposed to the social stratification of the society in the West, which is based on family, labor, social class, and official educational system, the Muslim community is based on close kinship and family ties, master-pupil relationship, religious brotherhood, and neighborhood.

Family cohesion is the prime tribal value that informs the social relations in the Middle East. Loyalty to the family becomes an important feature of these societies. According to Mardin, the linkages between these figures are pictured as consisting of "filial piety," "keeping one's engagements," "the sacredness of an oath," "establishing bonds of friendship," "fitting into the neighborhood," and "trying to establish a respectable status as a member of a (partly) religious community."[16] The combination of traditional and modern systems of political authority in the modern world presents confusion to the individuals in terms of where the loyalty should be invested (i.e. state vs. family). Understanding this confusion becomes an important aspect of the study of Middle Eastern society.

Palestinian society reflects these Middle Eastern characteristics in terms of its social organization. The values mentioned above and systems of authority form the bases of power relations in the society. They enable certain people (e.g. religious leaders) to come into positions of power. They give legitimacy to the institutions they are narrating from, and also to their narratives. The social structure, combined with particular historical developments since the Ottoman period, has led to the emergence of a particular political group as the dominant force within the society. As stated in previous chapters, this dominant political group in the Palestinian community was the 'notables' in the nineteen and twentieth centuries as intermediaries between the Ottoman government and the population, similar to other Middle Eastern societies. However, while the politics of notables were generally overthrown in the Arab world during the post-independence period, in Palestine notables remained as a major political force, since the dominant states (first the British, then Egypt and Jordan, and later Israel) continued to utilize notables as useful intermediaries between them and the Palestinian population. Co-opting the notables and distributing resources through them was perceived as the best way to maintain social control. The internal conflict between the notables made this task easier for the foreign powers.

As stated in Chapter Three, it is possible to identify three types of traditional notables in the Palestinian context.[17] These are the "religious leaders" (*ulema*), who gained their legitimacy from the Islamic tradition and also controlling large religiously owned lands. The second group of notables was the "military leaders" who owed their status due to their arms and soldiers then commanded. Finally the third group consisted of "secular notables," who derived their wealth from land and trade.[18] Although leaders like al Qassam, who was not coming from this elite background, had become popular among the population, the politics of notables continued to be an important aspect of the Palestinian society until the 1980s. The authority of notables was not really challenged even after the Israeli occupation, as the Israeli authorities encouraged them, and took over the same policy of co-opting the elites practiced by the Ottoman, British, Egyptian, and Jordanian regimes. As Glenn Robinson points out, "the economic wealth of the notables, both in land and in capital, their religious and social preeminence in West Bank society, and their monopoly of higher education were valuable assets that worked to preserve the authority and influence of these pro-Jordanian politicians under early Israeli occupation."[19]

However, in the 1970s many of these traditional ways of organizing were replaced with new ones. This altered the power relations in the society and created new leaderships. During the 70s, resistance to the occupation increasingly took a cultural turn. There was a revival of an authentic Palestinian musical and theatrical tradition, independent of the Arab world. Various voluntary youth movements, which focused on community work, were established. An adult education program, aiming to wipe out illiteracy among working adults and rural women was launched. In this period, we also see nationalist notables in West Bank and Gaza increasingly replacing the traditional notables. This was reflected in a number of institutional sites, such as the creation of the Palestine National Front (1973-77) and National Guidance Committee (1978-82). Furthermore, two nationalist newspapers (*al-Fajr* and *al Sha'b*) were established in this period. And with the April 1976 municipal elections nationalists started to become a major political force. These new nationalist elites were younger, better educated and more ideological, but they still came from wealthy local families.[20]

The most significant change came in 1980s, especially with the *Intifada*. Robinson observes that this resulted from three major changes within the society. He identifies these changes as the virtual elimination of the Palestinian peasantry, land confiscation, and the establishment of the Palestinian University system.[21] Following the 1967 war, Israel opened its labor market to Palestinians. Since there were not many job opportunities in the West Bank and Gaza, the labor market offered more income then staying in agriculture especially for the peasants and refugees. For that reason many Palestinians chose to work in Israel, although their income was much lower then their Israeli counterparts. However, this shifted the Palestinian economy from agriculture to labor and proletariazed them. This shift had significant ramifications as it created a working class of people less tied to village life, exposed them to exploitative relations and to a much advanced industrial society, diminishing rural reliance on notable politics, damaging long-standing patron-client networks. Thus, it created new social relations and relations of power. It made the workers open to political recruitment. As Robinson states, "it turned peasants into Palestinians."[22]

The other crucial development was land confiscation by the Israelis, which altered the landholding pattern in the Palestinian society, as it was an attack on the sources of power and wealth of the notables, namely the land. Land confiscation increased, especially after the Likud Party came to power in Israel in 1977. Under this policy, some lands were taken with the state recognizing their legal owners and seizing their land to build Jewish settlements. Israeli state also declared some lands 'state lands,' using the 1858 Ottoman law as justification. Other times, Israel confiscated lands for 'security reasons' with little or no explanation. In all cases, eventually these confiscated lands were used to build Jewish settlements, which created resentment among the Palestinians. This policy of land confiscation also created extreme bitterness among the notables who lost the basis of their power.

Finally the other significant development was the establishment of Palestinian University system in 1972. Before this system was established, only the sons of wealthy notables could go to universities in countries like Egypt, Lebanon, and Jordan. Establishment of universities in the West Bank and Gaza allowed many Palestinians who otherwise could not have gone to a university. This new university student group reflected the large Palestinian population with about 70 per cent coming from refugee camps, villages, and small towns. This new educated group was to produce the counter-elite, which posed a direct challenge not only to Palestinian notables, but also to the Israeli occupation. This new elite initiated a mobilization campaign and established social networks that would become the basis of not only the Palestinian civil society, but also of resistance.

This mobilization occurred at several levels of the Palestinian society. Non-notable urban professionals in the medical and agricultural sectors built institutions that linked the urban and rural populations, student organizations established Voluntary Works Program to politicize villagers who were often removed from nationalist life, and also established factional grassroots organizations to promote health care, agricultural relief, and women's rights. In this period, the Israeli policies unwillingly helped to strengthen these mobilization efforts as they undermined the notables for being too "nationalistic." Especially the invasion of South Lebanon in 1982 to destroy the PLO and to leave the Palestinians leaderless resulted in contributing to the mobilization process and strengthening of the counter-elites that were largely autonomous. It was these autonomous elite that coordinated the activities during *Intifada*.

Another contribution to the development of these counter elites was the Israeli imprisonment of Palestinian political activist. Israeli prisons had become a major locale for political socialization of the Palestinians. Prisoners from West Bank and Gaza were held in the same detention centers, which enabled relationships to be formed, political strategy to be discussed, and ideologies to circulate. These prison veterans were later to become local leaders at the university blocks and other sectors of the society.

In his study, Robinson argues "the most significant sociopolitical phenomenon to come out of the *Intifada* was creation of alternative structures of authority at the local level-primarily neighborhood, popular, and relief communities."[23] He observes that although these structures were generally based on the modern principles of individual association and democratic hierarchy, they often operated within the local clan or *hamula*, configuration. Salim Tamari also observes that these alternative structures challenged traditional institutions such as the family system,[24] and argues that:

> [y]oung people, including women, found legitimate 'national' justification for spending prolonged periods outside their homes, and therefore away from the controlling of the parents (escape from arrest, organizing activities etc.). Parental authority was challenged directly by youth claims for a authority consecrated by political commitments to their political groups and therefore to the 'national cause'. These claims were furthermore deemed acceptable and legitimate by society at large.[25]

The vulnerability of the visible nationalist leadership in the form of elected mayors, PLO-affiliated Palestine National Front and National Guidance committee to arrest, deportation and imprisonment, and the absence of a "state proper" under Israeli occupation led to the growth of various grassroots organizations and nongovernmental organizations. The rapid increase of informal institutional sites, or NGOs in 1970s and particularly 1980s was aimed at disengaging from the network of control established by the Israel occupation, as well as providing social services such as health, education, etc. As stated by Denis J. Sullivan, when communities suffer from either the hurdles of poverty and inadequate resources, or a government that is unable to satisfy their needs, often turn to NGOs, and other community based organizations such as mosques, churches, private clubs, and so on.[26] Palestinian society suffers from both. Sullivan observes two main reasons for the development of NGOs in the West Bank and Gaza.[27] The first reason, he notes is that NGOs in Palestine have played an historic role advancing the social, cultural, and economic needs of hundreds of local communities as well as the national unit. Second, in the absence of a state and a government with institutions established to provide direct assistance to its people, Palestinian NGOs (PNGOs) in effect took on the additional task of filling in for the non-existent or absent state.

As the situation on the ground has been worsening gradually after the Israeli occupation, but especially since the conclusion of the Oslo negotiations in 1993, Palestinians have increasingly started to rely on various local and international NGOs and other civil society organizations to overcome the hurdles of the daily life. These included traditional religious charity organizations; human rights groups; professional associations, such as trade unions; popular organizations such as women's associations; student unions and cooperatives. In order to counteract the Israeli measures against the visible leadership, nationalist groups utilized these diffuse arrays of NGO's and local institutions.

Among these organizational structures, Islamist groups, particularly the Muslim Brotherhood, contributed to the new social relations and political ties between various strata of the Palestinian society. As Rex Brynen has observed, "[w]ith the growing influence of social and political Islam in the 1980s, parallel growth [of NGOs] occurred among religious charitable organizations, schools, clinics and social services."[28] These organizations provided a substantial share of education, health care, and other social services. According to Sara Roy, Islamic institutions comprise anywhere from 10-40 percent of all social institutions in West Bank and Gaza, and according to the records of Ministry of education, 65 percent of all Gazan educational institutions below secondary level are Islamic.[29]

The most obvious institutional expression of the growing Islamist movement [before the *Intifada*] was the increasing number of mosques found in the Occupied Territories,[30] which were linked to Islamic endowments. These mosques provided a critical space for communicating information, organizing protests, and getting financial support through religious endowments. Individuals, who were connected to organizations such as Muslim Brotherhood, utilized these spaces for political and strategic planning, distributing leaflets, and carrying their messages to the masses. Imams oriented their audience against occupation during their Friday sermons.

In this process, financial aid, obtained from various different sources, become an important resource. In that respect, the PLO, especially prior to the Gulf War was able to provide support from various Arab and Western donors mainly channeled through NGOs. This donor support, according to Brynen, reached a peak of $140 million and $220 million in the early 1990s.[31] Among different groups, the dominant Fatah mainstream had direct access to PLO financial resources. The smaller Leftist groups were able to get financial support both locally and also benefiting from the Cold War policies, from Western donors through NGOs. On the other hand, Islamic groups raised most of their financial resources locally, and from sympathetic states, religious individuals, and even some Western donors.[32] Some Western donors have contributed to Islamist health clinics and other social institutions, especially in Gaza.[33]

When the Palestinian National Authority was established in 1994, many NGO leaders merged their institutions and activities into the PNA structure, especially the education and health institutions. Others did not. Those leaders, who chose to do so were mostly associated with PLO affiliated NGOs. PNA attempted to suppress those institutions that did not want to merge into its system, especially those of opposing groups such as Leftist-Marxists, or the Islamists. For the PLO, the various component organizations of the PLO, and the Islamist movement, support for NGOs was thus an increasingly important part of the broader struggle against occupation."[34] As Sullivan notes, based on his interviews with various PNA officials, and NGO representatives, there remains a vocal and strong minority within the PNA that declares Palestinian NGOs as the enemy of PNA, as either Islamist or communist opponents of

Arafat and the structure of the PNA, and asserted itself against the NGOs in an aggressive way, through the actions of the secret police.[35]

NGOs and other voluntary institutions play an essential part in delivering economic and social services in Palestinian Territories. According to the World Bank, in early 1996, it was estimated that NGOs provided about 60 percent by value of all primary health care services and up to one-half of secondary and tertiary health care.[36] Furthermore, the same paper states that NGOs run all disability and preschool programs as well as most agricultural services, low-cost housing programs and micro-enterprise credit schemes. Under these circumstances three major groups have been influential in the Palestinian social and political life and competed for the legitimacy of their narratives in institutional sites. As stated earlier, these groups are Fatah, the Left, and the Islamists. Among these groups, Fatah, headed by Arafat since the late 1960s until his death in November 2004, has been by far the largest Palestinian nationalist organization and historically dominated the institutional machinery of the PLO.[37] Fatah was able to draw support from a broad segment of Palestinian society, and some of its leaders are known for their conservative Islamic views. For that reason it was able to enjoy significant support among the highly religious and conservative Palestinians. The bulk of the Fatah leadership supported the Palestinian participation at the Madrid peace process, and majority of them supported the Oslo Agreement. However, the breakdown of the Oslo process had a negative impact on the popular support of Fatah.

The second group consisted of the Palestinian leftist groups such as, Popular Front for the Liberation of Palestine (PFLP), the Democratic Front for the Liberation of Palestine (DFLP), Palestinian Democratic Union (FIDA), and Palestinian People's Party (PPP), which was formerly the Palestinian Communist Party (PCP). These groups played a significant role in the evolution of Palestinian politics, and the NGOs. They consisted of Palestinian intellectuals, and benefited greatly from the Cold War politics. However, the fall of the Communist Block had a negative impact on the Leftist movement in Palestine. The fall of the Communist block left these groups in financial distress, as they could get support from outside anymore. For that reason they are weakened. Moreover, among the leftist groups the FIDA and PPP supported the peace process, while PFLP and DFLP opposed to the process. This debate divided the Left further and contributed to its weakening.

The third group, which is also the focus of this study, is the Islamist groups. Islamist groups (initially the Muslim Brotherhood, later Mujama, and then Hamas; the Islamic Jihad, and also the Liberation Party *-Hizb-u Tahrir-*) have been outside the framework of PLO, indeed challenged it. Although the roots of the Islamic movement in Palestine can be dated to the initial years of the British mandate, as stated earlier, the Islamic movement started to re-emerge as a political force in 1970s. In the 1980s it became a major political force in the Palestinian political balance.

One of the strengths of this new Islamic movement that emerged in the 1970s was its links directly or indirectly to a growing number of clinics, educational institutions, and other social welfare NGOs in the territories. Realizing the critical role played by the "population" as a potent force in the process of establishing their regime of truth, Islamic groups such as the Muslim Brotherhood, and Mujama focused on especially previously neglected segments of the society, such as the dispossessed peasants, villagers, and refugees. Especially the influence of Western trends such as democratization, which emphasized the role of the population, the success of Islamic popular movements in other parts of the Arab world, such as Algeria, Sudan, among others, and the success of the Iranian revolution contributed to the policy of reaching out to the Palestinian population to gain support. For that reason, gaining access to crucial Palestinian institutions has been an important goal of the Islamic movement to influence the population.

Another crucial development that affected the institutional sites has been the Oslo Process. This process created a new dynamic in the social and political life of the Palestinian society. Many PLO members and leaders, including Arafat returned to Gaza and West Bank, after being in diaspora for a very long time. Arafat and the new Palestinian National Authority, which envisioned a Palestinian state to be established at the end of this process, started to create a huge bureaucracy and a public sector. This new regime was consolidated by the partial return of Palestinian investors, and also the increasing foreign aid to the reconstruction of the Palestinian society and the future Palestinian State. In accordance with the Oslo Accords, Arafat initially focused on consolidating security by eliminating opposition groups, especially Islamists.

In that direction, they invested in building prisons, and strengthening the police force to control the population. Palestinians are critical of the PNA for establishing only oppressive institutions such as prisons and police forces against its own population instead of establishing institutions that provide crucial social services such as schools and medical centers. Furthermore, the autocratic and anti-democratic structure of the administration, combined with mismanagement of the financial aid received from outside, created resentment among the population. Widespread corruption was another major criticism directed at the PNA in general and Arafat in particular. As the PNA invested most of its financial resources in building prisons and the police force, it attempted to overcome the hurdles of establishing institutions that provide social services by taking over the NGOs that were already operating in these fields since 1970s.

The PNA attempted to control the NGO sector by merging them into its own system, and benefiting from their expertise and experience in providing services to the public. Palestinian Authority's approach to NGOs was that: "we needed you for the liberation struggle, but now we are here to take over and the government knows everything, does everything for its people."[38] Various NGOs chose to merge into the Palestinian Authority system, some were forced to do so, others resisted. Therefore, rejecting taking part in the Palestinian Authority system became a form of resistance and also a way of denouncing the legitimacy of the peace process. Thus, competition for controlling the institutional sites became a part of the power struggle between rival groups.

As the Oslo Process unfolded with no improvement in the lives of Palestinians, these criticisms started to become more pronounced. In this period, the economic life of Palestinians declined further,[39] settlement construction increased there was no progress on some of the central issues such as the borders of the Palestinian State, the status of Jerusalem, and the right of return. Palestinian Territories were divided into cantons and grouped under three different administration patterns. The first group was Group A, in which the administration and security was handed to the PNA. "In total this made up 2.7 percent of the West Bank and around 36 percent of its population (excluding Jerusalem)."[40] The second group was Group B, and involved administration being handed to the PNA, while Israel retained overriding responsibility for security. This area represented 25 percent of the West Bank and 60 percent of the population.[41] The third group, the Group C, was still under complete Israeli control. Palestinians were not able to travel from one place to another without the permission of the Israeli authorities. Furthermore, over sixty new Israeli military bases were established, and Israel still retained the control of exits and entries of main towns, in addition to controlling the roads. Additionally Israel periodically adopted general or comprehensive closures, which prevented movement between population centers. All these developments had a devastating impact on the Palestinian population, which eventually lost hope in the peace process.

Furthermore, the Oslo Process created a heated debate over the "step-by step" approach of the Oslo Process, in which Israel did not commit itself legally to anything in terms of final status. Others, such as the Islamic groups, rejected the Peace Process altogether. This debate impacted the institutions and other organizations in the society. These institutions had to decide whether they were supporting the process and the authority or not. Many institutions were polarized and the society was further fragmented over this debate. Therefore two different concerns emerged within the Palestinian social and political arena. The first one was the liberation of Palestine, since independence was still not achieved, and the second one was the nature of this state when it was established. Many Palestinians were determined not to let another autocratic regime to replace the previous ones. The undemocratic and autocratic nature of Arafat's rule was not the preferred system for many Palestinians, including the Islamists.

In terms of mobilizing the Palestinian society, both Islamic and non-Islamic groups utilized various religious and cultural values, vocabulary, and institutions. Especially in times of social crises, "pre-existing social structures provide resources and organization that are crucial to the initiation and spread of collective action" as Aldon Morris also observes.[42] When that is the case, historic and central institutions, such as cultural and religious institutions, play a major role in the mobilization process. In addition to familiarity with how these institutions work, religious and cultural values that are knitted into the fabric of these institutions gives credibility and legitimacy to these institutions in the eyes of the population. These institutions become sites for communicating ideas, pushing forth various narratives utilizing various values, vocabulary and existing social networks embedded in the society.

For example, Palestinians adopted an indigenous economic strategy to resist Israeli policies. "Throughout the 1970s and 1980s, the dominant motif of Palestinian economic strategy was that of *sumud* (steadfastness), intended to foster the ability of Palestinian institutions, lands, and infrastructure to resist Israeli pressures."[43] This must be seen in conjunction with the penetration of capitalism into Muslim societies, which dissolved the traditional economic structuring of the society and its institutions. Today, Muslim societies are struggling with the market economy in their own terms. Contemporary understanding of Western economics, which seems to be devoid of ethics, reduced to motive of gain, and increases injustice in the world and within societies created a critical re-evaluation of capitalism and the role of societal life in the Muslim world. The transformation from a traditional society to modern one created difficulty for the individual and damaged the feeling of security. The fabric of society is disrupted; population is decimated. The distanced and cold nature of the new relationship destroyed the previous identity, which found its meaning in the traditional social structure of the rural areas. Unequal distribution of income, high inflation rate, increased unemployment, and alienation, creating a sense of resentment, resulted in a search for a substitute within these societies. Especially in Palestine, this development was linked to Zionist occupation, reflected in the unequal treatment of Palestinians and Israelis, with a huge gap between economic success and welfare between two communities. Such a platform created the adequate conditions for a discourse of social justice.

Providing effective services in the areas of health, education, and agriculture to alleviate the suffering of the Palestinian population became an important discourse of resistance and also a crucial aspect of the struggle for power within the society. In their responses to Israeli policies, together with Marxist-Leftist narratives, nationalists to connect the Palestinians to this process and to mobilize them adopted an Islamic narrative, with its emphasis on social justice. This economic strategy stressed social integration and harmony as the main goals to be achieved in society. In this totality, economic sphere is just one aspect of the social life, and the primacy is given to maintenance of social order, and harmony. In this picture, it is clear that social relations are privileged over economic relations, and the society is governed by cultural/religious norms. A balance between material and spiritual needs is considered necessary to survive the purpose of creation. As opposed to the Western understanding of economy-society relations, which sees economy as the primary determinant of social structuration of the society, this approach focused on the embeddedness of economy within the existing social relations and institutions.

In that sense, the Palestinians stressed the traditional characteristics of their culture, which emphasized village life, peasant attachment to the land, and women as caregivers and mothers of the nation. *Sumud* was directed toward maintaining Palestinian presence on the land, and being self-sufficient, emphasizing on agriculture, home produce, growth of cooperative movement, and "buy Palestinian" campaign in association with boycotting Israeli goods. In this process, although it was not a religious strategy, various Islamic values, such as sharing, fasting, self-sufficiency were used to connect the population to these strategies. In order to understand this phenomenon, it is necessary to understand the role of social institutions in the Middle East.

Social Institutions and Their Role in the Modern Islamic Societies

Within the institutional structures, religious and cultural establishments played a crucial role in Palestine. Islam is a comprehensive religion that lurks into all aspects of the daily life. According to Islamists, Islamic social order must be at the core of all aspects of society. Under the pressure of modernization, Westernization and Israeli occupation, reviving certain Islamic institutions became an important aspect of reorganizing the society. Associations or organizations that consist of dedicated and trained Muslims become important tools for fighting against corruption and social injustice, and establishing regimes of truth. Combining modern and traditional elements, Muslim societies in general and Palestinian society in particular are in the process of transformation.

Islamic societies are home to various traditional institutions that are specific to their socio-religious character. Traditionally, in the Islamic societies there is no distinction between religion and the state. For that reason, there has been a blending of formal and informal religious institutions at times. Groups that have been traditionally called "*ulema*" have represented the formal religious institutions, which were in charge of the official religious discourse of the state, although various independent institutions were operating in Islamic societies. Historical evidence suggests that there has been an organic relationship between the *ulema* and the sultans, in the sense that religious texts have been utilized to legitimize the interests of the state. Informal Islamic institutions, on the other hand, were made independent through the establishment of *awqaf*, religious endowments. These institutions are themselves divided into subunits, and the cement holding them together is religion. These institutions differ from mosques, *medreses* (Islamic educational institutions), hospitals, schools, *tekkes* (Sufi lodges), to *Shariah* Courts. "The independent charters of the establishments, together with their generous endowments, enabled these institutions to be effective in ways that the state-controlled universities and research centers of the Muslim world cannot."[44] The same was true for the hospitals, clinics, even roads and canals.

After the introduction of modern state system, new institutions began to emerge within Muslim societies. These modern institutions are secular, bureaucratic and rational. Yet, the reminiscence of religious practices can be clearly found in these organizations. Besides, these institutions have not been able to erase the legitimacy and popularity of the previous institutions completely. Rather than losing legitimacy, these previous institutions became a resource, a base for the modern institutions to function. For that reason, the local religious authorities have been a major source of guidance and organization. As stated earlier, this view is supported by Aldon D. Morris, who argues, "Pre-existing social structures provide the resources and organization that are crucial to the initiation and spread of collective action."[45] For instance, under Israeli occupation, where there is a major conflict and confusion between the Israeli legal system, Palestinian secular institutions, and traditional institutions, these pre-existing social structures become important locales of resistance within Palestinian population.

The modern state systems in the region demolished traditional structures and atomized individuals, eliminated all the intermediary forces between them and the state, instead of building upon and improving this socio-religious structure.[46] Islamic social movements in these societies, criticize these modern institutions for subverting political, economical, cultural, and military hegemony of the West. By drawing legitimacy from religious vocabulary, they attempt to re-center society and politics around Islamic values.[47] In these attempts, traditional institutions become an important locale of organization, communication, and education of the population. These institutions also come to be symbols of reaction and resistance to the Western institutions, and Israeli occupation in Palestine.

Charles Amjad Ali argues that, in order to understand reactions towards West in the Middle East, it is necessary to recognize how West is perceived in the Middle East; the tension between nation-state system and Islamic identity which transcends the states borders; and also the search for a instrumental rationality for the application and efficiency of the systems and institutions.[48] He argues that there is a tension between the traditional symbols for evoking political activity and the anti-Western sentiments and the current nation-state system with authoritarian leaderships, which are supported by the West. Such a contradiction between the traditional values and symbols, and use of power against the status quo colors the political discourse in the Middle East. In Palestine, resentment towards and resistance against Israel accompany this mood.

Group solidarity, traditional religious precepts, and norms concerning honor and shame retain their place in the social life of the modern Muslims. Worshiping (*ibadat*) simultaneously also creates a common experience for Muslims that contributes to the solidarity among Muslims. "*Ibada*(*t*) rationalizes life by framing it in a set of moral constraints which switch all persons who simultaneously in the same direction."[49] This personalized approach gives meaning to the social relations, and creates a bond that ties the society together. Informal institutions such as mosques, Quran schools, and *tekkes* become important resources to shape the way that society views the world. At times of discontent, these institutions become centers for local movements. The social-change oriented *imams* and individuals use these institutions as coordinating units. They also coordinate indigenous financing through mosques. Friday sermons and other religious gatherings serve as forums where local residents are informed of relevant information and strategies regarding the movement. These meetings are also used to build solidarity and deepen commitment to the struggle among the participants. Such strategies have been widely used during the Iranian Revolution and *Intifada* in Palestine. Especially in the Palestinian case, universities were also another space together with mosques that have contributed to the mass mobilization of the Muslim population against the Israeli occupation.

Today, traditional Islamic institutions have become locales for communicating various ideas of the Islamic social movements. An important development in this respect is the communication revolution. Since the end of the 19th century, the technological advancement in the communication systems has contributed to a new configuration of social life in the world. The Muslim world was not excluded from these developments.[50] Islamic vocabulary, socio-religious festivals, and norms, which are common in all the Muslim countries, have been more effectively communicated to transmit the ideas of various Islamic movements and mobilize the populations. Utilizing modern means of communication such as cassette tapes, videos, and internet, speeches, *fetwas* (legal rulings), and sermons of influential *imams* and Islamic scholars have reached many Muslims all around the world, and thus united them in many respects.

Such a development in the communication network of these institutions sheds new light onto the increasing role of mosques, Islamic educational and economical institutions in the modern world. Going back to Morris' argument on the role of religious institutions during social movements, this adds to the organizational capacity of these institutions. Observed in this light, these informal structures are becoming more influential in the current world for organizing and orienting the societies towards their constructed ends. They are locales for emergence, reinforcement, or reproduction of narratives on social and political issues. It is through these institutional sites that various groups legitimize their narratives using religio/cultural myths, vocabulary, knowledge systems as technologies of power. Various Islamic groups in Palestine utilize these institutional sites for mobilizing the population towards their goals, and legitimize their narratives.

Islamic Groups and Institutional Sites in Palestine

The growing influence of Islam in Palestinian society since the 1980s is visible at a number of levels, including social practices, institution building, student body elections at universities, and public opinion surveys. In terms of social practices, the number of women, especially young women began wearing modest Islamic dress, which had disappeared from the Palestinian scene a generation earlier. The traditional dress code, thus, became a symbolic form of resistance. In addition to that there has been an increase in the observance of other Islamic practices such as daily prayer, Quranic recitation, and fasting, according to a 1984 survey.[51] More importantly there has been an increase in the institutions that are geared toward an Islamic reorganization of social life.

Islamic institutions play an important and visible role in relief and charity work; preschool, primary and elementary education; library development; the education and rehabilitation of physically and mentally disabled children and adults; primary and tertiary health care (one of the best hospitals in the Occupied Territories is Islamic, i.e. founded, administered and financed by Islamists); women income-generating activities; literacy training; the care of orphans; the care of the elderly; the care and placement of "illegitimate" children, who come as abandoned infants; and youth and sports activities.[52]

Most of these services that the Islamists provide to those previously neglected areas such as small villages and refugee camps. In most of the cases, they conduct activities in areas where other NGOs could not reach or did not reach. However, their services are not limited to these areas and Islamist services directly or indirectly reach out to thousands of people in the Palestinian Territories.

The flourishing of Islamic institutions was in part a response to a similar process under taken by the PLO. Observing that the PLO was formulating a policy of grass-roots organizing as a means to widen and deepen the resistance to the occupations, the Islamists felt that there should be a parallel movement to widen the Islamic base, and to provide an alternative to the secular nationalist PLO through a process of religio-socialization of the Palestinian society. One of the main characteristics of Islamic institutions is their management and staffs are very well educated, highly trained and professional. The services provided in these institutions are of very high quality and are perceived as such by the population.[53] Islamic institutions have been legally registered first with Israeli authorities and then with Palestinian Authority. Islamic institutions take financial aid from who ever is willing to support them. This includes also Western donors such as the US, EU secular and religious NGOs all around the world.

There has been a rise of Islamic institutions since mid 1970s. The most obvious institutional expression of this was the increasing number of mosques in the Occupied Territories. In addition to mosques a number of Islamic learning centers were established in the years preceding the *Intifada*, such as the Islamic University in Gaza in 1978 and Colleges of Islamic Law in Jerusalem and Hebron. These schools produced many well-educated Muslim clerics, which replaced the traditional *ulema*. Moreover, other Muslim institutions included charity (*zakat*) institutions and committees that collected money and distributed to the needy, Islamic nurseries, elementary and secondary schools and Muslim associations for young men and women in Jerusalem and Gaza.

Mujama and Hamas

One of the first groups to recognize the potential power of population to alter the dominant narratives in the society was the Muslim Brotherhood. The Brotherhood utilized charity organizations, mosques, educational and health institutions to expand their message to the masses. They made use of existing religious values and institutions to create the needed base support. Mujama, an offshoot of the Brotherhood (which later became the basis of Hamas), based its activities upon the networks created and utilized by the Brotherhood. Like the Brotherhood, Mujama, and later Hamas (headed by Sheikh Yassin) was aware that in order to legitimatize its narrative and dominate the socio-political arena of Palestinian life had to access social institutions. Since the beginning of his religio-political career, Yassin concentrated especially on the education system.

However, knowing that the popular tide of support favored a Palestinian nationalist-secularist solution to the problem, during these initial years he concentrated on religious education in his community, preaching, and social services. He surrounded himself with educators, doctors, and others who could offer services to the population, and he did not emphasize the importance of Islam playing a political role. In 1973, *al-Mujamma al-Islami* the Islamic Center was established as a mosque with a medical clinic, a sports club, a nursing school, and Islamic festival hall, a zakat committee, and a center for women's activities and for training young girls were also attached to it.[54] Most of the activities of the Brotherhood were pursued through this center.

Also, as stated before, the Israeli authorities supported the Mujama to counteract the nationalist movement. In 1978, the Israeli authorities encouraged Mujama to submit an application to register as a charitable society. The permission was granted in 1979, in a period when it was extremely hard for other Gazan groups to get such permission. Israel was aware of the implications of their decision, yet they hoped that an Islamic challenge like Mujama will cripple the nationalist movement and dissolve it. As Edwards observes "[w]hen the Mujama started to exert its influence over already existing institutions as a means to undermine the nationalists, the Israelis stood by."[55] In the meantime Mujama refrained from confrontation with the nationalists and took a more gradualist approach, and remained a religious organization dedicated to a program of social reform. However, as it started to expand its base, the Mujama took a more confrontational attitude towards the nationalist. This attitude was reflected in the clashes that took place at various institutional sites.

The Mujama consisted of two parallel organizations under the same name. The first one was the charitable and welfare organization, which was the public face, and was located in Gaza City. The second one was the clandestine political organization, which directed the political activities of the movement and was directed from the home of its leader Sheikh Yassin and the Jawrat Mosque. The charitable wing established a welfare structure that consisted of kindergartens, clinics, and drug rehabilitation programs and youth associations. During religious festivals, the organization would distribute candies and toys for children. The crucial aspect of this organization was its decision to operate in previously neglected areas of the society by the institutions of national movement.

Sheikh Yassin also established small clinics in the refugee camps, organized classes in the study of the Quran and the Hadith in mosques. He also set up a public address system for the call to prayer.[56] Furthermore, he organized sporting activities that focused on martial arts and soccer. The Mujama founded and opened soccer stadiums throughout Gaza. It was through its charitable and social outlook the Mujama was able to disseminate its message. And through their mosques, libraries, health clinics and educational centers (including kindergartens) they were able to reach out to wider segments of the society and start a new generation of Islamists. As Kepel states "Islamic welfare networks were coming to play an essential part in assimilating those elements of the population who aspired to taste the fruits of modernity and prosperity but could not get at them."[57]

In their work among the youth the Islamic groups prioritized laying conditions for an Islamic moral order, and emphasized the importance of remolding the Muslim individual in the face of the dangers presented by secular and godless society in which Muslims were forced to live in. They guarded their reputation as hardworking, disciplined, serious individuals. They also eschewed "frivolous" student activities such as folk dancing, theatre etc. and focused on study circles, communal prayers and commemorating religious occasions in public events and rallies.[58] At the community level mosques and charitable societies founded by Islamic organizations such as the Brotherhood served as the foci of their educational and social efforts. They also brought women from refugee camps and cities to the mosques with the help of charismatic women, and increasing number of young women adopted the "uniform" of the Islamic movement- the distinctive head covering and coat.

Soon the organization extended its activities into other areas of Gazan society, with the aid of Israeli policy of non-interference. The secularization of the society and increasing support for the nationalist movement was a real challenge for Mujama, as they identified the nationalist movement the real enemy of Islam. They perceived the nationalist-secularists and communists as traitors to Islam, and worse then non-believers. They also blamed the nationalists for the failure to liberate the land arguing that this was a result of abandoning the faith. This caused violent clashes between the two camps and, in line with the argument of this work, this struggle for domination the discursive space of the Palestinian society was most obvious at various institutional sites.

When the *Intifada* began, the Islamists were strong at the local level due to the growth of university-educated elites who had spent much time during the 80s expanding grassroots Islamic organizations. Furthermore, various Islamic institutions such as the mosques have been extensively utilized to organize the uprising. Mosques present one of the most effective means to expand Islamic ideas and influence. Mosques are open at all times. They are sanctuaries. These aspects of mosques allow them to be used as spaces for political work away from the interference of Israeli authorities. Mosques, therefore, are used to recruit followers and expand influence. Imams are also considered men of God, who have a deep understanding of the Quran, the Hadith and the Sunna. Hence, they are considered as having access to the "Truth." Therefore religious clerics enjoy a strong and credible position within the community and can incite religious feelings concerning important issues.

The institutional base inherited from the Brotherhood created an opportunity for Mujama to build their policies and actions on. In this period, Mujama had also come to the conclusion that in order to widen its support base, it had to adjust itself to the realities on the ground and take the public mood and will into consideration. As stated earlier, Mujama had close ties to its Brotherhood background, and did not adopt a nationalist agenda. Following the developments during *Intifada*, the Mujama leadership established Hamas on February 1988 to compete with the PLO, with a new narrative of resistance against Israeli occupation and nationalized Islam. Lisa Taraki, who observed in 1989 that "Hamas appears to be engaged in a competitive race with the Unified National Leadership of Uprising for direction of the daily struggle of the people of the occupied territories", supports this view.[59] Indeed, Hamas was able to call a general strike in the West Bank and Gaza on various occasions.[60]

Contrary to the image it has in the West, Hamas is not merely a military faction. It is also a charity and welfare organization that provides services to the Palestinian population. In doing that it utilizes the institutional network and organizational structure of Mujama. Both Hamas and Islamic Jihad disseminates their ideas through books, pamphlets and leaflets, which they promote through bookshops, book fairs, mosques, libraries, market-stalls and hawkers,[61]and until recently, through the internet.[62] It is a political, cultural, and social grassroots organization that has a separate military wing specializing in armed struggle against the Israelis. This military wing has its own leadership and recruiting mechanism. All other sections within Hamas function through overt public platforms and institutions concerned with social, medical or educational services to the public, and have no direct say in the military operations. The most successful effort of Hamas was to mobilize hundreds and thousands of people to join Islamist student and youth groups, which coincided with the rise and proliferation of mass organizations affiliated with the nationalist movement, particularly student blocks at schools, colleges, and universities.[63]

One of the important aspects of these Islamic institutions is channeling funds into the region, which plays a significant role in expanding their message to broader masses. For both Mujama and Hamas fund-raising has been a very important aspect of their work. Each project (establishing a kindergarten, school, clinic, mosque, or undertaking a suicide attack) needs funds. Mujama had encouraged Palestinians to contribute to its projects through *zakat* (alms money), and through *zakat* committees it was able to control the funding projects for the poor. However, local funds were not enough to undertake all the projects. External funding, coming from countries like Saudi Arabia, Jordan, Islamic welfare organizations around the world, among others have been extremely important in raising the necessary funds. Since Mujama took a gradual approach to the conflict, did not challenge the Israeli authorities, and concentrated on welfare and charity activities, it was much easier for them to establish a network of funds from abroad. Additionally, in order to bolster the Mujama in its anti-nationalist campaign, the Israeli authorities contributed indirectly to its funds. As stated by an Israeli military governor for the Gaza Strip, Brigadier-General Yitzak Sager testified that:

> The Israeli government gave me a budget and the military government gives it to the mosques... the funds are used for both mosques and religious schools, with the purpose of strengthening a force that runs counter to the pro-PLO leftists.[64]

Founded of the Mujama background, Hamas was able to benefit from the existing networks of Mujama, and utilized the same fund-raising techniques. Hamas enjoys strong financial backing from various sources that include, but not limited to unofficial bodies in Saudi Arabia, the Gulf States, Iran, as well as Muslims living in the West. [65] According to the IDF (Israeli Defense Force) spokesman in 1993, the amount of money Hamas receives is estimated at one million dollars.[66] As stated earlier Hamas' financial situation, especially compared to PLO, strengthened after the Gulf war in 1990,[67] and in May 1991 it was reported that the US$ 28 million a month from Saudi Arabia that the PLO had received before Gulf Crisis was going to Hamas now.[68] In addition to these external donors, Hamas collects alms money, which it distributes to the needy. According to Nidal, Islamic groups, and Hamas in particular, "get funding from religious endowments, *Zakat*, they promote ideas at mosques and collect money there as well as for their *Dawah* (mission)."[69] Handling the *Zakat* (alms) money, is one of the five pillars of Islam and different groups attempt to collect this alms money. As a religiously oriented group that provides good and credible services to the community, Hamas is better at collecting this money than other groups. As Bassam stated,

> Hamas gets money from *Zakat*. In terms of *zakat*, local communities collect it. Although Palestinian Authority wants to control the money flow in the society, they are not successful and still Hamas collects them.[70]

Hamas has been using *Zakat* to bring people closer to Islam and to broaden its own ranks. In addition to *Zakat*, Hamas has been receiving money from religious endowments. Bassam argued that "Hamas members [....] are able to draw money from religious endowments" through their connection with the local communities that manage these endowments.[71] Although parts of these funds are used for charity, some of it is used to sponsor and organize attacks against the Israeli targets. The network of charity associations serves to transfer funds to field operatives, and identification of potential recruits. All these activities and facilities were funded by the alms money they collected and funding they received from donors. The same funds are also used to assists the families of those who die during Hamas operations and defined as charity. The return of the PLO from exile has had major implications for Hamas and its position in the areas of local politics, religion, charity, education, and welfare. The secular nationalist position, represented by the PLO was strengthened and empowered as a result of foreign donor funds that supported the peace process and the Palestinian economy. Nationalists adopted a policy of re-opening of locales of entertainment, relaxing the dress codes and re-secularization if the society. The PNA suppressed many NGOs that were not supportive of its policies. In order to comply with the Accords, the PNA also tightened its security measures to crackdown on terrorist groups such as Islamic Jihad and Hamas. Foreign aid to support the peace process and assist PNA to build infrastructure contributed to PNA's financial resources, and strengthened them. This had a negative impact on Hamas, as many Palestinians supported this policy and the peace process.

However, as the peace process started wear thin and peace process started to be seen as a failure, the PNA began to loose support. Failure to deliver the crucial social services to the population also added to their loss of credibility. Under these circumstances institutions operated by Hamas remained as the most credible and valuable services. Hamas' social and educational activities in the Occupied Territories have become so entrenched within the Palestinian community that neither Israelis nor the Palestinian Authority have been able to extricate them. Hamas acts as an infrastructure to the numerous cultural, education and social institutions within the society that renders invaluable and irreplaceable services to the public. Neither the Israelis, nor the Palestinian Authority have been able to close down these institutions since that would mean declaring war not only against Hamas but also against the Palestinian community as a whole. In addition to that neither Israel nor Palestinian Authority have been able to provide alternatives to these indispensable institutions run by Hamas. The quality of the services provided in these institutions not only gives them credibility among the Palestinian population, but also among foreign donors.[72] Furthermore their honest conduct and industriousness makes them preferable to the PLO institutions that are believed to be corrupt. Therefore, institutions run by Hamas have become one of the important pillars of the society and rendered them indispensable. This contributes to their legitimacy among the population and increasing popularity of their narrative. As the director of one of the Christian conflict resolution institutions in the West Bank have put it:

> Most of these [Islamic] groups such as Hamas work at grassroots level and provide many social services. They are the only ones doing anything. I do not see them as a threat...[73]

However, the current international embargo which withholds much needed financial support presents a main challenge to Hamas led government's ability to provide for the Palestinian society. Many Palestinians view this embargo "yet another plot to undermine Palestinian society and its institutions.[74] "For that reason they have been patient so far."[75] Nevertheless, in the light of recent violence in the region, how Hamas will manage this situation will be a decisive element in its success and legitimacy as a political organization and representative of the Palestinian people.

Sites of Struggle

Various institutional sites have been utilized to deal with the problems of the Palestinian people under occupation. Some of these institutional sites are modern institutions, such as international and local human rights groups, health care institutions. The secular nationalists and leftist with the support of various international organization and group created many of these modern institutions. However, even these groups used various traditional locales and, cultural and religious vocabulary and symbols and existing power relationships to make their message acceptable to the population in general. Furthermore, in the absence of a formal government with proper institutions, and lack of experience in managing these modern institutions, traditional sites have provided resources and legitimacy. Since religion has been a major source of legitimacy and religious institutions has had a long tradition and experience in the region, religious leaders and institutions have been a significant source of guidance and organization in Palestine.

Institutional sites provide spaces for local power relations to function, and make certain kinds of narratives possible. These organizations place certain individuals in positions of knowledge/power. In the Palestinian context, religious institutions—which are considered one of the most legitimate and trustworthy institutions—place religiously oriented people in positions of power to speak the 'truth.' Their knowledge of the Quran, *Hadith* and their affiliation with religious institutions provide their bases of power. In the establishment of narratives as regimes of truth multiple discursive elements come into play in various strategies. Religious myths, texts and symbols are used to legitimate narratives. If Hamas was able to develop its narrative of "just war" and "legitimate means to fight that war", it was because the relations of power in the Palestinian context had enabled it. Hamas leadership used religio/cultural symbols, texts and myths as discursive elements to justify their narratives.[76] In the following paragraphs I will briefly expand on two of these traditional sites that played a crucial role in the mobilization of the population and legitimation of narratives.

Medical Institutions

Medical institutions, such as hospitals, clinics, dentistries are important institutional sites in the organization of societies. Besides providing health services to patients, these institutions play a critical role in the legitimation of narratives. These institutions reflect the power/knowledge relations within the society and have the potential to influence the way populations think and act. Medical institutions in Palestine are an example of this. Medical institutions in Palestine are closely effected by the developments within the society. For example, the development of a new elite as a result of the establishment of the Palestinian university system had consequences for the medical institutions in Palestine. This new elite aimed at developing the civil society in Palestine and established various relief committees, including medical and agricultural relief committees. These committees attempted to help Palestinians overcome their problems and also mobilize the population towards their constructed ends.

Medical Relief Committees were established to deal with the health problems of the Palestinians. The health care standards in West Bank and Gaza lagged behind Israel and Jordan. According to Physicians for Human Rights "Throughout the occupation, Israel has neglected medical services in the Occupied Territories, intentionally creating a dependency on Israeli health services."[77] Moreover, "no new medical centers were opened, no beds were added to existing ones and doctors were impeded in their efforts to obtain professional expertise."[78] The number of doctors and hospitals available to the Palestinians were low. The life expectancy was lowest in the region, health services were absent in rural areas, and there was no coordination between health care providers. Furthermore access to health care was too expansive for most of the Palestinians. The Israeli soldiers and Jewish settlers intensified these problems during the *Intifada* as need for medical care increased due to the increasing attacks on Palestinians. Curfews, closures and detentions, denial of referrals to Israeli hospitals, periodic cut-offs of running water to Palestinian camps and villages contributed to the deterioration of the Palestinian health problems. Under these conditions providing health care services became one of the major issues of different groups.

According to Mustafa Barghouti and Rita Giacaman, there have been three distinct phases in the Palestinian response to the occupation when medical care is considered.[79] The first phase lasted until mid 70s and was dominated by the "old medical establishment" comprised of well-to-do doctors, who understood health, disease, and medical care as simple and pure biological phenomena, divorced from social, economic, and political contexts.[80] These doctors were interested in centralized hospital, state of the art medical technology, within the framework of Israeli law. In the second phase the autonomy from the military government in the field of health care was emphasized, although still operated within that framework. These doctors were more nationalists, but still came from the wealthy social strata. In the third phase the emphasis was on decentralization, volunteerism, and non-compliance with Israeli regulations. Providing health care to rural areas, through education, mobile clinics, small permanent clinics, and an emphasis on prevention were the focus of this movement. These young specialists had close ties with the grassroots organizations and committees. Female doctors were particularly active. Thus, medical institutions became locales for resistance and non-compliance with the Israeli rule.

In order to coordinate these health care efforts Palestinian Communist Party founded the Union of Palestinian Medical Relief Committees in 1979.[81] The existing health care community initially dismissed this new movement for being "communists" who "were cheapening medicine by going to the villages."[82] Between 1979 an 1987 this Committee established seventeen permanent clinics, emphasizing prevention, education, and first aid training. Training villagers in first aid and establishing first aid centers in villages helped the Palestinian population especially during the *Intifada*.

During the *Intifada* one of the most important contributions of this committee was to institutionalize a computerized blood donor system. This was particularly important since many of the Palestinians were not comfortable with accepting blood from outsiders with the fear of contamination as it is the case with many traditional societies.[83] The system was a success.

The success of this health care initiative, and its popularity among the population resulted in competing groups to launch similar services. Providing better and more effective health services increased the popularity of groups and gave the movement they were affiliated with more credibility. It enabled them to disseminate and legitimize their narratives and placed them in positions of power. In addition to the Medical Relief Committee, PFLP-affiliated Union of Health Work Committees were established in 1985 with similar objectives, and also DFLP, closely associated with Women's Action Committee started providing health care in the 1980s and formalized these services in 1985 under the title Union of Health Care Committees. The last Palestinian health committee to be established was the Fatah affiliated Health Services Council in 1986.[84] After its establishment it became the best-funded health NGO in Palestine due to its close relations with the PLO. Furthermore, in contrast to other health care organizations, it was not political.

After the Oslo process many of the health care grassroots organizations and committees faced financial problems as the donors diverted their resources to the Palestinian Authority, who sought to suppress NGOs, which were not affiliated with the PLO and were in opposition to its policies. During this time, Islamic groups had already laid down the foundations of various services within the society. Unlike other Palestinian factions the Islamic movement, and particularly the Mujama was not proscribed and so was free to organize, recruit, and receive funds more easily before the *Intifada*. Its charitable status allowed Mujama to establish rapidly and openly an organization network rivaling that of the other political groups. As stated before, this was made possible by the Israeli policy of divide and rule, to undermine the Palestinian nationalism. Under these conditions, Mujama was able to establish its own clinics and health centers with its own doctors and dentists. As its influence was becoming more wide-spread, Islamists targeted some of the central medical institutions, which played a crucial role in the Palestinian social and political space. Edwards, who states, "local health-care institutions soon became the arena of competition between the newly-registered Mujama and the national movement,"[85] support this view. One such site was the Palestinian Red Crescent.

One of the first encounters of the nationalist and Islamist narratives in an important Palestinian institutional site has been at the Palestinian Red Crescent (PRC). Founded in 1972 as a welfare and relief organization, funded, administered and operated by the Palestinians, the PRC was an important nationalist institution associated with the PLO and its supporters. Its director was a well-recognized Palestinian leftist, who was a strong supporter of national rights.

Having a strong position in this organization was considered as an important step towards establishing hegemony and control of the discursive space. 1979 elections for the administrative committee was an important opportunity for Mujama to gain influence in one of the key Palestinian institutions. For that reason they put their candidates up. However, Mujama supporters were able to win only three seats. This defeat infuriated them. One of the committee members, who was supportive of Mujama took the complaint to Israeli authorities, and asked to investigate the matter. After the Israeli investigation, the PRC was cleared but the organization dismissed the committee member from his post.[86]

The conflict between the nationalists over the PRC was not over after that. Combined with a conflict over influencing another key institution (the rumor that the nationalists were going to set up their own university in Gaza as an alternative to the Islamic university there), the struggle between the nationalist and Mujama supporters took a violent form, in which many Mujama supporters attacked cafes, video shops, liquor shops, and set the PRC building on fire. Taking control over a key institution that is revered and respected by a great majority of Palestinians was perceived by the Islamists to gain control over the political narrative within Palestine, and consolidate their power within the society.

Educational Institutions

Educational institutions have a direct political role in creating the intellectual and institutional technologies that generate distinctly new social groups, not just an indirect role diagnostic of a standing distribution of power.[87] Educational institutions play an important role in the cultural production, social reproduction, and orientation of the individuals. Being educated is considered a great merit in the Middle East. Especially in the Palestinian Territories, education is linked with resistance to occupation. For instance in an interview, Thahini stated that

Hamas, which is the strongest faction in her university in Hebron consider education as one of the important tools for mobilizing the resistance. She added that, "they [Hamas] insist that we have to learn Hebrew, because they argue that in order to be able to defeat our enemy we have to learn their language."[88] Also Dr. Abbad emphasized the role of education, and reverence to education in Islam, especially for women and quoted a Hadith from the Prophet that states "any Muslim who educates his/her daughter will be safe from the fire in the last day."[89] Therefore looking at the educational institutions, such as universities becomes helpful for understanding the position of the Islamic discourse within the society.

As stated earlier one of the important developments in the Palestinian political life was the establishment of Palestinian University system, which led to the emergence of new, ideologically motivated, and well-educated elite. This system politicized the Palestinian discursive space more then before, as students from the refugee camps and small villages were now able to get university education and organize more efficiently. Realizing the role universities played in mobilizing and politicizing the Palestinian population, especially during the *Intifada*, Israel closed down all schools, including kindergartens and elementary schools. In response to this policy, Palestinian groups organized popular committees in urban neighborhoods to cater the educational needs of the population. Since the number of university trained Palestinians were abundant who could undertake teaching. These underground educational activities would take place in hotels, mosques, churches, or homes. With this initiative, education became a subversive activity and the locale of narratives of resistance. In order to prevent these underground educational activities, Israel resorted to house to house searches arrested those who were engaged in these activities.

The first Palestinian University to be founded was the Bir Zeit University in Ramallah, established in 1972. The second Palestinian University was the University of Bethlehem, established in 1973-4 by Christian Brothers, affiliated with Vatican. Al-Najah University was the third and the establishment of Islamic universities in Hebron and Gaza followed this. The first student block in the Territories was established by the PFLP at the Bethlehem University in 1980. In two years time other major PLO factions also established political blocs. The leadership of these blocs consisted of those Palestinians that were imprisoned by the Israeli authorities. With the rise of Islamic bloc various PLO affiliated student blocs joined to counter-balance the Islamic movement. During this period, with the exception of Islamic University in Gaza, PLO related student blocs were able to maintain their political hegemony. As Robinson observes, prior to the *Intifada*, PLO related blocs, such as Fatah had the hegemony, while the Islamists generally won between a quarter and a third of the total vote.[90]

In Gaza, however, Islamic bloc had the hegemony at the university elections. An important development that had a significant affect in this line was the establishment of various Islamic learning centers and universities by the end of

1970s. The strength of student Islamic blocks at Palestinian universities reflects the increasing power of the Islamist movement in the region. Especially after the Iranian revolution, Islamist blocs in the West Bank and Gaza gained control of a number of student councils.[91] These universities enjoyed a relative autonomy from the Israeli pressure. Also by concentrating on social Islamication and not on confrontation with Israel, Mujama was able to act with less constraint from the Israeli authorities. These qualities became particularly important for the successful use of Islamic institutions in the Occupied Territories.

The relations with the nationalist student blocs were fraught with tension and conflict especially in the mid-80s. Throughout the 1980s there was a clear pattern of heavy politicization at Palestinian universities; it centered primarily on the PLO factions but had, at most universities, a strong Islamist current.[92] Several violent conflicts between nationalist and Islamist students erupted on campuses, at times spilling over into the community and requiring great conciliation efforts.[93] These clashes were particularly intense at Bir Zeit and al-Najah Universities and at the Islamic University at Gaza. These violent methods of the Islamic bloc were denounced by the prominent nationalist figures, newspaper editorials, public statements and institutions associated with the nationalists.

Recruitment of students into various camps was an important endeavor at the universities. Incoming students prior to the *Intifada* were actively recruited to one or another political faction, however, the intensely politicized atmosphere of the society changed the recruiting activities.[94] People joined various factions as a result of social utility and self-identity, albeit family ties and social relations played an important role in this process. Recruitment was often done through social activities, such as helping students to register, choose classes, and inviting them to informal gatherings. Nevertheless a screening or probationary period was always employed to avoid Israeli collaborators.

University based political activities usually spilled over into the community. For example each faction at Bir Zeit University had a particular restaurant, which the members usually gathered.[95] Furthermore, student activities were not restricted to campus life, but involved activities that created and strengthened their ties to the wider Palestinian community. In that line, various projects undertaken in rural areas helped politicize the villagers and expanded the mass organizations, in addition to establishing factional related grass-roots organizations by the university groups. These included education and literacy programs, health care programs, women's programs, and agricultural relief programs among others. These extracurricular activities were aimed at mobilizing the population and to establish a network of alliances and relations. These networks were crucial during the *Intifada* to mobilize the population and organize mass demonstrations. Additionally the experience garnered at the universities and relations established were crucial both in the formation of mass mobilization outside of the universities and in the establishment and leadership of the popular committees during the *Intifada*. Thus universities played a critical role in the re-configuration of power relations within the Palestinian society.

The above analysis of the role of educational sites, especially universities in Palestine shows their crucial role in mobilization of the population towards certain ends of different groups. Gaining the upper hand in these institutions provided wider access to the population and dissemination of their message to broader segments of the society and legitimization of their narratives and also recruiting followers among different levels of the society, and also placing them in positions of power. For that reason, especially universities became important locales for different groups that competed with each other.

One such institutional site, where the struggle between nationalists and Islamist was severe, was the Islamic University of Gaza. A harsh competition, similar to the one that took place at the PRC took place at the Islamic University at Gaza. Edwards states that "[t]he attempt to win influence over and control the PRC was just one element of a wider policy and was soon followed by targeting another institution: the Islamic University of Gaza (IUG)."[96] Since the idea of educating the population was at the heart of both the Brotherhood and the Mujama, controlling an important institutional site like the IUG was a crucial aspect of the struggle over establishing their regime of truth in the Palestinian arena. It was believed that if the illiterate and uneducated were taught to read the Quran and other religious literature, then their hearts and minds would follow.[97] A university would give the organization a great opportunity to disseminate their message with the pretext of advancing the education of the population and also influence the local political scene.

Until 1978 most Palestinians were educated in Egyptian universities. Following the Palestinian demonstrations protesting the peace treaty signed between Egypt and Israel, Egyptian President Sadat closed the Egyptian universities to Palestinians. Until that time the only higher education institution in Gaza was the al-Azhar religious college and the Mujama was able to establish a close affiliation with this institution. The locals had decided to establish a university by transforming this religious college into an Islamic University of Gaza. Although the religious orientation of the emerging university caused conflict, initially the new university tried to give the impression that it was representative of the political spectrum of Gaza by giving a part to the secularists.[98]

The university was soon to increasingly fall under the influence of leaders and activists of the Mujama, as Edwards states, "[t]his was Gaza's only institution of higher education and the Mujama were keen to establish its hegemony over it."[99] By 1981, a Mujama backed group attempted to eliminate the secularists. And the Israeli authorities, which ordered seven of the thirteen members of the consulting committee to resign, supported this move. This Israeli-Mujama alliance was noticed with great concern by the Palestinian press as they reported; "One claims the removal was a coincidence of the authorities suppression of Palestinian education opportunity and Awwad's[100] desire to 'control the university and fill the staff with Sheikhs rather than Ph.Ds.''[101] Soon, from the highest to lowest position (including the porters and gatekeepers), the university posts were filled with supporters of Mujama.

By the mid-80s, the Islamic University in Gaza had 4,500 students, making it the largest campus in the Occupied Territories.[102] The form of education was also reflecting the Islamic perspective of the Mujama. As Edwards states "behind the walls of the institution the message of Islam was all pervasive."[103]For example, separate entrances were assigned to women and men. The courses that were taught and the ideas that were disseminated reflected the Islamic message of the Mujama. Mujama activists and their supporters were in charge of the organization of all the student life and student activities. These non-textual gestures and textual content of the education was aimed at sending a message to the rival groups regarding their power.

Furthermore, Islamists dealt severely with the leftists, liberalists, and progressives expressing a view that differed from theirs. "Mujama students, easily identifiable by their beards and Islamic inspired dress, contested Palestinian nationalist activity among their fellow students where ever they found it."[104] PLO was criticized for being a coalition of atheists. Supporters of the PLO were singled out and ridiculed. At times beating was involved against them, including women who refused to wear headscarf. The same phenomena took place at the Islamic University in Hebron, where Islamic dress code became a symbol of political affiliation and a form of resistance not only against Israel but also nationalists. As one of my interviewees, Thahini professed that she was harassed for not covering her hair at the Islamic University of Hebron during the *Intifada.*[105] These practices and confrontations with the non-Mujama supporters created an intimidating and authoritarian atmosphere. This Islamication trend had spilled over into the community life. Cinemas, liquor stores, restaurants selling alcohol, and casinos were closed down due to the pressure of the movement. Those that did not close were attacked and vandalized. Weddings that were not consistent with Islamic tradition were attacked and forcibly disrupted.[106] By 1987 this Islamic movement was able to penetrate into the political life as well, as many Gazans chose to become religious.[107] Eventually, the Mujama's strategy of starting from the education system and controlling the highest educational institution in Gaza to control the discursive space in the area, mixed with its intimidating and oppressive tactics and legitimated its narrative by using a familiar and powerful use of religious symbols and texts was successful. This student base was to become the limbs for expanding their narrative deeper into the society and become a major challenge for both the Israeli occupation and the policies of the PLO.

To conclude, by focusing on the institutional sites where different narratives compete of legitimacy and domination within the social fabric of the Palestinian context this chapter aimed to show how these narratives are disseminated through various influential institutions and grassroots organizations within the society. Here, I argued that institutions play an important role in legitimation of narratives and becoming the dominant political force that controls the discursive space in Palestinian Territories. In their attempt to do so various groups utilize cultural and religious vocabulary and symbols that the population is familiar with and considers legitimate. Furthermore, these groups utilize pre-existing social structures as resources to mobilize the society. In that process various institutional sites become important locales for reaching out to the population. The effectiveness and the popularity of their institutions and the services that are affiliated with these groups not only assist them in reaching out to the population, but also gives them credibility and legitimacy.

Within these institutions, various values that are embedded within the cultural context are emphasized. These values may include, for example, those such as steadfastness, sharing, fasting, patience, sacrifice, doing good, serving the community, alms giving among other, derived from the Islamic tradition. Bringing people together in a religious context such as mosques, rituals of prayer, fasting or alms giving revives these values and gives the moral, spiritual, and psychological strength to face and resist the occupation. Combined with the other traditional sources of legitimacy (such as kinship ties, lineage, etc.), these values position certain individuals in ranks of authority and power to proffer various narratives as legitimate. The power/narrative nexus that operates through these institutions enables these people to claim legitimacy to the 'Truth.' The historical situatedness of the Palestinian people and various critical events draw the limits of what can be said and what cannot be said in these sites.

Understanding the workings of power/narratives through these institutional sites to establish regimes of truth gives us clues for developing conflict resolution strategies that are appropriate for the conflict under study. In developing a conflict resolution strategy, understanding how various narratives are formed, transformed and legitimated becomes important. This requires an analysis of the sources of legitimacy within the context of the affected community. Understanding what can be said and what cannot be said within the context of community and to find ways to transform those narratives that incite hatred and animosity into ones that are more prone to peace. In this process engaging hermeneutically with the textual, inter-textual and contextual factors, involving those religious and traditional leaders that are peace oriented becomes critical to replace the extremist narratives with more peaceful ones. Furthermore, the effectiveness and the credibility of the institutions where these narratives are operationalized through the workings of power must also be comprehended. Understanding the workings and functions of various institutions operated by various groups that provide key services to the population are important to address the needs and frustrations of the community. Encouraging and empowering those institutions that work for a just solution to the conflict through nonviolent means by assisting them through technical, political and financial support become decisive to delegitimize extremist voices. Thus, based on the analyses presented in these chapters, the final chapter will attempt to provide a framework for developing an effective conflict resolution strategy in the region.

Endnotes

1. Hardy Roger Analysis: "What was achieved in Mecca?" BBC News February 9, 2007 at www.news.bbc.co.uk
2. Foucault M. *History of Sexuality*. (New York: Vintage Books, 1978), 86-87.
3. Foucault 1978, 94.
4. Foucault 1978.
5. Foucault 1978.
6. Foucault 1978, 96.
7. Alec McHoul, and Wendy Grace.. *A Foucault Primer: Discourse, power and the subject*. (London: UCL Press, 1993), 65.
8. McHoul and Grace, 1993, 70.
9. McHoul and Grace, 1993.
10. McHoul and Grace, 1993.
11. See page 31.
12. Here I used the term "non-textual domain" similar to the way Foucault uses the term "non-discursive domain." Foucault uses "non-discursive domain" to refer to "institutions, political events, economic practices and processes. See Foucault 1972, 162.
13. Foucault 1972. 68.
14. Foucault 1972, 227.
15. Irani and Funk Rituals of Reconciliation: Arab-Islamic Perspectives" in Said, *Peace and Conflict Resolution in Islam: Precept and Practice* Abdul Aziz, et. al .eds. New York: University Press of America. (2001): 169-191
16. See Serif Mardin *Religion and Social Change in Modern Turkey: The Case of Bediuzzaman Said Nursi* (State University of New York Press 1989 , 163.
17. See Mardin 1989
18. Hourani 1971.
19. Glenn E. Robinson. *Building a Palestinian State: The Incomplete Revolution*. (Bloomington and Indianapolis: Indiana University Press, 1997), 9.
20. Robinson 1997, 10-11.
21. Robinson 1997, 14.
22. Robinson 1997, 15.
23. Robinson 1997, 67.
24. Selim Tamari. "Palestinian Social Transformations : the Emergence of Civil Society," in *Civil society: Democratization in the Arab World* (A monthly publication of the Ibn Khaldun Center for Development Studies.) at http://www.ibnkhaldun.org/newletter/1999/feb/essay3.html:2 (1999).
25. Tamari, 1999.
26. Denis J. Sullivan.n.d. "NGOs and Development in the Arab World: the Critical Importance of a Strong Partnership Between Government and Civil Society" at http://www.mideastinfo.com/arabngo.htm.
27. Sullivan n.d.,7.
28. Rex Brynen. *A Very Political Economy: Peacebuilding and Foreign Aid in the West Bank and Gaza*. (Washington D.C.: United States Institute of Peace, 2000), 51.
29. Sara Roy. "Transformation of Islamic NGOs in Palestine," in *Middle East Report no. 214 (spring)*. at http:/www.merip.org/mer/mer214/pitner_214.html (2000).

30. Robinson 1997, 136.

31. Robinson 1997, 50.

32. Robinson 1997, 51.

33. See Robinson 1997. footnote 56.

34. Robinson 1997.

35. Sullivan n.d., 8-9.

36. World Bank, "The Palestinian NGO Project, Public Discussion Paper" 15 July, 1997 al-Ram: 1-1.

37. World Bank 1997, 51.

38. Interview with Fateh Azzam. In *Civil Society: Democratization in the Arab World.* (A Monthly Publication of the Ibn Khaldun Center for Development Studies) at http://www.ibnkhaldun.org/newsletter/1999/feb/interv.html (1999)

39. According to the UN, between 1992 and 1998 real per capita GNP fell by 21 percent. UNSCO. *The Economy of West Bank and Gaza Strip: A Retrospective on the 1990s and Future Challenges.* (January, 1999), 6.

40. Brynen 2000, 60.

41. Brynen 2000.

42. Morris, *1948 and After* New York: Oxford University Press, (1987), 91.

43. Brynen, 2000, 48.

44. Ahmad, Imad-ad Dean "Building Muslim Civil Society from the Bottom Up" Paper presented at the Meeting of the American Muslim Social Scientists (Washington D.C: Georgetown University, 2000) October 13-15 at http://www.minaret.org/CivilSociety.htm.

45. Morris, 1987, 91

46. Emmanuel Sivan "Arab Nationalism in the Age of Islamic Resurgence" in James Jankowski and Gershoni eds. in *Rethinking Nationalism in the Arab Middle East.*(New York: Columbia University Press, 1997), 219.

47. Musa. Budeiri, 1997 "The Palestinians: Tensions Between Nationalist and Religious Identities" in Sivan 1997, 192.

48. Charles Amjad Ali. "Democracy and Islam" in Elise Boulding eds. *Building Peace in the Middle East: Challenges for States and Civil Society.* (Boulding and London.: Lynne Reinner Publishers. 1998).

49. Mardin 1989, 165.

50. For an analysis if the impact if communication revolution and its impact on the Ottoman Empire see Mardin 1989, 148-149.

51. Robinson, Glenn E. *Building a Palestinian State: The Incomplete Revolution.* Bloomington and Indianapolis: Indiana University Press, (1997), 136.

52. Roy, Sara. *The Gaza Strip: The Political Economy of De-development* Washington D.C.: Institute for Palestinian Studies, (1995), 3. See also "Transformation of Islamic NGOs in Palestine," in *Middle East Report no. 214 (spring).* at http:/www.merip.org/mer/mer214/pitner_214.html, 2000. (2000)

53. Roy 1995.

54. Abu-Amr 1994, 16.

55. Edwards 1996, 105.

56. Edwards 1996, 102.

57. G. Kepel. *The Revenge of God, The Resurgence of Islam, Christianity and Judaism in the Modern World.* (Cambridge, 1994), 24.

58. Taraki 1989, 31.

59. Taraki 1989, 30

60. Taraki 1989.

61. see Edwards 1996, 183, 198.

62. In April 2002, hackers bombarded the web site with pornographic material and debilitated the web page of Hamas. However, Hamas renewed its website following that incident. See Hamas website at http://:www.hamasonline.org

63. Edwards 1996.

64. Edwards 1996, 128.

65. Finding the sources of Hamas funding has not been easy. Some information has been gathered by Israel Ministry of Foreign Affairs. See http://www.mfa.gov.il/MFA/MFAArchive/2000_2009/2003/7/The%20Financial%20Sources%20of%20the%20Hamas%20Terror%20Organiza and http://www.mfa.gov.il/MFA/MFAArchive/2000_2009/2003/9/Hamas-s%20use%20of%20charitable%20societies%20to%20fund%20and%20su

66. see http:/www.fas.org/irp/world/para/docs/930100.htm

67. PLO's Support for Saddam Hussein undermined its relations with especially Gulf countries. On the other hand, Hamas leaflet 64 had called Saddam Hussein to withdraw its troops, to maintain support from its Gulf funders.

68. Edwards 1996, 155.

69. Interview with Nidal, Dheisheh Refugee Camp, Bethlehem June 30, 2000.

70. Interview with Bassam Bethlehem July 18, 2000.

71. Interview with Bassam.

72. Interview with Nidal, Dheisheh Refugee Camp, Bethlehem June 30, 2000.

73. Interview with Zoghby, Bethlehem July, 18 2000.

74. Interviews, Tel Aviv, January 2007.

75. Interviews Tel Aviv.

76. It must be noted that not all religious institutions are under the control of Hamas and Hamas' narrative (although it has increasingly become more popular) is not the only Islamic narrative in Palestine. Nevertheless, this thesis focuses mostly on Hamas.

77. See http://english.phr.org.il/phr/Pages/PhrArticle_Unit.asp?Cat=15&art=229&Pcat=4

78. See http://english.phr.org.il/phr/Pages/PhrArticle_Unit.asp?Cat=15&art=229&Pcat=4.

79. Barghuti, M. and Giacaman, R cited in Brynen 2000, 40.

80. Brynen 2000.

81. Brynen 2000, 41.

82. Brynen 2000.

83. Brynen 2000, 42.

84. See Brynen 2000

85. Edwards 1996, 100.

86. See Edwards 1996, 106-108.

87. Gregory Starrett.. *Putting Islam to Work: Education, Politics, and Religious Transformation in Egypt,(*Los Angeles: University of California Press, 1998), 11.

88. Interview with Thahini Hebron July 6, 2000.

89. Interview with Dr. Abbad (a Sufi sheikh) Bethlehem July 19, 2000.

90. Robinson 1997, 22.

91. Robinson 1997, 138.

92. Robinson 1997, 27.

93. Taraki 1989, 30.
94. Robinson 1997, 27.
95. Robinson 1997, 28.
96. Edwards 1996, 108.
97. Edwards 1996.
98. Edwards 1996, 109.
99. Edwards 1996, 110.
100. Sheikh Awwad used to run the al Azhar religious college in Gaza before the establishment of IUG and has been known to be a supporter of Mujama.
101. *Al fajr*, 16-22 August, 1981,9 Quoted by Edwards, 110.
102. Edwards 1996, 111.
103. Edwards 1996.
104. Edwards 1996.
105. Interview with Thahini Hebron, July 6, 2000.
106. Edwards 1996, 116.
107. Edwards 1996.

Chapter 8

Conclusion: Musalaha

The Israeli-Palestinian conflict has been an unceasing area of interest for the scholars of conflict resolution. The "famous" handshake between Arafat and Rubin in 1993 at the White House in Washington D.C. inspired tremendous hope for those in the field and for the common people in general. It was considered a crucial step in the minds of many, showing that the 42-year of conflict was about to come to an end and conflict resolution techniques in general, and second track diplomacy and mediation in particular were proving fruitful. Yet the failure of the Camp David Summit in July 2000 and the re-escalation of the conflict in September 2000 resulted in great disappointment, not only for both Israeli and Palestinian communities, but also for the pundits of conflict resolution.

The intensity of the conflict only increased since then. Islamic militant groups such as Hamas and Islamic Jihad increased suicide attacks, whereas Israel is responded with war helicopters, missiles, and closure of Palestinian territories. Both communities are extremely frustrated with the failure of the long "Peace Process" and their daily lives are interrupted with never-ending violence. Although the death of Arafat and the latest truce negotiated by the elected Head of the Palestinian Authority, Abu Mazen, had initiated a more hopeful current, these did not last. The election of Hamas government, Israeli-Lebanese conflict of Summer 2006, clashes between Hamas and Fatah supporters, and attempts to form a new coalition government following the Mecca Agreement in February 2007 obscures the future. In the meantime, violence over the last five years seems to have nurtured the radicals in both communities.

Mecca Agreement in February 2007 obscures the future. In the meantime, violence over the last five years seems to have nurtured the radicals in both communities.

However, violence begets more violence. To break this cycle of violence and to renew faith in peace requires first, an understanding of why the previous attempts to resolve the conflict failed, and second, to develop an innovative approach that has the potential to offer alternative avenues for transforming the current situation into a new peace process that is sustainable. This requires an in-depth analysis of key factors influencing the conflict and the role of religion/culture.

Shortcomings of Previous Attempts to Resolve the Conflict

The Israeli-Palestinian conflict is a very complex one with its multi-dimensional aspects, involving issues including territory, security, identity, confrontation of religions, and cultures, sharing of resources such as water, and etc. There have been many attempts to resolve this conflict, albeit with limited access. For example, Herbert Kelman and his friends have been working on bringing together politically active and influential Israelis and Palestinians for private and direct communication since the early 1990s. [1] Their work has involved the "intensive application to the Israeli- Palestinian conflict of the concepts and methods of interactive problem solving - an unofficial 3rd party approach to Conflict Resolution derived from the work of J. Burton, and based on social-psychological principle"[2]. They organized a series of meetings between 1990-1993, all of which had different purposes, different contributions, and different outcomes.

In these workshops the participants came from a significant proportion of the political elites of the two communities.[3] They were aimed at increasing the participants' knowledge about the other side and sensitivity to their concerns and at enhancing their experience and skills in communicating with the other side, as well as their commitment to such communication. As a consequence, workshop participation was expected to strengthen the qualifications and effectiveness of the participants in a negotiating role.[4] Their approach emphasized transmitting the lessons learned during the workshops to political leaders and others to help create a political atmosphere conducive to negotiations and to impact the decision making processes. These Problem-Solving workshops were considered a great success, as it led to the Oslo Peace Process, which was considered a breakthrough, was a formal agreement between the Israeli-government and the PLO.[5]

However, Oslo process failed to bring the hoped-for peace, as it crumbled following the Camp David Summit of 2000. As stated earlier, the Oslo process excluded critical actors such as the fundamentalist groups, peace actors and grassroots movements.[6] The negotiations failed to account for the civil society and the alternative leaderships that have been gaining support among the population, such as the Islamic groups. In his analysis of the Oslo process, William Zartman argues that, "the best Oslo could accomplish was a settlement, not a resolution, and that settlement was possible in large measure because reconciliation took place on a personal level among the negotiation teams."[7] He adds that, by its nature and by the problems inherent in its implementation, this settlement made reconciliation more difficult."[8] As stated by Bercovitch and Kadayifci, "the secrecy of the process and the exclusion of other segments in both societies, created problems of re-entry for the negotiators."[9] Thus, hard-liners in both societies rejected the Oslo process and actively worked to undermine it.[10]

Moreover, the implementation of the agreements proved to be much harder than signing the agreements. The negotiations were mostly focused on Israel's security concerns, and mutual recognition, leaving difficult issues such as the status of Jerusalem, the settlements, refugees, and the borders of the Palestinian State for the permanent talks anticipated in 2000.[11] Additionally, the Oslo process set no mechanism for implementation of the agreement, nor it established a mechanism to monitor or enforce the implementation of the agreement. The mediators pulled out following the settlement, and no services were offered to assist reconciliation between the communities. These were left the parties themselves and both sides neither had the time nor the program to bring the "Spirit of Oslo" back to Israel and Palestine.[12] Faced with problems of implementation, negotiators had difficult time convincing their constituencies of the benefits of the agreements and that it was possible to reach a mutually acceptable solution to the conflict.

Furthermore, previous attempts to resolve the conflict, including the Oslo Process, ignored the power asymmetry, which is a critical aspect of this conflict. Israel is an internationally recognized state with one of the world's strongest armies and a wealthy diaspora with strong ties in the government to the United States. Whereas "Palestine" still only consists of scattered lands controlled by Israel, and has no official army. Palestinian people lack a recognized state and are represented by an authority whose legitimacy is challenged within the community. There is also the fact that United States – the only superpower in the global arena—who has deep vested interests in the region, and whose close relations and alliance with Israel is no secret to anyone, has been the mediator of the conflict for the final agreement. Such a situation raises concerns in terms of justice and fairness of the peace process. As Edward Said states "...to place the Palestinian and the Israeli sides within the opposition on what appears to be an equal, opposite and symmetrical footing is also to reduce the claims of the one by elevating the claims of the other."[13] An uneven handed pressure on the Palestinian side to end the violence, without pressuring Israel to limit its use of violence and fulfill the terms of the agreement have undermined the sense of justice, fairness, and impartiality among the Palestinian population. Finally, these attempts to end the conflict failed to recognize the need for communal reconciliation, and the need to address the mutual hatred, mistrust among both communities as well as the deepening feeling of desperation and frustration of the Palestinian people. Cultural and religious sources that could provide a basis for reconciliation were ignored.

In deep-rooted and intractable conflicts, like the Israeli-Palestinian conflict, conflicting communities suffer from mutual hatred, and deep mistrust as a result of a long-going violence. Both Israelis and Palestinians view each other as existential threat. Both communities are under the influence of a history filled with resentment, dehumanization, anger, and rage. Both suffer from deep injuries, and traumas, which prevent any true reconciliation process to take place. However, as stated before, for peace to be sustainable it must be seen as legitimate by a critical majority, the agreement must be signed by a leadership that is viewed as legitimate; the mediators and the peace-making process must also be considered legitimate. Furthermore, in addition to addressing the needs and interests of all the parties involved, it must be accompanied by a communal reconciliation process that will lead to a change in the negative perceptions of the 'enemy' and to establish constructive relations that can re-generate itself. In this process, religio/cultural values, traditions and institutions can be rich sources for altering the mind frames of the communities as well as assist healing deep social traumas and injuries.

Culture/Religion and Conflict Resolution

Most of the scholarship concerning the Israeli-Palestinian conflict takes a secular perspective and ignores its religio/cultural dimension.[14] There are two main reasons for this negligence in my opinion. First of all, it is to many people's concern that if the religious character is emphasized, it will turn into a self-fulfilling prophecy, whereby the conflict will acquire a heavy religious stand. It is believed that this would lead to a war of two religions, namely Judaism and Islam with enormous spillover effect in a region, which is already marked by intense religious tension. The second reason is that, the traditional Western conflict resolution models and approaches do not leave space for issues such as the role of culture and religion. As stated earlier, until recently, traditional Western scholarship had valued a secular approach to understand sources of conflict and its resolution.

Although culture has been viewed with great suspicion by the traditionalist international relations and conflict resolution scholars for not being "quantifiable," current scholars have come to recognize its importance for resolving conflicts in non-Western contexts.[15] The realist perspective, which focuses on unitary actors, rational decision-making and interests defined in terms of power, does not leave space for culture. Those who include beliefs and images in their analysis refer to psychological factors rather then culture. Idealists, or liberalists, on the other hand, believe in a single human nature and homogenous values that stem from this nature. Edward Tylor's inclusive definition of culture as "the complex whole which includes knowledge, belief, art, morals, law, custom, and any other capabilities and habits acquired by men as a member of society"[16] explains why many scholars do not want to deal with a complex phenomenon such as culture.

Culture affects the behavior and actions of individuals, plays a profound role in the molding of social structures. "Because culture provides the structure through which people interpret experience, it informs and guides both intention and action."[17] Here, structure is used to indicate the way a society organizes itself in terms of social, economic, legal and political institutions. Since social structures are produced and reproduced through culturally mediated social action and interaction, culture becomes the link between the individual and the social structures. As Bercovitch states, culture helps us interpret and structure incoming information.[18] Therefore, culture and action are interdependent, and culture itself is reproduced and produced in this process as Sewell argues, "Events ...shape history by changing the cultural meanings or signification (of) political and social categories and consequently changing people's possibilities for meaningful action."[19]

Nevertheless, it is important to note that culture is not the answer to all the problems, and "culture" is not a unified whole, even within a single community. There is more than one culture within each community. "By linking cultures to individuals and emphasizing the number and diversity of social and experiential settings that individuals encounter," Kevin Avruch "expands the scope of reference of culture to encompass not just quasi- or pseudo-kinship groupings (tribes, ethnic group, and nation are the usual ones), but also groupings that derive from profession, occupation, class, religion, or region."[20] His definition of culture holds up that "culture is always psychologically and socially distributed in a group."[21]

In order to operationalize culture as an analytical tool, Avruch and Black develop a useful distinction. According to this, there are two faces of culture: generic and local. Generic culture develops as a result of the adoptive feature of human beings and "directs our attention to the universal attributes of human behavior," whereas "local cultures are those complex systems of meanings created, shared, and transmitted (socially inherited) by individuals in particular social groups" and "direct[s] our attention to diversity, difference, and particularism."[22] Based on Theodore Schwartz definition of culture Avruch and Black argue that,

> Culture consists of the derivatives of experience, more or less organized, learned or created by the individuals of a population, including those images or encodements and their interpretations

> (meanings) transmitted from past generations from contemporaries, or formed by individuals themselves.[23]

This definition locates culture simultaneously inside and outside of individuals. Connecting culture with individual experience makes culture situational, flexible, and responsive to the requirements of the external world that the individuals live in and thus links the generic and local cultures, and allows for diversity and plurality of cultures, even within the same society. Cultures exist in different but overlapping layers, and these different layers interact with each other and produce outcomes that may be unexpected.

Culture is a living, growing social reality, created and continually recreated by people through their social interaction, rather then imposed upon them.[24] Itis manifest in the capacity with which it endows people to practice meaning in, or attach meaning to social behaviour. Behavior does not contain meaning intrinsically, but it is found to be meaningful by an act of interpretation.[25] It is the individual who makes sense of what s/he observes. Social interaction is contingent upon such interpretations and it is a transaction of meanings.[26] Thus, it is through interaction with the community that the individual acquires and developes cultural codes and symbols.

The role of culture in international relations and conflict resolution has become an important area of study in the recent years, as the scholars have come to see identities and divergent values as major factors in ethnic conflicts. The role of culture can be detected in various aspects of conflict studies. Culture plays a significant role in conflict situations, as perceptions, enemy images, interests are socially constructed therefore directly linked to identities and culture. "Power is also seen as a complex phenomenon, closely associated with legitimacy, and therefore with culture."[27] And as Avruch states projections of power are never unambiguous and culturally based stereotypes may influence the degree of credibility given to threats or commitments.[28] Culture provides us with a vocabulary that enables us to talk about the relationship of individuals to social groups and institutions. Therefore, culture also provides us with the vocabulary regarding conflicts and their resolution. Cultural values can be used to justify violence and legitimate conflictual narratives, or condemn violence and call for reconciliation.

Culture has many dimensions, and one of the crucial dimensions is religion. This study will focuses on the religious dimension of culture in particular and use the words interchangibly, although these concepts differ significantly.[29] One reason for this is that "religious values and norms are central aspects of the cultural identity of many people involved in conflict dynamics."[30] On the other hand, although most Palestinians are Muslim by faith, Islam is more a cultural trait then a strict religious conviction. Religion, as a system of beliefs and practices relating to the sacred, and uniting its adherents in a community, has a powerful hold on people's way of thinking, acting and perception of interests. "Religious values, like other values, can motivate people to fight or to reconcile their differences, and similar to culture, play an active role in escalating or de-escalating a conflict as it influences the issues, parties, strategies, outcomes, and interveners.[31]

Many political leaders have used this unique power of religion for legitimating their discourses and for mobilizing people towards their constructed ends. [32] Although the main reasons and issues of a conflict may not be of religious character, religion plays a significant role at times of conflict where different religious systems encounter each other. In such cases, political leaders do not hesitate to resort to religious myths and sacred documents of their religion to justify their acts, and policies. By doing that they try to get the support of their communities and reinforce their power. As it is stated by Anthony Giddens, "there has been no shortage of religions that have glorified war and which, in so doing, have helped to knit a state cult tightly to the military pursuits of a dominant class."[33] In addition to that, religious institutions have been supportive of violence and repression at times of conflicts where religious identity plays a significant role using their capacity to reach out to masses. As Donoald W. Shriver, Jr. quotes, "Huntington was not far from the sociological reality when he called the Philippine Catholic Church a "latent national political machine", able to influence and communicate with members in every village of the country."[34]

Use and abuse of religion for justification of acts and policies by the leaders as a means to reach their constructed political ends have not been fully examined. Justification and legitimation is a crucial factor for maintaining political power, especially today, when principles of democracy and the opinion of domestic and international public is valued more then before. According to Kokosalakis, religion can act as a legitimizing force both for governments and those who oppose them.[35] He argues that, although the current justification of state power in the Western world rests on ideologies such as nationalism, the pursuit of democracy and humanitarian values, a "strong residual element of religion, which clearly exists even in the Western societies, can still perform basic legitimizing and oppositional functions within such ideologies." [36] In a similar vein, Little also argues that religious beliefs play an active and prominent part in defining group identity and in picking out and legitimating particular ethnic and national objectives, because of the human need to "elevate given political and economic arrangements in reference to sacred or cosmic standards."[37]

Like secular ideologies, religious ideology conceive of the world in coherent manageable ways, provide explanations for worldly events, provide the authority that gives social and political order its justification, and define what is proper individual behavior.[38] As the secular nationalisms are going through a "crisis of legitimacy," religion has become a powerful challenge in the modern world.[39] This condition presents opportunities for leaders and opposition groups to use and abuse religion in order to pursue their goals and establish their regimes of truth.

On the other hand, religious narratives can also be rich resources for managing conflicts creatively and constructively. As Abu-Nimer notes, "[f]raming the interventions within a religious context and deriving tools from a religious narrative have made possible for interveners to gain access and increase their potential impact on the parties."[40] Most religious systems incorporate ideals of peace and promise peace as the outcome of its applications. All religions embody a wide variety of cultural and moral resources, which have configured the basis of personal and communal values that support or prevent conflicts. Religious traditions offer rich resources for resolving conflicts by advocating values such as repentance, forgiveness, justice and patience, among others. Thus religion can bring social, moral, and spiritual resources to the peace-building process, and can inflict a sense of engagement, and commitment both to peace and to transforming a relationship of a missing dimension from the mechanical and instrumental conflict resolution models.[41] According to Marc Gopin, the way sacred texts are used to foster peace or promote violence and destruction:

> ... seems to depend on the complex ways in which the psychological and sociological circumstances and the economic and cultural constructs of a particular group interact with the ceaseless human drive to hermeneutically develop religious meaning systems, texts, rituals, symbols, and laws.[42]

Religion offers a language and symbolism through which human beings interpret reality as well as get comfort for trauma and injuries. Under extreme conditions such as at times of war, the sacred religious texts are interpreted through deep fears and concerns. At such times, various texts, ideas, or spiritual images may meet the cognitive and emotional needs of the individuals as Gopin states.[43] When that is the case, it becomes important to understand which sacred phenomena motivates violent actions and how did religions in the past and how can they in the future contribute to peacemaking.

In fact, using religious precepts to resolve conflicts is not a new phenomenon. Religion, as a source that provides a language, a set of values, and institutions with which groups identify them selves, has been widely used by different communities to promote peace and reconciliation. Religious actors have been involved in peacemaking and reconciliation in many instances, and recently their efforts begun to grab the attention of scholars and other actors involved in conflict resolution.

Although there is an increasing literature on religion and conflict resolution, the state of knowledge in this area has been mostly centered around the role of religion in identity creation and the role of religious institutions in resolving conflicts. Douglas Johnston, Marc Gopin, Cynthia Sampson, Adam

Curle, John Paul Lederach.[44] are among the major scholars who have been looking at the role of religion as a foundation of peace and conflict transformation. Their argument is that some aspects of peace building and reconciliation are best found in concepts and approaches of various religious traditions such as forgiving, mercy, confession, repentance, and acceptance of personal responsibility. Most of the scholarship on religion and conflict resolution has been concerned with religious groups such as Quakers,[45] Mennonites,[46] Moral Re-Armament, and their contribution to peace in Latin America, Asia, and Africa.[47] Islam, on the other hand, has been used as a synonym for terrorism and extremism. Indeed, like other traditions, Islam has not been immune to being used and abused by different groups to establish their regimes of truth and gain dominance within a community. However, various Islamic institutions such as *al-Watan* Center and Islamic University in Hebron in Israel and Palestinian Territories have been actively working for peace building during the Israeli-Palestinian Conflict, together with religious groups such as Rabbi's for Human Rights, and Christian Theologians.

In this work, I focus on the religious values that inform the cultural codes in the Palestinian Territories and how these codes impact the Palestinian community's views on peace and war. This project is based on the observation that conflict, as an aspect of social systems requires justification for mobilization of support for the acts and policies of the leaders. In order to understand the ability of a leadership to mobilize the entire population, common beliefs and sentiments must be observed. To observe religion from this aspect is to identify the most basic elements, which connect signification and legitimation in such a way as to favor dominant interests. The role of social institutions in the generation of narratives and the creation of a collective mind is central in the process of linking the masses to this process.

Conflict Resolution in the Middle East

If we accept that conflict is universal and atemporal, we should also expect to see that different societies have developed techniques and measures to deal with this issue. From indigenous peoples of Americas, to Middle Eastern and to various Asian cultures, societies have been utilizing mechanisms for dealing with their conflicts for so long. These communities have assumptions that differ significantly from their counterparts in the United States and Europe. Today, most of the conflicts that the conflict resolution specialists deal with involve non-Western communities. Most of these communities come from the third world and a significant number of them involve Muslim communities. When practitioners of conflict resolution attempt to introduce the techniques developed in a different context and try to resolve the conflicts, or even communicate with such communities, they face certain difficulties. These difficulties lie in the fact that these techniques, based on Western cultural norms, traditions, and assumptions, differ greatly from that of the local communities.[48] In that respect it becomes vital for the practitioners to get to know and understand the cultural norms, values, and assumptions of the society they are working with.

This, however, does not mean that one has to ignore or deny the contributions made in terms of peace and conflict resolution studies by scholars in the United States and Europe. On the contrary, this literature and models should be reviewed critically to extract principles, models, and techniques, which then could be adopted in different cultural contexts to enhance indigenous mechanisms, and should exclude those, which are specific to the Western culture and alien or unacceptable to the locals. These models and techniques should be viewed in the light of various cultural values, and after a careful examination and assessment, should be combined with the indigenous mechanisms that are available for resolving conflicts. In order to do that, scholars should gain a better understanding of the culture and value systems that they are working with.

When the region is Middle East, understanding Islam becomes important as an integral aspect of the culture. Even though many non-Muslim communities, such as Christians, Druze, and Jews among others, coexist with Muslim community, the long Islamic dominance in the region has had an affect of Islamization of the other groups to a great extend. Moreover, since this paper focuses on Islamic social movements in Palestine as its case study, Islam will be the focal point.

Amr Abdalla[49] notes that social researchers have raised two issues related to conducting social research in an Islamic context using tools developed in the West. The first issue he raises is related to the question "is it possible to use tools developed in the West?' He states that both Western and Islamic scholars agree that researchers should adopt an approach that describes a cultural phenomenon in terms of its own units. This approach is called an *emic*[50] approach. But since there is a lack of *emic* tools to analyze conflicts in Islamic settings, researchers adopt an approach that imposes categories that are external to the phenomenon. This approach is called *etic* approach.[51] Application of an *etic* approach developed in the Western context and refining it through the process enables scholars to contrast the conflict resolution models of two societies. But as Islamic researches indicate, modifications to the Western models are necessary until new and more appropriate tools are developed.

The second issue, according to Abdalla is the existence of two conditions with Western-developed research models. These are universal conditions and specific conditions. The universal conditions are those that can be found in all societies, and the specific conditions are the ways in which the universal conditions present themselves in each culture and society.[52] When universal conditions, such as class, nation, social stratification, etc. are being applied to an Islamic setting, scholars should be aware of the specific conditions that are based on the Islamic theoretical model, which is influenced by its own social reality.

According to Abu Nimer, there are at least three objectives for application and intervention of Western conflict resolution in Middle East:

1. Teaching and exporting conflict resolution to Islamic groups, assuming that it is better then the authentic ones.
2. Exploring alternatives to learn how to control radical groups within the existing frameworks of their countries.
3. Learning more and understanding better the background and context of the movements and utilizing such knowledge to increase degree of legitimacy and credibility of conflict resolution by implementing modified conflict resolution tools.[53]

According to Abdalla,[54] developing models for conflict resolution within the Islamic setting requires two methodological parameters. First, scholars must recognize that they are entering an inter-disciplinary realm, where there is an interaction of sociology, culture, psychology, and religious interpretive traditions. The second parameter, he argues is the emphasis on social justice and social change functions of dispute resolution in relation to Islamic culture and theory. This requires distinguishing between Islamic theory consisting of the main sources of Islam, namely the Quran, the *Hadith* and the *Sunna,* and the Islamic culture that evolved over the centuries of integrating Islamic theory with cultural and traditional practices in different parts of the world.

In Middle Eastern societies, conflict is considered a negative phenomenon, destructive to the social order, and thus, should be avoided. Whereas in the Western tradition conflict is perceived as a normal phenomenon, that can also bring growth and creativity. In the Middle Eastern understanding of the conflict, the group affiliation is the primary concern therefore the conflict resolution technique must be directed at protecting this affiliation. Also, spontaneous and emotional acts are considered as part of conflict since codes of honor, shame, and dignity are integral parts of the conflict. Invoking acknowledgment, apology, compensation, forgiveness and reconciliation are crucial to resolving conflicts. Thus, social and religious norms and values play an important role when resolving conflicts. Especially Quran is a very important source for comprehending conflict resolution and reconciliation processes in the Muslim world. Whereas Western conflict resolution approaches consider individual interests, positions, desires, and needs more important and an agreement on these can be reached through human reason. Furthermore, the unity of the social group is the ultimate goal in Middle Eastern conflict resolution mechanism, and hierarchical and authoritarian procedures, and relationships are central in the processes.[55]

Facilitators and mediators in the Middle East are chosen among the respected people who have political, religious, or military power and are mostly people of age, as opposed to conflict resolution professionals of the West. These Middle Eastern mediators are expected to know the history of the community, the conflict, and be familiar with the social, religious, and cultural norms of the parties involved. The third party might have a direct or indirect interest in his/her involvement in the conflict and this intervention is based on traditional social and religious norms and values. The third party uses norms such as honor, shame, unity of the village, city, family, considering the future of the next generations, association with religious values, respect to elders, attention to the history of relationships, and forgiveness.[56]

Abu Nimer states that in the Middle East conflict resolution practices mainly exist where traditional norms legitimize such actions.[57] A critical combination of Western and Middle Eastern conflict resolution approaches can play a constructive role to bring sustainable peace to the Middle East. Abu Nimer states:

> There are few newly established government-related offices for labor management in Arab countries such as Lebanon, Jordan, and Egypt.[58] In addition, there is another type of mediation which is conducted on the interstate level (inter-Arab state) in which specific leaders intervene to settle emerging diplomatic crises between different countries.[59] Such distinctions (in regard to professionalization) point out one type of learning that can be transferred from the West to the Middle East.[60]

Looking at the Middle Eastern assumptions of conflict and the way to resolve it, one can observe that the legitimation of war and conflict resolution has different sources from its Western counterpart. These differences are related to the way that the individual and society is viewed. The individual is not conceptualized as autonomous and self-regulating, but in terms of his/her place within the network of social relations. There is a strong sense of community, solidarity of people and a collaborative understanding of freedom that is embedded in the notion of *Ummah,* the community of Muslims. The society comes before the individual. As opposed to the individual of the West, who has rights, the Middle Eastern/Islamic individual has obligations towards the community. The freedom of the individual exists only within the limits of the community traditions and well-being. While in the Western liberal tradition freedom signifies the ability to act, in Islam it is the ability to exist. Existence is the reflection of the Supreme Being itself. As the reflection of God, who is complete freedom and complete necessity, the human being participates in both freedom and necessity. Personal freedom lies in surrender to the Divine Will, and this must be sought within oneself. And yet, its limit is the freedom of the community.

This idea of the individual and community informs the sources of legitimacy. The tradition validates the legitimacy of the social order in

Weberian terms. Islam is the tradition that underscores the Middle Eastern communities under observation here. Obedience is owed to the persons who occupy a position of authority according to Islamic tradition. The authority of these persons are legitimized either partly in terms of the Islamic tradition that are believed to be valid within the limits of the Quran, the *Sunna* and the *Hadith*, or partly in terms of those persons' discretion in that sphere which Islamic tradition leaves open to him, to paraphrase Weber.[61] Here the rules and regulations are derived from the sacred sources, and new rules can be legitimized by claiming that they have been there and are now recognized because of the application of various Islamic techniques such as *ijtihad* to the current circumstances. Therefore, when working in this region, one must accept and recognize that Middle Eastern societies contain beliefs, customs, attitudes, and a rich history that may serve as rich bases for identifying constructive conflict resolution frameworks and processes.

Re-visioning Religion and Peace

This work argues that nonviolent approaches, as active resistance to oppression and injustice, are an authentic part of the Islamic tradition, and history provides us examples of when this strategy has been successful.[62] Even though "justice," rather than "nonviolence" is considered the ultimate goal of Islamic faith, it can easily be argued that there is nothing in Islam that denounces pursuing justice through nonviolent strategies. Although Hamas and Islamic Jihad attempt to justify suicide attacks based on their interpretation of Quranic verses, suicide attacks are a contentious matter within the context of Islamic tradition. In order to promote an Islamic approach that is not extremist there is a need to uncover those Islamic values and beliefs, together with Quranic verses and the Prophet's sayings that encourage active resistance against injustice, through effective nonviolent strategies.

To promote nonviolent active resistance as an alternative avenue for dealing with the Israeli-Palestinian conflict, and to undermine the acceptance of suicide attacks as a legitimate form of self defense, there is a great need to utilize existing authorities (e.g. religious leaders, traditional peacemakers), institutions (e.g. charity organizations, mosques), vocabulary (e.g. *sulha*, *sabr* or patience), values (forgiveness, mercy, etc.), and stories (e.g. tolerance of Salah ad Din Ayoubi, Prophet's conduct during war, etc.). As a first step, peacemaking and reconciliation efforts should involve working with legitimate religious authorities who are peace oriented and have a deep understanding of the religious texts and the culture of the people, their needs and frustrations. Conflict resolution practitioners must then, identify those leaders who are peace oriented and have resources to reach out to the community. These efforts need to be supported both by financial and institutional resources.

The increasing interest in involving religious actors in building peace by the conflict resolution field is a hope-inspiring development. As Cynthia Sampson observes "[g]rowing numbers of religious actors of many sorts- laypersons, individual religious leaders, denominational structures, ad hoc commissions and delegations, and interdenominational and multireligious bodies- have been involved in a range of peace-building efforts over the past couple of decades."[63] However, these initiatives must not be viewed as substitutes for official mediation attempts, problem-solving workshops, or other secular peace-building efforts. They must be seen in addition to and in conjunction with other efforts, and official mediators. Western practitioners should make an effort to understanding cultural and religious particularities, needs and potentials of the communities they work with. They should identify the particular roles religious actors can play in the peace-building process.

Various peacemaking roles that religious leaders can assume have been identified.[64] These include advocate, intermediary, observer, and educator. For example advocates may be catalysts for empowering the weaker party, restructuring relationship, and transforming unjust social structures.[65] Intermediaries, on the other hand, may be effective in bringing parties together to resolve the conflict and transform the conflictual relationships. Observers may be effective in preventing violence and transforming the conflict dynamics.[66] Finally, educators may work towards conflict transformation by reaching out to the community through sermons, training seminars, and other social activities. However, it is equally important that conflict resolution scholars and practitioners develop religious peace-building training workshops that engage religious actors.

Scholars such as Marc Gopin, David Smock, and Mohammed Abu-Nimer have introduced groundbreaking research in this area for conflict resolution literature. These scholars point out that cultural religious attributes play an important role in conflict resolutions since religious and cultural values have the potential to motivate people to fight or reconcile, and rituals can be powerful tools in transforming hatred and animosity into cooperation. Religious commitment can become a strong impetus for engaging in peace-building activities and bringing about social change. Engaging in religious peace-building can provide a spiritual basis for transformation and compensate for the mechanistic and instrumental conflict resolution models. Based on his research and practical experience, Abu-Nimer argues that "the intervention within a religious context and deriving tools from a religious narrative have made it possible for interveners to gain access and increase their potential impact on the parties."[67] Thus, religious peace-building becomes a major tool for training, empowering, and motivating religiously oriented people towards peace.

Secondly, scholars and practitioners need to address the events (e.g *naqba*), and how these catastrophic events are perceived, remembered, or interpreted by the population as well as perceptions of injustice that lead people to invoke texts that promote violence or nonviolence. Myths that have provided the basis for violence should be identified, and how these myths have been manipulated should be analyzed thoroughly.[68] Myths translate complex problems into manageable cognitive structures and make them comprehensible to the human mind. During times of conflict myths become tools to make sense of human atrocities, to "explain" the reasons and sources of the conflict to the people in a "clear" way. In this process religious narratives serve to mobilize people. Conflict resolution scholars need to identify myths that serve to perpetuate violence and conflict, as well as myths that promote peace and reconciliation. This should be accompanied by identification of those myths that call for justice and promote nonviolence. These "positive" myths can be woven into the fabric of narratives of peace to mobilize people towards reconciliation and co-existence through the active involvement of religious actors. These myths should also be supported with religious texts and images.

Thirdly, those religious and cultural values that promote peace and coexistence should be identified and included in conflict resolution in order to facilitate reconciliation between communities. As Said et. al. articulate "[t]he ideal of peace spans religions and cultures, incorporating conceptions of security as well as human dignity and well-being."[69] As stated in Chapter Four, Islam, like other religions includes values that promote peace and coexistence with fellow human beings. Some of these values—supported by innumerable verses in the Quran and *Hadith*—have been identified by Abu-Nimer.[70] These values include, but are not limited to: showing love, kindness, affection, forgiveness, patience, compassion and mercy to other human beings; pursuing justice; social empowerment through doing good; the universality of human dignity; equality based on oneness and the common origin of all people; sacredness of human life; a quest for peace and peacemaking; showing creativity and innovation; demonstrating individual responsibility and choice; solidarity; as well as encouraging pluralism and diversity. As discussed in Chapter Six, Islam also incorporates values that promote the pursuit of justice through nonviolent means. This potential for nonviolence should be put into practice by engaging religious leaders that are committed to peace and the nonviolent pursuit of justice. Furthermore, they must be supported by religious texts and myths.

Finally, since institutions play a major role in the legitimization of narratives and mobilization of society, those institutions that uphold nonviolent values and are committed to justice should be identified and empowered. Or, new civil society institutions compatible with the traditions and customs of the region should be established. One of the main reasons for the emergence of extremist Islamic narratives in Palestinian Territories was that the institutions these narratives were affiliated with have been able to provide effective and good services in key areas such as health, education, and poverty relief. Neither the PLO, nor other groups have been able to match the institutional base and strength of these Hamas led institutions.

Israeli security concerns have forced the PLO to concentrate mainly on developing institutions such as prisons and the police force. These institutions are necessary for providing security not only for Israelis but also for Palestinians. However, the establishment of other crucial institutions to provide medical, agricultural, and educational services did not back these institutions. In order to enhance the well-being of the Palestinian population and to give them a sense that their life conditions were improving as a consequence of the peace process, they also needed to establish institutions to develop a healthy social infrastructure.

The financial aid received from international financial institutions such as the IMF and the World Bank, as well as donations from various states, were handed to the PLO without effective mechanisms for accountability and monitoring how this money was used. Widespread corruption within the PLO has hindered the effective use of these resources and undermined the legitimacy of the leadership that was in charge of representing the Palestinian people and implementing the agreements. Most of the work of international aid and financial institutions (e.g. the World Bank, USAID, the IMF, etc) has focused on developing a market economy in Palestinian society in order to prepare them for entering the global economic system once they have established their state. Considering the difficulties of implanting a market economy, even in countries that are not conflict-thorn, this approach also failed to address the existential needs of the Palestinian community. Moreover, since these donations and development projects had to be approved by the Israeli authorities, they were considerably slowed in reaching the Palestinian community, and thus ineffective.

Taking these factors into account, conflict resolution scholars and practitioners should first identify institutional sites that could contribute to peace-building and reconciliation. Next, they should empower these institutions technically, financially, and also by providing necessary training. They could open channels through which these institutions could then connect to a wider network of peace-building initiatives across the social, political, and economic spectrum. Working with religious groups first individually to develop an understanding of their cultural and religious peacemaking resources, and then providing them with training, financial and technical support, would prepare them for dialogue with the other religious groups. All major religions in the region (Judaism, Christianity, Islam, and Druze) value peace as one of their central themes and incorporate values of sharing, forgiving and healing. They also contain rituals of peacemaking and reconciliation. Conflict resolution practitioners could help identify those common values that promote peace and reconciliation, and those values that differ significantly in each tradition. Following that they could then facilitate reconciliation between religious groups from both sides through various peace-building activities.

A number of religious peacemaking and peace-building mechanisms can be identified in Israel and the Palestinian Territories. Among them, interfaith dialogue groups and study sessions are particularly based on religious identities and their respective texts. For example, there are Interfaith dialogue groups in which a balanced representation of religious community members are gathered in an environment that is sensitive to the power disparity between groups on the ground to learn and listen each other and to address similarities and differences to establish understanding and peaceful relations. Interfaith dialogue groups try to move participants towards peace by utilizing their religious identity, sacred texts and rituals in order to develop understanding between religious communities.[71]

Another interfaith initiative that has emerged within the context of this particular conflict is the study sessions of Yehuda Stolov, of the Israel Interfaith Association, and Yakar Institute. These study sessions derive their legitimacy from the text-centered reverence in Judaism and Islam to discover shared values and traditions before engaging in difficult exchanges with the 'enemy' about inflicted injuries.[72] According to Gopin this approach maximizes the possibility of honesty but minimizes the possibility of dishonor and shame for respective religious traditions and may work best for conservative traditions of the region.[73] This indigenous approach evolved from within the context of the region and although other peace initiatives and dialogue groups seem to have dissolved after October 2000, these study groups not only continued their sessions but also intensified them.[74]

It is crucial to remember that reconciliation cannot be done without engaging with the adversary. However, every religious community contains various groups with different approaches and interpretations of sacred texts, and because texts are ambiguous there is confusion and contending approaches. Therefore it becomes necessary to engage in an inner dialogue which addresses the motivations of reconciliation, and their internal disagreements over various issues, such as the concept of jihad, justice in Islam, and requirements for peacemaking (*sulha*) with the enemy, before attempting reconciliation with the "other." This requires working separately with trainers and teachers in each community utilizing various conflict transformation training activities. Conflict resolution practitioners who work with these groups separately and together can utilize various traditional and religious values and mechanisms embedded in these communities, analyze differences and similarities between different traditions and develop approaches that would lead to reconciliation. In this respect, analyzing and incorporating traditional conflict resolution mechanisms becomes important in developing an authentic and effective conflict resolution strategy.

Palestinian Institutions for Conflict Resolution

Palestinian society, like other Middle Eastern societies, hosts a variety of mechanisms to resolve internal conflicts. These include mediation (*wasta*), arbitration (*tahkim*), reconciliation (*musalaha* or *sulha*), truce (*hudna*), and negotiation. These mechanisms pre-date Islam, but Islamic precepts and guidelines have been integrated into these mechanisms after the emergence of Islam. The purpose of Palestinian conflict resolution mechanisms is to resolve communal conflicts in order to restore social harmony. Since the Palestinians have not had a state of their own, they were not able to develop their own modern legal system. In the absence of these legal institutions, traditional conflict resolution mechanisms assumed a vital role in upholding harmony amongst Muslims and Christians alike, especially during the *Intifada*.

The evolution of a Palestinian legal system was crippled with the British Mandate, and later under the other foreign states. Since Palestinians were under the control of foreign powers, including the British, Egyptian, Jordanian, and Israeli states, Palestinians were not able to develop their own legal system. The legal system under the occupation was a mishmash of courts and jurisdictions in which Palestinians cohabited but never cooperated.[75] This multifaceted legal system included civil and criminal courts, which handled most cases involving taxes, land and petty crimes, and Islamic *Shariah* Courts, which handled personal status matters but were limited in their jurisdiction by the requirement of mutual consent.[76] Other courts included municipal courts, administrative tribunals and settler courts, and most importantly, Israeli military courts, which handled all security cases, many financial cases, and other cases that the military considered appropriate. In addition to these courts, the High Court of Justice in Israel would also hear some special cases involving Palestinians.

The *Intifada* brought significant changes in the way Palestinians attempted to solve their internal problems, since one aspect of the *Intifada* was resisting occupation by not engaging with any Israeli institutions to delegitimize them. Also the *Intifada* brought economic hardships and as a result Palestinians could not afford to take their cases to civil and even religious courts. Moreover, during the *Intifada*, Israel adopted a policy, in which the military courts handled all cases. Military courts were designed to discipline the Palestinian society through collective punishment. These developments following the *Intifada* overloaded the legal system and made it almost impossible for Palestinians to seek justice.

Under these circumstances, in order to deal with internal conflicts, Palestinians created their own bodies to achieve justice, such as *tahkim*, *sulha* and *wasta*: "Such bodies were often based on customary law and traditional mediation institutions, but were sometimes self-appointed 'revolutionary' committees."[77] These community-based justice systems were derived from traditional mechanisms that existed within the society. As a part of the cultural repertoire, the local populations –Christian, Muslim, Druze and Jew alike – used these mechanisms to resolve their communal, family and religious conflicts over the course of history. The particular religious values of each community have been woven into the fabric of general principles and modes of these mechanisms to promote harmony and avoid future conflict. These mechanisms provide rich resources for reconciliation efforts in the region. *Sulha* has especially become a major conflict resolution tool once again. In the following section, the tradition of *sulha* and possibility of applying it to the Israeli-Palestinian conflict as a framework of reconciliation is explored.

Reinvigorating Sulha

Sulha is an authentic conflict resolution mechanism in the Middle East, dating back to pre-Islamic times, that attempts to reconcile conflicts between rival parties. Today, *sulha* is used in many inter-/and intra-communal disputes in Lebanon, West Bank and Gaza, and Kingdom of Jordan officially recognizes *sulha* as a traditional conflict resolution practice of the Bedouins. In its modern day application, *sulha* does not replace the modern civil/criminal law but is an addition to it, and its purpose is to restore peace so that normal life can be resumed. Especially in Palestine and Lebanon, where official institutions are not well established or have lost their power, it is still widely accepted as a means for resolving conflicts.

Sulha is important both from the Islamic law and tribal customs points of view. According to Islamic law, "the purpose of *sulh* is to end conflict and hostility among believers so that they may conduct their relationship in peace and amity….In Islamic law, *sulh* is a form of contract (*'aqd*), legally binding on both at individual and community levels."[78] Many verses in the Quran also refer to *sulha* and the establishment of peace among the members of the community. The following Quranic verse is an example:

> If two parties among the believers fall into a fight, make ye peace [*sulh*] between them … make peace between them with justice, and be fair; for Allah loves those who are fair (and just). (49: 9)

Sulha is also deeply embedded in tribal culture, wisdom, and experience. It combines tribal, religious and customary practices to provide social control and cohesiveness. It claims to restore peace between individuals, families, tribes and villages. It is supported by well established and long standing rituals, and is sensitive to the values, such as honor, dignity, and continuity of the community, that are essential to Middle Eastern culture.

"According to Jordanian judge Abu-Hassan there are two types of *sulh* processes: *public sulh* and *private sulh*."[79] Public *sulh* can be compared to a peace treaty between two countries to end conflict for a period of time. It takes place to resolve conflicts between tribes, or communities, or different religious groups. Private *sulh* takes place when there is a conflict between the members of a community who know each other. The aim of private *sulha* is to avoid revenge and to restore harmony within a community. The outcome of *sulha* can be a total peace where two parties of the conflict forgive each other, forget what happened, and do not hold any resentment towards each other. The outcome of *sulha* can also be partial or conditional where the conflict between two parties ends according to the agreed conditions set in the peace process.

Sulha is a ritualistic event that involves the whole community and is based on forgiveness. It is related very closely to matters of survival, honor respect, hospitality, integrity, and justice. Following an event (such as murder) that can result in a conflict, a group of delegation called *jaha* forms. *Sulha* is based on the principle that the offender or his or her family, immediately asks a delegation—*Jaha*—of influential people to mediate between the two conflicting parties in order to resolve the conflict and avoid a circle of vengeful responses. *Jaha* are usually composed of elderly people who are respected in their communities due to their religious, political or social status. This delegation serves as the mediators between the parties and initiates a fact-finding process while questioning the parties. These mediators use their kinship connections and social standing as a tool to exert pressure and gain access during the negotiation process. Furthermore, *jaha* members are expected to know the history of the communities or families, know the customs and religious values well, and must be perceived as just and impartial.

The nature of the issue and the parties determines the number and status of the people make up the *jaha*, and the intensity of the reconciliation process. If the conflict is between two individuals, the *jaha* may be as small as one or two members, who are respected in the community. If the conflict involves two villages or two different religious communities, the number of *jaha* can rise up to twenty or more people, and in addition to the elected community leaders, the process usually involves the highest religious authorities in the region. The task of *jaha* is not to judge, condemn or punish but to preserve the good names of the parties involved and reaffirm the necessity of ongoing relationships within the community.[80]

Symbolic gestures and rituals play a crucial role in the process of *sulha*. Once the *jaha* is formed, its members decide upon a specific date to visit the offended family. Protecting honor and dignity are key to the process, and the *jaha* aims to restore the honor of the offended family by paying a visit to them. *Jaha* tells the offended that the offender asked them to pay a visit in order to have the honor of offering their repentance and to express their sorrow for what happened, and asks them to agree on their intervention, using a special code and terminology. They also ask the offended family for forgiveness and transmit the offer of repentance on behalf of the offender. Thus accepting responsibility over one's actions, offering repentance and also forgiveness are crucial aspects of *sulha*.

After the offended side gives its consent to the intervention of the *jaha*, a *hudna*, or truce is established between the parties to prevent revenge and further bloodshed. Once the parties agree on the third party intervention, *sulha* becomes socially binding. An elderly person, who can ensure implementation of the final decision, is also chosen as a guarantor. During this time *atwa* (compensation in the form of money or word of honor) is paid to back the truce. After that, the *jaha* starts negotiating with the parties separately on a settlement. In this process, confidentiality and impartiality are central principles. After negotiating with the parties, the *jaha* meets as a delegation in a neutral place and decides on a ruling. Usually a certain amount of money *(diya)* is given to the offended family to compensate their loss. However, *diya* is a symbolic act and the crucial aspect of *sulha* is restoring honor to the offended family. The rituals and gestures of *sulha* aim at restoring the honor of the parties, and the *jaha* in many cases becomes the anger or shock absorber.

Once the negotiations are completed, and a ruling has been decided, the *jaha* invites the whole community, and depending on the case, notables from all over the country to join the final ritual of reconciliation. The reconciliation is done openly so that the whole community knows about it. This creates a social pressure on the parties to abide by the agreement reached. The ritual itself is a complex and symbolic process, and the details differ according to the customs of the region and the community. Nevertheless, the basic principles of the *sulha* ritual are based on forgiveness (*musamaha*) shaking hands (*musafaha*), sharing a meal and bitter coffee (*mumalaha*) between the opponents. It is also important to note that the reconciliation is declared binding to those who are present and not present at the ritual, including those that are not yet born.

Sulha lifts the burden of revenge and emphasizes collective responsibility, circles of loyalty, and aims to build trust as well as restore justice and satisfy all the parties involved—an important dimension of conflict resolution. It is based on the values of honor, saving face and dignity, wisdom, generosity, respect, forgiveness, and repentance. Compared to the impersonal and indifferent courts, *sulha* is personal. Elias Jabbour (a Christian *jaha*) explains brilliantly why *sulha* continues to be an important mechanism:

> [t]he person who loses in the court always leaves unhappy, because he has lost the case. The person who wins the case leaves the court happy, because he has gained. A civil court cannot satisfy two sides, it can only satisfy one...
>
> Making the *sulha* satisfies both parties-there is no loser and no winner. No unhappy or unsettled party. All are happy at the end. Even the whole village is happy ...[81]

Today, *sulha* is widely used in Palestine. As one of my interviewees, Nidal, pointed out "after *Intifada*, with the economic situation worsening and with the disappointment of Oslo, which offered no benefits for the Palestinians, there was much disillusionment among the community, more conflict."[82] This, according to Nidal, led to resolving internal conflicts through traditional ways and added that:

> when there is a conflict within the society, today a *jaha* goes to the prison and tells the soldiers that they will resolve the issue through *sulha*. Jaha is more important then the police in Palestine ... Police also suggest resolving community conflict with the involvement of *jaha*.[83]

Sulha is often used to resolve conflicts within the Palestinian community by different groups and offered conflict resolution centers such as Wi'am. For example Wi'am applies *sulha* to conflicts over land and resources between Christian, Muslim, Druze and at times Jewish (since most of the employers are Jewish) individuals and communities. Participants are often in relationships as neighbors, land owner-tenant, and employer-employee, among others.[84] Thus, *sulha* takes place not only among communities who share the same faith, but also between those who come from different faiths. For example, when there is a conflict between a Christian and a Muslim Christian *sulha* delegates (*jaha*, *wujaha* pl.) come together with their Muslim counterparts, who consist of Muslim dignitaries that have leverage within their communities, to resolve the conflict. These *jaha* members resolve the conflict between the two communities by resorting to the common principles and values of *sulha*.

There have been attempts to apply *sulha* to resolve the conflict between Arabs and Jews in the region. During the Shavout weekend of May 25-28, 2001, amidst all the violence and hostility that had been going on for eight months, a "*sulha*" (reconciliation) village was set up, which was co-sponsored by the Peacemaker Community in Israel. After a blessing by the Sufi Sheikh Abu Salih, Muslims joined the Jewish community for the festival. The six Sufi delegations made a joint speech in which the spokesman said, "when I was born from my mother's womb I wasn't called a Muslim, Christian or a Jew, but (firstly) a *Bani Adam* (human being)... no religion says destroy another human being, for each and every one is a temple of G-d's [sic] creation."[85] Teachings about *sulha* were explained and peace between Arabs and Jews in the Holy Land was called for. At this festival the Rabbi Mordechai Gafni also made a call for peace and proclaimed that "we can't do without *sulha*: forgiveness, rapprochement, healing."[86] Unfortunately the constructive efforts of such groups go unnoticed behind the scenes of exploding bombs. Still this example indicates that, if used correctly, *sulha* has a great potential for facilitating reconciliation between Palestinians and Israelis.

However, transporting these traditional mechanisms and values into a broad conflict resolution and reconciliation framework requires a careful study and examination of the conditions, expectations, and values of all the participants involved. As Dr. Abbat stated, the application of *sulha* to the Israeli-Palestinian conflict is not so easy, because the conflict involves the issue of land, and the fate of 6.5 million people.[87] In spite of this, combining the experience of Western conflict resolution practitioners with these traditional mechanisms—

which the populations of the region are familiar with and perceive as legitimate and acceptable—would contribute significantly to establishing peace.

As indicated also by Elias Jabbour, the crux of the *sulha* practices is to restore the rights and the honor of both parties.[88] Gopin notes:

> *sulh* [sic] and its Jewish counterpart, *teshuva*, may speak to peoples' hearts and deeper needs in a way that virtually nothing currently proposed by diplomacy is accomplishing for the majority of people affected and injured by the Arab-Israeli conflict that has lasted several generations now. This disconnect between the deeper needs of the people and elite diplomacy is exactly what has undermined the Oslo peace process so many times.[89]

The peace process between the government of Israel and the PLO failed to restore the rights and honor of both sides, and also failed to address the needs and injuries of both communities in general. Palestinians felt that their honor and dignity was ignored and their sacrifices were not acknowledged. The U.S. mediation was not considered just or impartial and thus, not legitimate by Palestinians. My interviewees stated that a group of states, rather than one state alone would form a better *jaha* in resolving the conflict between Israelis and Palestinians. For example, Dr. Azzam suggested that a *jaha* consisting of states such as Japan, China, France, Germany, Italy, and some Muslim countries could play a role in resolving the conflict[90] at the official level. However, a simultaneous process of reconciliation between the two communities that involves the highest religious authorities is also crucial for a sustainable peace. It is also important to have a strong and influential state (such as the U.S.) to serve as a guarantor for the implementation of the signed agreements.

It is hopeful to note that there are various attempts to bring together Jewish, Christian, and Muslim religious leaders to sign a declaration of peace and coexistence. For example, Gopin records that a treaty was developed between a number of Jewish and Islamic leaders that refers to the traditions of peace and tolerance of each religion, supported by sacred texts.[91] Also, in 1998 a document was signed by the highest religious leaders on both sides under the leadership of the USA during the Clinton administration, and religious peace activists proposed formation of an interfaith committee that would parallel the peace process. This proposal was taken to President Clinton, who gave an affirmative response in 1999.[92] Regrettably, it was not possible to pursue this offer further before the Bush administration replaced the Clinton administration. Nevertheless, this initiative suggests that there are an increasing number of religious leaders who are interested in reconciliation with the 'other' to establish peace in the region. Given the necessary financial and institutional support, such efforts could prove fruitful for reaching a just and sustainable peace between the two communities.

Sufis as Peace-Brokers

As this study shows, there are multiple approaches to peace and conflict resolution within the Muslim community, and Hamas antagonism is only one of the voices, although a loud one, that does not represent the Palestinian Muslim community in general. I have argued that it is important for conflict resolution scholars and practitioners to identify those peace-oriented religious leaders and individuals who are respected in their communities. Working with these leaders could help facilitate reconciliation between the conflicting communities.

Observing Islamic peace-oriented religious leaders, one can see that most of them are affiliated with Sufi orders. Sufi orders are significant informal institutions that play an important role in Muslim societies. Sufism is the Islamic mystic path of love that combines individualist denunciatory piety and a community oriented approach within the framework of the doctrine of *Tawhid* (unity). "From a Sufi perspective, *tawhid* expresses the Islamic ideal of the fundamental unity of all mankind and of all life, and rejects a vision of reality rooted in exclusiveness."[93] Sufism is an interior path concerned with the duties and rights of Muslims and sees the real basis of peace as the transformative knowledge of unity. Jihad, from a Sufi perspective, indicates the internal struggle of the individual to overcome egoism and to attain human dignity via a cleansing of the self and establishment of harmony with God and God's creation. Thus, Sufism underscores the need for harmony and equilibrium in all relationships and appeals to the creative capacity of human beings through affirmation, rather than inducing fear[94] as the basis of peace.

As a popular movement within Islam, Sufism has a deep impact upon Muslim societies. While the traditional Islamic way of life was expressed officially and formally in Islamic law, there developed within the Islamic community individuals for whom mere obedience to the will of God was not totally satisfying.[95] Many of the early Sufis were critical of the political authorities, opposed to their practices and attempted to refocus the vision and goals of the community. Sufism as a mass movement soon was also critical of the *ulema* for being co-opted by power, tolerating and even supporting the authorities' sociopolitical abuses. Therefore, they claimed their own authority and guides in opposition to the official religion, and government. This resistance-oriented dimension of Sufism gained many supporters among the people who were feeling oppressed, and it offered an alternative way to deal with social and political pressures.

Sufi centers are called *tekkes* or *zawiyyas* and are organizationally built on the pre-existing relations of spiritual guide (*Sheikh*) and student or disciple (*murid*).[96] Deriving their legitimacy from links to early pious predecessors, they were considered spiritual guides and models. Sufi lodges served as the spiritual, social and cultural centers in their communities. Sufi masters lead prayers, instruct and train, guide and advise individuals, and oversee communal life.[97]

These centers were usually established and supported by pious endowments. Members of the Sufi Orders were engaged in everyday activities, participated in community services and were involved with financial support of the order. Due to their involvement in the everyday lives of individuals, Sufi orders have been the location of a more popular form of religion where daily life and the contemporary needs of common people have been addressed. Sheikhs, as local religious authorities, have been a major source of guidance and organization within society.

During the 19th century there was a resurgence of the Sufi movement as a reaction to Western cultural influence and the colonization of the Muslim world. Mardin states that this neo-Sufi movement shifted to a worldlier stance in which Sufis were increasingly involved in socio-political mobilization and were politicized.[98] Today, Sufi Orders provide important centers for the organization of social movements due to their well-established networks in the Muslim world and their respected position within society. They often have more direct access to, and better understanding of, the workings of the society then the governments. Thier crucial role can be seen in how Sultan Abdulhamid of the Ottoman Empire utilized Sufi Orders to carry out his proto-nationalist propaganda.[99] Thus, Sufi Orders became a major component of the informal structures that play a critical role within Islamic societies.

Sufi Orders are very active in Palestine today. The Sufi Council convenes regularly; its members attend meetings at home and abroad and meet with religious scholars from all faiths. In these encounters and meetings they discuss the problems that the Palestinians are facing and try to find a just and sustainable resolution to the conflict. Compared to the extremist groups such as Hamas and Islamic Jihad they hold a much more moderate view, which is derived from their conception of *tawhid* and peace, and are strong supporters of democracy. In general, Sufis are known to be more inclusive and liberal than their conservative counterparts. However, Sufis are not a unified whole and there exists various different opinions among them, some of which are more conservative than others.

In order to reach out to people, Sufis give lectures at universities, organize seminars and conferences, give sermons at mosques and try to utilize the media.[100] They also publish three magazines entitled *Al-Isra, Huda al Islam*, and *Al-Mimbar*. Due to their religious role in society, they are connected to various religious groups and institutions. Nevertheless, until now they have not been as well organized as groups such as Hamas and Islamic Jihad. Nor have they been able to establish a unified political agenda and a viable strategy for resolving the conflict, although they agree with the other Palestinian groups that before they can normalize their relationship with Israel the Palestinians must have their rights. These rights basically include self-determination, Jerusalem as their capital, right of return, freedom of movement, and the dismantling of Jewish settlements in West Bank and Gaza. Still, many Sufis have been in touch with other religious groups to discuss ways to resolve the conflict and to promote tolerance and coexistence between Israelis and Arabs. Thus their inclusive approach to peace and justice and their respected status within the Palestinian Muslim community renders Sufis as potentially effective peace-brokers in the region. Based on their social status, competency in religious matters and approach to peace, Sufis can easily assume the roles of advocate, intermediary, observer, and educator within their society, facilitate reconciliation in the region and undermine the legitimacy of violence to achieve justice.

Afterwords

The analyses presented in this study provide evidence that religion and culture matter in conflict, and its eventual resolution. Based on that assumption, throughout this work, I have argued that for peace to be sustainable, the official track of negotiations must be complemented with community-based reconciliation tracks based on their cultural and religious values and practices. I have also argued that conflict resolution practitioners should address the material, psychological and spiritual needs of the parties and develop strategies to engage hermeneutically with religious and cultural texts that provide justification for either violence or nonviolence.

This work has many shortcomings. One of the major shortcomings is that it focuses more on the dynamics of the current situation in the Palestinian Territories and the rise of extremist Islamic movements, than developing sufficiently how this situation can be transformed into a cultural peace. It briefly provides a framework of how this may be done by introducing indigenous conflict resolution institutions such as *Sulha*, using alternative leaderships like Sufis, and identifying various values such as forgiveness, restoring honor, harmony, etc. that can be utilized in resolving the Israeli-Palestinian conflict. A more detailed analysis on how to effectively combine Western and indigenous conflict resolution approaches and how to apply *sulha* on a broader scale to resolve the Israeli-Palestinian conflict, which has endured more then fifty years now, remains to be undertaken. Fortunately, there are an increasing number of works that deal with such issues in the conflict resolution field.

Furthermore an analysis of the similarities and differences between conflict resolution practices of all the religious communities in the region would be essential for a comprehensive reconciliation project in the region. Such a task would necessarily involve the exhaustive efforts of many conflict resolution scholars, practitioners and religious experts. Completion of such a project would not only take years, but also would need to be supported by generous grants. However, this analysis would lead to a more profound and comprehensive peace process and would facilitate reconciliation and healing for all the communities. This volume fills several gaps in the field of conflict resolution. It provides a framework for understanding the process of the legitimization of violence and nonviolence via religious texts and institutions. It contributes to the development of knowledge, theory, and practice by hermeneutically engaging with the Islamic tradition on the issues of peace and war. Finally, it identifies areas for further research on the constructive role Islam can play in resolving conflicts and peace-building.

Endnotes

1. See H. C. Kelman "Contributions of An Unofficial Conflict Resolution Effort to the Israeli- Palestinian Breakthrough" *Negotiation Journal.* Vol.11, No.1 (January 1995), 19-20.

2. Kelman 1995.

3. Kelman 1995.

4. Kelman 1995.

5. Kelman 1995.

6. See also Galtung "40 Conflicts, 40 Perspectives" In *Searching For Peace: The Road to Transcend.* Galtung J and C. G. Jacobsen eds (London: Pluto Press. 2000), 130.

7. William I. Zartman "Explaining Oslo," *International Negotiation,* No 2, (1997), 195-215; 209. See also Dean Pruitt, "Ripeness Theory and the Oslo Talks," *International Negotiation* No.2, (2001), 237-250

8. Zartman 1997.

9. Jacob Bercovitch and S. Ayse Kadayifci "Conflict Management and Israeli-Palestinian Conflict: The Importance of Capturing the 'right Moment'" *Asia-Pacific Review* Vol. 9, No. 2 (2002); 113-129, 123

10. Bercovitch and Kadayifci 2002.

11. Bercovitch and Kadayifci 2002.

12. Zartman 1997, 209

13. Edward Said. "The Burdens of Interpretation and the Question of Palestine" paper presented to the conference of *International Society of Political Psychology.* (Amsterdam, July 1986). Cited from Jabri, 155.

14. For information on religiously motivated attempts to resolve the Israeli-Palestinian conflict see Marc Gopin *Holy War Holy Peace* Oxford University Press, 2002.

15. See. Kevin Avruch *Culture and Conflict Resolution.* (Washington D.C.: United States Institute of Peace Press, 1998) Kevin Avruch, Peter Black and J. A. Scimecca eds. *Conflict Resolution: Cross- Cultural Perspectives* (Westport, CT.: Greenwood Press. 1991); R. Cohen *Culture and Conflict in Egyptian/Israeli Relations* (Bloomington: Indiana University Press, 1990); *International Negotiation* (Washington D.C.: United States Institute of Peace, 1997 second edition); 145-163.; G. O. Faure and J. Z. Rubin *Culture and Negotiation* (Thousand Oaks, CA: Sage, 1993); D. W. Augburger *Conflict Mediation Across Cultures* Louisville, KY: Westminister/ Knox Press, 1992); and Bercovitch, J. and Ole Elgstorm "Culture and International Mediation: Exploring Theoretical and Empirical Linkages," in *International Negotiation* vol 6 no.1 2001

16. Tylor, Edward. *Primitive Culture* (1870); (New York Reprint Harper and Row, 1958), 1.

17. Anne E. Kane "The Centrality of Culture in Social Theory" in *Social Theory and Sociology: The Classics and Beyond.*_Stephen P. Turner eds. (Blackwell Publishers, 1996), 162.

18. Bercovitch and Elgstorm 2001, 3.

19. W. R. Sewell. "Three Temporalities: Toward an Eventful Sociology," in *The Historic Turn in the Human Science,* ed. T. J. McDonald Ann Arbor: University of Michigan Press, 1996, 548 quoted as in Kane, 162.

20. Avruch, 1998, 5.

21. Avruch, 1998.

22. Avruch, 1998., 10.

23. T. Schwartz. "Anthropology and Psychology: An Unrequited Relationship," in T. Schwartz, G. White, and C. Lutz, eds. *New Directions in Psychological Anthropology.* (Cambridge: Cambridge University Press, 1992.): 324. (quote taken from Avruch, 17).

24. Clifford Geertz,. *Interpretation of Cultures.* (New York: Basic Books, 1973),.

25. Geertz. 1992

26. Cohen, Anthony. *The Symbolic Construction of Community: Key Ideas* Peter Hamilton Eds. (Ellis Horwood Ltd. And Tavistock Publications Ltd./Routledge, 1985, 1989.), 17

27. Bercovitch and Elgstorm 2001.

28. Avruch, 1998, 48-55.

29. For religion as a cultural institutions see Geertz, 79.

30. Abu Nimer, Mohammed. "Conflict Resolution, Culture, and Religion: Toward a Training Model of Interreligious Peacebuilding," *Peace Research.* (38:6, 2001), 685-704, 686.

31. Abu Nimer. 2001, 688.

32. For examples regarding use of religion to justify violence, see Kadayifci-Orellana 2003

33. Giddens, Anthony; *The Nation-State and Violence;* (Berkeley: University of California Press, 1987),72

34. Huntington, S; 'Religion and the Third Wave' pp. 29-42, as quoted in Donald W. Shriver, Jr. "Religion and Violence Prevention" in. *Cases and Strategies For Preventive Action,* Barnett R. Rubin eds. (New York: The Century Foundation Press, 1998)

35. Nikos Kokosolakis,. "Legitimation, Power and Religion in Modern Society," *Sociological Analysis* 46(4) (winter, 1985), 367-376,371.

36. Kokosolakis 1985

37. David Little, *Ukraine: The Legacy of Intolerance.*(Washington D.C.: United States Institute of Peace Press, 1991), xx.

38. Mark Juergensmeyer. *The New Cold War?* (Berkeley, CA: University of California Press, 1993), 30-31.

39. Juergensmeyer 1993

40. Mohammed Abu-Nimer "Conflict Resolution, Culture, and Religion: Toward a Training Model of Interreligious Peacebuilding," *Peace Research.* vol. 38 no.6, 685-704 (2001), 686

41. Abu Nimer, 2001.

42. Marc Gopin *Between Eden and Armageddon: The Future of World Religions, Violence, and Peacemaking.(* Oxford University Press, 2000.), 11

43..Gopin. 2000, 17.

44. D. Johnston and C. Sampson, eds. *Religion: The Missing Dimension of Statecraft.* (New York: Oxford University press, 1994.), Marc Gopin 2000.; "Confronting the Secular/Religious Conflict in Israel: Suggested Solutions." In *Religious Secular Relations in Israel: Social and Political Implications,* ed. Ephraim Ya'ar and Tamar Herman (Tel Aviv: Steinmetz Center for Peace Research, Tel Aviv University, and the Konrad Adenauer Foundation, 1998.); "Forgiveness as an Element of Conflict Resolution in Religious Cultures: Walking the Tightrope of Reconciliation and Justice." Unpublished paper delivered Feb 19, 1999 at American University; J. P. Lederach. 1997 and Lederach, 1995).

45. C. H. Yarrow. *Quaker Experiences in International Coalition.* (New Haven: Yale University Press, 1978).

46. Sampson and J. P. Lederach eds. *From the Ground Up: Mennonite Contributions to International Peacebuilding.* (New York: Oxford University press, 2000).

47. Cynthia Sampson. "Religion and Peacemaking" in *Peacemaking in International Conflict: Methods and Techniques.* I. W. Zartman and L. Rassmussen, eds. (Washington D.C: United States Institute of Peace Press, 1997.

48. See also Abu-Nimer, 1996.

49. Amr Abdalla, "Principles of Islamic Interpersonal Conflict Intervention: A Search within Islam and Western Literature," *Journal of Law and Religion.* (15:1-2,2000-2001), 151-184; 155-156.

50. Avruch, 1998.

51. Avruch 1998.

52. Abdalla 2000.

53. Abu-Nimer, "Conflict Resolution Approaches: Western and Middle Eastern Lessons and Possibilities." *The American Journal of Economics and Sociology.* vol. 55 no.1 (January, 1996): 35-55, 23.

54. Abdalla, 2000 158-159.

55. For more information on Middle Eastern Conflict Resolution Assumptions see Abu-Nimer 1996 and Abu-Nimer. "Conflict Resolution in an Islamic Context: Some Conceptual Questions" in *Peace and Conflict Resolution in Islam: Precept and Practice.* Abdul Aziz Said, Nathan C. Funk and Ayse S. Kadayifci eds. (University Press of America, 2001),

56. Said et. al. 2001. See also Abu-Nimer. 1996; Abdul Aziz Said. "Cultural Context of Conflict Resolution: A Reference to an Arab Islamic Perspective." (American University Washington DC.) (Unpublished paper).

57. Abu-Nimer. "Conflict Resolution in an Islamic Context: Some Conceptual Questions" in *Peace and Conflict Resolution in Islam: Precept and Practice.* Abdul Aziz Said, Nathan C. Funk and Ayse S. Kadayifci eds. (University Press of America, 2001), 130.

58. Abu Nimer states "In 1993 and 1992, the first two regional Conflict Resolution conference were held in Cyprus and Turkey to discuss the development and promotion of Conflict Resolution in the Middle East." In Said et.al. 2001, 130

59. See A, Yosuf-Ahmad,. *Arab-Arab Conflicts 1945 1981: An Exploratory Study* (Beirut, Lebanon: The Center for the Studies of Arab, 1988).

60. Yosuf-Ahmad, 1988.

61. Weber. 1978. 227.
62. See Chapter Four.
63. Sampson 1997, 273-274.
64. See A. Curle Making Peace (London: Tavistock Publications, 1971) and Sampson 1997, 279-290.
65. Sampson. 1997, 279.
66. Sampson., 1997, 280.
67. Abu-Nimer. 2001, 686.
68. For use of myths in peace-making see also Gopin 2002.
69. Said, et. al. 2001, 1.
70. Abu-nimer 2003.
71. For an analysis of interfaith dialogue groups see Abu- nimer op.cit. 2001; abu-nimer, "The Miracles of Transformation Through Interfaith Dialogue: Are You A Believer?" in *Interfaith Dialogue and Peacebuilding*; David Smock ed. (Washington D.C. United States Institute of Peace, 2002), 15-32; Ronald Young "American Jews, Christians, and Muslims Working Together for Peace in the Middle East" in Smock, 2002.; and also Jaco Cilliers "Building Bridges for Interfaith Dialogue" in Smock, 2002.
72. Gopin, 2002, 152.
73. Gopin, 2002
74. Gopin, 2002
75. Glenn. E. Robinson. *Building a Palestinian State: The Incomplete Revolution.* Bloomington and Indianapolis: Indiana University Press, 1997, 110.
76. Glann, 1997.
77. Glenn, 1997 112.
78. Khadduri M.. "Sulh" in *The Encyclopedia of Islam. vol IX* C.E. Bosworth, E. van Donzel, W.P. Heinrichs, and the late G. Lecomte (Holland, Brill. Leiden, 1997), 845-846.
79. Irani George E. and Nathan C. Funk. "Rituals of Reconciliation: Arab-Islamic Perspectives" in *ASQ* vol. 20. No. 4, (Fall, 1998), 64.
80. Irani, 1998, 65.
81. Elias. Jabbour. *Sulh: Palestinian Traditional Peacemaking Process*: (Israel: House of Hope Publications, 1996), 59.
82. Interview with Nidal Dheisheh Refugee Camp, Bethlehem June 30, 2000.
83. Nidal, 2000.
84. Interview with Zhoughby Zhoughby (Director of Wi'am- Palestinian conflict Resolution Center), july 18, 2000 Bethlehem.
85. Eliyahu McLean. Director, Peacemaker Community in Israel. *[copred] message of Peace: Muslim and Jewish leaders Meet.* Wed 06 Jun 2001, 12:19:02., 2.
86. Eliyahu, 2001 .
87. interview with dr. Abbat, bethlehem, July 19, 2000.
88. Jabbour, 76.
89. Gopin 2002, 138-139.
90. Interview with Dr. Azzam, 20 July, 2000 hebron.
91. For more information on this and also for the whole text, see gopin, 2002, 53-54.
92. For more information on this and also for the communication with Clinton see Gopin 2002., 46-52.
93. Said, Abdul Aziz, and Nathan Funk "Peace in the sufi Tradition: An Ecology of the Spirit" in Said et al. 2001, 248.

94. Said et. a.l. 2001, 257.
95. Esposito 1998, 101.
96. Literally meaning he or she who seeks knowledge.
97. Esposito 1998, 106.
98. See Serif Mardin. *Religion and Social Change in Modern Turkey: The Case of Bediuzzaman Said Nursi* (New York: State University of New York Press. 1989), 149.
99. Mardin, 1989.
100. Interview with Dr. Abbat Bethlehem July, 19 2000.

Appendix I

The Covenant of the Islamic Resistance Movement[1] 18 August 1988

In The Name of The Most Merciful Allah

"Ye are the best nation that hath been raised up unto mankind: ye command that which is just, and ye forbid that which is unjust, and ye believe in Allah. And if they who have received the scriptures had believed, it had surely been the better for them: there are believers among them, but the greater part of them are transgressors. They shall not hurt you, unless with a slight hurt; and if they fight against you, they shall turn their backs to you, and they shall not be helped. They are smitten with vileness wheresoever they are found; unless they obtain security by entering into a treaty with Allah, and a treaty with men; and they draw on themselves indignation from Allah, and they are afflicted with poverty. This they suffer, because they disbelieved the signs of Allah, and slew the prophets unjustly; this, because they were rebellious, and transgressed." (Al-Imran - verses 109-111).

"Israel will exist and will continue to exist until Islam will obliterate it, just as it obliterated others before it "(The Martyr, Imam Hassan al-Banna, of blessed memory).

"The Islamic world is on fire. Each of us should pour some water, no matter how little, to extinguish whatever one can without waiting for the others." (Sheikh Amjad al-Zahawi of blessed memory).

In The Name of the Most Merciful Allah

Introduction

Praise be unto Allah, to whom we resort for help, and whose forgiveness, guidance and support we seek; Allah bless the Prophet and grant him salvation, his companions and supporters, and to those who carried out his message and adopted his laws—everlasting prayers and salvation as long as the earth and heaven will last. Hereafter:

O People: Out of the midst of troubles and the sea of suffering, out of the palpitations of faithful hearts and cleansed arms; out of the sense of duty, and in response to Allah's command, the call has gone out rallying people together and making them follow the ways of Allah, leading them to have determined will in order to fulfill their role in life, to overcome all obstacles, and surmount the difficulties on the way. Constant preparation has continued and so has the readiness to sacrifice life and all that is precious for the sake of Allah. Thus it was that the nucleus (of the movement) was formed and started to pave its way through the tempestuous sea of hopes and expectations, of wishes and yearnings, of troubles and obstacles, of pain and challenges, both inside and outside.

When the idea was ripe, the seed grew and the plant struck root in the soil of reality, away from passing emotions, and hateful haste. The Islamic Resistance Movement emerged to carry out its role through striving for the sake of its Creator, its arms intertwined with those of all the fighters for the liberation of Palestine. The spirits of its fighters meet with the spirits of all the fighters who have sacrificed their lives on the soil of Palestine, ever since it was conquered by the companions of the Prophet, Allah bless him and grant him salvation, and until this day.

This Covenant of the Islamic Resistance Movement (HAMAS), clarifies its picture, reveals its identity, outlines its stand, explains its aims, speaks about its hopes, and calls for its support, adoption and joining its ranks. Our struggle against the Jews is very great and very serious. It needs all sincere efforts. It is a step that inevitably should be followed by other steps. The Movement is but one squadron that should be supported by more and more squadrons from this vast Arab and Islamic world, until the enemy is vanquished and Allah's victory is realised.

Thus we see them coming on the horizon "and you shall learn about it hereafter"

"Allah hath written, Verily I will prevail, and my apostles: for Allah is strong and mighty." (The Dispute - verse 21).

"Say to them, This is my way: I invite you to Allah, by an evident demonstration; both I and he who followeth me; and, praise be unto Allah! I am not an idolator." (Joseph - verse 107).

Definition of the Movement

Ideological Starting-Points

Article One:

The Islamic Resistance Movement: The Movement's programme is Islam. From it, it draws its ideas, ways of thinking and understanding of the universe, life and man. It resorts to it for judgement in all its conduct, and it is inspired by it for guidance of its steps.

The Islamic Resistance Movement's Relation With the Moslem Brotherhood Group:

Article Two:

The Islamic Resistance Movement is one of the wings of Moslem Brotherhood in Palestine. Moslem Brotherhood Movement is a universal organization, which constitutes the largest Islamic movement in modern times. It is characterised by its deep understanding, accurate comprehension and its complete embrace of all Islamic concepts of all aspects of life, culture, creed, politics, economics, education, society, justice and judgement, the spreading of Islam, education, art, information, science of the occult and conversion to Islam.

Structure and Formation

Article Three:

The basic structure of the Islamic Resistance Movement consists of Moslems who have given their allegiance to Allah whom they truly worship,— "I have created the jinn and humans only for the purpose of worshipping" —who know their duty towards themselves, their families and country. In all that, they fear Allah and raise the banner of Jihad in the face of the oppressors, so that they would rid the land and the people of their uncleanliness, vileness and evils.

"But we will oppose truth to vanity, and it shall confound the same; and behold, it shall vanish away." (Prophets - verse 18).

Article Four:

The Islamic Resistance Movement welcomes every Moslem who embraces its faith, ideology, follows its programme, keeps its secrets, and wants to belong to its ranks and carry out the duty. Allah will certainly reward such one.

Time and Place Extent of the Islamic Resistance Movement:

Article Five:

Time extent of the Islamic Resistance Movement: By adopting Islam as its way of life, the Movement goes back to the time of the birth of the Islamic message, of the righteous ancestor, for Allah is its target, the Prophet is its example and the Koran is its constitution. Its extent in place is anywhere that there are Moslems who embrace Islam as their way of life everywhere in the globe. This being so, it extends to the depth of the earth and reaches out to the heaven.

"Dost thou not see how Allah putteth forth a parable; representing a good word, as a good tree, whose root is firmly fixed in the earth, and whose branches reach unto heaven; which bringeth forth its fruit in all seasons, by the will of its Lord? Allah propoundeth parables unto men, that they may be instructed." Abraham - verses 24-25).

Characteristics and Independence:

Article Six:

The Islamic Resistance Movement is a distinguished Palestinian movement, whose allegiance is to Allah, and whose way of life is Islam. It strives to raise the banner of Allah over every inch of Palestine, for under the wing of Islam followers of all religions can coexist in security and safety where their lives, possessions and rights are concerned. In the absence of Islam, strife will be rife, oppression spreads, evil prevails and schisms and wars will break out. How excellent was the Moslem poet, Mohamed Ikbal, when he wrote:

"If faith is lost, there is no security and there is no life for him who does not adhere to religion. He who accepts life without religion, has taken annihilation as his companion for life."

The Universality of the Islamic Resistance Movement:

Article Seven:

As a result of the fact that those Moslems who adhere to the ways of the Islamic Resistance Movement spread all over the world, rally support for it and its stands, strive towards enhancing its struggle, the Movement is a universal one. It is well-equipped for that because of the clarity of its ideology, the nobility of its aim and the loftiness of its objectives.

On this basis, the Movement should be viewed and evaluated, and its role be recognized. He who denies its right, evades supporting it and turns a blind eye to facts, whether intentionally or unintentionally, would awaken to see that events have overtaken him and with no logic to justify his attitude. One should certainly learn from past examples.

The injustice of next-of-kin is harder to bear than the smite of the Indian sword.

"We have also sent down unto thee the book of the Koran with truth, confirming that scripture which was revealed before it; and preserving the same safe from corruption. Judge therefore between them according to that which Allah hath revealed; and follow not their desires, by swerving from the truth which hath come unto thee. Unto every of you have we given a law, and an open path; and if Allah had pleased, he had surely made you one people; but he hath thought it fit to give you different laws, that he might try you in that which he hath given you respectively. Therefore strive to excel each other in good works; unto Allah shall ye all return, and then will he declare unto you that concerning which ye have disagreed. "(The Table, verse 48).

The Islamic Resistance Movement is one of the links in the chain of the struggle against the Zionist invaders. It goes back to 1939, to the emergence of the martyr Izz al-Din al Kissam and his brethren the fighters, members of Moslem Brotherhood. It goes on to reach out and become one with another chain that includes the struggle of the Palestinians and Moslem Brotherhood in the 1948 war and the Jihad operations of the Moslem Brotherhood in 1968 and after. Moreover, if the links have been distant from each other and if obstacles, placed by those who are the lackeys of Zionism in the way of the fighters obstructed the continuation of the struggle, the Islamic Resistance Movement aspires to the realisation of Allah's promise, no matter how long that should take. The Prophet, Allah bless him and grant him salvation, has said:

"The Day of Judgement will not come about until Moslems fight the Jews (killing the Jews), when the Jew will hide behind stones and trees. The stones and trees will say O Moslems, O Abdulla, there is a Jew behind me, come and kill him. Only the Gharkad tree, (evidently a certain kind of tree) would not do that because it is one of the trees of the Jews." (related by al-Bukhari and Moslem).

The Slogan of the Islamic Resistance Movement:

Article Eight:

Allah is its target, the Prophet is its model, the Koran its constitution: Jihad is its path and death for the sake of Allah is the loftiest of its wishes.

Incentives and Objectives:

Article Nine:

The Islamic Resistance Movement found itself at a time when Islam has disappeared from life. Thus rules shook, concepts were upset, values changed and evil people took control, oppression and darkness prevailed, cowards became like tigers: homelands were usurped, people were scattered and were caused to wander all over the world, the state of justice disappeared and the state of falsehood replaced it. Nothing remained in its right place. Thus, when Islam is absent from the arena, everything changes. From this state of affairs the incentives are drawn.

As for the objectives: They are the fighting against the false, defeating it and vanquishing it so that justice could prevail, homelands be retrieved and from its mosques would the voice of the mu'azen emerge declaring the establishment of the state of Islam, so that people and things would return each to their right places and Allah is our helper.

"...and if Allah had not prevented men, the one by the other, verily the earth had been corrupted: but Allah is beneficient towards his creatures." (The Cow - verse 251).

Article Ten:

As the Islamic Resistance Movement paves its way, it will back the oppressed and support the wronged with all its might. It will spare no effort to bring about justice and defeat injustice, in word and deed, in this place and everywhere it can reach and have influence therein.

Strategies and Methods

Strategies of the Islamic Resistance Movement: Palestine Is Islamic Waqf:

Article Eleven:

The Islamic Resistance Movement believes that the land of Palestine is an Islamic Waqf consecrated for future Moslem generations until Judgment Day. It, or any part of it, should not be squandered: it, or any part of it, should not be given up. Neither a single Arab country nor all Arab countries, neither any king or president, nor all the kings and presidents, neither any organization nor all of them, be they Palestinian or Arab, possess the right to do that. Palestine is an Islamic Waqf land consecrated for Moslem generations until Judgment Day. This being so, who could claim to have the right to represent Moslem generations till Judgment Day?

This is the law governing the land of Palestine in the Islamic Sharia (law) and the same goes for any land the Moslems have conquered by force, because during the times of (Islamic) conquests, the Moslems consecrated these lands to Moslem generations till the Day of Judgment.

It happened like this: When the leaders of the Islamic armies conquered Syria and Iraq, they sent to the Caliph of the Moslems, Umar bin-el-Khatab, asking for his advice concerning the conquered land—whether they should divide it among the soldiers, or leave it for its owners, or what? After consultations and discussions between the Caliph of the Moslems, Omar bin-el-Khatab and companions of the Prophet, Allah bless him and grant him salvation, it was decided that the land should be left with its owners who could benefit by its fruit. As for the real ownership of the land and the land itself, it should be consecrated for Moslem generations till Judgement Day. Those who are on the land, are there only to benefit from its fruit. This Waqf remains as long as earth and heaven remain. Any procedure in contradiction to Islamic Sharia, where Palestine is concerned,
is null and void.

"Verily, this is a certain truth. Wherefore praise the name of thy Lord, the great Allah." (The Inevitable - verse 95).

Homeland and Nationalism from the Point of View of the Islamic Resistance Movement in Palestine:

Article Twelve:

Nationalism, from the point of view of the Islamic Resistance Movement, is part of the religious creed. Nothing in nationalism is more significant or deeper than in the case when an enemy should tread Moslem land. Resisting and quelling the enemy become the individual duty of every Moslem, male or female. A woman can go out to fight the enemy without her husband's permission, and so does the slave: without his master's permission.

Nothing of the sort is to be found in any other regime. This is an undisputed fact. If other nationalist movements are connected with materialistic, human or regional causes, nationalism of the Islamic Resistance Movement has all these elements as well as the more important elements that give it soul and life. It is connected to the source of spirit and the granter of life, hoisting in the sky of the homeland the heavenly banner that joins earth and heaven with a strong bond.

If Moses comes and throws his staff, both witch and magic are annulled. "Now is the right direction manifestly distinguished from deceit: whoever therefore shall deny Tagut, and believe in Allah, he shall surely take hold with a strong handle, which shall not be broken; Allah is he who heareth and seeth." (The Cow - Verse 256).

Peaceful Solutions, Initiatives and International Conferences:

Article Thirteen:

Initiatives, and so-called peaceful solutions and international conferences, are in contradiction to the principles of the Islamic Resistance Movement. Abusing any part of Palestine is abuse directed against part of religion. Nationalism of the Islamic Resistance Movement is part of its religion. Its members have been fed on that. For the sake of hoisting the banner of Allah over their homeland they fight. "Allah will be prominent, but most people do not know. "

Now and then the call goes out for the convening of an international conference to look for ways of solving the (Palestinian) question. Some accept, others reject the idea, for this or other reason, with one stipulation or more for consent to convening the conference and participating in it. Knowing the parties constituting the conference, their past and present attitudes towards Moslem problems, the Islamic Resistance Movement does not consider these conferences capable of realising the demands, restoring the rights or doing justice to the oppressed. These conferences are only ways of setting the infidels in the land of the Moslems as arbitraters. When did the infidels do justice to the believers?

"But the Jews will not be pleased with thee, neither the Christians, until thou follow their religion; say, The direction of Allah is the true direction. And verily if thou follow their desires, after the knowledge which hath been given thee, thou shalt find no patron or protector against Allah. " (The Cow - verse 120).

There is no solution for the Palestinian question except through Jihad. Initiatives, proposals and international conferences are all a waste of time and vain endeavors. The Palestinian people know better than to consent to having their future, rights and fate toyed with. As in said in the honourable Hadith:

"The people of Syria are Allah's lash in His land. He wreaks His vengeance through them against whomsoever He wishes among His slaves It is unthinkable that those who are double-faced among them should prosper over the faithful. They will certainly die out of grief and desperation."

The Three Circles:

Article Fourteen:

The question of the liberation of Palestine is bound to three circles: the Palestinian circle, the Arab circle and the Islamic circle. Each of these circles has its role in the struggle against Zionism. Each has its duties, and it is a horrible mistake and a sign of deep ignorance to overlook any of these circles. Palestine is an Islamic land which has the first of the two kiblahs (direction to which Moslems turn in praying), the third of the holy (Islamic) sanctuaries, and the point of departure for Mohamed's midnight journey to the seven heavens (i.e. Jerusalem).

"Praise be unto him who transported his servant by night, from the sacred temple of Mecca to the farther temple of Jerusalem, the circuit of which we have blessed, that we might show him some of our signs; for Allah is he who heareth, and seeth." (The Night-Journey - verse 1).

Since this is the case, liberation of Palestine is then an individual duty for very Moslem wherever he may be. On this basis, the problem should be viewed.This should be realised by every Moslem.

The day the problem is dealt with on this basis, when the three circles mobilize their capabilities, the present state of affairs will change and the day of liberation will come nearer.

"Verily ye are stronger than they, by reason of the terror cast into their breasts from Allah. This, because they are not people of prudence." (The Emigration - verse 13).

The Jihad for the Liberation of Palestine is an Individual Duty:

Article Fifteen:

The day that enemies usurp part of Moslem land, Jihad becomes the individual duty of every Moslem. In face of the Jews' usurpation of Palestine, it is compulsory that the banner of Jihad be raised. To do this requires the diffusion of Islamic consciousness among the masses, both on the regional, Arab and Islamic levels. It is necessary to instill the spirit of Jihad in the heart of the nation so that they would confront the enemies and join the ranks of the fighters.

It is necessary that scientists, educators and teachers, information and media people, as well as the educated masses, especially the youth and sheikhs of the Islamic movements, should take part in the operation of awakening (the masses). It is important that basic changes be made in the school curriculum, to cleanse it of the traces of ideological invasion that affected it as a result of the orientalists and missionaries who infiltrated the region following the defeat of the Crusaders at the hands of Salah el-Din (Saladin). The Crusaders realised that it was impossible to defeat the Moslems without first having ideological invasion pave the way by upsetting their thoughts, disfiguring their heritage and violating their ideals. Only then could they invade with soldiers. This, in its turn, paved the way for the imperialistic invasion that made Allenby declare on entering Jerusalem: "Only now have the Crusades ended. "General Guru stood at Salah el-Din's grave and said: "We have returned, O Salah el-Din. "Imperialism has helped towards the strengthening of ideological invasion, deepening, and still does, its roots. All this has paved the way towards the loss of Palestine.

It is necessary to instill in the minds of the Moslem generations that the Palestinian problem is a religious problem, and should be dealt with on this basis. Palestine contains Islamic holy sites. In it there is al- Aqsa Mosque which is bound to the great Mosque in Mecca in an inseparable bond as long as heaven and earth speak of Isra' (Mohammed's midnight journey to the seven heavens) and Mi'raj (Mohammed's ascension to the seven heavens from Jerusalem).

"The bond of one day for the sake of Allah is better than the world and whatever there is on it. The place of one's whip in Paradise is far better than the world and whatever there is on it. A worshipper's going and coming in the service of Allah is better than the world and whatever there is on it. "(As related by al-Bukhari, Moslem, al-Tarmdhi and Ibn Maja).

"I swear by the holder of Mohammed's soul that I would like to invade and be killed for the sake of Allah, then invade and be killed, and then invade again and be killed." (As related by al-Bukhari and Moslem).

The Education of the Generations:

Article Sixteen:

It is necessary to follow Islamic orientation in educating the Islamic generations in our region by teaching the religious duties, comprehensive study of the Koran, the study of the Prophet's Sunna (his sayings and doings), and learning about Islamic history and heritage from their authentic sources. This should be done by specialised and learned people, using a curriculum that would healthily form the thoughts and faith of the Moslem student. Side by side with this, a comprehensive study of the enemy, his human and financial capabilities, learning about his points of weakness and strength, and getting to know the forces supporting and helping him, should also be included. Also, it is important to be acquainted with the current events, to follow what is new and to study the analysis and commentaries made of these events. Planning for the present and future, studying every trend appearing, is a must so that the fighting Moslem would live knowing his aim, objective and his way in the midst of what is going on around him.

"O my son, verily every matter, whether good or bad, though it be the weight of a grain of mustard-seed, and be hidden in a rock, or in the heavens, or in the earth, Allah will bring the same to light; for Allah is clear-sighted and knowing. O my son, be constant at prayer, and command that which is just, and forbid that which is evil: and be patient under the afflictions which shall befall thee; for this is a duty absolutely incumbent on all men. Distort not thy face out of contempt to men, neither walk in the earth with insolence; for Allah loveth no arrogant, vain-glorious person." (Lokman - verses 16-18).

The Role of the Moslem Woman:

Article Seventeen:

The Moslem woman has a role no less important than that of the moslem man in the battle of liberation. She is the maker of men. Her role in guiding and educating the new generations is great. The enemies have realised the importance of her role. They consider that if they are able to direct and bring her up they way they wish, far from Islam, they would have won the battle. That is why you find them giving these attempts constant attention through information campaigns, films, and the school curriculum, using for that purpose their lackeys who are infiltrated through Zionist organizations under various names and shapes, such as Freemasons, Rotary Clubs, espionage groups and others, which are all nothing more than cells of subversion and saboteurs. These organizations have ample resources that enable them to play their role in societies for the purpose of achieving the Zionist targets and to deepen the concepts that would serve the enemy. These organizations operate in the absence of Islam and its estrangement among its people. The Islamic peoples should perform their role in confronting the conspiracies of these saboteurs. The day Islam is in control of guiding the affairs of life, these organizations, hostile to humanity and Islam, will be obliterated.

Article Eighteen:

Woman in the home of the fighting family, whether she is a mother or a sister, plays the most important role in looking after the family, rearing the children and embuing them with moral values and thoughts derived from Islam. She has to teach them to perform the religious duties in preparation for the role of fighting awaiting them. That is why it is necessary to pay great attention to schools and the curriculum followed in educating Moslem girls, so that they would grow up to be good mothers, aware of their role in the battle of liberation.

She has to be of sufficient knowledge and understanding where the performance of housekeeping matters are concerned, because economy and avoidance of waste of the family budget, is one of the requirements for the ability to continue moving forward in the difficult conditions surrounding us. She should put before her eyes the fact that the money available to her is just like blood which should never flow except through the veins so that both children and grown-ups could continue to live.

"Verily, the Moslems of either sex, and the true believers of either sex, and the devout men, and the devout women, and the men of veracity, and the women of veracity, and the patient men, and the patient women, and the humble men, and the humble women, and the alms-givers of either sex who remember Allah frequently; for them hath Allah prepared forgiveness and a great reward." (The Confederates - verse 25).

The Role of Islamic Art in the Battle of Liberation:

Article Nineteen:

Art has regulations and measures by which it can be determined whether it is Islamic or pre-Islamic (Jahili) art. The issues of Islamic liberation are in need of Islamic art that would take the spirit high, without raising one side of human nature above the other, but rather raise all of them harmoniously an in equilibrium. Man is a unique and wonderful creature, made out of a handful of clay and a breath from Allah. Islamic art addresses man on this basis, while pre-Islamic art addresses the body giving preference to the clay component in it. The book, the article, the bulletin, the sermon, the thesis, the popular poem, the poetic ode, the song, the play and others, contain the characteristics of Islamic art, then these are among the requirements of ideological mobilization, renewed food for the journey and recreation for the soul. The road is long and suffering is plenty. The soul will be bored, but Islamic art renews the energies, resurrects the movement, arousing in them lofty meanings and proper conduct. "Nothing can improve the self if it is in retreat except shifting from one mood to another."

All this is utterly serious and no jest, for those who are fighters do not jest.

Social Mutual Responsibility:

Article Twenty:

Moslem society is a mutually responsible society. The Prophet, prayers and greetings be unto him, said: "Blessed are the generous, whether they were in town or on a journey, who have collected all that they had and shared it equally among themselves."

The Islamic spirit is what should prevail in every Moslem society. The society that confronts a vicious enemy which acts in a way similar to Nazism, making no differentiation between man and woman, between children and old people—such a society is entitled to this Islamic spirit. Our enemy relies on the methods of collective punishment. He has deprived people of their homeland and properties, pursued them in their places of exile and gathering, breaking bones, shooting at women, children and old people, with or without a reason. The enemy has opened detention camps where thousands and thousands of people are thrown and kept under sub-human conditions. Added to this, are the demolition of houses, rendering children orphans, meting cruel sentences against thousands of young people, and causing them to spend the best years of their lives in the dungeons of prisons.

In their Nazi treatment, the Jews made no exception for women or children. Their policy of striking fear in the heart is meant for all. They attack people where their breadwinning is concerned, extorting their money and threatening their honour. They deal with people as if they were the worst war criminals. Deportation from the homeland is a kind of murder.

To counter these deeds, it is necessary that social mutual responsibility should prevail among the people. The enemy should be faced by the people as a single body which if one member of it should complain, the rest of the body would respond by feeling the same pains.

Article Twenty-One:
Mutual social responsibility means extending assistance, financial or moral, to all those who are in need and joining in the execution of some of the work. Members of the Islamic Resistance Movement should consider the interests of the masses as their own personal interests. They must spare no effort in achieving and preserving them. They must prevent any foul play with the future of the upcoming generations and anything that could cause loss to society. The masses are part of them and they are part of the masses. Their strength is theirs, and their future is theirs. Members of the Islamic Resistance Movement should share the people's joy and grief, adopt the demands of the public and whatever means by which they could be realised. The day that such a spirit prevails, brotherliness would deepen, cooperation, sympathy and unity will be enhanced and the ranks will be solidified to confront the enemies.

Supportive Forces Behind the Enemy:

Article Twenty-Two:
For a long time, the enemies have been planning, skillfully and with precision, for the achievement of what they have attained. They took into consideration the causes affecting the current of events. They strived to amass great and substantive material wealth which they devoted to the realisation of their dream. With their money, they took control of the world media, news agencies, the press, publishing houses, broadcasting stations, and others. With their money they stirred revolutions in various parts of the world with the purpose of achieving their interests and reaping the fruit therein. They were behind the French Revolution, the Communist revolution and most of the revolutions we heard and hear about, here and there. With their money they formed secret societies, such as Freemasons, Rotary Clubs, the Lions and others in different parts of the world for the purpose of sabotaging societies and achieving Zionist interests. With their money they were able to control imperialistic countries and instigate them to colonize many countries in order to enable them to exploit their resources and spread corruption there.

You may speak as much as you want about regional and world wars. They were behind World War I, when they were able to destroy the Islamic Caliphate, making financial gains and controlling resources. They obtained the Balfour Declaration, formed the League of Nations through which they could rule the world. They were behind World War II, through which they made huge financial gains by trading in armaments, and paved the way for the establishment of their state. It was they who instigated the replacement of the League of Nations with the United Nations and the Security Council to enable them to rule the world through them. There is no war going on anywhere, without having their finger in it.

"So often as they shall kindle a fire for war, Allah shall extinguish it; and they shall set their minds to act corruptly in the earth, but Allah loveth not the corrupt doers. "(The Table - verse 64).

The imperialistic forces in the Capitalist West and Communist East, support the enemy with all their might, in money and in men. These forces take turns in doing that. The day Islam appears, the forces of infidelity would unite to challenge it, for the infidels are of one nation.

"O true believers, contract not an intimate friendship with any besides yourselves: they will not fail to corrupt you. They wish for that which may cause you to perish: their hatred hath already appeared from out of their mouths; but what their breasts conceal is yet more inveterate. We have already shown you signs of their ill will towards you, if ye understand." (The Family of Imran - verse 118).

It is not in vain that the verse is ended with Allah's words "if ye understand."

Our Attitudes Towards:

A. Islamic Movements:

Article Twenty-Three:

The Islamic Resistance Movement views other Islamic movements with respect and appreciation. If it were at variance with them on one point or opinion, it is in agreement with them on other points and understandings. It considers these movements, if they reveal good intentions and dedication to Allah, that they fall into the category of those who are trying hard since they act within the Islamic circle. Each active person has his share.

The Islamic Resistance Movement considers all these movements as a fund for itself. It prays to Allah for guidance and directions for all and it spares no effort to keep the banner of unity raised, ever striving for its realisation in accordance with the Koran and the Prophet's directives.

"And cleave all of you unto the covenant of Allah, and depart not from it, and remember the favour of Allah towards you: since ye were enemies, and he reconciled your hearts, and ye became companions and brethren by his favour: and ye were on the brink of a pit of fire, and he delivered you thence. Allah declareth unto you his signs, that ye may be directed." (The Family of Imran - Verse 102).

Article Twenty-Four:

The Islamic Resistance Movement does not allow slandering or speaking ill of individuals or groups, for the believer does not indulge in such malpractices. It is necessary to differentiate between this behaviour and the stands taken by certain individuals and groups. Whenever those stands are erroneous, the Islamic Resistance Movement preserves the right to expound the error and to warn against it. It will strive to show the right path and to judge the case in question with objectivity. Wise conduct is indeed the target of the believer who follows it wherever he discerns it.

"Allah loveth not the speaking ill of anyone in public, unless he who is injured call for assistance; and Allah heareth and knoweth: whether ye publish a good action, or conceal it, or forgive evil, verily Allah is gracious and powerful." (Women - verses 147-148).

B. Nationalist Movements in the Palestinian Arena:

Article Twenty-Five:

The Islamic Resistance Movement respects these movements and appreciates their circumstances and the conditions surrounding and affecting them. It encourages them as long as they do not give their allegiance to the Communist East or the Crusading West. It confirms to all those who are integrated in it, or sympathetic towards it, that the Islamic Resistance Movement is a fighting movement that has a moral and enlightened look of life and the way it should cooperate with the other (movements). It detests opportunism and desires only the good of people, individuals and groups alike. It does not seek material gains, personal fame, nor does it look for a reward from others. It works with its own resources and whatever is at its disposal "and prepare for them whatever force you can", for the fulfilment of the duty, and the earning of Allah's favour. It has no other desire than that.

The Movement assures all the nationalist trends operating in the Palestinian arena for the liberation of Palestine, that it is there for their support and assistance. It will never be more than that, both in words and deeds, now and in the future. It is there to bring together and not to divide, to preserve and not to squander, to unify and not to throw asunder. It evaluates every good word, sincere effort and good offices. It closes the door in the face of side disagreements and does not lend an ear to rumours and slanders, while at the same time fully realising the right for self-defence.

Anything contrary or contradictory to these trends, is a lie disseminated by enemies or their lackeys for the purpose of sowing confusion, disrupting the ranks and occupy them with side issues.

"O true believers, if a wicked man come unto you with a tale, inquire strictly into the truth thereof; lest ye hurt people through ignorance, and afterwards repent of what ye have done." The Inner Apartments - verse 6).

Article Twenty-Six:

In viewing the Palestinian nationalist movements that give allegiance neither to the East nor the West, in this positive way, the Islamic Resistance Movement does not refrain from discussing new situations on the regional or international levels where the Palestinian question is concerned. It does that in such an objective manner revealing the extent of how much it is in harmony or contradiction with the national interests in the light of the Islamic point of view.

C. The Palestinian Liberation Organization:

Article Twenty-Seven:

The Palestinian Liberation Organization is the closest to the heart of the Islamic Resistance Movement. It contains the father and the brother, the next of kin and the friend. The Moslem does not estrange himself from his father, brother, next of kin or friend. Our homeland is one, our situation is one, our fate is one and the enemy is a joint enemy to all of us.

Because of the situations surrounding the formation of the Organization, of the ideological confusion prevailing in the Arab world as a result of the ideological invasion under whose influence the Arab world has fallen since the defeat of the Crusaders and which was, and still is, intensified through orientalists, missionaries and imperialists, the Organization adopted the idea of the secular state. And that it how we view it.

Secularism completely contradicts religious ideology. Attitudes, conduct and decisions stem from ideologies.

That is why, with all our appreciation for The Palestinian Liberation Organization - and what it can develop into - and without belittling its role in the Arab-Israeli conflict, we are unable to exchange the present or future Islamic Palestine with the secular idea. The Islamic nature of Palestine is part of our religion and whoever takes his religion lightly is a loser.

"Who will be adverse to the religion of Abraham, but he whose mind is infatuated? (The Cow - verse 130).

The day The Palestinian Liberation Organization adopts Islam as its way of life, we will become its soldiers, and fuel for its fire that will burn the enemies. Until such a day, and we pray to Allah that it will be soon, the Islamic Resistance Movement's stand towards the PLO is that of the son towards his father, the brother towards his brother, and the relative to relative, suffers his pain and supports him in confronting the enemies, wishing him to be wise and well-guided.

"Stand by your brother, for he who is brotherless is like the fighter who goes to battle without arms. One's cousin is the wing one flies with - could the bird fly without wings?"

D. Arab and Islamic Countries:

Article Twenty-Eight:

The Zionist invasion is a vicious invasion. It does not refrain from resorting to all methods, using all evil and contemptible ways to achieve its end. It relies greatly in its infiltration and espionage operations on the secret organizations it gave rise to, such as the Freemasons, The Rotary and Lions clubs, and other sabotage groups. All these organizations, whether secret or open, work in the interest of Zionism and according to its instructions. They aim at undermining societies, destroying values, corrupting consciences, deteriorating character and annihilating Islam. It is behind the drug trade and alcoholism in all its kinds so as to facilitate its control and expansion. Arab countries surrounding Israel are asked to open their borders before the fighters from among the Arab and Islamic nations so that they could consolidate their efforts with those of their Moslem brethren in Palestine.

As for the other Arab and Islamic countries, they are asked to facilitate the movement of the fighters from and to it, and this is the least thing they could do.

We should not forget to remind every Moslem that when the Jews conquered the Holy City in 1967, they stood on the threshold of the Aqsa Mosque and proclaimed that "Mohammed is dead, and his descendants are all women." Israel, Judaism and Jews challenge Islam and the Moslem people. "May the cowards never sleep."

E. Nationalist and Religious Groupings, Institutions, Intellectuals, The Arab and Islamic World:

The Islamic Resistance Movement hopes that all these groupings will side with it in all spheres, would support it, adopt its stand and solidify its activities and moves, work towards rallying support for it so that the Islamic people will be a base and a stay for it, supplying it with strategic depth an all human material and informative spheres, in time and in place. This should be done through the convening of solidarity conferences, the issuing of explanatory bulletins, favourable articles and booklets, enlightening the masses regarding the Palestinian issue, clarifying what confronts it and the conspiracies woven around it. They should mobilize the Islamic nations, ideologically, educationally and culturally, so that these peoples would be equipped to perform their role in the decisive battle of liberation, just as they did when they vanquished the Crusaders and the Tatars and saved human civilization. Indeed, that is not difficult for Allah.

"Allah hath written, Verily I will prevail, and my apostles: for Allah is strong and mighty." (The Dispute - verse 21).

Article Thirty:

Writers, intellectuals, media people, orators, educaters and teachers, and all the various sectors in the Arab and Islamic world—all of them are called upon to perform their role, and to fulfill their duty, because of the ferocity of the Zionist offensive and the Zionist influence in many countries exercised through financial and media control, as well as the consequences that all this lead to in the greater part of the world.

Jihad is not confined to the carrying of arms and the confrontation of the enemy. The effective word, the good article, the useful book, support and solidarity—together with the presence of sincere purpose for the hoisting of Allah's banner higher and higher—all these are elements of the Jihad for Allah's sake.

"Whosoever mobilises a fighter for the sake of Allah is himself a fighter. Whosoever supports the relatives of a fighter, he himself is a fighter." (related by al-Bukhari, Moslem, Abu-Dawood and al-Tarmadhi).

F. Followers of Other Religions: The Islamic Resistance Movement Is A Humanistic Movement:

Article Thirty-One:

The Islamic Resistance Movement is a humanistic movement. It takes care of human rights and is guided by Islamic tolerance when dealing with the followers of other religions. It does not antagonize anyone of them except if it is antagonized by it or stands in its way to hamper its moves and waste its efforts.

Under the wing of Islam, it is possible for the followers of the three religions—Islam, Christianity and Judaism—to coexist in peace and quiet with each other. Peace and quiet would not be possible except under the wing of Islam. Past and present history are the best witness to that.

It is the duty of the followers of other religions to stop disputing the sovereignty of Islam in this region, because the day these followers should take over there will be nothing but carnage, displacement and terror. Everyone of them is at variance with his fellow-religionists, not to speak about followers of other religionists. Past and present history are full of examples to prove this fact.

"They will not fight against you in a body, except in fenced towns, or from behind walls. Their strength in war among themselves is great: thou thinkest them to be united; but their hearts are divided. This, because they are people who do not understand." (The Emigration - verse 14).

Islam confers upon everyone his legitimate rights. Islam prevents the incursion on other people's rights. The Zionist Nazi activities against our people will not last for long. "For the state of injustice lasts but one day, while the state of justice lasts till Doomsday."

"As to those who have not borne arms against you on account of religion, nor turned you out of your dwellings, Allah forbiddeth you not to deal kindly with them, and to behave justly towards them; for Allah loveth those who act justly." (The Tried - verse 8).

The Attempt to Isolate the Palestinian People:

Article Thirty-Two:

World Zionism, together with imperialistic powers, try through a studied plan and an intelligent strategy to remove one Arab state after another from the circle of struggle against Zionism, in order to have it finally face the Palestinian people only. Egypt was, to a great extent, removed from the circle of the struggle, through the treacherous Camp David Agreement. They are trying to draw other Arab countries into similar agreements and to bring them outside the circle of struggle.

The Islamic Resistance Movement calls on Arab and Islamic nations to take up the line of serious and persevering action to prevent the success of this horrendous plan, to warn the people of the danger eminating from leaving the circle of struggle against Zionism. Today it is Palestine, tomorrow it will be one country or another. The Zionist plan is limitless. After Palestine, the Zionists aspire to expand from the Nile to the Euphrates. When they will have digested the region they overtook, they will aspire to further expansion, and so on. Their plan is embodied in the "Protocols of the Elders of Zion," and their present conduct is the best proof of what we are saying.

Leaving the circle of struggle with Zionism is high treason, and cursed be he who does that. "for whoso shall turn his back unto them on that day, unless he turneth aside to fight, or retreateth to another party of the faithful, shall draw on himself the indignation of Allah, and his abode shall be hell; an ill journey shall it be thither." (The Spoils - verse 16). There is no way out except by concentrating all powers and energies to face this Nazi, vicious Tatar invasion. The alternative is loss of one's country, the dispersion of citizens, the spread of vice on earth and the destruction of religious values. Let every person know that he is responsible before Allah, for "the doer of the slightest good deed is rewarded in like, and the does of the slightest evil deed is also rewarded in like."

The Islamic Resistance Movement considers itself to be the spearhead of the circle of struggle with world Zionism and a step on the road. The Movement adds its efforts to the efforts of all those who are active in the Palestinian arena. Arab and Islamic Peoples should augment by further steps on their part; Islamic groupings all over the Arab world should also do the same, since all of these are the best-equipped for the future role in the fight with the warmongering Jews.

"...and we have put enmity and hatred between them, until the day of resurrection. So often as they shall kindle a fire of war, Allah shall extinguish it; and they shall set their minds to act corruptly in the earth, but Allah loveth not the corrupt doers." (The Table - verse 64).

Article Thirty-Three:

The Islamic Resistance Movement, being based on the common coordinated and interdependent conceptions of the laws of the universe, and flowing in the stream of destiny in confronting and fighting the enemies in defence of the Moslems and Islamic civilization and sacred sites, the first among which is the Aqsa

Mosque, urges the Arab and Islamic peoples, their governments, popular and official groupings, to fear Allah where their view of the Islamic Resistance Movement and their dealings with it are concerned. They should back and support it, as Allah wants them to, extending to it more and more funds till Allah's purpose is achieved when ranks will close up, fighters join other fighters and masses everywhere in the Islamic world will come forward in response to the call of duty while loudly proclaiming: Hail to Jihad. Their cry will reach the heavens and will go on being resounded until liberation is achieved, the invaders vanquished and Allah's victory comes about.

"And Allah will certainly assist him who shall be on his side: for Allah is strong and mighty." (The Pilgrimage - verse 40).

The Testimony of History

Across History in Confronting the Invaders:

Article Thirty-Four:

Palestine is the navel of the globe and the crossroad of the continents. Since the dawn of history, it has been the target of expansionists. The Prophet, Allah bless him and grant him salvation, had himself pointed to this fact in the noble Hadith in which he called on his honourable companion, Ma'adh ben-Jabal, saying: O Ma'ath, Allah throw open before you, when I am gone, Syria, from Al-Arish to the Euphrates. Its men, women and slaves will stay firmly there till the Day of Judgement. Whoever of you should choose one of the Syrian shores, or the Holy Land, he will be in constant struggle till the Day of Judgment."

Expansionists have more than once put their eye on Palestine which they attacked with their armies to fulfill their designs on it. Thus it was that the Crusaders came with their armies, bringing with them their creed and carrying their Cross. They were able to defeat the Moslems for a while, but the Moslems were able to retrieve the land only when they stood under the wing of their religious banner, united their word, hallowed the name of Allah and surged out fighting under the leadership of Salah ed-Din al-Ayyubi. They fought for almost twenty years and at the end the Crusaders were defeated and Palestine was liberated.

"Say unto those who believe not, Ye shall be overcome, and thrown together into hell; an unhappy couch it shall be. "(The Family of Imran - verse 12).

This is the only way to liberate Palestine. There is no doubt about the testimony of history. It is one of the laws of the universe and one of the rules of existence. Nothing can overcome iron except iron. Their false futile creed can only be defeated by the righteous Islamic creed. A creed could not be fought except by a creed, and in the last analysis, victory is for the just, for justice is certainly victorious.

"Our word hath formerly been given unto our servants the apostles; that they should certainly be assisted against the infidels, and that our armies should surely be the conquerors." Those Who Rank Themselves - verses 171-172).

Article Thirty-Five:
The Islamic Resistance Movement views seriously the defeat of the Crusaders at the hands of Salah ed-Din al-Ayyubi and the rescuing of Palestine from their hands, as well as the defeat of the Tatars at Ein Galot, breaking their power at the hands of Qataz and Al-Dhaher Bivers and saving the Arab world from the Tatar onslaught which aimed at the destruction of every meaning of human civilization. The Movement draws lessons and examples from all this. The present Zionist onslaught has also been preceded by Crusading raids from the West and other Tatar raids from the East. Just as the Moslems faced those raids and planned fighting and defeating them, they should be able to confront the Zionist invasion and defeat it. This is indeed no problem for the Almighty Allah, provided that the intentions are pure, the determination is true and that Moslems have benefited from past experiences, rid themselves of the effects of ideological invasion and followed the customs of their ancestors.

The Islamic Resistance Movement is Composed of Soldiers:

Article Thirty-Six:
While paving its way, the Islamic Resistance Movement, emphasizes time and again to all the sons of our people, to the Arab and Islamic nations, that it does not seek personal fame, material gain, or social prominence. It does not aim to compete against any one from among our people, or take his place. Nothing of the sort at all. It will not act against any of the sons of Moslems or those who are peaceful towards it from among non-Moslems, be they here or anywhere else. It will only serve as a support for all groupings and organizations operating against the Zionist enemy and its lackeys.
The Islamic Resistance Movement adopts Islam as its way of life. Islam is its creed and religion. Whoever takes Islam as his way of life, be it an organization, a grouping, a country or any other body, the Islamic Resistance Movement considers itself as their soldiers and nothing more.

We ask Allah to show us the right course, to make us an example to others and to judge between us and our people with truth.

"O Lord, do thou judge between us and our nation with truth; for thou art the best judge." (Al Araf verse 89).

The last of our prayers will be praise to Allah, the Master of the Universe.

Endnotes

1. Originally from Hamas web site at : http://209.204.204.153/hamas/documents/charter_text/2000/7_aug_00.htm. The first Hamas webpage was attacked by hackers in 2002. A second Hamas website was launched at http://www.hamasonline.com/indexx.php?page=Hamas/hamas_convenant. This site too has been attached by hackers. However a copy of the Charter can also be found at Avalon Project website at Yale Law School at: http://www.yale.edu/lawweb/avalon/mideast/hamas.htm, 2007

Bibliography

Abbad, Abdul Rahman. "Peace and Pacifism in Islam." *International Journal of Nonviolence* vol. 3, (1996): 60-71

Abboushi, W. *The Unmaking of Palestine* Brattleboro: Amana Books, (1990)

Abdalla, Amr. "Principles of Islamic Interpersonal Conflict Intervention: A Search within Islam and Western Literature," *Journal of Law and Religion.* 15 (1, 2), (2000-2001): 151-184

Abedi, Mehdi and Gary Legenhausen eds. *Jihad and Shahadat: Struggle and Martyrdom in Islam.* The Institute for Research and Islamic Studies (IRIS), (1986)

Abduh, Muhammad. "The Necessity of Religious Reform" in *Contemporary Debates in Islam: An Anthology of Modernist and Fundamentalist Thought.* Moaddel, Mansoor and Kamran Talattof eds. New York: St. Martin's Press, (2000): 45-51

Abou El-Magd, Nadia "Politics of Fatwa" in *Al-Ahram Weekly On-line* 3 - 9 May Issue No.532, (2001)

Abu-Amr, Ziad. *Islamic Fundamentalism in the West Bank and Gaza: Muslim Brotherhood and Islamic Jihad.* Bloomington and Indianapolis: Indiana University Press, (1994)

Abu-Ghazaleh, A. *Arab Cultural Nationalism in Palestine.* Beirut: Institute for Palestine Studies, (1973)

Abu Laila, Muhammad. "Islam and Peace." *The Islamic Quarterly* Vol.35 No. 1 (First Quarter, 1991): 55-69

Abu-Nimer, Mohammed "Conflict Resolution Approaches: Western and Middle Eastern Lessons and Possibilities." *The American Journal of Economics and Sociology.* vol. 55 no.1, 35-55 (January, 1996)

———. *Dialogue, Conflict Resolution, and Change* SUNY, (1999)

———. "Conflict Resolution, Culture, and Religion: Toward a Training Model of Interreligious Peacebuilding," *Peace Research.* vol. 38 no.6, (2001): 685-704

———. "Conflict Resolution in an Islamic Context: Some Conceptual Questions" in *Peace and Change* 22-40 (January, 1996)

———. *Nonviolence and Peacebuilding in Islam* Florida: University Press of Florida, (2003);

Abul-Fadl, Mona. "Community, Justice, and Jihad: Elements of the Muslim Historical Consciousness" in *The American Journal of Islamic Social Sciences.* Vol. 4 No. 1, (1987): 13-30

AbuSulayman, AbdulHamid A. *The Islamic Theory of International Relations Herndon, VA.:* International Institute of Islamic Thought, (1987)

———. "Islamic Jurisprudence and Modern Needs: The Challenge of Renewal" in *Peace and Conflict Resolution in Islam: Precept and Practice.* Eds. Abdul Aziz Said, Nathan C. Funk and Ayse S. Kadayifci University Press of America, (2001): 59-72

Abu Yusuf *Kitab al-Kharaj* trans. Ben Shemesh, London, (1969)

Adams, Charles *"Mawdudi and the Islamic State"* in Esposito *Voices of Resurgent Islam* Oxford University Press. New York, (1983): 99-133

Ahmad, Khurshid *Islamic Law and Constitution (Collection of Mawdudi's Speeches)* Lahore: Islamic Publications, (1967)

Ahmad, Mumtaz ed. *State, Politics, and Islam.* Indianapolis: American Trust Publications, (1986)

Alberoni, Fransesco. *Movement and Institution.* Cambridge: Cambridge University Press, (1984)

Alexander, Yonah. *The Role of Communications in Middle East Conflict: Ideological and Religious Aspects* New York: Preager, (1973)

Allardt, Erik *"Ethnic Mobilization and Minority Resources"* in *Zeitschrift Fur Soziologie.* Vol. 10 (1981): 427-437

Amnesty International *Human Rights in the Gaza Strip and Jericho Under Palestinian Self-Rule Vol*.6 No.10 (September 1994)

Antonius, G. *The Arab Awakening: The Story of Arab National Movement* New York: Capricorn Books, (1965)

Antoun, Richard T. *Low-Key Politics: Local-Level Leadership and Change in the Middle East.* Albany, N.Y.: SUNY Press, (1979)

Antoun, Richard T. and Lilly Harik eds. *Rural Politics and Social Change in the Middle East.* Bloomington: Indiana University Press, (1972)

Appleby, R. Scott ed. *Spokesmen for the Despised: Fundamentalist Leaders of he Middle East.* Chicago: University of Chicago Press, (1997)

Arbery, Arthur, J. *Religion in the Middle East: Three Religions in Concord and Conflict* (two volumes) London: Cambridge University Press, (1969)

Arberry, Arthur, J. *Sufism: An Account of the Mystics of Islam.* London: Unwin Paperbacks, (1979)

Arkoun, Mohammed *Rethinking Islam Today.* Washington. D. C: Center For Contemporary Arab Studies, (1987)

———. *"The Concept of Authority in Islamic Thought: 'La Hukma illa lillah'"* in *Islam, State and Society* K. Ferdinand and M Mozaffer eds., London: Curzon Press, (1988): 53-73

Arouri, N. H. *The Obstruction of Peace: The U.S., Israel and the Palestinians* Monroe, ME., Common Courage Press, (1995)

———. *Occupation: Israel over Palestine,* 2nd edition. Belmont, MA.: Association of Arab-American University Graduates, (1989)

Asad, Muhammad. *The Principles of State and Governance in Islam*. Berkeley: University of California Press, (1961)

Ashley, Richard K. "Living on Borderlines: Man, Poststructuralism, and War." In *International/Intertextual Relations: Postmodern Readings of World Politics*. Eds. James Der Derian and Michael J. Shapiro, New York: Lexington Books, (1989): 259-321

Ashrawi, Hanan. *This Side of Peace* New York: Touchstone Books, (1995)

Augburger D. W. *Conflict Mediation Across Cultures* Louisville, KY: Westminister/ Knox Press, (1992)

Aveni, Adrian. F. "Organizational Linkages and Resource Mobilization: The Significance of Linkage Strength and Breadth." *Sociological Quarterly* vol.19, (1978): 185-222

Avruch, Kevin. *Culture and Conflict Resolution*. United States Institute of Peace Press: Washington, DC., (1998)

Avruch, Kevin and Peter Black and J. A. Scimecca eds. *Conflict Resolution: Cross-Cultural Perspectives* Westport, CT.: Greenwood Press. (1991)

al-Ayid, Khalid. This interview was published under the title of "The Movement of Islamic Jihad and the Oslo Process" in *Journal of Palestinian Studies* Vol. 28 No.4, (Summer, 1999): 61-73

Ayubi, Nazih N. *Political Islam: Religion and Politics in the Arab World*. London: Routledge, (1991)

Azar, E. "Management of Protracted Social Conflict in the Third World," paper prepared for the Fourth ICES Annual Lecture at Columbia University (unpublished) New York 10 (June, 1986)

al-Azmeh, Aziz. *Islams and Modernities* London: Verso, (1993)

Badran, N. "The Means of Survival: Education and the Palestinian Community, 1948-67" *Journal of Palestine Studies* vol. 9 no. 4, (Summer 1980): 44-74

al-Banna, Hasan *Five Tracts of Hasan al-Banna (1906-1949)* Charles Wendell tr., Berkeley: University of California Press, (1978)

———. *Majmu'at Rasa'I al-Imam al-Shahid Hasan al-Banna* new legal ed. Cairo: Dar al Da'wa, (1990)

Barnett, Micheal. "Institutions, Roles and Disorder: The Case of the Arab States System." *International Studies Quarterly* Vol. 37, (1993): 271-296

Bawa, Muhaiaddeen, M. R. *Islam and the World Peace: Explanations of a Sufi* Philadelphia: The Fellowship Press, (1987)

BBC News "Voices from the Conflict." at http://news.bbc.co.uk/hi/english/static/in_depth/middle_east/2002/voic es/abu.stm (2002)

Becker, Howard S. "Notes on the Concept of Commitment." *American Journal of Sociology*. vol.66, (1960): 32-40

———. "Practitioners of Vice and Crime." In *Pathways to Data*. Ed. R.W. Abstein, Aldine, , Chicago, (1970): 30-49

Beckford, J. *Cult Controversies: The Societal Response to New Religious Movements*. Tavistock. New York, (1985)

Beetham David *The Legitimation of Power*. Houndmills: Macmillan, (1991)

Beinin, J. *Was the Red Flay Flying There? Marxist Politics and the Arab-Israeli Conflict in Egypt ad Israel, 1948- 1965* Berkeley, CA.: California University Press, (1990)

Benvenisti, M. *Intimate Enemies: Jews and Arabs in a Shared Land* Berkeley: University of California Press, (1995)

———. *Report: Demographic, Economic, Legal, Social, and Political Development in the West Bank* Boulder, CO.: Westview Press, (1986)

Bercovitch, Jacob and S. Ayse Kadayifci "Conflict Management and Israeli-Palestinian Conflict: The Importance of Capturing the 'right Moment'" *Asia-Pacific Review* Vol. 9, No. 2 (2002): 113-129

Bercovitch Jacob and Ole Elgstrom. "Culture and International Mediation: Exploring Theoretical and Empirical Linkages," in *International Negotiation* vol. 6 no.1 (2001)

———. "Mediation in International Conflict: An Overview of Theory, A Review of Practice" in *Peacemaking in International Conflict: Methods and Techniques.* eds. I. William Zartman, J. Lewis Rasmussen. Washington D.C.: United States Institute of Peace Press, (1997): 125-154

———. "International Mediation: A Study of Incidence, Strategies and Conditions of Successful Outcomes." *Cooperation and Conflict* vol. 21 no.3, (1986): 155-168

Berger, E. *Peace for Palestine: First Lost Opportunity* Gainseville: University Press of Florida, (1993)

Berger, Peter and Thomas Luckmann. *The Social Construction of Reality: A Treatise in the Sociology of Knowledge.* Garden City Doubleday N.Y. Anchor Books. (1966)

Berryman, Phillipe. *Liberation Theology.* Philadelphia Temple University. (1987)

Blalock, Jr. H. M. *Power and Conflict* Thousand Oaks, CA: Sage. (1989)

Boulding, Elise. *Building Peace in the Middle East: Challenges for States and Civil Society* Boulder, CO.: Lynne Rienner Publishers, (1994)

Boulding, Kenneth E. *Three Faces of Power* London: Sage Publications. (1989)

Boullata, Kamal *Faithful Witnesses: Palestinian Children Recreate Their World.* New York: Olive Branch Press, (1990)

Borhek, James T and Richard F. Curtis . *A Sociology of Belief* Wiley. New York. (1975)

Bourdieu, Pierre. *Language and Symbolic Power.* Cambridge, Mass: Harvard University Press, (1991)

Galtung, J. and C. G. Jacobsen eds *Searching For Peace: The Road to Transcend.* London: Pluto Press, (2000)

Brynen, Rex. *A Very Political Economy: Peacebuilding and Foreign Aid in the West Bank and Gaza.* Washington D.C.: United States Institute of Peace, (2000)

———. *Echoes of the Intifada: Regional Repercussions of the Palestinian-Israeli Conflict* Boulder, Co.: Westview Press, (1991)

———. "The Dynamics of Palestinian Elite Formation" *Journal of Palestine Studies* vol. 24 no. 3, (Spring, 1995): 31-43

———. Rex "Adjusting to a New World Order: the PLO and the Twilight of the Soviet Union," in *The Decline of the USSR and the Transformation of the Middle East* ed. David Goldberg and Pail Marantz Boulder, Colo.: Westview Press, (1994)

Budeiri, Musa. "The Palestinians. Tensions Between Nationalist and Religious Identities." In *Rethinking Nationalism in the Arab Middle East.* Eds. James Jankowski and Israel Gershoni. New York: Columbia University Press, (1997): 191-206

Burke, Edmund, III and Ira M. Lapidus *Islam, Politics, and Social Movements* Berkeley: University of California Press, (1988)

Childress, James *Moral Responsibility in Conflicts: Essays on Nonviolence, War ad Conscience.* Baton Rouge, Louisiana State University Press: (1982)

Chittick, William C. "Theological Roots of Peace and War According to Islam." *The Islamic Quarterly* vol.34, no. 3, (Third Quarter, 1990): 145-163

Churchill, R. Paul. "Interpreting the Jehad of Islam: Militarism versus Muslim Pacifism," *The ACORN: Journal of the Gandhi-King Society.* vol. 6, no.2, (Fall, 1991): 20-28

Clegg, S. *Frameworks Of Power*, London: Sage, (1989)

Cobban, H. *The Palestinian Liberation Organization: People, Power and Politics.* Cambridge: Cambridge University Press, (1984)

Cohen, Anthony. *The Symbolic Construction of Community: Key Ideas* ed.er Hamilton. Ellis Horwood Ltd. And Tavistock Publications Ltd./Routledge, (1985, 1989.)

Cohen, Jean L. *"Strategy or Identity: New Theoretical Paradigms and Contemporary Social Movements."* n *Social Research* vol. 52, (1985): 663-716

Cohen R. *Negotiating Across Cultures: Communication Obstacles in International Diplomacy* Washington D.C.: United States Institute of Peace, (1991)

———. *Culture and Conflict in Egyptian/Israeli Relations* Bloomington: Indiana University Press, (1990)

———. *International Negotiation* (second edition) Washington D.C.: United States Institute of Peace, (1997)

Cohen, Abner. *Arab Border Villages in Israel: A Study of Continuity ad Change in Social Organization.* Manchester: Manchester University Press. (1965)

Colebrook, C. *New Literary Histories*, Manchester: Manchester University Press, (1997.)

Coleman, James. *"Social Theory, Social Research, and Theory of Action"* in *American Journal of Sociology.* vol. 91, (1986): 1309-1335

Combs-Schilling, M. Elaine "Sacred Refuge: the Power of a Muslim Female Saint" in *Fellowship* vol. 60, (May/ June, 1994): 5-6

Committee of Muslim Scholars (Assisted by Mahmud Y. Zayid). *The Quran: An English Translation of the Meaning of the Quran.* Lebanon: Dar al-Choura, (1980)

Cox, Harvey, AbdulAziz Sachedina, Arvind Sharma, Moshe Idel and Massao Abe. *World Religions and Conflict Resolution.* Paper produced for the Center for Strategic and International Studies. *Program on Religion and Conflict Resolution.* (August 31, 1992)

Cunningham, Robert B. and Yasin K Sarayrah. *Wasta: The Hidden Force in the Middle Eastern Society.* Preager Publishers. Westport, CT. (1993.)

Crenshaw, Martha. "The Causes of Terrorism." *Comparative Politics.* Vol. 13, (1981): 379-99

———. "An Organizational Approach to the Analysis of Political Terrorism." *Orbit.* 29, (1985): 465-489

———. "Theories and Terrorism: Instrumental and Organizational Approaches". In David Rappaport, eds. *Inside Terrorist Organizations.,* Columbia University Press. New York, (1988): 13-31

———. "The Subjective Reality of Terrorists: Ideological and Psychological Factors in Terrorism." In *Current Perspectives on International Terrorism* eds. Robert O. Slater and Michael Stohl, London: Macmillan, (1988): 12-46

Crow, Karim Douglas. "Islamic Ethics and Changing Behavior" in International Journal of Nonviolence. 3 (Third issue), (1996): 72-87

———. "Divided Discourse: Muslim Discussion On Islam And Peace," *Nonviolence International,* unpublished paper. Washington D.C July, (1997)

———. Ralph E., Philip Grant, and Saad Eddin Ibrahim eds. *Arab Nonviolent Political Struggle in the Middle East.* Boulder, CO.: Lynne Rienner, (1990)

Curl, A. *Making Peace* London: Tavistock Publications, (1971)

Dajani, Souad R. *Eyes Without a Country: Searching for a Palestinian Strategy of Liberation.* Philadelphia: Temple University Press, (1994)

Davidson, Lawrence. *Islamic Fundamentalism.* Westport, Connecticut: Greenwood Press, (1998)

Davies, Joyce M. *Between Jihad and Salaam: Profiles in Islam.* St. Martin's Griffin, (1999)

Della Porta, Donatella. *Social Movements, Political Violence, and the State: A Comparative Analysis of Italy and Germany.* New York: Cambridge University Press, (1995.)

———. *"Institutional Responses to Terrorism: The Italian Case." Terrorism and Political Violence.* Vol. 4, (1992): 151-170

Della Porta Donatella eds. *Social Movements and Violence: Participation in Underground Organizations.* Greenwich Conn. JAI Press. (1992.)

Della Porta Donatella and Dieter Rucht. "Left Libertarian Movements in Context: Comparing Italy and West Germany, 1965-1990." *Discussion Paper FS III* No.91-102. Wissenschaftszentrum Berlin, (1991.)

Denzin, Norman K. and Yvonna S. Lincoln eds *Handbook of Qualitative Research,* London: Sage Publications, (1994)

Der Derian, James, *Antidiplomacy: Spies, Terror, Speed, and War* Cambridge and Oxford: Blackwell, (1992)

Dessouki, Ali E. Halil "The Resurgence of Islamic Organizations in Egypt." in *Islam ad Power* Alexander S. Cudsi ad Ali E. Hillal Dessouki eds. Baltimore: John Hopkins University Press, (1981)

Diani, Mario, and Ron Eyman eds. *Studying Social Movements*. London: Sage, (1992)

Dickey, Christopher "Inside Suicide, Inc." *Newsweek* at http://www.msnbc.com/news/735266.asp, (2002)

Donnan, Hastings ed. *Interpreting Islam.* London: Sage Publications, (2002)

Donner, Fred M. "The Sources of Islamic Conceptions of War" in *Just War and Jihad: Historical and Theoretical Perspectives on War and Peace in Western and Islamic Traditions.* Eds. John Kelsay and James Turner Johnson New York: Greenwood Press, (1991): 31-69

Doob, L. W. *Resolving Conflicts in Africa: The Fermeda Workshop.* New Haven, CT: Yale Univ. Press, (1970)

Dougherty, James E. and Robert L. Pfaltzgraff, Jr. eds. *Contending Theories of International Relations: A Comprehensive Survey.* (Fourth Edition) Longman, (1996)

Drummond, James. "Martyrdom Debate Points to Harder Islamic Line" *The Muslim News* 04/04/2002 at http://.muslimnews.co.uk/news/news.php?article=2134, (2002.)

Easwaran, Eknath. *A Man to Match His Mountains: Badshah Khan: Nonviolent Soldier of Islam* Petaluma, California: Nilgiri Press, (1984)

Edwards, Beverly-Milton. *Islamic Politics in Palestine.* London: Tauris Academic Studies, (1996)

Eickelman, Dale F. and James Piscatori. *Muslim Politics.* Princeton, N.J.: Princeton University Press, (1996)

Ellingson, Stephen "Understanding the Dialectic of Discourse and Collective Action: Public Debate and Rioting in Antebellum Cincinnati," in *Social Movements: Readings on Their Emergence, Mobilization and Dynamics.* Eds. Dough McAdam and David A. Snow. Los Angeles, CA. Roxbury Publishing Company, (1997): 268-280

el-Tigani Mahmoud, Mahgoub Dr. "Islamic Law, Human Rights and International Law: A Critique of Mahmoud Taha and An-Naim Part II" in *Islamica. The Journal of The Islamic Society of The London School of Economics in Association with the Muslim Academic Trust* Vol.2 No.4, (Spring 1998): 62-71

Erikson, Bonnie H. "Secret Societies and Social Structures." *Social Forces.* Vol. 60, (1981): 188-210

Esack, Farid. *Quran, Liberation, and Pluralism: An Islamic Perspective of Interreligious Solidarity Against Oppression* Oxford, Oneworld Press, (1998)

Esposito, John. *The Islamic Threat: Myth or Reality?* Oxford University Press. New York, (1992)

———. *Islam and Politics.* Syracuse, New York: Syracuse University Press, (1991)

———. *Islam: The Straight Path.* (Third Edition) Oxford: Oxford University Press, (1998)

Esposito John ed. 1983.*Voices of Resurgent Islam* New York: Oxford University Press, (1983)

Farrag, A. "The Wastah Among Jordanian Villagers." in *Patrons and Clients* E. Gellner and J. Waterbury eds. London: Duckworth, (1977)

Farsoun, Samih K. and Christina E. Zacharia *Palestine and the Palestinians.* Westview Press, (1997)

al Faruqi Isma'il Raji. *Al Tawhid: Its Implications for Thought and Life* Herndon, Va.: International Institute of Islamic Thought fifth printing, (2000)

Faure, G. O. and J. Z. Rubin *Culture and Negotiation* Thousand Oaks, CA: Sage. (1993)

Fernea, Elizbeth W. and Mary E. Hocking *The Struggle for Peace: Israelis and Palestinians.* Austin, TX.: University of Texas Press, (1992)

Finkelstien, N. G. *Image and Reality of Israeli-Palestinian Conflict* Vondon: Verso, (1995)

Fisher R. J. and L Keashley. "The Potential Complementarity of Mediation and Consultation Within a Contingency Model of Third Party Intervention." In *Journal of Peace Research.* Vol. 28 No. 1, (1991): 29-42

Fischer, Micheal M. J. and Mehdi Abedi *Debating Muslims: Cultural Dialogues in Postmodernity and Tradition* Madison: University of Wisconsin Press, (1990)

Flapan, S. *The Birth of Israel: Myths and Realities* New York: Pantheon, (1987)

Francis, Dana ed. *Mediating Deadly Conflict*, World Peace Foundation, (1998)

Folberg, Jay and Alison Taylor. *Mediation.* San Francisco: Jossey-Bass, (1984)

Foucault, M. *Archeology of Knowledge and Discourse on Language* New York: Pantheon Books, (1972)

———. *History of Sexuality: An Introduction, Volume I.* New York: Vintage Books, (1978)

———. *Power/Knowledge: Selected Interviews and Other Writings 1972-1977.* London: Harvester Press, (1980)

Fox, Jonathan. "The Influence of Religious Legitimacy on Grievance Formation by Ethno-Religious Minorities" *Journal of Peace Research* vol. 36 no. 3, (1999): 289-307

———. "The Salience of Religious Issues in Ethnic Conflicts: Large-N Study" *Nationalism and Ethnic Politics* vol. 3 no. 3, (1997): 1-19

Francis, Dana ed. *Mediating Deadly Conflict* World Peace Foundation, (1998)

Franck, Thomas. "Legitimacy in the International System" in *American Journal of International Law*. Vol. 82, (1988)

Fry, Douglas P. and Kaj Bjorkqvist eds. *Cultural Variation in Conflict Resolution: Alternatives to Violence* Mahvah, NJ: Lawrence Erlbaum Associates, (1997)

Gadamer, Hans-Georg. *Truth and Method.* Tans. Joel Weinsheimer and Donald G. Marshall. Second revised edition New York: Crossroad, (1989)

———. Universality of the Hermeneutical Problem (1966)" in *Philosophical Hermeneutics: Hans Georg Gadamer* translated and ed. By David E. Linge. Los Angeles: University of California Press, (1997): 3-17

Galtung, J. *Solving Conflicts: A Peace Research Perspective* Honolulu: Hawa'i (1989)

———. "Peace and Conflict Research in the Age of The Cholera: Ten Pointers to the Future of Peace Studies." in *Peace and Conflict Studies* Vol. 2 No.1 (June, 1995) at http://www.gmu.edu/academic/ijps/vol1_1/Galtung.htm

———. "Violence, Peace and Peace Research" in *Journal of Peace Research*. Vol. 6 No.3 (1996): 167-191

Galtung J and C. G. Jacobsen eds. In Searching *For Peace: The Road to Transcend.* London: Pluto Press. (2000)

al-Ghannouchi, Rachid "The Battle Against Islam, " in *Middle East Affairs Journal* Vol.1 No. 2 (Winter, 1993)

al-Ghunaimi, Muhammad Talaat. *The Muslim Conception of International Law and the Western Approach.* Martinus Nijhoff, The Haugue, (1968)

Geertz, Clifford. *Interpretation of Cultures*. New York: Basic Books, (1973)

———. "Centers, Kings and Charisma: Reflections on the Symbolics of Power" in *Culture and its Creators* Joseph Ben-David and Terry Nichols Clark eds. Chicago, IL.: University of Chicago Press, (1977)

Gerber, Haim *The Social Origins if the Modern Middle East* Boulder, CO.: Lynne Rienner, (1987)

Giddens, Anthony; *The Nation-State and Violence;* Berkeley: University of California Press, (1987)

Gerner, Deborah J. *Understanding the Contemporary Middle East.* London: Lynne Reinner Publishers, (2000)

Gershoni, Israel. "The Muslim Brothers and the Arab Revolt in Palestine, 1936-1939" *Middle Eastern Studies* vol. 22, (1986): 367-397

Ginat, Joseph *Blood Disputes among Bedouin and Rural Arabs in Israel: Revenge, Mediation, Outcasting and Family Honor* Pittsburgh, PA: University of Pittsburgh Press, (1987)

Gopin, Marc. Confronting the Secular/Religious Conflict in Israel: Suggested Solutions." In *Religious Secular Relations in Israel: Social and Political Implications*, Ephraim Ya'ar and Tamar Herman ed. Tel Aviv: Steinmetz Center for Peace Research, Tel Aviv University, and the Konrad Adenauer Foundation, (1998): 81-94

———. "*Religion, Violence, and Conflict Resolution*" in Peace and Change. vol. 22. no.1, (January 1991): 1-31

———. "Forgiveness as an Element of Conflict Resolution in Religious Cultures: Walking the Tightrope of Reconciliation and Justice." Unpublished paper delivered Feb 19, at American University, (1999)

———. *Between Eden and Armageddon: The Future of World Religions, Violence, and Peacemaking.* Oxford University Press, (2000)

———. *Holy War Holy Peace* Oxford University Press, (2002)

Graham Allen. *Inter-textuality.* London: Routledge, (2000)

Gresh, Alain *The PLO: The Struggle Within* A. M. Berrett trans. London: Zed Books, (1985)

Groom, A.J.R. "Problem Solving in International Relations," *International Conflict Resolution: Theory and Practice,* eds. Edward E. Azar & John W. Burton. Sussex: Wheatsheaf Books, (1986)

Groom A.J.R. and Keith Webb "Injustice, Empowerment and Facilitation in Conflict" in *International Interactions.* vol. 13, no. 3, (1987): 263-280

Groves, Joseph W. "Nonviolence in an Islamic Context: A Study of the Palestinian Intifada" Unpublised Paper October 6, 1(989)

Habbeb, William Mark *Power and Tactics in International Negotiation; How Weak Nations Bargain With Strong Nations.* London: The John Hopkins University Press, (1988)

Habermas J. *Legitimation Crisis* Oxford: Polity Press, (1988)

Haddad, Yvonne Y. "Sayyid Qutb: Ideologue of Islamic Revival" in Esposito ed. *Voices of Resurgent Islam* New York: Oxford University Press, (1983): 67-98

Haddad, Yvonne Y., Byron Haines, and Ellison Findley eds. *The Islamic Impact* Syracuse, N.Y.: Syracuse University Press, (1984)

al-Hakim Suad. "Islam and Peace" Paper presented at the Symposium *Islam and Peace in the 21st Century.* Trans.Tara Aziz and Karim Crow, February, (1998)

Hamidullah, Muhammad. *Muslim Conduct of State* Lahore: Sh. Muhammad Ashraf, 3rd ed, (1953): 164-165

Hamzeh, A. Nizar ad R. H. Dekmejan. "A Sufi Response to Political Islamism: Al Ahbash of Lebanon *International Journal of Middle East Studies* Vol. 28, No. 2 (May, 1996): 217-229

Hanafi, Hassan. *Islam, Religious Dialogue and Liberation Theology, and Islam and Reconciliation.* Birmingham: Center for the Study of Islam and Christian-Muslim Relations, (1997)

———. "Arab Nationalist Thought in the Balance," *Qadaya Arabiyya*, (March-April 1978)

Hannigan, John, A. "Social Movement Theory and the Sociology of Religion: Toward a New Synthesis" *Sociological Analysis* vol. 52 no. 4, (1991): 311-331

Harkabi, Y. *Fedayeen Action and Arab Strategy* London: Institute for Strategic Studies, (1968)

Hashmi, Sohail. "Is There an Islamic Ethic of Humanitarian Intervention?" *Ethics and International Affairs.* Vol.7, (1993):55-73

———. "Interpreting the Islamic Ethics of War and Peace." In *Ethics of War and Peace: Religious and Secular Perspectives.* Ed.Terry Nardin. Princeton: Princeton University Press, (1996)

Hazrat Mirza Tahir Ahmad *Murder in the Name of Allah.* trans. Syed Barakat Ahmat Cambridge: Lutterworth Press, (1990)

Hefner, Robert W and Patricia Horvatich ed. *Islam in an Era of Nation-States: Politics and Religious Renewal in Muslim Southeast Asia.* Honolulu: University of Hawa'i Press, 1997

Heiberg, m and G. Ovensen. *Palestinian Society in Gaza, West Bank and Arab Jerusalem: A Survey of Living Conditions* FAFO Report 151 Oslo: FAFO, (1993)

Helick, Raymond G. S. ed. *The Role of Religious Values in the Search for Peace* (Panel Discussion from Convocation, "Towards Peace in the Middle East. held at Boston College, February 16) Philadelphia, PA.: The U.S. Interreligious Committee for Peace in the Middle East, (1990)

Hill, B. J. "An Analysis of Conflict Resolution Techniques: From Problem-Solving Workshops to Theory." *Journal of Conflict Resolution* vol. 26, no. 1, 109-138 (March, 1982)

Hobbes. *Leviathan* London: Penguin Classics, 1651, reprint (1985)

Hoffman, Valerie. "Muslim Fundamentalists: Psychological Profiles." in *Fundamentalisms Comrehended* volume 5 of *The Fundamentalism Project,* Martin Marty and Scott Appleby eds., Chicago, IL.: University of Chicago Press, (1995): 199-230

Holsti, K. J. *International Politics: A Framework for Analysis.* Eaglewood Cliffs, NJ: Prentice-Hall, (1967)

Hourani, Albert. "Ottoman Reform and the Politics of Notables." In *Beginnings of Modernization in the Middle East.* William R. Polk and Richard L. Chambers eds. Chicago: University of Chicago Press, (1968)

———. *Arabic Thought in the Liberal Age, 1798-1939* Rev. ed. London: Oxford University Press, 1971

Hroub, Khaled *Hamas: Political Thought and Practice* Washington, D.C.: Institute for Palestine Studies, (2000)

Hudson, M. ed. *The Palestinians: New Directions* Washington, D.C.: Center for Contemporary Arab Studies, Georgetown University, (1990)

Humphreys, R. Stephen. *Between Memory and Desire: The Middle East in A Troubled Age* Berkeley, CA.: University of California Press, 1999

Hunter, Robert F. *The Palestinian Uprising: A War by Other Means* Berkeley, LA: University Press of California, (1991)

Huntington, Samuel "If Not Civilization, What?" in *Foreign Affairs* Vol.72 No. 5, (December-November, 1993): 186-194

Hurewitz, J. C. *The Struggle for Palestine* New York: W. W. Norton, (1950)

Ibn Asakir, *Ta'rikh Madinat Dimashq* Damascus, (1977)

Ibn Hanbal. *Kitab al Sunna* Cairo, n.d.

Institute for Social and Economic Policy in the Middle East, John F. Kennedy School of Government, Harvard University, *Securing Peace in the Middle East: Project on Economic Transition* Cambridge: Harvard University Press, (1993)

Imad-ad Dean, Ahmad. "Building Muslim Civil Society from the Bottom Up" Paper presented at the Meeting of the American Muslim Social Scientists Washington D.C: Georgetown University October 13-15 at http://www.minaret.org/CivilSociety.htm, (2000)

Israeli, Raphael. *Muslim Fundamentalism in Israel.* London: Brassey's, (1993)

Iqbal, Afzal. *Diplomacy in Early Islam.* (Fifth Edition) New Delhi. India: International Islamic Publishers, (1992)

———. *Diplomacy in Islam: The Art of Negotiation as Conceived and Developed by the Prophet.* Lahore: Institute of Islamic Culture, (1965)

Iqbal, Muhammed *Six Lectures on the Reconstruction of Religious Thought in Islam* Ashraf Lahore, (1986)

Irani, George. *"Reconciliation and Peace: Rituals For the Middle East."* in *Middle East Insight.*, (September-October. 1998):24-26

———. "Islamic Mediation Techniques for Middle Eastern Conflicts" *MERIA (Middle East Review of International Affairs) Journal* Vol. 3 No. 2 at http://www.bui.ac.il/SOC/meria/journal/1999/issue2/jv3n2a1.html (June 1999)

Irani, George E. and Nathan C. Funk. "Rituals of Reconciliation: Arab-Islamic Perspectives" in Said, *Peace and Conflict Resolution in Islam: Precept and Practice* Abdul Aziz, et. al .eds. New York: University Press of America. (2001): 169-191

Jabbour. Elias. *Sulh: Palestinian Traditional Peacemaking Process*: Israel: House of Hope Publications, (1996)

Jabri, Vivienne. *Discourses On Violence: Conflict Analysis Reconsidered*, Manchester University Press, (1996)

Jamilah Jitmoud. " Principles of Jihad in the Quran and Sunnah" in *State Politics and Islam* Mumtaz Ahmad ed., (American Trust Publications, n.d):133- 146

Janowski, James and Israel Gershoni eds. *Rethingking Nationalism in the Arab Middle East.* New York: Columbia University Press, (1997)

Johansen, Robert C. *"Radical Islam and Nonviolence: A Case Study of Religious Empowerment and Constraint Among Pashtuns"* in *Journal of Peace Research* Vol. 34. No. 1, (1997):53-71

Johnston, Douglas M. *Religion and Conflict Resolution* Paper presented at Fletcher Forum of World Affairs. (Winter/Spring 1996)

Johnston, Douglas M, and Cynthia Sampson eds. *Religion, The Missing Dimension of Statecraft.* Oxford University Press. New York. (1994)

Juergensmeyer, Mark Terror in the Mind of God: The Global Rise of Religious Violence University of California Press,(2000)

———. Fightng Fair: A Nonviolent Strategy for Resolving Everyday Conflicts. San Francisco: Harper and Row, (1986)

———. *The New Cold War?* Berkeley, CA: University of California Press, (1993)

Kadayifci-Orellana S. Ayse, "Religion, Violence and the Islamic Tradition of Nonviolence" Turkish yearbook of International Relations No.34, (2003)

Kane, Anne E. "The Centrality of Culture in Social Theory" in *Social Theory and Sociology: The Classics and Beyond.* Stephen P. Turner eds. Blackwell Publishers, (1996): 161-180

Kazziha, W. *Palestine in the Arab Dilemma* New York: Barnes and Nobles, (1979)

———. *Revolutionary Transformation in the Arab World: Habash and His Comrades from Nationalism to Marxism* London: Charles Knight, (1975)

Kelley, Jack. "Devotion, Desire Drive Youths to 'Martyrdom'" *USA TODAY* 07/05/2001 (2001)

Kelman, Herbert C. The Interactive Problem-Solving Approach. In C.A. Crocker and F.O. Hampson and P. Aall. eds. *Managing Global Chaos: Sources of and Responses to International Conflict:.* Washington, DC: United States Institute of Peace Press,(1996): 501-519

———. Interactive Problem-Solving: A Social -Psychological Approach to Conflict Resolution. In. *Conflict: Readings in Management and Resolution* J. Burton and F. Dukes: New York: St. Martin's Press. (1990): 199-215

———. "Contributions of An Unofficial Conflict Resolution Effort to the Israeli-Palestinian breakthrough" *Negotiation Journal* Vol. 11, No. 1 (January 1995): 19-27

———. "Social-Psychological Dimensions of International Conflict" in *Peacemaking in International Conflict: Methods and Techniques.* eds. I. William Zartman, J. Lewis Rasmussen. Washington D.C.: United States Institute of Peace Press, (1997): 191-238

Kelsay, John and James Turner eds. *Just War and Jihad: Historical and Theoretical Perspectives on War and Peace in Western and Islamic Traditions.* New York: Greenwood Press, (1991)

Kepel, G. *The Revenge of God, The Resurgence of Islam, Christianity and Judaism in the Modern World.* Cambridge, (1994)

Khadduri, Majid. *War and Peace in the Law of Islam.* The John Hopkins Press. Baltimore, MD. 1955

———. *Islamic Law of Nations: Shaybani's Siyar.* The John Hopkins Press. Baltimore. MD. (1966)

———. "The Islamic Theory of International Relations and Its Contemporary Relevance," in *Islam and International Relations.* J. Harris eds. Frederick A. Preager Inc. (1965)

———. "Sulh" in *The Encyclopedia of Islam. vol IX* C.E. Bosworth, E. van Donzel, W.P. Heinrichs, and the late G. Lecomte, 845-846 Holland: Brill. Leiden. (1997)

———. "Theory of State" in Abdul Aziz Said et al.eds. *Peace and Conflict Resolution in Islam: Precept and Practice*: 35-38 New York: University Press of America. (2001)

Khalaf, I. *Politics in Palestine* Albany: SUNY, (1991)

Khalidi, R. "A Palestinian View of the Accord with Israel" *Current History* Vol. 93, (February, 1949):62-66

Khalidi, T. ed. *Land Tenure and Social Transformation in the Middle East* Beirut: American University of Beirut, (1984)

Khan, Inamullah. "Nuclear War and the Defense of Peace: The Muslim View," in *International Peace Research Newsletter* vol. 23, no. 2 (April 1985)

Khan, Mohammed A. Muqtedar. "*Peace and Change in the Islamic World*" paper presented at the conference *Islam and Peace in the 15/20th century.* Washington DC. (February 6- 7, 1997)

Khan, Maulana Wahiduddin. "Non-Violence and Islam" Paper prepared for the Symposium: *Islam and Peace in the 21st Century* Washington D.C. (February 6-7, 1998)

el-Khatib, Husam "The Jurisdiction of Classical Islam" in *Islamica* Vol. 3 No. 1, (Summer 1999): 79-88

Khuri, Richard. *Freedom, Modernity, and Islam: Toward a Creative Synthesis.* Syracuse: Syracuse University Press, (1998)

King, Martin Luther, Jr. "Nonviolence and Racial Justice" in *Christian Century.* (February 1957)

Kipper Judith ad Harold H. Saunders eds. *The Middle East in Global Perspective* Westview Press, (1991)

Klandermans, Bert. "The Social Construction of Protest and Multiorganizational Fields in A.D. Morris and C.McClurg eds. Frontiers of Social Movement Theory. New Haven. Conn.: Yale University Press, (1992):77-103

———. "The Formation and Mobilization of Consensus," in Bert Klandermans, H. Kreisi and S. Tarrow eds. *International Social Movement Research*, Vol. I, Greenwich, Conn.: JAI Press, (1988): 77-92

Kishtani, Khalid. *Towards Nonviolence*. Amman: Dar al-Karmil, (1984)

Kristianasen, Wendy. "Challenge and Counterchallenge: Hamas's Response to Oslo" in *Journal of Palestine Studies*. Vol 28, No 3, (Spring, 1999): 19-35

Kokosolakis, Nikos. "Legitimation, Power and Religion in Modern Society," *Sociological Analysis* Vol. 46 No.4, (Winter1985): 367-376

Kolas, Ashild. "Tibetian Nationalism: The Politics of Religion" in *Journal of Peace Research* Vol. 33. No.1, (1996): 51-66

Kuftaro, Sheikh Ahmad. "Islam is Always for Peace and for Reconciliation...An Interview with Sheikh Ahmad Kuftaro" *The World and I*. Vol. 6, (February, 1991): 532-533

Lang, Chris. n.d. www.xenos.org/essays/litthry3.htm,2

Lapidus, Ira. *Contemporary Islamic Movements in Historical Perspective*. Center of International Studies. University of California, Berkeley (1983)

Lazarus-Yafeh, Hava "Contemporary Fundamentalism in Judaism, Christianity, Islam." in *Jarusalem Quarterly*. No. 47, (Summer 1988): 27-39

Lederach, J. P. *Preaparing for Peace: Conflict Transformation Across Cultures*. Syracuse: Syracuse University Press, (1995)

———. *Building Peace: Sustainable Reconciliation in Divided Society*. United States Institute of Peace Press. (1997)

Le Strange, G. *Palestine Under Moslems* London: A. P. Watt, (1890)

Lincold, Bruce. *Religion, Rebellion, and Revolution*. London: Macmillan. (1985)

Little, David. *Ukraine: The Legacy of Intolerance*. Washington D.C.: United States Institute of Peace Press. (1991)

Little, David, John Kelsay and Abdulaziz A. Sachedina. *Human Rights ad the Conflict of Cultures: Western and Islamic Perspectives on Religious Liberty*. Columbia, South Carolina: University of South Carolina, (1988)

Lockman, Z. and J. Beinin, eds. *Intifada: The Palestinian Uprising Against Israeli Occupation* Boston: South End Press, 1989

Louat. M Safi. "Islam and Peace' in *Islamic Horizons*, (September/October 1996):42-43

Lund, M. S. *Preventing Violent Conflicts* Washington D.C.: United States Institute of Peace. (1996)

Lustick, I. S. ed. *The Conflict with Israel in Arab Politics and Society* New York: Garland, 1994

———. *From Wars Towards Peace in the Arab-Israeli Conflict 1969-1993* New York: Garland, (1994)

Malik, Iftikhar H. *"Islamic Discourse on Jihad, War and Violence"* in *Journal of South Asian and Middle Eastern Studies* Vol. 21, No. 4, (Summer 1998): 47-78

Mallison, W. T. and S. V. Mallison *he Palestine Problem in International Law abd World Order* New York: Longman, (1986)

Mandaville, Peter. *Transnational Muslim Politics: Reimagining the Umma*. London: Routledge. (2001.)

Mardin Serif. *Religion and Social Change in Modern Turkey: The Case of Bediuzzaman Said Nursi* State University of New York Press. (1989)

Marty, Martin E. "Fundamentalism as a Social Phenomenon." *Bulletin of the American Academy of Arts and Sciences.* vol. 42, (1988): 15-29

Mattar, Philip. *Mufti of Jerusalem: Al-Hajj Amin Al-Husayni and the Palestinian National Movement.* New York: Columbia University Press. (1988)

McHoul, Alec and Wendy Grace. *A Foucault Primer: Discourse, power and the subject.* London: UCL Press. (1993)

Mellucci, Alberto. *Nomads of the Present: Social Movements and Individual Needs in Contemporary Society.* Hutchinson Radius. London. (1989.)

———. "Getting Involved: Identity and Mobilization in Social Movements" in *From Structure to Action: Comparing Social Movement Research across Cultures.* Bert Klandermans, Hanspeter Kreisi, and Sidney Torrow eds. Vol.1 of *International Social Movement Research* JAI Press Greenwich, Conn. (1988)

Mellucci, Alberto. "The Symbolic Challenge of Contemporary Movements" in Social Research. vol. 52, (1985): 789-816

Meyer, Ann Elizabeth "The Fundamentalist Impact on Law, Politics, and Constitutions in Iran, Pakistan, and the Sudan." In *Fundamentalism and the State: Remaking Polities, Economies and Militancy.* Martin Marty and Scott Appleby, eds. Chicago: Chicago University Press, (1992)

Migdal, J. S., ed. *Palestinian Society and Politics* Princeton, NJ: Princeton University Press, (1980)

Mitchell, Richard P. *The Society of Muslim Brothers* London: Oxford University Press. (1969)

MirzaBashir-ud-Din Mamud Ahmad. *Introduction to the Study of Holy Qur'an.* Islam International Publications Ltd. (1996)

Moaddel, Mansoor and Kamran Talattof eds. *Contemporary Debates in Islam: An Anthology of Modernist and Fundamentalist Thought.* New York: St. Martin's Press. (2000)

Moore, Christopher. W. *The Mediation Process: Practical Strategies for Resolving Conflict.* San Francisco: Jossey-Bass, (1986)

Morgan, Peter "Contested Native Forests: A Theoretical and Empirical Study", PhD dissertation, published by Mcmullan bros. at www.mcmullan.net/pmorgan/ (1997)

Morgenthau, Hans J. *Politics Among Nations: The Struggle for Power and Peace*. Fifth edition. New York: Alfred A. Knopf, (1973)

Morris, B. *1948 and After* New York: Oxford University Press, (1987)

Mousalli, Ahmad S. "An Islamic Model for Political Conflict Resolution: Tahkim (Arbitration)" in Paul Salem eds. *Conflict Resolution in the Arab World: selected Essays.* American University of Beirut. Lebanon. (1997.)

Moulavi Chiragh Ali "War and Peace: Popular Jihad" in. *Contemporary Debates in Islam: An Anthology of Modernist and Fundamentalist Thought* Moaddel, Mansoor and Kamran Talattof eds. New York: St. Martin's Press, (2000)

Muslih, M. Y. *The Origins of Palestinian Nationalism* New York: Columbia University Press, (1988)

Nachmani, Amikam. "The Palestinian *Intifada* 1987-1993: The Dynamics of Symbols and Symbolic Realities, The Role of Symbols, Rituals and Myths in National Struggles" *Civil Wars* Vol. 4 No. 1, (Spring, 2001): 49-103

Nardin, Terry *Peace: The Ethics of War and Peace: Religious and Secular Perspectives.* Princeton University Press, (1996)

Nasr, Sayyed Hossein. *Islam and the Plight of Modern Man.* Longman. London. (1972)

———. *Traditional Islam in the Modern World.* London: KPI. (1987)

Nietzsche, Fredriech *In the Genealogy of Morals and Ecce Homo* Walter Kaufmann trans. New York: Vintage Books, (1989)

Norton, Augustus R. ed. *Civil Society in the Middle East* (Two Volumes) New York: Brill, (1995)

Nusse, Andrea. *Muslim Palestine: The Ideology of Hamas* (Australia: Harwood Academic Publishers, (1998)

———. "The Ideology of Hamas: Palestinian Islamic Fundamentalist Thought on the Jews, Israel, and Islam" In *Studies in Muslim- Jewish Relations,* Oxford, (1993): 97-125

Ott, Mervin C "Mediation as a Method of Conflict Resolution." *International Organization* Vol.26 No.4, (1972): 595-618

Ovensen, G. *Responding to Change, Trends in Palestinian Household Economy,* FAFO Report 166 Oslo: FAFO, (1994)

Palumbo, M. *The Palestinian Catastrophe: The 1948 Expulsion of a People from Their Homeland* London: Quartet Books, (1987)

Peters, Rudolph. *Islam and Colonialism: The Doctrine of Jihad in Modern History* The Hague: Mouton, (1979)

Peters, Rudolph ed. *Jihad in Classical and Modern Islam: A Reader.* Princeton. NJ, (1996)

Piscatori, James P. *Islam in a World of Nation-States.* Cambridge University Press. New York, (1986.)

———. *Law, Personalities, and Politics of the Middle East: Essays in Honor of Majid Khadduri* Boulder, CO.: Westview, (1987)

Porath, Y. *The Emergence of the Palestinian Arab National Movement, 1918-1929* London: Frank Cass, (1974)

Porath, T. "Social Aspects of the Emergence of the Palestinian Arab National Movement" in *Society and Political Structure in the Arab World* Menahem Mislon, ed. New York, (1973): 93-144

Pouluantzas, Nicos. *State, Power, Socialism.* Trans. Patrick Camiller. London, New Left Books, (1980)

Princen, Thomas. *Intermediaries in International Conflict.* Princeton: Princeton University Press, (1992)

Quandt, William B., Fuad Jabber, Ann Mosely Lesch. *The Politics of Palestinian Nationalism.* Berkeley, Los Angeles; University of California Press. (1973)

Qurashi, M.M. "The Concept of Islamic Jehad" in *Islamic Thought and Scientific Creativity,* Vol. 2, No. 1 (1991): 57-71

Qutb, Sayyid *Khassas al-Tassawwur al-Islami wa-muqawwamatuhu* Cairo: Issa la Babi al-Hilabi wa Shurakauhu, (1962)

———. *Nahwa Mujtama Islami* Dar al-Shuruq, Beirut, 2nd printing (1975)

———. *Ma'alim fi al tariq* 13th legal ed. Dar al Shuruq, Cairo (1989)

———. "War, Peace and Islamic Jihad" in *Contemporary Debates in Islam: An Anthology of Modernist and Fundamentalist Thought.* Mansoor Moaddel and Kamran Talattof eds. New York: St. Martin's Press, (2000): 223-245

Rabinow, P and W. M. Sullivan eds. *Interpretive Social Science: A Second Look* Berkeley: University of California Press, (1987)

Rabinowitz, Dan *Overlooking Nazareth: The Ethnography of exclusion in Galilee* Cambridge: Cambridge University Press, (1997)

Rahman Fazlur. *Islam and Modernity: Transformation of an Intellectual Tradition.* (Chicago and London: University of Chicago Press, (1982)

Rapoport, David. "Some General Observations on Religion and Violence. *The Journal of Terrorism and Political Violence.* Vol. 3 No. 3, (1990): 118-139

Rawls. J *A Theory of Justice* Oxford: Oxford University Press, (1971)

el-Rayyes, R. and D. Nahhas. *Guerrillas for Palestine: A Study of the Palestinian Commando Organizations* Beirut: An-Nahar Press, (1974)

Reuck, A. de, "A Theory of Conflict Resolution by Problem-Solving," *Conflict: Readings in Management and Resolution,* John Burton and Frank Dukes eds. New York: MacMillan Press, (1990)

Reuven, Paz. "Saudi Fatwah against Suicide Terrorism. [sic]" *Peace Watch,* The Washington Institute's Special Reports on the Arab-Israeli Peace Process, No. 323, (May 2, 2001)

Richmond, Oliver *Maintaining Order, Making Peace* London: Palgrave, (2002)

Ricoeur, Paul. *Hermeneutics and the Human Sciences*: Edited and Translated by John London and New York: Cambridge University Press, (1982.)

Robinson, Glenn E. *Building a Palestinian State: The Incomplete Revolution.* Bloomington and Indianapolis: Indiana University Press, (1997)

Rothman, J. *Resolving Identity-Based Conflict* San Francisco, CA: Jossey-Bass. (1997)

Roy, Oliver. *The Failure of Political Islam* Cambridge, MA, (1994)

Roy, Sara. *The Gaza Strip: The Political Economy of De-development* Washington D.C.: Institute for Palestinian Studies, (1995)

———. "Transformation of Islamic NGOs in Palestine," in *Middle East Report no. 214 (spring.* at http:/www.merip.org/mer/mer214/pitner_214.html, 2000. (2000)

Rubin, Barry "Religion and International Affairs" in *Religion, The Missing Dimension of Statecraft* eds. Douglas Johnston and Cynthia Sampson New York: Oxford University Press, (1994): 20-34

Rubin, J. D. Pruitt and S. H. Kim *Social Conflict: Escalation, Stalemate and Settlement* New York: McGraw-Hill. (1994)

Rubin J. eds. *Dynamics of Third-Party Intervention: Kissinger in the Middle East.* New York: Praeger, (1981)

Runciman, W. G. "The Sociological Explanation of 'Religious' Beliefs" *Archiv. Europ. Sociol.,* (1969): 149-191

Rupesinghe, Kumar. *Civil Wars, Civil Peace: An Introduction to Conflict Resolution.* London: Pluto Press, (1988)

Sabbagh, Suha ed. *Palestinian Women of Gaza and West Bank.* Bloomington: Indiana University Press, (1998)

Sahlins, M. "The Return of the Event, Again: With Reflections on the Beginnings of the Great Fijian War of 1843 to 1855 between the Kingdoms of Bau and Rewa." Aletta Biersack eds. in *Clio in Oceania: Toward a Historical Anthology.* Washington D.C: Smithsonian, (1991) 37-100

Salem, Paul eds. *Conflict Resolution in the Arab World: selected Essays.* Lebanon: American University of Beirut, (1997)

Sa'id, Jawdat *The Doctrine of the First Son of Adam. The Problem of Violence in Islamic Practice* (Fifth Edition) Dar al Fikr: Damascus, (1993)

———. *"Peace- or Nonviolence- in History and with the Prophets"* Paper written for Conference on *Islamic Values for Change* trans. By Dr. Abduhu Hammud al-Sharif, revised with notes by Dr. Karim Crow. Bi'r Ajam, Qunaytra, Syria. (April 3, 1997)

———. "Law, Religion and the Prophetic Method of Social Change." *Journal of Law and Religion*. Vol. 15 No.1 and 2, (2000-2001): 83-149

———. *The Doctrine of the First Son of Adam: The Problem of Violence in Islamic Practice,* 5th edition. Damascus: Dar al Fikr, (1993)

Said, Abdul Aziz. *Cultural Context of Conflict Resolution: A Reference to an Arab Islamic Perspective.* American University Washington DC. Unpublished paper (n.d.)

———. "Islamic Fundamentalism and the West." *Mediterranean Quarterly: A Journal of Global Issues* Vol. 3 No.4 (Fall, 1992)

Said, Abdul Aziz and Nathan Funk. "Islam and the West: Three Stories" paper presented at the *Conference on the Future of Islam-West Relations.* Center for Strategic Studies (June, 1998)

Said, Abdul Aziz, Nathan C. Funk and S. Ayse Kadayifci .eds. *Peace and Conflict Resolution in Islam: Precept and Practice* New York: University Press of America. (2001)

Said, Abdul Aziz, and Nathan Funk. "Peace in the Sufi Tradition: An Ecology of the Spirit" in Abdul Aziz Said et al.eds. *Peace and Conflict Resolution in Islam: Precept and Practice*: New York: University Press of America. (2001): 247-262

Said, Edwards "The Burdens of Interpretation and the Question of Palestine" paper presented to the conference of International Society of Political Psychology. Amsterdam, (July,1986)

———. *The Nation Feature Story* http://www.thenation.com/doc.mhtml?I=3D20020204&s=3Dsaid (February 4, 2002)

Salmi, Ralph H., Cesar Adib Majul, and George K. Tanham.. *Islam and Conflict Resolution: Theories and Practices* University Press of America. Lanham. (1998)

Salem, Paul ed. *Conflict Resolution in the Arab World: Selected Essays.* Lebanon: American University of Beirut, (1997)

Sampson, Cynthia "Religion and Peace Building" in *Peacemaking in International Conflict: Methods and Techniques.*_W. Zartman and L. Rasmussen eds. United States Institute of Peace Press. Washington DC. (1997): 273-316

Sampson and J. P. Lederach eds. *From the Ground Up: Mennonite Contributions to International Peacebuilding.* New York: Oxford University Press. (2000)

Sandole D. J. D. and H. van der Merwe *Conflict Resolution Theory and Practice* New York: Manchester University Press, (1993)

Sardar, Zaiuddin "The Other Jihad: Muslim Intellectuals and Their Responsibilities" in *Inquiry* (London) Vol. 2 No. 10 (October 1985)

Satha-Anand, Chaiwat. "Core Values for Peacemaking in Islam: The Prophet's Practice as Paradigm". in Elise Boulding eds. *Building Peace in the Middle East: Challenges for the States and Civil Society.* Boulder Co: Lynne Reinner Publishers. (1994)

———. "The Nonviolent Crescent: Eight Thesis on Muslim Nonviolent Action" in Said, *Peace and Conflict Resolution in Islam: Precept and Practice* Abdul Aziz, et. al .eds. 195-211 New York: University Press of America. (2001): 195-211

———. *Islam and Nonviolence*. Tampa, FL.: University of South Florida, (1987)

______. *Nonviolent Crescent: Two Essays on Islam and Nonviolence*. Alkmaar, The Netherlands: International Fellowship of Reconciliation, (1996)

Schelling, Thomas. C. *The Strategy of Conflict*. Cambridge, Mass.: Harvard University Press, (1960)

———. "Constructivist, Interpretivist Approaches to Human Inquiry" in *Handbook of Qualitative Research*, eds. Norman K. Denzin and Yvonna S. Lincoln ondon: Sage Publications, (1994): 118-137

Schwartz. T. "Anthropology and Psychology: An Unrequited Relationship," in T. Schwartz, G. White, and C. Lutz, eds. *New Directions in Psychological Anthropology*. (Cambridge: Cambridge University Press, (1992)

Seligman, Adam B. *Modernity's Wager: Authority, the Self, and Transcendence.* Princeton University Press. Princeton and Oxford. (2000)

Sewell, W.R. "Three Temporalities: Toward an Eventful Sociology," in *The Historic Turn in the Human Science*, ed. T. J. McDonald Ann Arbor: University of Michigan Press, (1996)

Shadid, M. "*The Muslim brotherhood Movement in the West Bank and Gaza*" in *Third World Quarterly*. Vol. 10 No.2 (1988.)

Shalev, Aryeh. *The Intifada: Causes and Effects*. Tel Aviv and Londin: Westview Press, (1991)

Sharoni, Simona and Mohammed Abu-Nimer, "The Israeli-Palestinian Conflict." in *Understanding the Contemporary Middle East*. Ed. Deborah J. Gerner, London: Lynn Reinner Publishers, (2000): 161-200

Sharp, Gene. *The Politics of Nonviolent Action* Boston: P. Sargent Publisher, (1973)

Shapiro, Michael J. "Representing World Politics: The Sport/War Intertext" In *International/Intertextual Relations: Postmodern Readings of World Politics*. Eds. James Der Derian and Michael J. Shapiro New York: Lexington Books, (1989): 69-96

Shifferd, Kent D. "*A Taoist Peace*" in *Religion, War and Peace.* Conference Proceedings. Ripon Collage. Ripon, WI. (November 1-2, 1996): 84-98

———. "The Greater Jihad and the Twentieth-Century Islamic Pacifism." in *Religion, War, and Peace*. Stevens-Point, WI: Wisconsin Institute for Peace and Conflict Studies, (1997)

Shipler, D. *Arab and Jew: Wounded Spirits in a Promised Land* New York: Penguin, (1987)

Shriver Donald W., Jr. "Religion and Violence Prevention" in *Cases and Strategies For Preventive Action* ed. Barnett R. Rubin. New York: The Century Foundation Press, (1998)

Simkin, William E. *Mediation and the Dynamics of Collective Bargaining*. Washington, D.C.: Bureau of National Affairs, (1971)

Singh, N. K. *Peace Through Nonviolent Action in Islam*. Delhi: Adam Publishers and Distributors, (1995)

Sisk, Timothy D. *Islam and Democracy: Religion, Politics, and Power in the Middle East* (Special Middle East Program in Peacemaking and Conflict Resolution with the

Jennings Randolph program for International Peace Washington D.C: United States Institute of Peace Press, (1992)

Sivan, Emmanuel. *Interpretations of Islam: Past and Present..* The Darwin Press, Princeton Jew Jersey, (1985)

———. "Arab Nationalism in the Age of Islamic Resurgence" in James Jankowski and Gershoni eds. in *Rethinking Nationalism in the Arab Middle East.* New York: Columbia University Press, (1997)

Smock, David R. *Religious Perspectives on War.* Washington DC.: United States Institute of Peace, (1992)

Smock, David R. eds. Interfaith Dialogue and Peacebuilding Washington D.C.: United States Institute of Peace Press, (2002)

Smoke, Richard *Paths to Peace: Exploring the Feasibility of Sustainable Peace* Boulder, CO.: Westview Press, (1987)

Snow, David A. and Susan Marshall "Cultural Imperialism, Social Movements, and Islamic Revival" in *Social Movements, Conflicts and Change* ed. Luis Kriesberg. Greenwich, CT.: JAI Press, (1984): 131-152

Snow, David A and Pamela Oliver. *Social Movements and Collective Behavior: Social Psychological Dimensions and Considerations"* in *Sociological Perspectives on Social Psychology.* Eds. K. Cook, G. Fine, and J. House, Boston: Allyn and Bacon, (1995): 571-599

al Sobki, Muhammad Abdul Lateef. "Al Jihad in Islam" *The Fourth Conference of the Academy of Islamic Research* Cairo: Al Azhar Academy of Islamic Research, (1968)

Sonn, Tamara. "Political Authority in Classical Islamic Thought" in *The American Journal of Islamic Social Sciences.* Vol. 13 No. 3, (Fall 1996): 309-324

Starrett, Gregory. *Putting Islam to Work: Education, Politics, and Religious Transformation in Egypt,* Los Angeles: University of California Press, (1998)

Steffek, Jens. *The Power of Rational Discourse and the Legitimacy of International Governance.* Paper presented at the workshop "Analysis of Discourse and Ideas in European and International Affairs" EUI, Florence, (12/13 May 2000)

Sullivan, Denis. "NGOs in Palestine: Agents of Development and Foundations of Civil Society" *Journal of Palestinian Studies* Vol. 25 No.3 (Spring, 1996)

———. "NGOs and Development in the Arab World: the Critical Importance of a Strong Partnership Between Government and Civil Society" at http://www.mideastinfo.com/arabngo.htm. (n.d.)

Spinzak, Ehud *"Models of Religious Violence: The Case of Jewish Fundamentalism in Israel"* in *Fundamentalisms and the State: Remaking Politics, Economies and Militance.* Marty Martin E. and R. Scott Appleby eds, 462-490. Chicago: University of Chicago Press, (1991)

Schwandt, Thomas A., "Constructivist, Interpretivist Approaches to Human Inquiry" in *Handbook of Qualitative Research,* eds. Norman K. Denzin and Yvonna S. Lincoln, London: Sage Publications, (1994): 118-137

Swedenburg, Ted. *Memories of Revolt: The 1936-39 Rebellion and the Palestinian National Past.* Minneapolis: University of Minnesota Press, (1995)

Tamari, Selim. "Palestinian Social Transformations: the Emergence of Civil Society," in *Civil society: Democratization in the Arab World* (A monthly publication of the Ibn Khaldun Center for Development Studies.) at http://www.ibnkhaldun.org/newletter/1999/feb/essay3.html (1999)

Tamimi, Azzam "The Legitimacy of Palestinian Resistance: An Islamic Perspective" paper presented at the 7th *Annual Conference of the Center for Policy Analysis on Palestine*, Washington, D.C. (11 September, 1998)

Tarrow, Sydney. *Power in Movement: Social Movements, Collective Action and Politics.* Cambridge, UK: Cambridge University Press. (1994)

Taraki, Lisa. "The Islamic Resistance Movement in the Palestinian Uprising" *Middle East Report,* (January-February, 1989): 30-32

Taussig, Micheal. *Colonialism, Shamanism, and the Wild Man: A Study in Terror and Healing* Chicago: University of Chicago Press,(1987)

Taylor, C. "Interpretation and the Sciences of Man" in *Interpretive Social Science: A Second Look* eds. P.Rabinow and W. M. Sullivan Berkeley: University of California Press, (1987)

Terri-Harris, Rabia. "Nonviolence in Islam: The Alternative Community" in Daniel L. Smith-Christopher eds. *Subverting Hatred: The Challenge of Nonviolence in Religious Traditions.* (Boston: Boston Research Center for the 21st Century, 1998), 95-113

Tessler, Mark and Jodi Nactwey. "Islam and Attitude toward International Conflict: Evidence from Survey Research in the Arab World" *Journal of Conflict Resolution* vol. 42, no.5., (October, 1988): 619-636

Tibi, Bassam. "War and Peace in Islam" in *The Ethics of War and Peace: Religious and Secular Perspectives* Terry Nardin eds. New Jersey: Princeton University Press Princeton, (1996)

———. "Jihad." in *Protest, Power, and Change* Roger S. Powers and William B. Vogele, eds. New York: Garland Publishing, Inc., (1997)

———. *Arab Nationalism: Between Islam and the Nation-State.* 3rd edition. New York: St. Martin Press, 1997

———. *Arab Nationalism: A Critical Enquiry.* trans. Mario Farouq-Sluglett and Peter Sluglett. New York, (1981)

Tilly, Charles. *From Mobilization to Revolution.* New York: Random House, (1978)

Tylor, Edward. *Primitive Culture* 1870, Reprint Harper and Row: New York. (1958)

UNSCO, *The Economy of West Bank and Gaza Strip: A Retrospective on the 1990s and Future Challenges.*(January, 1999)

Usher, G. *Palestine in Crisis: The Struggle for Peace and Political Independence* London: Pluto Press, (1995)

Varisco, Daniel Martin. "Metaphors and Sacred History of the Genealogy of Muhammad and the Arab "Tribe"" in *Anthropological Quarterly* Vol. 68 No. 3 (1995): 139-156

Veena Dan ed. *Mirrors of Violence: Communities, Riots and Survivors in South Asia.* Oxford University Press, India (1990)

Voll, John Obert. *Islam: Continuity and Change in the Modern World* Westview Press. Boulder, Colorado. (1982)

———. "Renewal and Reform in Islamic History: *Tajdid* and *Islah*" in *Voices of Resurgent Islam.* John L. Esposito eds. Oxford University Press: (1983): 32-47

Wall, James A, Jr. "Mediation: An Analysis, Review and Proposed Research." Journal of Conflict Resolution Vol. 25 No.1, (1981): 157-80

Wallach, J. and J. Wallach *The New Palestinians: The Emerging Generations of Leaders* Rocklin, CA.: Prima Publishers, (1992)

Wallensteen, Peter and Sollenberg, Margareta. "After the Cold War: emerging Patterns of Armed Conflict, 1989-1994" *Journal of Peace Research.* Vol.32 No. 3 (1996): 345-360

Wallis, Roy. *Salvation and Protest.* Fransic Pinter. London. (1979)

———. and S, Bruce. *Sociological Theory, Religion, and Collective Action.* The Queen's University. Belfast. (1986)

Waltz, Kenneth *Theory of International Politics.* Addison-Wesley, Reading, MA, (1979)

Watson, Geoffrey R. *The Oslo Accords: International Law and the Israeli-Palestinian Peace Agreements* Oxford: Oxford University Press, (2000)

Webb, Keith "Prediction in International Relations: The Role of Power, Interest and Trust" in *Kent Papers in International Relations.* Series I no. 11. Canterbury Kent: University of Kent at Canterbury, (1992)

Weber, Max *Economy and Society.* Guenther Roth and Claus Wittich eds. University of California Press. Berkeley, (1978)

World Bank, *Developing the Occupied Territories,* vol. 2, *The Economy* Washington D.C.: the World Bank, (1993)

———. *Developing the Occupied Territories,* vol. 3, *Private Sector* Washington D.C.: the World Bank, (1993)

———. *The Palestinian NGO Project, Public Discussion Paper* 15 July. al-Ram, (1997)

Yosuf-Ahmad, A. *Arab-Arab Conflicts 1945 1981: An Exploratory Study* Beirut, Lebanon: The Center for the Studies of Arab, (1988)

Young Ronald 2002. "American Jews, Christians, and Muslims Working Together for Peace in the Middle East" in David R. Smock eds. *Religious Perspectives on War.* United States Institute of Peace, Washington DC. (1992)

Spencer and Young "Lessons from the Field of Intra-National Conflict Resolution." *Notre Dame Law Review* Vol. 67, (1993): 1495-1512

Zakzouk, Mahmoud. "Peace from an Islamic Standpoint." in *Peace for Humanity: Principles, Problems and Perspectives for the Future as Seen by Muslims and Christians,* Andreas Bsteh ed., New Delhi: Vikas Publishing House Pvt. Ltd., (1996): 65-86

Zartman William "The Political Analysis of Negotiations: Who Gets What and When?" in World Politics. vol. 26, no.3. (1974)

Zartman, I.W. 1997. 'Explaining Oslo' *International Negotiation* Vol. 2 (1997): 195-215

Zartman and Rasmussen eds *Peacemaking in International Conflict: Methods and Techniques.* Washington, D.C.: United States Institute of Peace Press (1997, 2005)

Zureik, E. "Toward a Sociology of the Palestinians" *Journal of Palestine Studies* Vol. 7, No. 4, (Summer, 1977): 3-16

Index

About the Author

Born and raised in Turkey, Dr. S. Ayse Kadayifci-Orellana is currently Assistant Professor in the field of Peace and Conflict Resolution at the School of International Service at American University, Washington D.C. She is also the one of the founding members and the Associate Director of *Salam Institute for Peace and Justice*, a non-profit organization for research, education, and practice on issues related to conflict resolution, nonviolence, and development with a focus on bridging differences between Muslim and non-Muslim communities. She received her PhD from American University's School of International Service in Washington DC in 2002 with a Master's degree in Conflict Analysis from University of Kent in Canterbury, England.